TALKING JAZZ

BY

Max Jones

W. W. NORTON & COMPANY

NEW YORK   LONDON

First published in UK 1987 by
The Macmillan Press Ltd
Basingstoke and London

Published in the USA and Canada in 1988 by
W. W. NORTON & COMPANY
New York

Printed in Great Britain by
Anchor Brendon Limited
Tiptree, Essex

ISBN 0-393-02494-6

Contents

List of illustrations

Acknowledgments

Grateful acknowledgment is made to IPC Magazines Ltd, and in particular to Allan Jones, editor of *Melody Maker*, for permission to reproduce copyright material which has appeared in *Melody Maker*, and (in the case of Wingy Manone) in *Music Maker*. In addition, thanks are due to Allan Jones for giving free access to the cuttings and photographic files of *Melody Maker*, and to Roy Birchell and David Howling for their assistance in locating copy and photographs. Acknowledgments are made also to *Wire* magazine for permission to quote from 'The Trouble with Billie'; to *Jazz Music* for the 1948 interview with Bob Wilber and to Eddie Cook, editor of *Jazz Journal*, for parts of 'Joe Bushkin's Tapeology'. The author extends his grateful thanks to John Chilton, Dick Sudhalter and Ernie Anderson for their contributions to the pieces on Preston Jackson, Bobby Hackett and Joe Bushkin respectively.

Thanks are also due to all those who have helped with illustrations, including Beryl Bryden, Hans Harzeim, Val Wilmer, Howard Lucraft, Bob Thiele, Nancy Miller Elliott, Jack Bradley and Capitol Records. The author and publishers have made every effort to trace the copyright ownership of photographs reproduced in this book, but if any acknowledgment has inadvertently been overlooked they will be pleased to rectify matters at the first opportunity.

Finally the author wishes to express his appreciation of his editor, Alyn Shipton, whose enthusiasm for the book exceeded the call of duty.

Preface

Readers with long memories, as they glance through this book, will realise I am deeply in debt to the *Melody Maker* for much of the contents. To others I should explain that this singular periodical figured prominently in my life from the age of 13 until semi-retirement at 65. And since then, scrutinising back issues and cuttings files, I have been happy to revive memories not only of 38 years on the paper's strength but of an earlier decade and a half as regular reader. The pieces offered here are a mixture of straight interviews, personal impressions, attempted portraits of a few artists I met, and bits of biography and fancy. Some are reprinted as they first appeared, or have been 'restored' to what they were before a sub-editor struck, others have not previously been written-up and several are composites drawn from various sources, including unpublished ones (see Acknowledgments for details). I feel sad about a number of omissions. Trummy Young, Kenny Davern, Earl Hines, Ralph Sutton, Dick Wellstood, Eubie Blake, Jabbo Smith, Roy Eldridge, Arnett Cobb, Illinois Jacquet, Buddy Tate, Quentin Jackson, Billy Butterfield and a dozen more... where have they gone? In the end, sheer lack of space dictated the exclusions.

It was not, in fact, the *MM* — then a fat, eagerly awaited monthly magazine — which introduced me to 'hot music'. It is hard to recall exactly what triggered my obsession, even girls, but so far as music went, for me and brother Cliff (two years older) it was a few attractively exotic gramophone records by the Denza Dance Band, Sam Lanin, Ted Wallace's Campus Boys and the like which ignited the sacred spark. We bought pawnshop instruments, including a Swanee Sax, and some kazoos and formed various off-the-cuff bands, rather like skiffle groups with friends in the Primrose Hill area of London. School fellows initiated us into the mysteries of real hot jazz, and Christopher Stone's radio record programmes furthered our education by leaps and bounds. We tied up with Bert, an alto-playing schoolmate, and planned a proper 'dance outfit'. Cliff owned an alto by now, while I bought a second-hand soprano and some instruction manuals. We taught ourselves to play — badly! — but doing something is better, most times, than watching it or listening.

Our amateur band was born at the Polytechnic in London's Regent Street, well placed next door to Boosey and Hawkes music store and within walking distance of the Palladium, Selfridge's Roof Garden (with its lunchtime record sessions), the Mayfair Hotel, the Astoria dance hall in Charing Cross Road, and esoterically named clubs and bottle-party premises located in Soho. Considering our ages and ignorance and the comparative obscurity of the jazz phenomenon in Britain, this band was an ambitious project. It boasted eight pieces — trumpet, three saxes, piano, guitar, string bass and drums — and featured a book of 'small orchestrations' of tunes of the day, plus a few special arrangements of hot numbers. We called ourselves the Campus Club Dance Band, to convey a hint of US campus boys.

Enlightenment was shed by the study of 'Rhythm Style' records, dissected at weekly band meetings and rehearsals, and perusal of the *Melody Maker*. It is impossible to overstate the importance of this journal to enthusiasts in those dark ages, around 1930, when dance music was popular but widely despised, while hot jazz was a half-secret subject whose excitements were revealed only to the few. To us, the *MM* was 'the Bible', the only regular source of jazz information and wisdom. It was guide to which band played where and who was in it, what music and records were available and worth getting, who was arriving in town, how much chance there might be of buying a new instrument, and (of prime interest to us) what was afoot on the American jazz scene. We were all, writers and readers, innocents then.

In a short time the CCDB, the name emblazoned on our music-stand banners, had become a semi-pro outfit, in which I played tenor and soprano and Cliff doubled alto/baritone. The *MM* — 'organ of the profession' — offered the chance of finding gigs, or of entering one of its band contests. It announced rousing, and usually totally unexpected, events such as the imminent arrival at the London Palladium of Louis Armstrong, Duke Ellington's Band, the Mills Brothers or Boswell Sisters. For jazz obsessives, the paper was indispensable.

I engrossed myself in the romance of the dance-music world, and hoped to grow into a real musician, as did other members of the band. Only two or three reached acceptable standards but we continued after leaving school until 1934/5. Upon the Campus Club Band's demise I joined a new group fronted by trumpeter Johnny Claes and played happily alongside him until a close encounter with the sound of Coleman Hawkins convinced me of the futility of that ambition. After selling both tenor and soprano but hanging onto my silver clarinet, I got hold of an alto and a car and commenced lessons with the highly regarded George Evans. When he suggested a complete change of embouchure I threw in the towel. Hope, they say, never dies and I clung to the metal clarinet for a year or two more.

Jazz was still a way of life but now I was on the outside, looking at the inside through my association with Johnny Claes and with the aid of the good old *MM*, for long now a weekly: 'Every Friday, 3d' and excellent value. In the 14 or 15 years between discovering the *MM* and joining it, there could have been few issues I did not see. I also read *Rhythm*, its sister periodical, and *Hot News* (6d) when I had time and money. The latter was pretty scarce around me in the later 1930s, and other interests — girls, cricket and motor racing in particular — claimed energy and cash. Here, I'll stick to the music, though that was almost invariably intertwined with one romantic endeavour or another, most of them unfruitful.

Ever since the *MM* launched the Rhythm Club movement in 1933 I had sporadically visited two or three London clubs, also the Gig Club (near Swiss Cottage) where I heard the Great Man of violin jazz, Joe Venuti. That was in '34, a good year for maestros visiting Britain because we had Armstrong touring until the spring, and the incomparable Hawkins among us from about the time Louis left for Paris. As fringe benefits we had nifty Valaida Snow in 'Blackbirds of 1934' — with the Pike Davis band in the pit — and Cab Calloway's band on tour during March and April. No wonder I look back on the early 1930s as enchanted years, despite an economic depression and political storms a-brewing.

In those times anything in the jazz garden seemed lovely. Criticism had hardly raised its head, jazz history was obscure, and we accepted the styles as they came to us, on record or in person. Instruction, from John Hammond, an early guru, was printed in the *MM* and let us know that, say, a rival to Hawkins (Chu Berry) was 'out of this world'. But we had little analysis or weighty criticism to go on, and tell us how to react. So we listened to all we could, relying on our ears to form our taste; I imagine we were none the worse for it. As time passed I got very involved in the jazz club scene, gave record recitals, lectured under the Council for Adult Education in the Forces, began to broadcast on the BBC, wrote for a diversity of small publications and, in the summer of '42, founded the magazine *Jazz Music* with Albert McCarthy. I began to think I was an expert, even a critic. What an illusion! My studies helped me acquire knowledge of jazz history and pre-history, of territory styles and New Orleans traditions, but seriously restricted my outlook. Time taught me the errors of purism.

Though in touch with the *MM* on club matters, I entertained no notion of working for it until by chance jazz colleague Rex Harris invited me to join him on the paper's Collectors' Corner feature. That was late in '44 and January the following year saw me hired full-time. From then on, it was a life of jazz absorption allied to deadlines and the word — when I was at work, that is, and I observed pretty eccentric hours. But what work it has been . . . paid to enjoy myself. True, I never was paid much; however, with freelancing, I made enough to live comfortably.

As I was saying at the start, many of these 'prints' were rushed out for popular consumption in the *Melody Maker*. One of my editors used to declare: 'If it's good, let it run.' Another's motto was: 'There's nothing that's not improved by cutting.' A third had a saying: 'I don't want it good, I want it Friday.' Thinking back, I am astonished I ever succeeded in getting a series such as the McPartland, Eckstine or Mary Lou Williams into the pages of 'the Bible'. I'd like to add, boastfully I dare say, that I was quite proud of these lengthy interviews which have been extensively raided by *Hear Me Talkin' To Ya* and a generation of liner-note writers. There being no union rule about journalists' bylines then, I was never credited with these efforts. This book will at least put the record straight on that account.

MAX JONES
London, June 1987

This book is dedicated to
jazzologist supreme, Dave Bennett,
whose idea it was;
to Betsy, of course,
and to all the Dianas, Amys, Joans and Sheilas
who enjoyed jazz with me decades ago;
to Louis, Duke, Billie, Bix
and all the creators whose music shaped my life.

ONE

Clarinet

Paul Barnes

Shortly after Paul 'Polo' Barnes died in April 1981, Melody Maker *ran a long memorial article, based on a conversation I'd had with him a few years previously. Paul was one of the last few clarinet players in the real old New Orleans tradition. It was something of a red letter day for me, then, to have had the chance to talk to Paul when he appeared early in 1973 to play a handful of dates in Britain. He had never been tempted to travel to Europe before, but on this visit he played with several of our New Orleans type groups, producing a flowing Creole clarinet style which was pleasing and evocative, if not outstanding. For good measure he sang a few numbers in a casual and jocular fashion which seemed appropriate to the music.*

I found this semi-legendary figure, looking tired and somewhat frail, in the back room of the 100 club. To meet a man who had worked and recorded with Papa Celestin, Jelly Roll and King Oliver for openers was very much a special event, as I told him. I knew he had been quite seriously ill during the previous year, but he appeared fit enough — thin and lean in features, and with the well-worn toughness of many of the working-man school of New Orleans jazzmen. We talked at length about his early days playing fife, clarinet and alto, also about his record dates with Celestin, Morton and Oliver.

'Emile, in the first place he actually showed me how to play the clarinet. He was the first one, quite naturally; if he hadn't been a clarinet player I wouldn't have been one. Little brothers try to do what the big brothers do.'

The saxophone was nothing to do with Emile, though; Paul first saw a sax at a circus played by someone known as Jazzbo in a sideshow. Barnes claimed he introduced saxophone playing to New Orleans Jazz 'when he was seventeen going on eighteen'. This would have been in 1919. He said that one month after buying the alto he became a professional sax player, and soon after that formed a band of his own. He became so efficient on the alto that he turned a lot of New Orleans musicians on to the instrument.

One thing he mentioned about the '28 Morton session was having a solo on soprano sax on Jelly's *Deep Creek Blues*. And he thought he took another on one of Oliver's recordings, but couldn't remember and couldn't recognise himself when the old records were played. As for the historic discs by Celestin's Original Tuxedo Jazz Orchestra of 1926 and '27, Polo recalled that he played alto and clarinet on them and composed a few of the numbers that were cut. *My Josephine, Give Me Some More* and *As You Like It* were three he cited.

Like most of the older New Orleans players, Paul Barnes began his career with an Albert System clarinet. Later on he graduated to Boehm. 'That's because New Orleans was a French town and the Albert was a French-made instrument, whereas the Boehm was a German intrument.' Though the Albert model is often referred to as 'simple system', it is, Barnes agreed, rather more difficult to play. The Boehm, once mastered, is easier and more rewarding; in his words a much greater instrument. 'Sidney Bechet, Barney Bigard, most of all the New Orleans players at that time used to play Albert System clarinets. Everything was French there then, and Albert being French, why, everybody used that. Some of them changed in later years; others never did.'

The Barnes family was French, too, or more properly Creole. Paul's parents were Creoles of colour, and he recalled that they spoke French at home although the children, being the new generation, preferred to speak American.

When Emile and Paul started listening consciously to the new music which pervaded New Orleans it would have been the time of the first Great War, or just before — the period, in fact, when Nick LaRocca worked regularly in the city before leaving for Chicago (in 1916) and forming the history-making Original Dixieland Jazz Band. Some musicians, like Wingy Manone, have sworn that the Original Dixielanders were the first to play real jazz. Others claim that they copied what black bands were already playing. After laughing and refuting the 'Creators of Jazz' boast, Barnes nodded to signify that indeed he knew what 'those Dixieland boys' were doing.

'That's right,' he said with finality. 'They wasn't. No, those boys, they weren't even playing that kind of music. That came from way back, from Buddy Bolding (Bolden) and Jelly Roll Morton, from King Oliver and all those people. They played that music long before those fellows ...

'The white boys actually didn't play that music. And then again, they say Dixieland music. That's not Dixieland music. There's no such thing as Dixieland Jazz really. The only thing that's Dixieland music, if you want to know the truth, is all that hillbilly music. Now that's really Dixieland music.

'You must understand there was always a bad feeling between the northern part of the country and the southern part. After the Civil War they still battle against each other, and to those boys everything was Dixie and Dixieland as far as they were concerned. But to tell the facts, as far as we blacks were concerned it was New Orleans music — New Orleans, not Dixieland jazz. Those boys, they made that up.

'But they had a real good band. The Original Dixieland Band, they were what you call a first-class band. They made good records, and when they had a hit they put that out, that it was Dixieland music. But it was not. It was traditional New Orleans music. And when them boys said that, well, Jelly Roll Morton and people, they hit the roof. How could they come out with something like that?

'Like I told you, they went up north and put that out. They didn't know anything but they were Dixieland. They brought that in because they wanted to give praise to the South. We blacks weren't interested in the South. The South hadn't treated us right, nohow. So we weren't going to call it Dixieland music.'

From the question of racial origin, right on to geographical origin. New Orleans is the conventional answer to the query: where was jazz born? Is it a precise one, though? Did the jazz idea germinate in the southern and southwestern areas generally? Was jazz, or some very similar form of ragtime-influenced band music, being played in other parts of Louisiana during the final decade of the last century or the opening years of this one? Or was it performed in other more distant parts of the continent? His feeling was that jazz — what could truly be called jazz — started 'right there in New Orleans'. Because most of the music heard around was plain ragtime music. And that was altogether different from traditional jazz.

'You see, in ragtime music they had books and you read those parts, and you played what was written in them. Your Red Book, your Scott Joplin ... you just had to read that music, and when you read it you were reading another man's idea.

'But when traditional jazz happened along — Buddy Bolden was the first one — he start playing the way he felt the music go. So traditional jazz is really that: you play your feelings.

'What you play today, tomorrow you may not play the same thing. It's not like ragtime music. In that, what you play today you play tomorrow, like if you're playing opera, or in a symphony band. That's written there: you're not going to put anything else in.'

All very well, and the distinction between straight ragtime and improvised jazz was clear enough to most of us, but confusion arose when elderly jazzmen such as Bunk Johnson spoke of early jazz bands as ragtime bands. Paul, for example, was playing some sort of dance music in New Orleans during the second decade of this century. Was what he was playing ragtime proper or jazz?

'We played ragtime, but we couldn't read. And we played a different ragtime from those reading musicians who actually played it. We put our own version in there, so that our ragtime music was mixed up with traditional music. That's what Bunk Johnson was trying to tell you. Most of the traditional men, they couldn't read. So the music had to be different.'

So the Barnes family were not music readers as a whole. What of their relations, the Marreros? They weren't doing too much reading, either, according to Paul, though they learned later on to read. And trumpet player Kid Rena's band, in which Paul played during the early Twenties? What did that band play, and what was the standard of reading?

'Rena was playing jazz. That's right, not ragtime. He played jazz. But Kid Rena, like I was trying to get you to understand, he could read some music and he would play a rag ... and the rest of the fellows that couldn't read, they would fill in their own version like I was trying to explain you.

'But they would try to make some things that were how the music was written. They had great men that could play those instruments who couldn't read, but who were more familiar with their instrument than the men that read. But they weren't considered. Only the people that read music was considered great musicians. Of course some of the others were great, as I've told you, but they wouldn't give them any art.

'It's like being in medicine. Suppose some people would be sick and you'd made up your different medicines and cure those people where the doctors couldn't cure 'em; they still wouldn't give you credit as a doctor. You didn't go to school to learn to be a doctor, and you just wasn't considered although you might be greater than the doctors. Because you hadn't studied their way. Same thing with music.'

Barney Bigard

Everybody has childhood heroes and among my main men, leaving aside cricketers and the 'Bentley Boys' of Le Mans fame, were Louis Armstrong, Duke Ellington, Joe Venuti, Red Allen, Johnny Hodges and Barney Bigard. The choice was dictated by what records my brother and I could get hold of, and we were soon bewitched by the incomparable clarinet on Tiger Rag, The Mooche, Old Man Blues, Ring Dem Bells and Rockin' In Rhythm. So we knew Bigard's playing intimately when he was revealed in person, in the summer of '33 at the London Palladium, with Ellington's empyrean ensemble. The stage performance, though thinner than the recorded sound, confirmed that his effortless, liquid style differed from that of anybody we'd heard.

After the band left Britain there was a long wait before I saw B.B. again, and met him for the first time. That was at the Nice Jazz Festival of '48 and on that occasion I visited him, accompanied by clarinettist Wally Fawkes, at the Hotel Negresco. We were surprised to find him almost engulfed in cloud. It was bitterly cold for late February in Nice and Barney simply left the hot tap running in his bathroom in order to create steam heat. He beamed nevertheless and I conducted a lively interview (wish I could unearth the notebook) which touched on his work with Kid Ory in '46. Wal and I, keen on that band despite its flaws, could hardly fail to perceive that the Great Man was less enthusiastic. Even so it was a slight shock, when we mentioned the desirability of arranged elements in an improvised performance, to hear a snort of disgust.

'Arrangements? Papa Mutt couldn't play the shit he had in front of him,' was Barney's verdict.

Subsequently I met him in Paris on most of his visits, in London Airport during '49, in Nice, and in Britain in '75 when he was in the 'Night in New

Orleans' package show. In this interview, which the MM *printed in two chunks in May and June of '75, Bigard refers to his autobiography* With Louis and the Duke *which did not appear until 1985, five years after Barney's death on 27 June 1980.*

To meet Barney Bigard is to meet a real living legend, a jazz clarinettist who must be acknowledged as the greatest exponent of New Orleans clarinet still playing. Not that he plays all that often nowadays. He lapsed into a comfortable semi-retirement in the early Sixties in Los Angeles, and since then has contented himself with sporadic appearances in concerts and festivals and a very occasional tour away from home. To see Barney in this country is a rare experience indeed, also a rare pleasure. He last set foot in Britain in the summer of 1933*, when he made his first and only visit here with the Duke Ellington orchestra. His present brief visit was with Barry Martyn's *A Night in New Orleans* jazz package.

Barney has spent a good deal of time in France, where he has recorded and made many friends among the music community, and he reminisced for a while about some of his visits — with Ellington and, later, Armstrong. Bechet and Mezzrow came into the conversation, and there was reference to a time when Mezz tried to keep Bechet from coming into Louis' dressing-room.

'It's a wonder Mezzrow didn't get hit,' Barney said amid laughter. 'Well, I heard some bad things about Mezzrow, but no need to go into that now. He was about the worst clarinet player I ever heard, though, he was terrible. And that book of his, that was terrible, too.'

What about the Bigard book, then? I remembered from earlier meetings with Barney that he was in the publishing queue. Yes, he said, the book was coming along nicely.

'It'll be coming out; I'm doing it with Barry Martyn. Yeah, it was Barry persuaded me to leave home and come over here with this show.' We agreed it was odd that an Englishman had to go to LA to ignite a local New Orleans explosion. 'He's doing good, too,' said B.B.

Bigard also talked about the book which was being written by his old New Orleans clarinet colleague, Albert Nicholas, until his death in '73. Nick's friend, Rose, in Switzerland, aims to finish the book, and to this end she interviewed Barney at length about his childhood and youthful days with Albert.

'She's got some good pictures of Nick, some from the old days. She gave me a couple of them, real nice of her.' Barney smiled and added: 'She didn't think Nick had a temper. But I know; I worked with him long enough.'

Barney had worked on tenor sax with Nicholas at Tom Anderson's Cabaret in New Orleans on and off from 1922 to '24. Then they were together in King Oliver's reed section from late '24 to '26.

Bigard recorded with Jelly Roll Morton, as well as King Oliver, Luis Russell and Duke Ellington (to mention the most important), during the Twenties. It wasn't long before Morton's name came up.

* Late in 1949 Barney, with Louis Armstrong's All Stars, stopped off at Heathrow *en route* for the Continent but did not leave the airport.

'Jelly Roll, he was fabulous. He wrote so many tunes, and many of them have become jazz standards. Yet he was a playboy; money came easy to him and went just as easy.

'He had a diamond in his tooth, you know, and when he wanted money, in the Chicago days, he'd just write another tune and bring it over to Melrose Music. And Melrose would give him more or less what he wanted — a thousand dollars, two thousand even.

'And to get a band job he would simply talk himself into one, then talk himself right out of the job. He was something else, a big man. That's why he could go and get anything he wanted.'

Jelly Roll stated more than once that Omer Simeon was his ideal clarinettist, though he also had admiration for Bigard, Nicholas, Dodds and other good New Orleans practitioners. In 1929 Barney was honoured with the clarinet role on four Victor recordings by the Morton Trio, and I wondered how this had come about. Yes, said Barney, Simeon was his favourite but Simeon had to go somewhere and couldn't make the record date. So he got the job.

'Oh, Jelly was a fabulous man. A funny thing about him, in New York later, after say a Lafayette Theatre show, he'd get into arguments about how the music should be played and so on.

'Chick Webb was one musician he'd argue with. Chick liked to sing his arrangements through, he'd sing the whole arrangement to you if he had a new one. So he and Jelly would stand on the corner and get into one of these arguments and you'd swear it was a big fight. But they were just discussing the music and that sort of thing.

'Of course in those years he no longer had the success. I met him one time on 125th Street, and it was cold. I remember, and he just had on a little thin overcoat, you know, he was huddled up like this.

'I said: "Jelly," I just hardly recognised him. Said: "What's happening with you, man?" And he said: "Boy, I'm going to tell you something. Those white people, they know if they hold me down they hold the rest of us down."

'That's the way he was talking, because he couldn't get any work and he was frustrated. Then he came to California and died shortly afterwards.'

Despite all the set-backs, I speculated, did Morton continue to behave like a big-timer? Nodding swiftly, Barney pointed out that Jelly was exactly that.

'He was a big-timer. But he was also, you know, like a pimp. Well, he used to work in a sporting house when he was young, in Lulu White's in New Orleans. Yeah, a pool player, all those things you heard. He was an extraordinary man, all right. Jelly Roll was fascinating. I mean, you'd get a kick out of just talking to him. I used to get a big bang out of talking to Jelly all the time.'

And the sessions, such as the trio date with Bigard which produced *Turtle Twist, Smilin' The Blues Away* and the others? Whose arrangements and tunes were they, so far as arrangements were concerned, and how much preparation went into them? The clarinettist laughed and shook his head. There was no real rehearsal, he said, and not much preparation that he knew about.

'No, the way Jelly worked ... they'd call him for a date, and he'd maybe have a tune he wished to do, and then he'd make up a tune, or two or more, and we'd have a run over and see what he wants. And that's it: no music or nothing. Then we'd play it.

'He was quick, make up a tune just like that. He made up a lot of tunes, oh Lord, yes. And good ones, too. One I always used to be crazy about he wrote. I can't think of it now, but Benny Goodman made a big record of it. Right ... *King Porter Stomp*'

Bigard looked thoughtful reflecting over a period of nearly fifty years, then said weightily: 'At one time he swore to me, and he usually meant what he said, that he wrote the *St Louis Blues*. Of course, you can write a tune, or part of it, and neglect it and then lose it and see someone else work on it and register it. I don't know about all that. I do know he always told me that he wrote it. He said: "But I wouldn't put the old man down when he got old and sick".'

As so often happens, the references to Morton led on to Duke Ellington, with whose band Bigard had been working for almost two years when he cut his trio sides with Jelly. Why did Barney think the Duke was so slighting in all his mentions of Morton?

'Probably he was jealous of him in those days. Certainly it wasn't true if Duke said he couldn't play good, oh no. Ellington didn't like a lot of people, but he would never show it openly. He had his own way. Like in the band, he never fired anybody, but he could make it more miserable for you so that you'd want to quit, you know. But then he'd look after people who were sick, and dopeheads and everything. I never could understand some of those things, but of course they were long after my time.'

Barney left Ellington in June of '42 after some fifteen years' service, and he considers that original band — which existed in all its glory from about 1928 to 1942 — to have been something distinct from later Ducal aggregations; different musically and socially.

'Oh, that band was immaculate,' he told me of the nonpareil 1940 ensemble. 'Fine musicians who made a series of fine recordings, yes, but not only that. They were all gentlemen at that time. They all worked well, and they all were doing their best to try to do right, by the band and the music ... and the public. You know, we had many wonderful musicians in the band, long before 1940, that maybe the public didn't know much about over here: Arthur Whetsol, he played sweet trumpet; and Wallace Jones was in the band six or seven years; and another good one that was a singer, played the trumpet too ... Louis Bacon.

'But after the original band began to break up, Duke's orchestra was never the same. Never. Cootie Williams left, other people left, and later Tricky Sam took sick and died.

'Yes, many good musicians came into the band. But to me, those guys who were very fine musicians — Clark Terry and them — they never did fit the style of the band. So Duke had to change all his arrangements to fit those guys. See, that was the difference.

'No, Sonny Greer, he left the band some years after those others I mentioned, but he was another original. Sonny fit the band. That's what I'm saying; everybody used to fit the band for that style he wanted. They used to call it the Jungle Band, you know.

'So for me it deteriorated when the guys began to leave, and he had to get different people and change the music. It wasn't the same band any more. You know, the characters like Cootie and Rex had gone.'

Talk of the old band reminded Barney of the records he made with Rex Stewart in 1939, and which he liked.

'Yes, Rex and me, Billy Taylor and Django Reinhardt ... oh, Capitol reissued them in the States in a big album. It was funny, they couldn't find the drummer — he'd gotten drunk — and when they finally found Django he didn't know where his guitar was. So they got him a guitar with the back split open and that's the way we went to the studio, no drum or nothin'. And of course Django was fantastic, played just beautiful. And when I wasn't playing clarinet I was beating with some sticks on somethin' or other. That's right ... I was the ghost drummer that someone referred to.'

Towards the end of the conversation we spoke of Kansas City drummer Jesse Price, who had spent many years on the West Coast and who had died during 1974. Barney had known him pretty well, and he told me that Price had Chick Webb's drums. Well, he said, Jesse's widow has them now and someone should be interested in buying them. Mrs Price still lives in Los Angeles.

Another friend of Barney's, also of mine, is trombonist Trummy Young, now flourishing in the sunshine of Hawaii.

'He was supposed to be at the Nice Festival last year with us,' Barney said. 'But he's got a good job there and they wouldn't let him off; and his job is more important to him than one week. So he couldn't come.

'Now last time Trummy came to the States we went to Denver. They put him in the jazz festival there. Yes, he brought his wife, Sally, over with him; and you know, Trummy, he looked just as young as when you saw him. I said: "Now come on, when are you going to grow old?" He just smiled. Such a nice guy ... he's a beautiful man.

'Oh, we had a ball, enjoyed ourselves up there. It's exclusive, you know, you have to be invited. It's over a four-day period and costs 175 dollars a couple.

'Now that was the last time I saw Tyree Glenn. He was there, and I remember he had been operated on — one of his legs was big like that round the ankle.

'We were on a set together and we were talking. I asked how he felt and he said the doctor told him to take it easy and build his muscles back up in his stomach. I believe he'd had some kind of liver operation.

'He was trying like mad to blow like he used to, you know. And that's the last I saw of Tyree. Next thing I heard he was ... ' Bigard paused for emphasis and quietly ended the sentence: 'dead.'

The time Barney Bigard spent with Ellington's orchestra — effectively from 1928 until 1942 – was fruitful for the band as well as for Barney. These years matured his style and shaped his career, musically speaking, but they didn't see only a one-way passage of ideas. Barney, like most of the other pivotal figures in the Thirties band, furnished his own ideas, his own jazz experience culled from six years or so of 'scuffling' on tenor sax and clarinet in New Orleans, Chicago, Milwaukee and New York. And he added a few compositions and part compositions to the band's repertoire.

In talking about composing and composer credits in connection with an improvisational music such as jazz, it is wise to proceed with caution. The story of jazz, from the Original Dixielanders, through Jelly Roll Morton and W. Ç. Handy, to Chick Webb, Benny Goodman, Ellington and on up to bop, is studded with confusions about who wrote what, who pinched what, and whose name was added to which tunes for 'business' reasons. Bigard, speaking from memory, said he 'wrote about thirteen songs' while he was with Duke. Among them he instanced *Mood Indigo, Saturday Night Function, Clarinet Lament, Stompy Jones, Clouds in My Heart, Rockin' in Rhythm* and *Lament For Javanette*. With the exception of *Stompy Jones* and *Rockin' in Rhythm*, all of these and five or six more are credited to Ellington and Albany Bigard (which is Barney's real name), *Mood Indigo* being actually credited to Ellington, Mills and Bigard in the listing of Duke's compositions in copyright order at the end of his book, *Music is My Mistress* (W. H. Allen).

It is clear, when Bigard reminisces about the old days and Duke's working methods, that mistakes could easily occur when jointly constructed tunes came to be copyrighted. *Rockin' in Rhythm*, for instance, that 1930 classic of Ellingtonia — and I refer to the date of its first recording — is credited to Ellington, Carney and Mills although the early versions give no sign that baritonist Harry Carney had a hand in its creation (Cootie or Hodges seem more likely contenders). Bigard, on the other hand, plays an important and typical solo variation of 16 bars on the A-minor theme, and it looks at least probable that he contributed this section to the piece, and perhaps he contributed more.

I say this not to minimise Ellington's role in the composition — the maestro's imprint is everywhere — but simply to illustrate the Ellington band's modus operandi.

There have been plenty of references in print to *Rockin'* being a Carney tune, and Barry Ulanov (in his book, *Duke Ellington*) even introduces this dialogue on page 93.

'"Don't forget my number," Carney said, "*Rockin' in Rhythm*." "Who could forget your number?" Barney asked.' Possibly poetic licence on Ulanov's part; at any rate, it doesn't square up with what Bigard said to me.

As it happened, *Rockin' in Rhythm* was the first Ellington record I ever bought, and it has remained a special favourite. So I asked Barney who actually wrote the tune, or tunes to be precise.

'Truthfully that was my number and Johnny Hodges' number,' he answered without hesitation. 'Carney is listed as part-composer,' I said. 'Carney never wrote nothin' in his life,' Barney replied.

Was he sure about *Rockin' in Rhythm* though? 'Yes, that was our number. How It came about, in the Palace Theatre then they had these two comedians, and they used to do a song by themselves — something about "I Got The Number," something like that.

'So Johnny and I we're sitting there and I says: "Come on, John, let's do something about this." And so we made up *Rockin' in Rhythm* for their act. Now Duke said that Carney wrote it, but Carney never did write nothin': that's what makes me angry.'

Though Bigard mentioned being angry, I should explain that his enthusiasm for the 'original' Ellington band and its illustrious leader is evident at all times. That band was, quite simply, one of the enduring loves of the clarinettist's life — his wife, Dorothe being the other.

As we talked in his hotel room, the years soon rolled back to the end of 1927 when Albany Leon Bigard's round, woody (Albert-system) clarinet sound was added to the Duke's orchestral palette.

Ellington made special visits to the club where Luis Russell was playing, in order, we imagine, to assess the brilliance of its clarinettist. And after 'talking things over', an offer was made which Barney didn't refuse.

'I'd been playing several years before I joined Duke. And let me say, his music was altogether different from what I'd been used to playing, which was New Orleans stuff, you know.

'Now when I joined Duke I used to have a lot of fuss with him at first. I'd ask if he was making the right arrangement in the chords, and we'd have fusses all the time.

'I remember that he would say: "Well, Barney, just sit and play what I've put in front, that's it. Don't worry about it." Then gradually I got acquainted with the sounds of the band, with his harmonies, and then I loved the music.'

Most Duke-followers have spent long wondering how strongly Ellington directed the ideas of individual players in their solo or duet or obbligato passages. How much was written down, how much decreed by Duke?

Bigard smiled. 'Now, if I had to play anything for myself he'd leave like 16 bars blank. Well, solo, that's all. Nothing was on the paper but "solo". You figure it out yourself.

'Duke, you see, was different from anyone else; he studied every man in the band, figured his style, what his character was, and if he made an arrangement to feature me, he knew exactly that it would fit me.

'He wrote it to fit me, and when I played it I'd use my own imagination in the performance. He did the same for Cootie, the same for Hodges. And this went on throughout my time with the band.

'I say he was different; well he was funny. Like we'd open up a show at the Cotton Club and he's making arrangements for it. Now he'd never write an introduction or an ending until the night of the opening. The half of the time he wouldn't give them to us on paper. He'd just give the notes from the piano and tell you that's what you're going to play, and it goes like this. That's the way you did it. Every show was the same.'

So he did direct operations pretty tightly, I said. Bigard shook his head.

'No, not so far as my parts were concerned. He always left everything to me. We were going into the Palace Theatre one time and we were rehearsin', and at that time *Black And Tan* was one of the big numbers. While we rehearsed I was foolin' with the horn and I made a glissando, you know, and Duke says at once; "Keep that in, that's what I want."

'That's how things happened in that band. The funny part of it was when we opened at the Palace Theatre in New York, and that was the big number. And Tricky Sam and I, we had solos in this.

'So when I get up there — this is my first stage appearance and I'm all trembling — I get to make the slur and all I can do is say "peep, peep, peep," and the people started laughing. Then I went into the blues and it was all right.

'Well, I turned green, you know, thinking I really did a good bit of messin' it up. Then Tricky Sam started his solo with the plunger, and he had it in so tight, the inner mute, that he blew the back of the horn out.' (I assume this means he blew the tuning slide out). 'The people started laughing again. They thought that was in the act.

'Did you know that Tricky played the way he talked? He talked with a sort of a growl, and he played just that way. Other people tried that style of his and some of them did it well. Tyree Glenn for instance, but not like Tricky. Never.'

While Barney reflected, I asked about *Mood Indigo*. He said he had composed the second section of the song. 'I had the original part and he put the top part on it. That was a thing; Duke once said in a piece in one of those magazines that he wrote *Mood Indigo* while his mother was fixing breakfast or something. Don't know how he did that,' Barney laughed shortly.

'That's the only thing I didn't like about Duke. He never gave the boys in the band the credit they deserved. Like Otto Hardwick and Lawrence Brown wrote *Sophisticated Lady* but their names are not on it. It wouldn't cost him nothing to credit them — he was a genius.

'By the way, I made a record last year for RCA. I had Dick Carey on trumpet, Ray Sherman on piano, Nick Fatool on drums and Ed Safranski on bass, and we played some nice, lovely tunes. I can name some of them: *Clarinet Gumbo, Satchmo's Dream* — well you know I wrote that — and *Offshore* and *Bows and Arrows*.'

Speaking of compositions, Barney went on, did I remember his '*Lament for Javanette*. I did, and he offered to tell me how he happened to write it.

'We were working in the Sherman Hotel in Chicago, and while the band had intermission they used to have coloured girls who looked like Hawaiians, and they went round with baskets selling cigarettes and things at the tables. One night I just got tired and started foolin' around on clarinet, and that's how I made up *Javanette*. Well, they looked like Javanettes to me.'

A highlight of Barney's early career was his first visit to Britain in the summer of '33. That, he vowed, he would never forget.

'The most impressive thing I ever remember is when we were getting off the train in London and all the people turned up at the station. As we stepped off the train they were calling everybody by their names: "Here's Barney, here's Hodges, here's Cootie, here's Tricky Sam." They recognised almost everyone. That was a surprise to me.'

While we said our goodbyes I asked the clarinettist if we'd be seeing him again in Britain. If so, would he not leave it another 42 years?

'I'll probably be back sooner than that,' he said, smiling. 'And with my own band. I will, too, if I get the chance. I'll bring a handpicked group here with me.'

Bob Wilber

Bob Wilber's account of studying with Sidney Bechet was given to me verbally at Nice, during the Jazz Festival held there in February, 1948. This note, which is a verbatim account, originally appeared in Jazzmusic *in 1948.*

Over the forty years or so since that meeting, Bob, now an honorary Englishman, has remained a close friend. Every time Bob and Pug Wilber are 'at home' in England, we see them and enjoy the conversation and music.

I have been playing clarinet and taking an interest in jazz since I was about 13 years old. And all that time I have been an admirer of Sidney Bechet. I never met him until I was 16. Then I met him through Mezz Mezzrow, whom I knew from Jimmy Ryan's, and found out there was an opening for a pupil out at Bechet's house in Brooklyn. So I became a Bechet pupil.

Outside his house was a sign saying: Sidney Bechet School of Music. But I guess I was one of his first pupils in that sense of the word, though many musicians have learned directly or indirectly from Bechet. Johnny Hodges is just one.

It was in the spring of 1945 that I started with Sidney, studying both clarinet and soprano saxophone. At first lessons were on a formal basis, and paid for at five dollars each. I had two a week and then more. Finally, because we were both so interested in the lessons and the music, I moved into the house. From Sidney I learned a great deal — about music and about living.

One of the few musicians you can rely upon always to give a first-class performance, Sidney never seems to have an 'off' day. He has the deepest well of inspiration of any musician I've heard, allied to complete confidence and relaxation. His fine broad tone and pronounced vibrato (steady and controlled and somewhat akin to a violin vibrato) are a natural part of his playing. His tone has a velvety quality; soft when he is playing in small clubs, it has amazing carrying power in larger premises. Sidney produces volume and power, when desired, without straining. His style, like his tone, is distinctive. But it is not a trick style, being mature and applicable to any music.

He shows some preference for the soprano saxophone as a means of expressing himself. Indeed, at New York clubs and concerts his clarinet is not often seen, which for me is a pity because I believe him to be the finest clarinettist playing jazz today. A point of interest is that his new clarinet is a hybrid instrument — a combination Boehm and Albert job, with no middle joint, which was made in Czechoslovakia, I think.

As a listener, Sidney has the intuitive ability to sense the value of any music he hears. I've never heard him say 'That's an awful tune.' He loves all music because he sees the way to play it. There are some things you cannot realise about Bechet just from a study of his records. For instance, in clubs he plays plenty of 'pop' tunes, and plays them for all he's worth. He plays the melody, and when he improvises it's improvising on the melody. That, in brief, is his theory of jazz.

Today, improvisation has tended to develop from variations on the melody to variations on the chord structure. In general, a passion for harmony is abroad. Most New Orleans jazz musicians — Bechet among them — believe rhythm to be the most important element of jazz. Melody comes next and then harmony, the latter serving as a dressing for the melody and rhythm. Primarily you play the tune.

I agree with Sidney on these things, except that I prefer playing clarinet to soprano. When Bechet was at Ryan's, last winter and the year before, I sat in pretty regularly with the trio and we two played together, Sidney on soprano and myself on clarinet. Pretty soon everyone came to expect these soprano–clarinet duets. That was my training ground. I need hardly stress that you cannot learn to play jazz by listening and individual practice alone. It is necessary to play regularly with good jazz musicians, and I was fortunate to be able to play with Sidney as well as have him teach me.

Perhaps I should add here that Sidney insisted on my concentrating on clarinet, the more difficult instrument to master. 'Get down your clarinet,' he would say, 'and then you can do what you like with soprano.'

Studying with Bechet has, of course, been an invaluable experience, for Sidney is a great musician — the greatest jazz musician living — and a great man apart from his music. I cannot begin to say how grateful I am to him, and to the other musicians who have helped me. Working with Mezz Mezzrow, Baby Dodds, Pops Foster and the rest at Nice has been a further tremendous chance for me, and an unexpected honour. Many of these men have little regard for the music the majority of youngsters are playing today. For that reason they really welcomed me into the band and looked out for me.

I am hopeful of getting a good break with my own band, the Wildcats, which has already made a number of records. In any case, I shall continue playing the way I learned from Bechet and try to help carry on a tradition which will presently be faced with extinction.

Edmond Hall

I admit to a certain bias in writing about Edmond Hall. It was via a few Claude Hopkins records that I became aware of his distinctive tone, his drive and biting attack, but there was not much of his work about in the Britain of the Thirties. Not until the arrival of the Café Society and Hall Sextet records did his hot, fiery music make a real impression. Though not a virtuoso of the clarinet to rank with Goodman or Bigard, Hall was a worthy performer who consistently gave good value in what he did with a band. Because his supercharged playing had been a bit of a secret, I probably went overboard about it for a while. That's the bias. In 1947 I wrote that his style was an apparent compromise between Pee Wee Russell's and the more fluid manner of the traditional New Orleans clarinettists. Whatever the truth of that observation, I continued to respond favourably to the Hall bravado.

Although I always loved the beautiful sound of Bigard's lyrical improvisations,

I confess to preferring Edmond Hall's more determined role in the Armstrong All-Stars' ensemble. It was a thrill, therefore, to cross the Channel in 1955 and spend time with him and his wife, Winnie, in Paris — along with Louis, Trummy Young, Billy Kyle and the rest of the group. Betty and I passed many agreeable hours with the Halls — in cafés, at the concerts, and in the Hotel Ambassador where they were staying — and the material for this feature (run in three parts by the Melody Maker *in April 1956) was gathered between the music sessions and over Parisian repasts.*

We kept in close touch with Winnie and Edmond after that, right up to the moment when she wrote in February, 1967 to say that he had died from a heart attack suffered while clearing snow from the front of his house in Boston. He was sixty-five.

Edmond Hall has never been one of the Publicised Men of jazz. He didn't take part in a single 'historic' record session during the music's New Orleans heyday, and thus, when the Revival came about, there were no choice examples of early Hall to be unearthed and admired. For some years, half-hidden in the Claude Hopkins orchestra, he performed skilfully, soloing often and with distinction. But Hopkins's band, though highly regarded by those that heard it and danced to it, did not achieve the fashionable status which leads to a world following and discussion in European magazines. By 1940, when he recorded four titles with Henry Allen and Zutty Singleton that were to carry his reputation a hefty step forward, there were still no records under Hall's name — and few enough besides Hopkins's on which he could be heard. For these and other reasons, Hall was an obscure musician to audiences outside America. And I cannot find much that was written about him in the States prior to 1940, though he had then been playing professionally for twenty years.

Since the early Forties, Hall has become well known for his strong and expressive clarinet work on a large number and variety of records — including the Blue Note series, some Wild Bill Davisons, Eddie Condons, George Wettlings, Frank Newtons and Mary Lou Williams sessions. His playing is widely praised and, less often, criticised adversely. Yet, somehow, he has remained under-publicised; to a surprising extent, when you reflect on his total performance (on records alone) over the past fifteen years, and his high standing with fellow musicians. The explanation, I fancy, must lie in Edmond Hall's nature. He seemed, if the impression gained from a week's acquaintance can be relied upon, an uncommonly modest man, not a little surprised by the interest shown in him during the recent strong tour. He is probably the last man to worry about the shortage of Hall publicity. I never saw him do or say anything to boost his musical reputation, outside of playing sound clarinet. Enthusiastic comments on his playing were accepted with a slight bow and a courteous thank you; the roughest criticisms of All Stars concerts would be read through with no visible sign of disturbance. If, on occasion, his own contribution had not been well received, he didn't remark on it. But when he felt that the whole band had been unfairly blamed for a promoter's shortcomings, he might take off his reading-glasses, raise his eyebrows, and suggest in the mildest terms that the report was misleading.

I suspect it is in consequence of this unassuming disposition and perhaps because he has not — so far as I am aware — been 'taken up' by any particular pundit, hot concourse or critical cult, that Edmond Hall has for so long been neglected by many of the people writing about jazz. His inclusion in the current All Stars should soon be righting the matter. Next month he will play in Britain for the first time and his performance should make a powerful impression.

Though a New Orleans man by upbringing, Hall was in fact born outside the city — in Reserve Louisiana. The date was May 1901. Like so many of the original sylists in jazz, Edmond Hall was largely self-taught. He profited from some instruction at home, but completely escaped an academic musical training. With homes like the Halls', music schools were hardly necessary.

'How it happened with me was this,' Edmond explained. 'The whole family was musicians. I mean everybody in it knew how to play a guitar. An uncle played trumpet. My father Edward Hall, he was a clarinet player — my brothers, too (I was the second boy).

'I'd fooled around on guitar like most kids then, and it was just chance I picked up a clarinet one day. Of course, it was a free instrument. My father had four of them: one B flat, a C, an A, and an E flat. In those days you had to have all these to play in different keys.

'I never had a teacher. My father, he played with the Onward Brass Band, and he played Albert system. I did likewise.

'I picked up playing with bands in the locality, taught myself to read music. Round about 1917 I was already realising what it was all about, and within two or three years I had decided to earn a living playing clarinet.

'Bands I worked with were Thomas Valentine, Lee Collins, Bud Russell, Jack Carey and Chris Kelly.'

But these jobs were only what Hall spoke of as 'working around'. Though he earned more than his father, it wasn't a lot of money. And he still had spare evenings. On one of these, a Saturday in the year 1920, he went to a dance at Economy Hall. It led to his first real job.

'When I got inside it was a revelation.' Edmond remembered. 'Buddy Petit was leading from up on the bandstand. His favourite number was the *Tin Roof Blues*, which I believe he originated. Then I heard tunes like *Climax Rag* and *That's A-Plenty*.

'I can't remember the clarinettist's name; he was fine, but a few days later he left the band, and the following Saturday I was sitting right up there in his place, trying to keep up with those fast New Orleans pioneers.'

Trumpeter Petit, to whose name he brings the French pronunciation of *petite*, was a player who stood very high in Hall's estimation.

'Petit was a man who influenced me,' Edmond says, 'and his band was one of the best around New Orleans in those early Twenties. So we were doing pretty good business there.

'After a while we left the city and went to Galveston, Texas. It was my first time away from home. I had money to spare, and I kept it in my pocket. Until one day I walked past a music store and saw an alto sax in the window. I'll never forget what I paid for it — 65 dollars, which was a lot of money to me. My age was about twenty. There was nothing much to learn about it, so that night I took it on the job and doubled clarinet and alto. That's how I started on the saxophone.'

When Buddy Petit's band broke up, Hall decided to go touring. 'Around New Orleans,' he explained. 'I always had an idea I could make a better living by leaving New Orleans. When a chance came to go, I took it — went to Florida with a trumpet player named Mack Thomas. I finally quit Thomas in Jacksonville. That town had a piano player called Eagle Eye Shields. He'd heard me, and had told me: "Any time you want to come to Jacksonville I can use you."

'So I went to work with Eagle Eye, pretty soon found that he needed a trumpet. That's when I got Cootie Williams from Mobile, Alabama. I'd played with Cootie once before this. As he was in his teens still, his father made me take care of him. I hope I did. We were together a long while.

'After the Shields deal came Alonzo Ross. He was playing at Miami, Florida, when he offered me the job. I'd take it, I said, if he would make room for Cootie. So we both joined Ross about 1926.'

It was as near as Hall could remember, and I found his memory to be in good shape. On this occasion there was an element of doubt — 1925 or '26. 'I'll tell you the year.' he said, thinking back. 'When they had that big hurricane.' I nodded. The doubt remained.

Hall returned to Alonzo Ross. 'That was a reading band. We had three brass, three reeds and four rhythm — the regular combination then. The other two in the saxophone section didn't double clarinets, only sopranos, so I had to dump my clarinet and change to soprano saxophone. I dropped clarinet for two long years. As soon as I got away from that orchestra I dumped my soprano, was tickled to death to get rid of that thing.'

Although he had travelled a fair amount in the South, Edmond Hall had never — at this time — been North. There seemed little likelihood of his doing so with Ross, for, in Hall's words the band spent nine months of the year in Miami and the rest touring the State (Florida).

'Then,' he said. 'it happened that we went to Savannah, Georgia. Victor wanted that tune, *Girl of My Dreams*, recorded by Blue Steele, and sent a mobile outfit to Savannah to get it. They had scouts out who heard our band. We were asked to Savannah to do some sides, and made a few records mostly original tunes. I think I had a few bars on baritone.'

For the information of researchers, these records were made for Victor in 1927 and six titles were released under the name of the Ross De Luxe Syncopators. The line-up included Cootie and Melvin Herbert (trumpets). Eddie Williams (trombone), Dick Fulbright (bass) and Alonzo Ross (piano). Two more sides were cut but not issued.

'When the records came out,' Hall continued, 'the manager of the Roseland heard them and sent for us. He had two places, the Roseland on Broadway and the Rosemont in Brooklyn. We played at the Rosemont.

'That's how I came to New York. I'll never forget the day I arrived: 15 March 1928. It was the first time I ever saw snow.

'So we worked at the Rosemont with Ross: not long, though — there about two weeks. We split up when he lost that job. I went into a dance hall, the Happyland, and took Cootie with me.

'This Happyland was what they called a taxi-dance hall, used to be all the rage. You paid so much for a ticket, for a girl to dance with if you chose — or you could sit it out. The band played ten numbers to each set, including one waltz, then took intermission for two minutes. Of course the numbers weren't long. Sometimes we'd have to cut 'em real short down to a chorus, to get the dancers off and get others on.'

Hall — today a man of some dignity — smiled about this, shaking his head in a manner that suggested he would prefer to give customers value for cash. But in those days steady band jobs were hard to find, and not well paid. You didn't argue with the management.

Edmond stayed at the Happyland some two years. Cootie left before 1928 was out, and joined Chick Webb at the Savoy. 'I was sorry to see him go,' says Hall. 'From Mobile to New York. I was with him all that time.'

Hall's next move was to Billy Fowler's band 'in another dancing school', then to Charlie Skeets. He says: 'Skeets had a bigger band and about 500 stock tunes, so you had to be able to read. I was playing mostly alto and clarinet.

'Those were funny days. The places were all run by gangs, and this was no exception. The band wasn't bad but the guys didn't feel happy, all getting different salaries and that sort of thing.

'So we got rid of Charlie, who, as it happened, was the pianist. This was when I'd been with the band around six months. After this we needed a pianist, and the name of Claude Hopkins came up. No one knew of Claude except our drummer, Pete Jacobs: he brought him along.

'Naturally, with Skeets gone, we also needed a leader. I was offered the job, so were others, but nobody wanted that headache. So Hopkins stepped right in. He had recently been to Europe with Josephine Baker as accompanist, and here he got to be leader of a pretty good band, about the year 1930.

'We were house band at the Roseland for four or five years and played against every name band that came in: Fletcher Henderson, Mal Hallett, Paul Whiteman, Guy Lombardo, Joe Haymes and Shep Fields among them. After a while they decided to send us out on the road.'

During this time the Hopkins band became an attraction. In May, 1932, it began a series of recordings (for the American Columbia, Brunswick and Decca labels) which continued fairly steadily until early in 1935. Most of the sides were released over here. So far as I know, Hall played on all of these. His clarinet can be heard on a number of them (including *Margie, How'm I Doin, Chasing All The Blues* and *King Porter Stomp*) and — to use his words — 'Practically all the baritone you hear, I played it.'

The state of the Hopkins saxophone section is in some doubt. Reference books give three reeds (Hall, Johnson and Sands) right through till 1935, but Hall told me the line-up was two altos, tenor and baritone for most of this time. Hilton Jefferson was first alto he said, Gene Johnson third alto, Bobby Sands on tenor and himself doubling baritone and clarinet.

'Gene Johnson played baritone, too,' said Hall. 'Most of the clarinet solos were mine, but Gene also took some.'

Just You, Just Me is one on which Johnson's clarinet may be featured behind the vocal, in which case the baritone would be by Hall.

Hall stayed with Hopkins until late in 1935. He says: 'We went up to the Cotton Club in Cab Calloway's place. We stayed a whole year and closed the Cotton Club uptown.'

After six years of big-band work with Claude Hopkins, Edmond Hall spent another among the saxophones of Lucky Millinder's orchestra. In print he was still hardly more than a name in a section. It was a shift back to small groups in 1937 that started off the recognition process. He joined Billy Hicks and his Sizzling Six. 'A good band,' Hall remembers, and one in which he was sensibly employed. Helen Dance, who heard Hicks at the Savoy, confirms that this trumpet player led an interesting band. People who 'knew' used to go and listen to it — principally because of the featured clarinettist.

Hall was beginning to be noticed; and one who noticed him was John Hammond, about the most discerning man that ever scouted for jazz talent.

'I saw a man signal to me at the Savoy one night,' Edmond related. 'I went over, and he told me he was John Hammond, said he could use me on some records. He didn't waste time. It was Saturday, and by Monday or so I was recording with Mildred Bailey. And within a week or two he had me on four tunes by Billie Holiday.'

These were all made in June, 1937; during that month also, Hall cut two or three sides with the Sizzling Six, and some more with this group accompanying singer Midge Williams. In the spring of '37, Hall had recorded with Frank Newton's Uptown Serenaders. He made a few more sides with Newton in July, four with Henry Allen in June, some more in September. It was a good year for Hall. He had got away from big bands (and he has never returned to one, even declining an offer from Duke Ellington), made record dates that count, and made the acquaintance of John Hammond.

'John also had me on a jam session,' Hall says. 'That was the onliest time I played with Tommy Ladnier, the first time I met him, in fact. After this period, I didn't hear from Hammond till late in '39. Then he invited me to play at Café Society Downtown with Joe Sullivan's band.'

Between these happenings, Edmond worked with the Zutty Singleton Trio at Nick's ('I was at Nick's when war broke out'). The Sullivan group was the sextet with Danny Polo, 'Andy' Anderson, Hall on baritone and clarinet.

'I was there a long while, got to be what we call a regular house man. After Sullivan, the Red Allen band came into the Café. I was in it. There was Allen in 1940, then it went back to Sullivan, then Teddy Wilson until 1944. Any band that came in, I was in it. Barney Josephson, the owner, made that clear. If a band had a clarinet player, they got rid of him or they didn't get the job.

'When Teddy gave the band up to teach, I took it over. I took Teddy's arrangements over — some were his, some were Mary Lou's — anyway, the whole book: I still have it.

'I tried a couple of piano players in place of Wilson before I got Ellis

Larkins; another time I had Billy Taylor, also Charles Bateman — a hell of a musician.

'I kept that band three-and-a-half to four years, in the Uptown and Downtown places, and we made some records during that time for Continental and Brunswick. One tune, *I Found A Good Deal In Mobile*, they wanted Josh White to sing it, so we had him on the record.

'When the Café went out of business I went to Boston, myself, and played — picked up some men and worked as relief band to Bob Wilber there. The man at the Savoy liked it so much he asked me for a band. I got Ruby Braff, Vic Dickenson, Kenneth Kersey, Jimmy Crawford and John Fields. That, they claimed, was the best band they'd had at the club.'

After Boston, Hall returned to New York and then took a job in San Francisco.

'I went out there, yes I did,' said Hall as though the thought of a man voluntarily journeying to the West Coast was scarcely credible. 'Took only Kersey, picked up the others out on the coast. Played three weeks. The night we opened I got a long-distance call from Eddie Condon asking me to join the band at his club. It was 1950 when I went into Condon's, and I stayed right in there until I joined Louis Armstrong on 12 September.'

I asked Hall if he found it very different from playing with Condon groups. He replied: 'I don't know . . . the band seems more unified. Of course an act or concert performance is different from Condon's where you play anything. This is more or less set. You know pretty well what's coming, though I have to keep an ear open.

'I'm enjoying playing with the band. When it's really hitting — my God, the tempo is right. Enjoying my first visit to Europe, too. The people, you know they've been listening to your records; they tell you about things you've forgotten you made. It makes you feel good.'

Hall didn't talk very much about other musicians, but I formed the impression that he holds Armstrong and Bechet in high esteem.

'I always did like his playing,' he says very reasonably of Louis. And of Bechet: 'I'd heard so much about him, but didn't get to meet him until we were in New York. I knew of him long, long before.'

At no time had Hall mentioned Benny Goodman, often put forward as his favourite clarinettist. A second run-through failed to produce BG's name, so I smuggled it in. 'Benny Goodman?' Hall considered it seriously. 'Yes, he gave me a little something.'

On Louis, Edmond had a further point to make. 'I think tone has a lot to do with it. He really has a trumpet player's tone, big. When Pops hits a note, high or low, it's not faked it's really the thing. The kind of tone he has, he don't have to do anything with it.

'You have to produce tone too, on clarinet. I play that Albert system because I think that is the clarinet you need in a Dixieland band. It has that tone in the low register, that big tone.'

Edmond has at least three of these Alberts. He showed me the one he brought with him, looking it over fondly with long, thin-looking hands. 'I got this six-ring Albert in Boston,' he said. 'Have you ever heard of a six-ring Albert? A guy just came up to me and asked 50 dollars for it. I wasn't interested. Later he said: "Give me 25 dollars." I said: "Now you're talking." It's a good instrument. I've used it ever since.'

He uses a medium reed with a medium open lay, and says: 'I usually work on them myself. Sometimes you have to spoil two or three to get one you like.' On the subject of squeaks he was philosophical, too: 'To be frank with you, you can sometimes squeak and sound good.'

Hall takes music seriously, but is not too serious over it; it doesn't exclude other interests. And a subject that interests him more than most is cars. Despite his gentle, benevolent-uncle look, Hall's taste in transport shows more than a touch of dash and elegance. He is a Jaguar man, no less — once the owner of an XK120 sports model, now the keen driver of a Mark 7 saloon. He even took the XK around the track in a non-competitive way, encouraged by wife Winifred.

Hall is full of tales of big American cars 'left on bends' and surprised at lights. In Paris we spent a lot of time peering at a 300SL 'Merc' parked outside the hotel and I could see the clarinettist was tempted.

I don't think he bought a Mercedes, but the last thing he told me, when I was saying goodbye, was the story of a man at home who had one, and was stopped for speeding.

'The man says to the cop: "*Speeding*? But she'll do 150!" The cop said: "Right. Tell that to the judge."'

Hall was very amused. 'He did, too, and the judge said "200 dollars!" He paid it just like that, and left. He was proud of that car.'

Albert Nicholas

I had been listening to Albert Nicholas' fast and fluent clarinet playing for almost 25 years before meeting him in Paris in the early Fifties. His beautiful New Orleans style had given me great pleasure, and it seemed to improve as he matured. So great a favourite had he become by 1948, as a result of many excellent performances with Jelly Roll Morton, Sidney Bechet, Baby Dodds and groups of her own, that it decided us in favour of the name Nick for our son, an action which afforded Albert a certain amused satisfaction once he realised we were not putting him on.

We went to hear him whenever we were in France, in Paris concert or cave, and at the Dunkirk Festival, and 'Nick' consistently gave a good account of himself. I interviewed him in his Left Bank hotel and in various parts of London, and towards the end of his life helped in the planning and production of a double album called Let Me Tell You *on which the Creole clarinettist spoke and blew most engagingly. 'Nick' played 'in the tradition' but followed his own path, sounding comfortable with his London-based quartet as he relaxed on some late-night ad-libbing, 'looking over his shoulder at styles half-remembered' (as I put it in the liner note). Only a few weeks before his death —*

in Switzerland in September of 1973 — Nicholas returned to Britain again to play a concert at the Victoria and Albert (how apt!) Museum and proved once more that age had not seriously diminished his instrumental artistry.

The first of these two features, which overlap in some respects, resulted from an evening with the clarinettist spent at the Bedford Park home of record collector Ralph Harding in 1956. The second dates from some 16 years later.

'Well, I was with Russell — including the time Louis Armstrong had the band — for almost ten years off and on,' Nicholas said. 'I went with him soon after returning from Shanghai, Egypt and Singapore, which was late in 1928.

'King Oliver had brought his band to New York. He wouldn't leave Chicago when everybody wanted him. Not until his lip petered out: then he came, and he flopped. He had got Henry Allen from New Orleans, and Omer Simeon and Barney Bigard were in.

'After about a couple of months, Joe went home to Chicago. Meanwhile, Russell formed, and got Mule (Moore) on tuba, Teddy Hill and Charlie Holmes on saxes, Louis Metcalf on trumpet, and Higgy on trombone.

'Russell said to me: "You get an alto and take any place you like." So I played alto and all the clarinet. When we followed Fletcher Henderson into the Roseland, they wanted to enlarge. Russell got Henry Allen, who was then playing on the style of Louis Armstrong, but with something different in there.

'The Saratoga Club was our stomping ground for quite a while, and Bill Coleman came into the band there. Metcalfe had left by now. Most times we had two trumpets, sometimes three. Otis Johnson was one of them, and Bill Dillard was in another time.

'We hadn't gone long into 1929 when Russell sent to St Louis for Pops Foster. The tuba was going out, and Russell wanted that string bass. Foster made the string bass popular, you know. They should give that man a medal for that. There was only Braud' (Nicholas pronounced it Bro') 'playing it, and one or two that no one took notice of, but Foster popularised it. John Kirby, coming up then, was one who took lessons from Pops.

'Now I was telling you about the Saratoga Club, on 140th and Lennox Avenue, up in Harlem. Our place and Small's Paradise had mixed audiences. Everybody came up to the club to hear us. Eddie Condon, Jack Teagarden, Gene Krupa (he was learning) and Jimmy Dorsey all used to come to the Saratoga when we played. And they all said ours was the swingingest band.

'Those were great days. All the men had a love of playing, and I don't know when we went to sleep. We had three books of numbers — over 150 arrangements. And they were good, I'll tell you the secret of that band: Luis never wrote too much, never wrote for the soloists, for instance. He'd write enough to keep the backgrounds together, riffs, and so on, and chords for the band — you know, one of those things. But you played what you thought and felt. And every man in that band could blow; every one was a soloist. That was the secret of that band, and it's the secret of Count Basie's band today. It never sounds mechanical. He's featuring rhythm ... and riffs ... and every other number is a blues. In too many bands these days some monkey's written something for you to play that doesn't even know you, know what you can do. How can it sound as good?'

Nicholas, when you first talk to him, is inclined to be reserved in his opinions. But when the discussion gets a hold on him he can let rip with some pretty crisp judgments. These, he makes clear, are not for publication: for he is genuinely anxious to avoid hurting people's feelings. Anyway, his enthusiasm for good playing heavily outweighs his distaste for the bad. His interest in music is intense, and on the several occasions that I have met him here and in Paris he has willingly spent hours talking about it. So, after a few shrewd strictures, he was back on the pleasures of the Saratoga days.

'Intermission at the club,' he said 'we had a cut and some of the band would go. But not all, Russell stayed at the piano, and the New Orleans guys would stay, Red Allen and me, Paul Barbarin and Pops Foster. 'We'd continue for 20 minutes, playing those tunes like *High Society, Clarinet Marmalade* and *Buckets Got A Hole In It*. Then we'd go off, and Russell would have Higgy double on drums, and with Charlie Holmes and those guys he'd play some pop tunes. Sometimes Benny Goodman or the Dorseys would sit in — and Krupa. He was up there listening to Barbarin. Paul was a very good drummer: he knew everybody's style. He had something to push me, and something for everybody. And wonderful fill-ins.

'Well, I remained with the band five years. It was still a great band, could keep swinging all evening, but Russell wanted to alter the style. We all told him: "Luis, don't change our band's style." But he was a hard-headed West Indian when he wanted to be: and when he got an idea, nothing shook him off it. So around 1934 or '35 he started fooling around with those phoney arrangements, and the band went down. I left and joined the new Chick Webb combination at the Savoy.

'He had Louis Bacon and Taft Jordan (just up from Baltimore) on trumpets; Pete Clark and Elmer Williams, saxes; Elmer James, John Truehart, Don Kirkpatrick and Chick were the rhythm; and Charlie Green was on trombone for a few months. That Big Green really could drink — four or five "fifths" in a day. He always had about a pint in his pocket, and he used to bring a straw with him on the bandstand so he could suck the stuff up while we were playing.

'At that time, I remember, Sid Catlett was around often, and Chick used to let him come up and play. I guess he could learn from Chick, too, because Chick certainly played with feeling. Listen to the Webb band play those arrangements down, and see where Chick put in the feeling. He played for the band, not for the people; that's why he was so much admired by musicians. Yes, he was the finest big-band drummer I ever heard.'

Nicholas stayed some ten months with Webb, then rejoined Russell when Louis Armstrong took over the leadership.

In the next part of the interview, we went back to Nick's early career in New Orleans. Nick got started on clarinet through his uncle, Wooden Joe Nicholas, a trumpet player still living in New Orleans.

'I was then around twelve and my uncle gave me my first instrument — a C clarinet,' says Nick. 'After that I had some tuition from the Tios, father, son and uncle. It was not a formal education. Papa Tio was a cigar maker as well as a clarinettist. He taught all the kids: it didn't cost anything, he gave us our learning. Also, I took a few lessons from Big Eye Louis Nelson and Alphonse Picou.

'In those days, our three major clarinettists were Lorenzo Tio, Big Eye and Picou. That Picou played too. I know because I heard that man. He had finished, really, even when they made those earlier records of him.

'Picou was in business, also had some kind of a tinsmith business. I remember he was a safe man with that dollar. Louis Nelson was another of my favourites: he used to have a sound like a voice, but he'd petered out by the time you heard him on records.'

Nicholas played a few dates with Kid Ory's band, then made his real professional start with Oke Gaspard's Maple Leaf Band. He worked with Gaspard before and after his period with the navy, did street parades with Manuel Perez and the Onward Band, and played (around 1920) with Buddy Petit. During 1922 or '23, Nick took his own group into Tom Anderson's Cabaret. He says: 'We played down there for one-and-a-half years: me on alto, Barney Bigard on tenor, Luis Russell (piano), Willie Santiago (banjo), Paul Barbarin on drums and Arnold Metoyer, trumpet.

'This is how Oliver came to send for me. Jimmie Noone came down home for Mardi Gras, heard our little band and was surprised — we were coming up then. He went back to Chicago and told Joe: "They got a band down there!"'

'The fact is that I joined King Oliver twice. The first time, just before Christmas' (1924?). 'I made a little tour with him and after three months went home. We were supposed to play at a place in Chicago — was it the Plantation then? — but it burned down.

'I know I was home about seven months when Joe sent for us. Paul Barbarin, Barney and me caught the same train to Chicago. It happened that we didn't go straight to Joe's band though. The union was very strict, and we didn't want to say we'd come up with the purpose of joining Joe at the Plantation. So we hung around in Chicago for four or five weeks. Then Joe changed the band and we were in. I stayed with him until the summer of '26. He'd sent for Luis Russell a little before us, and Russell was in that band. The reeds were: me on first alto and clarinet; Darnell Howard, third sax (alto), clarinet and violin; and Barney Bigard, tenor and clarinet. Most of the clarinet solos were on my part. We all had soprano saxes, too, but they were out of tune so we didn't bother with them.'

In August, 1926, Nicholas left America to go to Shanghai with Jack Carter's band. For this job he changed to tenor sax. Others in the band were Billy Page (alto), Valaida Snow (trumpet), Teddy Weatherford (piano), Frank Ethridge (guitar, banjo and violin) and Carter (drums).

'I worked in China more than a year,' Nicholas says, 'then left with Ethridge for Singapore and Egypt. After another year in Cairo and Alexandria, I found my way back via Europe, finally making New York towards the end of 1928.'

In these early years, Nicholas — like so many New Orleans players —

consistently used an Albert system clarinet, as the photographs with Oliver's band show. He told me:

'I changed over in Egypt. My Albert needed overhauling and I had to send it to France. A clarinet player in the Symphony lent me his Boehm and taught me the fingering. I practised on that Boehm, and when the Albert came back I'd forgotten the fingering for it.

'I studied real serious while I was there, playing second in the Symphony in Egypt. It was good training technically. They taught us the legitimate fundamentals; of course, the jazz comes from your head, and from what you're hearing.

'Omer Simeon and Barney and Edmond Hall are still on their Alberts, but I prefer the sound of that Boehm. It's a true clarinet. That experience helped me a lot when I got back in the States.'

I asked him for some details of his return to Luis Russell's band, to pick up our earlier conversation.

'After Webb, I came back to Russell — with Armstrong fronting the band. I only stayed a year, got tired of travelling and pulled out to go with a group at Adrian's Tap Room. We made some records then with Adrian and Ward Pinkett, others with Freddy Jenkins and pianist Joe Turner.

'Then I went back with Armstrong and stayed till 1939. In the band we had Louis, Scad Hemphill, Henry Allen and Louis Bacon on trumpets. Later, Otis Johnson came in for Bacon. At this time, 1937, I'd gone over to first tenor: Bingie Madison was on second. And that band could play. On some numbers, like *Alexander's Ragtime Band* and *Heart Full of Rhythm*, you had fifteen men swinging like a small band. And Louis ... there was a part in one of these numbers — in the key of F concert — where the trumpets ended on a G in unison.

'Now those guys could all blow, all loud, and they all hit that one note. And Louis would come and hit that note so big, an octave above them. Louis would hit that note as big as this house every performance, and afterwards Scad would say: "Goddam, how does he do it?"'.

When Albert Nicholas ended his long run with the Armstrong-Russell orchestra in 1939, he spent eight months (rather appropriately) at Nick's, then moved to the Village Vanguard as one of the Zutty Singleton Trio — with Eddie Heywood on piano. 1940 saw him with Bobby Barnet's band at Café Society Uptown, and working off and on with John Kirby ('The smoothest small group in the world'). The following year, with the USA in the war, Nicholas gave up music. For four years he worked at other things — among them a subway guard — and returned to the clarinet late in '45 with Art Hodes at the Stuyvesant. The next March he joined Kid Ory's Creole Band in Hollywood, playing alongside Ory and Mutt Carey.

Almost his last engagement before coming to France in 1953 was for six weeks with Rex Stewart ('Rex has some tough lips, man') at the Savoy, Boston. Now Nicholas plans to go home in the summer. 'But,' he says, 'I'd like to come back and buy a place of my own outside Paris.

'Over here, it's what you're putting down that counts. In the States it's

different. It's what they write about you. They can make a man overnight.
Here, they like you and they respect human dignity. I ain't worried. I'm not
trying to prove nothing. All I want's a good reed, I'm happy.

'My children? They're musical, yes. One plays piano, and one boy plays
clarinet. I wouldn't encourage them to take it up; I had it rough enough.'

Then, with a small Nicholas smile: 'I'd go through it again though; you
know that!'

*When we met again in 1972, it was shortly after Nick's 72nd birthday, which he
had celebrated in England. I heard him warming up on his specially made gold-
plated Selmer with Mike Casimir and the New Iberia Stompers. The tone and
style, fluid but with a popping kind of attack, spoke as eloquently of his Crescent
City upbringing as they did when I first met him almost two decades ago. And
as they did on records twenty years before that.*

*Later on, over a drink and a tape recorder, Nick agreed that the New Orleans
training and the influence of his youthful days were things which stayed with
you always.*

'That New Orleans feeling, you keep that in your playing. Louis never lost
that, neither will I; but you change of course with wider experience.

'That feeling, and the way you phrase the music in New Orleans, it was
natural for me. But I learned more after I left New Orleans to go to Chicago in
1924. Hearing different guys there, you see, I was changing up with the times.
Automatically you change, you go along. That's why I never sound like
George Lewis, you know, because I didn't stay; I moved from New Orleans. I
was playing this part, that part, saxophones and that kind of stuff. But I never
lost my mentality of New Orleans, see?

'But you come up through the years. I went to work with King Oliver until
1926, and Joe handled a band with plenty of discipline. You had to play your
part. Joe wanted to hear everybody in the band — no one man making all that
noise, he wanted to hear the ensemble. That was Joe Oliver. He was a bandsman, a good leader.'

And what of the swing element? Did Nicholas notice a difference in the way
bands were swinging when he reached Chicago?

'Well, yes, in Chicago and later New York it was a little different, sure, but
not necessarily better. When you talk of swinging, let me tell you something.
Buddy Petit had the swingiest little group I ever heard, but way back.

'Simon and John Marrero were on bass and guitar, or banjo, and those cats
were playing, man. No piano in that band and they would swing you into bad
health.'

How was Petit as a cornet player?

'Buddy was fine, too. He didn't play high like Louis Armstrong but he played
a full horn. What I remember especially, and I used to work with him sometimes,
is that Buddy had more gigs than anybody in New Orleans. He was always
booked up a year ahead, like from this Christmas till next, playing one-nighters.
That's the only band I know that was booked up from one year to the next.'

Armstrong had died since my previous meeting with Nick, and it was inevitable we should talk about him. Armstrong was born in New Orleans five weeks after Nicholas, though in a different district and into a more oppressive environment, and they knew each other slightly as boys and very well subsequently. Nick has said in past interviews, and still says today, that of all the musicians he's worked with in jazz, Armstrong was the greatest. He has pointed out how astonishing it is that Louis rose from the poorest ghetto to become the world's best.

I supposed that the clarinettist would not have run into Louis as a child, and he agreed. Were their circumstances very different? 'Yes, I think they were and I guess my life then was a good deal easier than his. You see Louis came up in the rough days in a rough part of New Orleans. He lived Uptown, right around from the Parish Prison. When I met him he was a little raggedy boy around ten, eleven years old. It was way before he got known at all, I mean before he even went into the boys home, and then when he came out, as a trumpet player, I started hearing him and hearing about him.' That would have been the year of 1914. The mention of the Waifs' Home refers to the fact of Armstrong's having received musical tuition there. This was another point of dissimilarity in the two men's upbringing. Nicholas came from a musical family, growing up with instruments around him and tuition on hand. So far as he (or I) know, Louis had no family musical background at all. Thus Nick was surprised to find him playing good cornet at the age of fourteen or so. And a bigger surprise awaited him five years later.

'I'll tell you what amazed me with Louis was when I came out of the navy in 1919. He was on the boats with Fate Marable's orchestra, and a young man by then. And clean, and blowing so much horn. So when I saw Pops I said: "My, well I'll be durned. What you been doing?" We got to talking, and he remembered me when I was a kid, you know, six or seven years before.

'But his playing! When I heard him I said: "Jesus, listen at this man." Well, I knew Louis Armstrong was great then, and Manuel Perez and all the trumpet players admired him too, when he was on the riverboats. They used to say: "You just watch this boy, he's going to cut everybody." Manuel was a hell of a musician himself, and he told me: "That Louis is something else".'

Manuel Perez — like Jelly Roll Morton, Sidney Bechet, Johnny St Cyr, Wooden Joe Nicholas and the clarinettists already cited — were Creoles who had social and cultural backgrounds which differed widely from those of the black Uptown musicians who were the immediate descendents of slaves. Was there much opposition between the Creoles and Uptown players such as Bolden, Bunk Johnson, the Dodds brothers, Oliver and Armstrong? Nick said there wasn't, although each district tended to cultivate its own style of playing.

'No, they all played together in the brass bands. Those were mixed bands, Creole and Uptown. In a brass band they were solid, they were one, you know: Joe Oliver and Manuel Perez, see? But the dance bands like the Magnolia and Buddy Petit, Kid Rena and all like that were different. We had our bands, you see, and your Uptown, you had Chris Kelly, you had Frankie

Dusen, and so on. They sounded a little different, more gut-bucket, but there were always many different styles of music in New Orleans.'

These differences stemmed naturally from the kind of training received by the boys Downtown and those Uptown. Nick, from Downtown, learned by what he calls the method. And he had an early advantage: his uncle was clarinettist-cornettist Joseph Nicholas.

'My Uncle Joe, Wooden Joe, he's playing his clarinet at home, I mean, and it was fascinating to me. So ever since I can remember I always wanted to play clarinet, and my uncle was the influence for that. My father, he wanted me to finish school and learn medicine and all that stupidity, and I said: "No, I want to play music." But my mother, she was against it, said I was too delicate and all like that.

'So my father told me: "All right, you want to be a musician, but I'm telling you something. You be a good one. First, you're going to study music. And I don't want none of that drinking. Don't let me catch you in no bar with no whisky or nothing like that." I promised.

'Anyhow, when I got to be nine or ten years old my uncle bought me this clarinet, an E flat instrument. He got it for me in the morning and then went out. What he didn't know, I'd been practising on his clarinet when he'd go out. I used to blow it, you know, and pick up some fingering. He didn't know it for almost a year.

'So the day I got the clarinet, when he came back he wanted to put it together for me. I said: "I know how to fix it," and picked up the horn, put it together, tried the reed out, and then I went broom-ti-boomadi boom . . .'

Here Nick launched into the opening four bars of *Oh, You Beautiful Doll.* Wooden Joe had looked at him in silence for a few moments and declared: 'How the hell? Now you didn't learn that in no one day. Wait a minute there.'

Then Albert's grandmother told Wooden Joe: 'Oh, shut your mouth, Joe. This boy's been fooling with your horn every day for months.'

After that, with the benefit of some training from Wooden Joe, Nick says he took lessons until he was about fourteen, 'with Big Eye Louis Nelson, with Papa Tio and then Lorenzo Tio, who was my real teacher.'

Papa Tio, real name Luis Tio, was a concert musician who worked with brass bands and dance groups. He played ragtime, as jazz was called then, with a legitimate touch and was very particular about pupils learning correctly, studying the rudiments and getting to know the instrument.

'He was a cigar maker by trade,' Albert recalls, 'and he'd retired from music. But he was a hell of a clarinet player who had performed opera and all kinds of classical music. No, you wouldn't describe him as a jazz player; he was legit. Papa was a fine teacher, though. He used to roll cigars while you were taking your lessons, but he'd hear every time you were scuffling with your notes.

'Now Junior, Lorenzo Tio Junior, was a fine clarinettist also, but he got many a whipping to play correctly. That's why he played so well. He used to tell us: "Man, if you got as many spankings as I got, why, you just had to learn."

'And Junior was quite young then, a tall, handsome guy who was in his middle twenties I think. And he could read, oh man. Give him a violin part and he'd transpose it at sight; I've seen him do it. That's quite a study, you know.'

So this musical tuition, which equipped Nick to enter the profession at the age of fifteen, would have been nothing unusual for a young Creole musician such as Noone, Bigard, or Albert Burbank.

And an Uptowner like Johnny Dodds — how did Nicholas regard him?

'I liked his playing very much and always liked the man. I followed him into the Oliver band, you know. Johnny was probably mostly self-taught, and he originated a style quite unlike ours.

'Yes, Dodds was more gutbucket, an absolute jazz player who could improvise things we wouldn't think of doing in those days. He was one of my early idols.

'Now Johnny was an ear man. They were mostly ear players from Uptown and during those times we used to call them big-ear guys. We'd say: "Man, those Big Ears." Yes, Johnny was a bitch.'

In the final section of the 1972 interview, Nick recalled Jelly Roll Morton. Albert Nicholas knew Jelly Roll intimately, played clarinet in his bands occasionally and recorded with him in 1919 and '30 and again in 1939 and '40. Morton admired Nick as much as any clarinettist outside of Omer Simeon; and Nick reciprocated the regard. A boaster he might have been, Nicholas admits, but one who could live up to his boasts, who was good to work for, and was a keen and honest judge of a man's musicianship. If Jelly seemed a know-all this was, in Nick's view, because he knew what was happening.

'When Jelly tell you something, you put your money on it. Because he knows already, he's done found out. He was a sure shot, you know; he didn't gamble at that foolishness. He was sure when he said he was sure — he'd gotcha. So that's what the guys didn't dig about Jelly, those who didn't like him. 'Cos a few of them, they dug Jelly as I did.

'When that man died, I never knew till then he had so many friends. And when he was living, no one had so many enemies. Well, maybe not real enemies, but guys who'd say: "Oh, man, you talk too much."'

History has told us that Morton was something of a pimp and gambler as well as a superb piano soloist, band player, leader and arranger-composer. Was it his extra-musical activities that incurred the envy or disappoval of fellow musicians? Nicholas didn't look too sure.

'Yes, he was a hustler but I don't think it was that. Of course Jelly had always been sharp, and in his young days he made his money easily.

'When I was a kid in New Orleans Jelly worked in the District, playing piano in the whore-houses, you understand? He was making 50 dollars a night then, and you know in 1910 and round there 50 dollars was a hell of a lot of money. People were making ten dollars a week if they were lucky. For the average musician a dollar, dollar and a half a day was good pay. So Jelly always looked sharp.

'He dressed sharp, with rings and diamond pins and everything, and knew all them big pimps and sporting people. He was in the circle, and he had women and things.

'I'll tell you one thing about Jelly, he used to leave New Orleans and go out West and come back with a suitcase full of money. No really, a suitcase full of money. That's Jelly.

'One time he went up to Memphis, Tennessee, this was before 1920, and they didn't know him up there then. There was a big pool room there where they had one of those piano parlours. Jelly heard this cat playing the back room, some of those piano tunes. Jelly was playing pool, and he was a sure shot at that game, too.

'So he'd won two or three hundred dollars and was getting ready to leave, and he asked who was playing piano. The man told him: "That's so-and-so," who was big there. Jelly Roll said: "Man, I can play what he's playing; then I'll play something that he can't play." This fellow only knew Jelly as a pool player, so he told him he was out of his mind and to put his money where his mouth was. Jelly says: "I'll play what he plays and fifty more, I bet you, I'll play something he can't play." So the man says: "All right, put your money up," and they put up the bets and give it to the bartender to hold.

'They go over to the piano player and explain the bet. The pianist says sure, and the man tells him: "Go ahead, play, I'm betting on you now."

'So he plays his piece and Jelly had him covered already, and when he got through they said to Jelly: "Okay, your turn." He sat down and played the same thing the other fellow just played, and well. They looked at him, you know, and the pianist said: "Hey, this guy is something else." Of course Jelly was laughing. He asked the cat: "Say, how'm I doin"?' Then he said he was going to play something difficult. "Now you hear this one," and he went into one of his own things, wham!

'That beat of his, you know, they'd never heard that before. This piano player listened and said to the bartender: "Give him the money."

'And Jelly announced: "You know who I am? I'm Jelly Roll Morton. The Greatest. I invented jazz." So they say: "What? Is that Jelly Roll?"

'You see, as far as they knew he was Wining Boy. That's what Jelly called himself when he was playing pool, and it's a name that applies to hustlers and such. Now he's telling them he's Jelly Roll.

'Oh man, he was funny. And Jelly was strict, you know, on his sessions. Didn't drink, and insisted on having his music played right. Another thing about him: "Don't you start in playing loud," he used to say. "A lot of these cats, especially these Northerners, they're playing double forte from the word go. But if you start double forte, where you going to go? There's nowhere to go if you need to come up." He was right about that, and a lot of other things. And he liked good players.

'He never bit his tongue, though. If you played, he'd tell you so; if you couldn't play, he'd say: "Man, you don't play nothin'". He'd tell you to your face, didn't go round behind your back. He would tell you: "Can't play nothing."

'That was Jelly. He was a lifeman. Later on in New York, when there was nothing happening, guys looking for gigs would come up to him on the corner. One cat would say: "Hi, Jelly, I heard you'd got a recording session. Why don't you hire me?" He'd say: "You can't play nothing, that's why." That was his nature, you see.'

Those days, in New York, Morton kept no regular band but went out on the road with pick-up groups. 'The only band Jelly ever had in New York,' publisher Harrison Smith once wrote me, 'was the one round his hat.' Nick had an amusing tale about this.

'We were in the Saratoga Club, New York, Luis Russell's band. One of the best in town and we worked there a year with no day off. Finally we got two weeks holiday, and Jelly heard about it and started to get his mind together. He came to Russell and asked to use his band for a short tour. Luis said it was okay if the guys agreed. 'Jelly said: "Russell, I'm going to pay you 40 dollars a night to stay home, I don't need you." That was Jelly. "But I'm going to book the band." He didn't say what he was going to give us and we didn't ask him. Most of the fellows knew him, and Jelly was always correct. So we agreed.

'He booked us into a park in Pennsylvania. When you blew, these windows were open in this hall, and the people didn't come in until they heard the sounds. If they liked them, the place filled up. Jelly told the booker he would pack his joint that night, and the man said: 'Oh, Jelly, I heard that before. If you bring me two hundred people I'll be happy.' Jelly says the second night he will need the police there to keep the people in line.

'That night Jelly told us not to say who we were, but to say Jelly Roll Morton's band. We weren't known much outside New York, and we were playing in Pennsylvania. This was back in 1930–31.

'Well, we hit, and we'd rehearsed these stomps of his and we had a good band: Red Allen, Bill Dillard, Otis Johnson, Higginbotham, Charlie Holmes, Greely Walton and myself was the front line. In other words, we were tight. And Jelly moved with us.

'The booker said: "That Jelly's got a band in there." It was nine o'clock and word got round fast. By ten the hall was full. The man asked what the hell was happening, and where we were from. We told him: "This is Jelly Roll's band."

'Jelly was so proud; told the man: "Hey, what did I tell you?" The next night at nine o'clock the place is filled before we get out there to play. When we get through the first set, there's lines of people outside and police is keeping them straight.

'"See what I tell you," Jelly is saying, and the man he can't believe it. He says: "Yeah, people are asking about this band. When can you come back?"

'Jelly says: "I'm booked out man, too busy. You're too late." The man asks if it's money. "No, it's not the money," Jelly says. "I'm booked right out for a year. Pity you didn't hire me before." Yes, Jelly could be funny.'

Nick said how sad it was that Morton should have died before benefitting from the renaissance of classic jazz.

'He died heartbroken, didn't have a dime,' Nick reflected. 'And millions of dollars must have been earned since then from his records and compositions. Heard his sister collected two hundred and something thousand dollars royalties.

'If he'd been able to come over to Europe, like Bechet and myself and many others did, oh man, he'd be a star attraction.'

This is assuming that Jelly Roll would have agreed the terms. He was, in Nick's words, hard to please and arrogant, especially in defeat. At the Rhythm Club in New York, during the times of his fading reputation, he used to sit in and play against all the best pianists in the East: Waller, Jimmy Johnson, Willie The Lion, even Tatum. The Lion has told how those New York professors cut Jelly to pieces, but Nick takes a different view. 'They were brilliant, sure, but Jelly had his own style and to me it was always perfect.' And he adds that when Duke Ellington came in, and Jelly asked him to take over at the keyboard when he'd done with it, Duke declined the invitation. Then, too, musicians used to ask Morton: 'Hey, Jelly, why don't you go and sit in the same street as Basie and all them cats swinging up there?' And Jelly would reply: 'Man, they can't pay me.'

The talk of Morton reminded Nick keenly of New Orleans in his young days when it was 'a nice place for musicians'. It was hard to make a living from music alone, but most of the old-timers had other trades.

'And we didn't have no discrimination when I was coming up, not where I lived in the Seventh Ward in the Creole section. We were all playing together. Well, we lived more or less together, right next door to each other — passing food over the fence and all that sort of stuff. That was New Orleans.

'New Orleans was the only city of its kind in the world. Nothing like it anywhere; it had no peer. I thought all the world would be like New Orleans. That's where I was wrong. I realised that when I started travelling, when I joined the Merchant Navy towards the end of 1916. Yes, I saw the world then. To me New Orleans was the best town for music, food and spirit, you know, the happiness of people.'

And today?

'Today it's good in a different way and I enjoy going again. Well, about a year and a half ago I had the chance to go back there. That was my first visit in thirty some years, since I'd been there with Louis Armstrong in 1937. Many a thing has changed and I got some big surprises, I tell you.

'My son and me, we were walking on Bourbon Street in the afternoon — we'd parked the car on Iberville — and I was getting the feeling of New Orleans again. We had walked all around Canal, you know, and I wanted to see Bourbon Street in the day time. Well, that part hadn't changed too drastically; they keep it much like it was when I was around that district. But the other part has changed considerably. I didn't know it. I was standing on Claiborne Avenue, looking around and I asked my son: "Where's Claiborne Avenue?"

'Roy said; "We're on Claiborne Avenue." I said: "What?" Overpasses and all that. See, it was place where we used to walk along the middle, you know? Anyway, that's all gone.

'Now I got another surprise. We saw a cab on Bourbon Street and we say; "Let's take this." We got in and sat in the back and began talking about the town. I was telling Roy how things had altered but it was beautiful to be back, seeing old friends and hearing them play in Preservation Hall. This driver, he's listening to the conversation and all at once he turns and asks my son: "Say, are you a musician?" Roy said no but that his father was.

'So this man said: "Well, my daddy was a musician, too. Maybe you might know of him."

'I asked who he was. He say: "Johnny Dodds." Well, I fell out. He looked around again and, man, he looked just like Johnny Dodds.

'"Do I know your Daddy? I should say I do," I tell him. "I been knowing your daddy since 1912." So he asked: "Well, who are you, man?"

'I said: "I'm Albert Nicholas." It was his turn to say "What?" He stopped the cab at once and got out. He said: "This calls for a drink."

'We went into a bar and got to talking. He's taller than Johnny used to be, but Johnny's face you know. He said he had old pictures of me with King Oliver, said: "My dad had some of those pictures at home."

'But he was a little baby then, about three or four years old. He was very interesting, and told me he had a brother in Chicago. Neither of the sons were in music. This younger brother — I never met him — had a good job in the insurance business. Young Johnny gave me his brother's card and said for me to call when I was in Chicago. I had to split, though, next day to come on back to Switzerland. But wasn't that some meeting? Sure reminded me of Johnny.

'Well, that's New Orleans.'

TWO
Saxophone

Bud Freeman

There was hardly ever a time in my life, after the age of twelve or thirteen, when Bud Freeman was not a name to be conjured with. The McKenzie–Condon recordings were among the first acquired by our amateur band, and when I graduated from soprano sax to tenor I invested more than I could afford in discs on which Freeman or Hawkins could be heard. My first experience of extended tenor solos were provided by Bud on Condon's The Eel *and Hawk on* I've Got To Sing A Torch Song, *both recorded in '33. I don't remember which hit me first but they both struck hard. Over the following decade, Freeman sandpapered his tone a little, increased his harmonic know-how and continued to boot out the tenor in distinctive fashion with his Summa Cum Laude Orchestra and Famous Chicagoans, and on such solo outings with big bands as his vigorous improvisatiom on Tommy Dorsey's* Stop, Look And Listen.*

By the time LPs took hold, Freeman was a recognised and always recognis-able 'Jazz Immortal', well placed to record frequently, tour widely, play festivals on an international scale and, since 1963, indulge his long-held taste for Shakespeare, England and what he presumed to be English manners and culture. I had heard about Bud's obsession, partly on the grapevine and partly from a listen to that eccentric recording called Private Jives, *a misrepresentation of Coward's* Private Lives *on which the aspiring actor was assisted by Minerva Pious, Everett Sloan and Joe Bushkin. So I thought it a stroke of luck in the summer of '63, when Bud was wafted off to Fort Belvedere, home of Gerald Lascelles (cousin of the Queen), directly from London Airport. Like Dizzy Gillespie, Buck Clayton and their American colleagues, Bud was impressed by the house and gardens, and especially the cannon overlooking the lawn. Humphrey Lyttelton, also at the Fort Belvedere reception, wrote that Freeman enthused to him: 'England is just as I always imagined it.'*

A lunch with me at the Wig & Pen club, opposite the Law Courts in the Strand, further strengthened the veteran tenorman's belief in the Old Country, though he was to suffer disillusionment later on. What follows is a group of three pieces on Bud (I wrote several more) covering a fifteen-year span. The first dates from December 1965 and the third from 1980 when he decided to return to the United States to live.

Bud Freeman has been playing professionally for forty years and more. In his young days in Chicago he heard the pioneer bands from New Orleans, and was actively associated with the development of what came to be called Chicago Style. Over lunch this week in London, Freeman talked about great musicians he had known, and I asked him to name the masters, the originators, who had impressed him most.

'Bix Beiderbecke, Louis Armstrong and King Oliver, they were the three important cornet players in those days. They were like James P. Johnson, Fats Waller, Teddy Weatherford and Lucky Roberts on piano. They were like Bessie Smith and Ethel Waters, the people who have said it. The great drummers would have to be Baby Dodds, Dave Tough and Sid Catlett — the greatest drummers of all time in this idiom.'

What about saxophone players, tenors in particular?

'Nobody seems to know about Jack Pettis, but he was the first swinging tenor player I ever heard. Since there was no one before him, playing that style, I have to call him a master.

'It must be realised that there was a Chicago school of tenor. There were many players who played in that style and didn't become well-known. Pettis was the king of that style.

'They called the style North-western then. It had the cool sound and a Louis-King Oliver beat. Lester Young, though he may not have known Pettis, was influenced by that particular school of tenor. A lot of saxophone players in the early Twenties were pretty corny, and this swinging style was played by very few.

'I think Lester was the finest player on the tenor of his time, but I don't believe he created that style. He played it better than anyone before him. Then Hawkins, he became the first authoritative voice on tenor.

'A point about these masters is that they were so fabulous in their time and they sound marvellous today. I was listening to Bix on records the other night, and everything he played sounded so alive. But the people he played with weren't jazz players.

'I think Bix was the perfect player; he had the perfect, profound understanding of jazz. Often, I'm asked what he was like as a person. To me, Bix was not only a master of his instrument but an artist who loved the theatre, loved to read, who loved the aesthetic life. When I was playing with Ben Pollack in New York's Little Club in '28, Beiderbecke came down to tell me that John Barrymore was back from England with the English company that had been playing *Hamlet*. He told me they were going to do *Hamlet* on radio that night, and I went with him to hear it. I remember being gone an hour and a half or more and missing the next set. Pollack was furious, but Bix and I were great friends from then on.'

How does Freeman feel about singers?

'Truthfully, there are not many singers I can stand. But I remember Bessie and Ethel vividly. It was Beiderbecke who took me to hear Bessie for the first time, at a place called Paradise Gardens where Jimmie Noone had the band. Jimmie was another musician we all listened to.

'It was a club which began at midnight and went on until eight in the morning. Bessie would come out unannounced and sing dozens of choruses of one song. Yes she was the singer so far as I am concerned.

'I believe a great jazz musician is no different from a great artist in any of the arts. If he hadn't been a player he would have written a poem or acted in a play or painted a picture. How many times have we heard musicians say: "I couldn't make a living so I got out of the business"? A real artist couldn't have said that. He has to play as he has to breathe.'

In the Twenties, Bud was a member of the Austin High School Gang, with Frank Teschemacher and Jimmy McPartland, which played a predominant part in the formation of Chicago Style. From where did the Austin group and Freeman get their inspiration?

'The Austin High Gang were not copyists. They were influenced by what they heard from the Oliver band and others, and inspired to create a new style. Really, they weren't trying to copy New Orleans jazz or anything.

'Yes, we listened to the New Orleans Rhythm Kings. But they were synthetic compared to the real thing when Dave Tough took us to hear King Oliver.'

What of Jelly Roll Morton?

'I think of Jelly Roll as an important composer and organiser. There was a big part of our jazz study that we were to learn from Jelly, who was one of the first musicians to get away from the corny style of playing — the dotted eighth style.

'As for myself, my style came from everything: from Bessie, Ethel, Louis, Bix, Oliver, Noone, Lucky Roberts and all the great pianists. And I like to think it rolled itself up into something belonging to me. Because if jazz is anything, it is the expression of the individual. And it is happy music. It's music come of oppression, and its final effect is of happy music. Jazz has powerful therapy.

'Isn't it interesting that the early masters of jazz did not react with hostility but reacted with love, and gave us this warm and powerful music?'

And now we move forward ten years to 1975, and away from general topics and into the recording studio.

'I want to be known as a Londoner, you understand that don't you? If one is going to do what I want to do, one has to be in London, at least for three months of the year.'

The precise, Anglicised American voice and careful enunciation are as instantly recognisable as the speaker's resilient tenor saxophone playing. Lawrence (Bud) Freeman is conversing. Bud is making his latest in-Britain album, which is the fourth he has cut over here, if memory serves me faithfully, and the third under his own name. I was present at the first, as it happens, which took place in the Philips-Fontana studio near Marble Arch one blazing day in June, 1966.

The tenorman worked very informally then with a rhythm trio comprising Dick Katz, Spike Heatley and Tony Crombie. They played a set of standards, most of which Bud had recorded on previous occasions, plus a blues in B flat and *The Eel*. They made thirteen tunes in the day. The result: twelve of those tracks in fact, appeared under the album title of *Bud Freeman Esq*. The cover picture showed the American in dark suit and bowler, brief case pressed to his side, standing on Westminster Bridge with Big Ben in the background. He looked like a retired Guards officer who'd found refuge in the City, and this ultra-English image is something Bud has been cultivating for years. It is said he first assumed a British accent back in the Chicago days when Mezz Mezzrow had the idea of making Freeman into a movie actor. However that may be, he's always been known to keen collectors as a mild Anglomaniac.

Now after many visits in the past dozen years, he has settled in Europe, dividing his time between this country, Northern Ireland, Germany, Denmark and other Continental countries. Most of all he feels at home here. But then, as he points out in well-modulated tones: 'We do speak the same language ... almost.' Right now, he insists, he is busier than he wishes to be. 'I'd like to cut my work down to about six months in the year so I can do more writing. By next year I'll have three books out.'

Bud has quite recently recorded with the Dutch Swing College Band, and has several other Continental record deals in the offing. But he was easily tempted to fly into London to be reunited on disc with his former reed partner in the World's Greatest Jazz Band, Bob Wilber, and to play alongside Bruce Turner for the first time anywhere. So he is back in the same studio near Marble Arch, though it is now known as Phonogram, putting down new versions of *Blue Room*, a Freeman original called *That D Minor Thing*, another original, *Song Of A Tenor*, and the tune *Keep Smiling At Trouble* he first recorded for British Parlophone in 1936 and again for Commodore two years later.

Bud explains the sequence, the horns try it out, then a routine is worked out quickly in the studio. 'Shall we run it down?' asks someone. Away they go, playing a unison then breaking out into free-sounding interplay followed by solos from one or other of the saxmen, over riffing, and perhaps from pianist Keith Ingham or bassist Peter Ind. A little chat, a run-through of a tricky passage, one more try at the whole thing, and producer David Baker says from the control room: 'O.K., this is take one.'

Once the arrangement is settled, and some of the tunes on the second session next day have scored sections written by Wilber, Bob tends to take charge — controlling the design and dynamics of a performance, pointing or gesturing at different musicians as they are required to come in or cut out. At one moment, as Freeman is about to begin a chorus, Wilber looks across at Bobby Orr and

draws a hand across his throat. The drums fall silent on cue. At the end there's
discussion, but not too much. Bob is dissatisfied with the intro, also the coda
come to that. Variations are developed, a chase between alto and soprano is
developed for one number, Bob sets the tempo and take two is cut.

Then it's; 'Let's do one more; we gotta get that last chord,' and 'Right. Take
three.' After that, everyone troops into the control room to hear them back.
People are congratulated for some particular musical felicity, also suggestions
are made, often jokily.

'After Bruce, we go back to the diminished,' instructs Wilber gently. 'Yes I
wish you would gentlemen,' says Bud pleasantly. 'You've been f—— about
long enough.' He sometimes employs ancient English.

For the final session, Freeman has allowed his sartorial taste to slip along
with his language, and he's clad in old jeans plus, on his dignified head, a
Scottish cap such as might be worn by chilren or golfers. The even, unstrained
progress of record-making is interrupted by tea being served with biscuits and
sandwiches, and musicians and recording staff fall on the provender, aided by
two or three onlookers. The latter included, at various stages, TV director
Colin Strong (who was quizzing Bud for a projected appearance on the
Parkinson Show), photographers Ole Bask (with CBS News in London) and
Fred Warren, a number of jazz buffs, World Jazz Records' Gerry Finningley,
Freeman's agent Robert Masters and, of course, the man from the *MM*.

I take advantage of the interregnum to ask Bud about a particular feature of
The Eel's Nephew, a modernish offspring of that serpentine classic invented by
Uncle Lawrence for a 1933 Eddie Condon date. At one point he had declared:
'I think it would be better if we all played in D flat.' Suggestions had been made
and accepted and, after a, 'Here we go,' Bruce and Bud on saxes and Bob on
clarinet indulged themselves in a collective improvisation which drew a spontaneous round of applause from the control-room hangers-on.

I speak of the technical expertise involved in one particularly free-wheeling,
swirling example of reedmanship. Bud Freeman is not a man to let a dubious
remark fly by unchallenged.

'Everything is technique,' he says with a rise of the eyebrows. 'One note can
denote technique. I mean, one note can be improvisation; it depends on the
interpretation.'

Freeman is a man whose individuality of approach on his instrument is allied
to firm views on how jazz should be enjoyed and regarded by those fortunate
enough to play it.

'I hope the fellows enjoyed that as much as I did,' he's inclined to say at the
end of a session. And, at the finish of this two-day recording stint, he advances
the opinion that it is one of the most interesting he's participated in for years.
All the musicians are 'just wonderful.' But then with Bud they almost always
are, at least in conversation with pressmen. He explains his attitude:

'The greatest mistake an artist can make, in my opinion, is if he says
something disparaging about another artist, because that is like saying he thinks
of himself as being the criterion. And it's so silly, really. No one is ever going to
know in that sense. Just think of all the great music that's been written and

created long before we were on this earth. People readily come along and say they don't like this sort of music or that. They come along and tell you they don't like Beethoven, for instance. Well, if they can say they don't like Beethoven then I suppose they can say they don't like anybody.

'But I believe, first of all, that it's a form of insecurity to have to say that another musician doesn't play well. And frankly, it does not matter all that much whether somebody thinks you play well or not. It's what one thinks of oneself that matters, not in an egomaniacal sense but rather in the sense of liking or disliking one's own work. I am most unhappy, not when a critic says he doesn't like my work, but when I feel I don't like my work. Then I'm troubled.

'Up to now, having played for fifty-one years, I've been able to feel that I improve a little with experience. I would rather hope that I'm playing better today. Of course one could ask, "What do you mean by better? Are you going to change your style?" No, I want to play what I play better to my taste as I go along. But I must play what suits me.'

Freeman is acknowledged to be one of the originals of jazz tenor playing. And it has often been remarked upon that he survives changes of popular taste in jazz, and is stimulated by new developments (studying with Tristano for example), without radically altering his strongly personal style.

I ask whether he has been, even temporarily, thrown off course by sudden advances in jazz thinking and technique. His smile is paternal as he shakes his head.

'It's never been a matter of being thrown off. It's a matter of having the experience of the great masters, of hearing the great masters and knowing that was the inception. And knowing also that it has not been exploited yet. The vein has not been fully mined.

'The old King Oliver, the old Louis Armstrong music has not been exploited yet. You must realise this was an esoteric kind of music, and it's marvellous what you can do with it. The New York Jazz Repertory performance is just one example of a creative approach.

'In my view Louis was the great player, he was the great master of jazz. And I know that Bix also was a great master. But one would have to have been there, you see. The kids can't hear through the other people's playing in the Whiteman band; they can't really hear Bix. If they could have heard Bix as I did, in person, and played with him, then they would have known that he was probably the genius of our times.

'Now when I say that, I'm not trying to influence others' opinions; I'm just talking of what I heard and what I feel and what I know about music. I've no intention of trying to convert anybody.

'Louis was the great influence. He was, unfortunately, copied by every untalented player in the world, as well as some very talented people. Whereas Bix Beiderbecke was perhaps a more estoric taste. You see, when you listen to anything that's played in jazz, any jazz figure played today, you can trace it back to Louis. He was the great inventor and innovator of our music.'

And the young Freeman, is he one of the many who came under Armstrong's spell?

'Well, I was very much influenced by Louis, very much by Bix, by Ethel Waters and Bessie Smith, very much influenced by the dancers and by the great clarinettists and pianists — specially influenced by James P. Johnson and Fats Waller.

'I loved the clarinet as an instrument, loved to hear others play, but never had any feeling for playing it myself. I always loved the tenor. Yes, I tried clarinet on records in the Thirties but never cared for it. If you'd been environed with all the great clarinet players I was, you wouldn't have touched the instrument.

'People often think that it will make a better living for them if they play more instruments, but I think a musician really has to play one instrument if he's going to play it well. I still dream that one day I'm going to play it the way I want, you know.'

In this respect, then, Bud feels as Coleman Hawkins used to, when towards the end of his life he told me he was studying the tenor still, learning new things about it, aiming for the mastery of, say, a Casals.

'Yes, yes,' Bud nodded his agreement. 'Hawkins was a truly great musician. It was sad that at the end he had no desire to live. He was another great master.

'But, you see, I never had the ambition to be a Hawkins. I used the tenor as a means of expressing the feeling I had for a given kind of music. One had to play as one had to eat; it was something that burned inside of you. Naturally, as you got deeper into the music business and saw the horrors of it, the terrible life it presented, you then became disillusioned. But with the business, not the music. The finality is that you love the music as I, having played for more than fifty years, love it now very much. I love concerts and recording. I don't like night clubs because they remind me of my childhood. There was always something very depressing about them. I had to play in them to learn how to play.'

The period Bud is looking back to would be around 1925, and he remained in Chicago, his birthplace, until early 1928. Before that, he had made his first records with the McKenzie and Condon Chicagoans, one of the titles being *Nobody's Sweetheart*. We are vividly reminded of it because the band plays it complete with opening and closing choruses written out by Bob Wilber after the original arrangement, which he explains was done by clarinettist Frank Teschemacker. Bob adds a few touches of his own, and a clean take is soon down and accepted. Gene Krupa played drums on the 1927 version, and the first discographies added 'Mezz Mezzrow (cymbals),' which may be said to be a euphemism. Wilber smiles at Bud and says he hears that Mezz was in the studio with the stuff, and that everyone started the session pretty high. Freeman doesn't disagree.

Drinks are unearthed during the next break, and I'm able to tell the tenorman I hear he's about to visit the States. He says yes, he'll be over there for about five days, making an album with guitarist Bucky Pizzarelli, of Cole Porter numbers.

'I don't live over there any more,' says Bud, 'so then I'll come back and do some concerts in Germany, make an album with strings in Holland, and play in various countries here before going to Australia.'

Bud has one book out already in the USA, *You Don't Look Like A Musician*, which is being boned-up on by the Parkinson team. His second, *If You Know Of A Better Life ... Will You Let Me Know*, is being published in Ireland sometime next month. It is a paperback of about fifty or sixty pages, and Bud thinks it contains some anecdotes and points of view which people will find amusing. Each little story has its own heading, and one tale recalls the gangster era and the work-places of Freeman's youth.

'This is the story: I was playing in one of these places, a club which was run by the underworld in Chicago, and as I walked in I saw a lot of men wearing hats, and with collars turned up, and knives and guns bulging. I was a little apprehensive about it all, and this certain tough Tony came over and put his arm around me, and he said: "Now Buddy, I don't want you to worry about nobody in this here joint. Because nobody in this here joint will hurt you unless he gets paid for it."'

Bud laughs at it now. 'So I call that piece *Consolation*,' he says, and turns to the task of mixing a vodka and tonic with ice. Then it's back into the studio to try one more before calling it a day.

The last of the three Freeman pieces ties up some of the loose ends left hanging in the earlier conversations, and also ranges much more widely over Bud's career. There is a little more detail about the Austin High School Gang, and references to the big band phase of Bud's life, with Tommy Dorsey, and Benny Goodman.

'Dance music is coming back, I feel sure of that.' Bud Freeman smiles hopefully, then looks serious. 'The world has had it with way-out improvisation. All this music used to be played as dance music, and is essentially dance music. Once it loses that beat it loses something vital to its survival.'

Bud, who is about to leave for 'Sweet Home Chicago' via Amsterdam, surveys his audience with the knowing look of someone who has seen it all come and go. As he started playing jazz in Chicago in the early Twenties, he has seen a great deal. I suppose that back then, in the gang-run clubs where Freeman first met the public eye, in a musical sense, customers would dance to the bands.

'Of course,' he replies, 'in those days they danced to everything. Naturally, with most of the bands I played in, we used to do *our* thing but you know they loved it. Nobody came up with a gun and told you how to play. No, I must say that from our point of view they were an excellent audience.'

Bud laughs a lot when telling stories, which is one of his favourite pursuits. At this particular time he is clueing-up his support team for an imminent performance and everything is very relaxed. The drummer asks if he has a preference for sticks or brushes and Bud says sticks please, because they give a little more drive.

'You must forgive me, gentlemen, if I seem to have changed my way of playing,' he goes on, 'but I'm into the ballad thing and I'm loving it. I don't mean those sweet, cloying tunes but swinging ballads, you know.' He hums a few bars, marking a swing tempo with snapping fingers. Everyone looks happy with the suggestion. A few more details out of the way and the set has been set-up. Turning to me with a slight apology for the instrusion of mundane matters, the jazz veteran picks up his theme again.

'I'd like to say that I believe we're running into a change of direction, which happens every now and then as you know in this music. I think melodic line is becoming very important again, and I approve of that personally. If a song is beautiful, beautifully constructed, why ruin it with improvisation?'

The eyebrows go up in polite enquiry. Bud, by the way, like so many Americans, stresses the second syllable of the word 'Improvisation'. He looks cautious for a second or two and adds that he doesn't intend to criticise those who believe in improvising at all times.

'A lot of people make a living doing just that. That's their privilege. I'm trying only to explain my own approach to music today. And I feel that when a composer has created something great, we should respect it. The one thing I loved about Benny Goodman in the Thirties — when Benny was playing, I think, his very best, in 1938 and '39 — was this. I played nine shows a day with his band for many months during 1938, and he regularly used to play *Body And Soul*. He had that lovely Teddy Wilson accompaniment and he just played the melody, because it is such a delightful song. What better was there to do? And we used to wait for that, 'cos he played it so beautifully.

'Yes, of course, improvisation is always present in a jazz performance, to a greater or lesser degree. Improvisation is phrasing or rather, phrasing is improvisation. One note can be improvisation; it depends on what you want to do, and what you feel about a song.'

In his fifty-five and more years of professional playing, Lawrence Freeman — who has been known as 'Bud' for about as long as he can remember ('You know sisters tend to call their brother Bud; my sister did, and so did everyone else pretty soon. Only a few use my real name — those who like the name Lawrence') — has worked in almost every conventional jazz situation and several unconventional ones. Big bands, small groups (sweet or hot), duos, trios ... Bud has done it all as bandsman, featured sideman, leader or guest soloist. In general he prefers the experience of playing in a small or fairly small improvising band, and for many years now he has preferred to leave the headaches of bandleading to somebody else. Today, as he says, he feels most contented when exploring the contours of a well-made song and expressing to the best of his ability its beauty and meaning.

'I've heard quite a few musicians doing this, and I think it will happen more and more. It's a thing I want to develop, and it is called the swing ballad, for want of a better term than "swing". Shall we say the ballad that moves? It has feeling of an unaffected kind, not the syrupy sort, and of course it has to have that beat.

'Now to my mind that is what Ruby Braff is most interested in doing. And his taste is so excellent, you see. I said to him not too long ago: "Where the hell do you get off being so good? I remember when you were taking lessons from me." And it broke him up. He was always a fine player, you know, but he's come along in the last, oh, five years to where he's one of the most interesting players you could hear anywhere.

'But to return to the swing ballad: it is the ballad that moves, but not too quickly. Because it is true that fast tempos, whether a man can play fast or not, do not swing. I remember when we were kids and we idolised Bix — who was a perfect cornet player and our inspiration in many things — that he once told us: "Look, if you want to learn to play fast, go ahead. You may need it to earn a living. But it doesn't swing; it never did." And the great Louis Armstrong, of course, Louis cut it all in half. He had such a wonderful beat in his body that he could do it. But how many people can do that?'

Freeman, though not a backward-looking man by inclination, can naturally salt his observations with references to Bix Beiderbecke, Louis, King Oliver, Bessie Smith, Tommy and Jimmy Dorsey, Dave Tough, Frank Teschemacher, Johnny and Baby Dodds and such illustrious jazz names. Bud was there, listening and absorbing and building his own musical personality (as we can clearly discern today), and now he is still here. Which is a constant source of wonder to me, at any rate, for I am intrigued by the notion of taking a drink with someone who poured a few for the thirsty genius, Bix. As I walk round to the Pizza Express after a celebratory meal with old man Bud, I ask if in fact he did pour many drinks for Beiderbecke. He looks surprised by that sudden question, so soon after the lobster and strawberries, but it is not in his nature to be shaken by avid jazz journalists, and he says, quietly and evenly: 'Pour out the drinks? Well, we used to drink together. I don't remember who did the pouring, if anybody. He used to drink a lot of gin, though.'

Memories of Bix remind Bud of one of the first, if not the first, public performances he took part in for a listening, as opposed to dancing, audience.

'Well, you must realise this was back in 1926, no, it would be '27 'cos it was the year I recorded *Nobody's Sweetheart* and *Liza* with the McKenzie and Condon Chicagoans. Now Bix and the Dorsey brothers were playing at the time with Paul Whiteman in the Chicago Theatre, and Bix naturally would find himself a nearby ginmill or some such place with a piano, you know. He loved to play piano. Anyway, he found a sawdust-floor cellar with piano and he'd play and sometimes get to have a jam session.

'So one night it worked out that all these famous musicians were going to be there. Eddie Condon called me up and said to bring my tenor down. "Bix is going to be there," he told me, "and he wants to hear you. And Jimmy and Tommy will be there." Of course we went out there and played, and the place was jammed and the people loved it. That was 1927, and it was kind of an informal jazz concert, the first jam session with an audience, and it was an accident.'

Where was the place exactly?

'The premises that subsequently became the Three Deuces in Chicago. The address was 222 North State Street, right across the street from the Chicago Theatre, and that place became the original Three Deuces run by Sam Beer and his partner. Roy Eldridge was later to play a residency there.'

Informal jam sessions before an audience are one thing, large public concerts another. And I guess the swing to jazz concerts, triggered off by Goodman's historic Carnegie Hall affair, was one of the major changes witnessed by

Freeman. He says yes and no. The scene has changed, of course, with the emphasis on concert and similar presentation. But he wants me to realise that concerts were done long before the Goodman and 'Spirituals To Swing' bashes in New York.

'The first one, the first important jazz concert I was at, took place at the Yale Club, where all the noted cartoonists used to hang out. That was the Yale Club in New York, and many graduates from the University were there. It was 1929 and we were playing a concert. We didn't know it was going to be a concert, though. Benny Goodman called us together, I think, and besides him and me we had Bix, Dave Tough or Gene Krupa, I'm not sure which, and I believe Joe Sullivan on piano. It's difficult to remember after all these years, but it was a hell of a thing, and all these famous people lapped it up. I do recall that when we got there Benny said in surprise: "This is a concert." He didn't know himself.'

So the stories go on. One good lesson remains in Bud's mind from the period ('36 to '38) with Tom Dorsey's orchestra. T.D. was a beautiful and precise trombonist and Bud, to this day, is always in tune, in command of his tone, confident in his phrasing. I mention the intonation and the fact that Bud is never seen fiddling with his mouthpiece during performance. He smiles and says Tommy Dorsey told him about that. '"Tune up once at the start," Tommy would say. "Put that mouthpiece there and leave it there. It's the messing around with it that gets you into trouble." That was good advice.'

Bud has been coming over to Britain, and loving it here, since the early Sixties. Now, after residing sporadically in our midst since 1974, he is threatening to move back to the USA and, he hopes, warmer (and cheaper) shores for good and all, though he expects to be back in Europe as a touring jazzman quite early next year. Bud says that whenever he speaks about going home for a visit, bookers and promoters blow it up into a 'Freeman's last date' situation. And the publicity results in fresh offers of work coming in, so that he is more-or-less compelled either to stay on longer or return sooner than expected, or both. 'I have so many offers now from Italy, I expect I'll have to come back in January.'

The publicity from Britain and the rest of Europe, plus a natural increase of interest in his work brought about by his long absences from the homeland, have brought Bud two or three offers he doesn't care to refuse. The first is his welcome-home Chicago concert on 27 August. Then he has jobs in Toronto and North Carolina.

'Apart from the questions of health, and I have to get away from your winters, I am going back to America with a view to doing some work on the strength of having been over here all these years. I seem to have become better known there since being in Europe. But for Christ's sake, I'm still the complete and utter Anglophile. I wanted to come to England ever since I saw *Macbeth* at the age of eight, and I'm always happy to be here and behave as much like an Englishman as I can.'

Bud smiles and gestures in our direction. 'I mean, you people are like Americans to me.' After a hearty laugh he resumes a grave expression and says there would be valid reasons for his saying — if he were to say it — 'No, I shan't be back this time, not to stay.' And the most pressing reason, I am sorry to have to admit, is one I thoroughly understand. London life has become too costly to make sense any more.

'The expense of the hotels,' Bud groans. 'If I'm living in a trap I become terribly depressed. If I live out of London to cut the cost I'm depressed because everything's in London. I'm a theatre man, and I see three or four plays every week when I'm not working, also several films. I saw the film *Nijinsky* by the way, and it's superb. They've done the story beautifully and Alan Bates is a marvellous actor I think.'

Anyhow, Bud leaves us this month for a date in Holland on the 25th, then off to Chicago next day for the concert on the 27th. He doesn't know the details of the Chicago concert but says the organisers are in the process of honouring a dozen native sons of the Windy City, and he's one of them.

'They put on one of these each year, and I believe this is the second. Benny Goodman, I understand, did it last year. So of course I was delighted when they got hold of Robert Masters, my agent, and asked if I'd come over and do it. Forgive me if I mention money, but they're paying tremendously well for the engagement, and giving me a round-trip ticket from Holland.

'No, I don't know where I'll be settling in America; I don't have a place to live. I may look around in North Carolina. I won't stay too long in Chicago — that wind would blow me right off the sidewalk — and I don't think I'll go back to Los Angeles. That can be a very lonely place unless you're a success in the movie industry. New York? No, I don't care to go there either. I have an estranged wife with a stranger lawyer.

'My real reason for going back to the USA is that after six years absence I think it may be worth while looking around at the work. While I was at my sister's in Hollywood last year I made an album for Irving Edelman Products, and there may be some action from that. But I'm sure to be back in Europe next year, and if there was a nice little tour fixed up for Britain I'd like to do that. So it's likely you'll be seeing me again.'

Bud smiles as I mention his age and says that as long as his health holds out he wishes to hang around. 'Let me put it to you this way, Max. So long as I can look at the crowd and see some beautiful women I'm going to want to play for them.' I say that if I played tenor sax I'd feel the same way. This reminds Bud of a champagne party he attended in a London hotel with an elderly man who was celebrating his 91st birthday. When a dream of a girl passed by, the old man's eyes lit up.

'I toasted him and asked: "Do you still adore women?"' says Bud.

'He said: "I do, but I can't remember why."'

'And I said: "Well, I can remember why."'

Stan Getz

One Monday evening back in the Seventies I was hanging around in the
Melody Maker offices long after normal departure time. Two other members of
staff, at that period the only others on the payroll devoted to jazz, demanded to
know why I was still there. I said I was waiting for Ronnie's to open up. (An old
Ronnie Scott joke goes: Telephone enquirer asks 'What time do you start?'
Ronnie replies: 'How soon can you get here?') I was asked: 'Who you going to
see?' 'Stan Getz.' Almost in unison they say 'Hard luck!' It struck me as odd,
even though I realised that many 'Young Turks' had become disenchanted with
the tenorman since his well-blessed flirtation with bossa nova. I remember
saying that nobody of discerning taste and with true knowledge of saxophonic
skill would utter so churlish a remark. A few hours afterwards I listened to tenor
playing of transfixing superiority.

Of course Getz could be churlish himself, off-hand and dismissive (after a
massive fall-out with him, Scott described Stanley G. as 'an idol with a head of
clay'), but truth compels me to insist that he has never given me a rough time.
Even when I quoted, with permission, Ronnie's bon mot to him, one balmy
night at the Nice Festival, Getz smiled approvingly and said: 'Tell him that next
time we meet I'm going straight for the jugular.'

The conversations written-up here took place between 1964 and 1971. For the
first, I joined him at a musicians' watering hole in Soho.

After a certain amount of waiting and false-starting, I managed to get Stan Getz
and me and a notebook together at one table when Getz had time to answer
questions. He chose the Downbeat Club in Old Compton Street, London,
where he could talk and drink and listen to Pat Smythe's piano more or less at
the same time. As his month's highly successful stay at the Ronnie Scott Club
was drawing to a close, I asked if we would be seeing him back there soon.

'I hope so,' he said. 'But you'll have to ask Ronnie if he'll have me. I've
certainly enjoyed it.'

'This being your first experience of London club work, have you felt *en
rapport* with the audiences? Do you find them attentive?'

'Oh yes, more so than back home. Yes, it's always more so here — I mean all
over Europe. They're inclined to hang on to every note, and they're very
responsive.

'I want to say this about the trip. I have a new feeling in my heart about
playing again, and living again; it's been revitalised by coming here.

'You know, on the few nights when my drummer has been ill, and I've had
to play with other men — all fine drummers, mind you, but they hadn't
rehearsed — I've been hurt because I couldn't play better for the people
there.

'That's how I feel about your audiences. They make me feel that I want to
play for them. You know I've been playing jazz for a long time, but meeting
people like this makes me feel young again and eager, eager to play my best.'

On the subject of audiences, I said, there doesn't seem to be much of one left for jazz in the States. I hear that business there is the worst it's been since the Depression.

'That's all wrong, you know. There never was enough audience for jazz,' Getz said with conviction. 'They're all bitching, but there's never been a jazz musician who did jazz work exclusively. They always worked with other kind of bands.

'You don't just play jazz all the time. You think it, you think music. It's a hard thing to explain, but you think it when you're playing with a rumba band, or a Mickey Mouse band. If you're a jazz musician, that is the music of your heart. It's just a personal, creative kind of music that you play, that is you.'

'But if business is so bad, what are the prospects for men, for keeping new groups alive?'

'There's no such thing as keeping a young musician in jazz. If he loves jazz music, no matter what he plays he is a jazz musician. And if he's good, he comes to play jazz most of the time.

'My point is, there never was enough work for a jazz musician. All of a sudden, jazz has become an art, and jazz musicians are beginning to complain that there's not enough opportunity to perform their art.

'It may seem from what is happening that people on the Continent appreciate jazz more than those in the States. They may appear to, but it's not really so. In America, they've been subjected to so much jazz, you see. They've heard so much for so long. That's our music; they hear it all the time, it's just a part of what's going on, so it's natural they don't applaud like mad when they hear it.

'But they know. Believe me, they're the most discriminating audience in the world. If you get by with an American audience, you can get by anywhere. They hear bad as well as good, and they know.

'In short, the US listeners are the best in the world, though they don't act like it.

'One more point: you mentioned jamming … I like some jam numbers, when they come off, and I like some prepared, when I want the format set. When you have the skeleton frame, then you can do what you want. Really, I like it to be half and half.'

'What about unusual time signatures, less usual I should say? You generally play something in 6/8, also in 12/8. Do you like them?'

'Oh, they all end up 4/4, don't they? They all end up rhythm. It's just a feeling, and you use the time signature to express it.

'When I recorded *Focus*, it was the first time I'd seen 5/4, 6/4, 9/8 and so forth. I asked Eddie Sauter: "What am I going to play?" and he said: "Just play what comes in to your heart, and it'll come out right".'

On the subject of tone, of which he is clearly a master, Getz had this to say:

'I believe you should try to make music as beautiful as you can. It should not be done with ugliness. There's so much hate in the world, you have to counteract it with loveliness. Just as a singer tries for a beautiful tone, so should a horn player.'

On new styles: 'Well, I've heard a lot of styles that are new, but they sound forced. A style in music has to evolve, not be forced. Everyone today seems to think he has to find a new style in order to be recognised.'

The next talk occurred at a Verve/MGM press reception mounted for Stan Getz in London during November 1967. The commercial success enjoyed by such an accomplished artist was a paradox which added spice to a jazz addict's life. I put it to the guest of honour that, having broken the big public's alleged resistance to jazz with items like Desafinado, *he had returned with relief to the straight and narrow with his then-recent* Sweet Rain *album. It was a deliberate move, the tenor ace agreed, and yes, he was a little tired of bossa nova.*

'Everybody wanted more bossa, but I wanted to go back where I came from,' said the very fit-looking and sun-tanned Stan (he picked up the tan in Bangkok). His latest album, *Voices*, is self-explanatory but his next venture will once again combine his talents with a Brazilian musician, this time guitarist Baden Powell who played in this year's Berlin Jazz Festival.

'It won't be a bossa album, really,' Getz explained. 'Baden is from the North East of Brazil, not from Rio where the traditional bossa nova comes from. Bossa is a big city music, sophisticated and so on. This will be earthier, less sophisticated. There's very much heat in this kind of music. I don't believe you'll even think of bossa nova when you hear it.'

Getz also disclosed that he's planning a big band album.

'I do like working with a big band, and I'm planning to record one soon. We'll use at least five or six different arrangers on the session.

'No, I won't be doing any one of them; I don't arrange and I don't write.'

For many, the peak of Getz's recorded achievement is still the *Focus* album where Eddie Sauter surrounded the tenorist with strings.

'It's still my favourite album,' Stan affirmed. 'I think it's great. You know, those strings inspired me. Eddie Sauter left the tenor part entirely free, and there was a lot of "me" in that album.

'I like playing with strings — when they're good. I don't like people to write for strings so that they sound like molasses.

'I worked with the Boston Pops. Eddie Sauter had written a Concerto for Saxophone and with the Boston Pops I was working with one of the three greatest string sections in the world.'

The title track of the *Sweet Rain* album was composed by trombonist Mike Gibbs, now resident in Britain. Getz said he was introduced to Gibbs' music by vibist Gary Burton who was with Stan's quartet until he left to form his own group last year.

'Gary and Mike studied together at Berklee and it was from this association that I got to know Mike and the fine things he writes. I intend to do some more of his things as well.'

Over and above being what Stan described as a 'strictly jazz album', *Sweet Rain* illuminated a depth and development which while not avant-garde, was certainly a new direction for the tenorist.

He agreed: 'I'm going to be as modern as I want, but what I believe is that you must let it come slowly. A lot of people come up and their attitude is "let's play modern" and they go away from the basics. I'm not saying "let's play bullshit just for the hell of it." Let it develop slowly.'

At the next Getz/MGM press shindig I attended Stan looked more tanned and prosperous than ever. This time he had caught the sun in Nassau, where wife Monica was still vacationing. He had not gone to Nassau to work, but had enjoyed a couple of blows, jamming with the local talent. Something about the Stanley steamer appeared to be different, and it turned out to be contact lenses.

'I've only had them three weeks,' he explained, 'and they're still giving a bit of trouble. No, it's not vanity. When you wear glasses your vision is very restricted, don't you think? But with contact lenses you see with your own eyes. Of course I'm not quite used to them yet. One night when I was playing, one of the things jumped out and fell on the floor. I stopped at once and shouted "Nobody move! These lenses cost me 140 dollars and one's missing." Eventually I found it.'

Another thing is new about Getz. He's joined the ranks of the soprano blowers and, from what I heard one night, is producing a softly persuasive tone on it somewhat similar to his tenor sound. But he is self-denigrating on the subject.

'Playing soprano?' he echoes. 'Well, I'm holding it. The saxophone company sent it to me, this little toy. That's a Boston instrument if ever I heard one. A cross between a tin whistle and a flute.'

I couldn't help wondering what Sidney Bechet would have made of that description; I said only that it was none too easy to make a good sound on. Stan agreed that it was 'hard to play in each octave'.

In the way of special events, Getz said he was working at home on a one-and-a-half hour TV programme in colour. In it he plays two movements of an Alex Wilder four-movement work, and is heard in a short piece by Teo Macero.

'Also I'm attempting to ad-lib over Ravel's String Quartet in F. What could you add to something that perfect? Well, you try to add something, but I ask you ... Ravel's String Quartet. Since *Focus*, people think I can ad-lib to anything.'

Did the picture have a documentary content? Getz said it did.

'They introduce the home thing, you know. I'm walking about the estate with one of my daughters and a son. It's supposed to draw a tear here and there.'

So far as contemporary happenings are concerned, did Stan keep his ears open?

'No, my heart. It's not hearing the new things that matters; it's knowing what to do with them.'

'Do you agree it is a good thing that people should be playing, and listening to, these new styles?'

'What new styles? I haven't heard any new styles since Charlie Parker. I think I've said before that I agree with Hindemith when he said the ear is the first and last court of appeal in music. That's how I feel. I'm interested in making music, not in experimenting.'

To hear and chat with Getz during his visit to Britain early in 1971, I drove a short distance to the West End studio where he was recording with an organ-guitar-drums combo. This dispatch was run in the Melody Maker *of 23 January 1971.*

Stan Getz and his trio (Eddie Louiss, Rene Thomas, Bernard Lubat), his daughter, producer George Martin, the recording engineer and jazz buff Spike Milligan were listening to playbacks at AIR studios in Oxford Street. The day's music-making, repeated on tape, came to an end with a sensuous improvisation on tenor. The silence which followed was broken as musicians put down coffee cups, stretched, and got to their feet. Getz and Martin congratulated each other and a beaming tenorman expressed pleasure at the results of the date. 'A good day's work, fellows. Thank you,' he told the group.

For a while he engaged in a conversation with Milligan and Martin, which sped bewilderingly from one subject to another. I caught strands of it as Spike mused over the situation that would have existed if the Queen had been triplets ('It's your turn on the throne today')!

'I want to buy shares in World War Three,' Milligan told me in the manner of one offering friendly advice, 'while they're still cheap.'

At about this point, George Martin offered to give Spike a lift home, then remember he hadn't brought the car in that morning. Spike thanked him and said never mind, they'd hire a fleet of taxi cabs. As they left I could hear a Milligan duologue with himself: 'I'll drive you home.' 'You haven't got a car.' 'No, but I've got a whip.'

Getz, looking fitter and more relaxed than when I last met him, was showing huge enthusiasm for his current trio.

'You know how every few years I come up with a cyclone group,' he asserted. I said I did. He recited a few names.

'Like with Al Haig, Jimmy Raney, Teddy Kotick and Tiny Kahn in the early Fifties. And the Bob Brookmeyer group in 1953 with Johnny Williams on piano. And after that came the group with Gary Burton, Steve Swallow and Roy Haynes, and then it was the Chick Corea group with Miroslav Vitous and what's-his-name who's on *Bitches Brew.*' I guessed it was Jack De Johnette.

'Now this is one of those cyclone bands. I'm taking them to America in mid-March. It's something different. We have a dynamic sound.'

The group, as alert readers will have spotted, sports neither string bass nor piano. And Stan Getz is not a player I would have expected to find in the ranks of the organ-fanciers.

In this, my instinct would have been right. 'I've had a group with no piano before. There was no piano with Gary. But I never thought I'd want to play with organ, not until I heard this guy. As for the bass, Eddie takes care of that — he can do it so great.'

So far as I knew, this Continental Rhythm of Getz's was new to him. Certainly it was their first recording with him.

'When I heard them just before summer I immediately thought this is going to be my group. We played a week together in the fall and now we're recording.

'So we're completing this double album for MGM which, as you know, was interrupted because I flew to New York when my father died. I was across the ocean twice in one day in the middle of recording.

'The title? Yes, it's called *Dynasty* and is dedicated to my father. He was a printer, by the way, and a great man. George liked the title because he thought of it as something passing down from one king to another.

'All of the group except the drummer have composed this music. All originals except for a German song, *Mona*, and *Invitation* by Billy Strayhorn. The one you heard was called *Our Kind of Sabi*. That's a Japanese word meaning some special kind of beauty.'

Thinking it an appropriate word for what I'd been listening to, I went on to ask why the tenorman chose to record in Britain these days.

'I think New York has lost it and London is now the place in which to live and operate. Then, too, I like working with George. He's a super guy — like Spike he's beautiful.'

I wondered how Getz planned his recording schedule and, for that matter, his working life in general. It seemed he took it all pretty easy. He explained that he always had to record three albums a year. It was an arrangement which suited his musical temperament — and his pocket.

'When you have a contract that involves half a million dollars over five years, and calls for three records a year, you don't have to worry about money. I wouldn't have to do any work other than that.

'I can take fifty thousand a year and invest it and live on the rest. And it's best to have some cash properly invested because you don't go on for ever in this business. You have to put so much in it all the time, playing jazz. It's a hard thing to get out of somebody; people don't always realise that. It wears you out emotionally to get up there and play, maybe an hour three times a night, if you're to produce something that's heartfelt, meaningful and exciting.

'So I could just live like that, on my recordings, but the point is I love to play. The improvisation part of jazz, that is what's so interesting. It's always a challenge to you.'

And is Getz still as intrigued by the ad-lib possibilities of the music as he was in his junior days? He nodded emphatically.

'More so than ever. The deeper you get into it the more you get out of it and the more you want to get into it. And with a good group it's easier, of course.

'A bad group now, that will deteriorate your playing quicker than anything. But the good group improves it, and the exciting thing is that each new group brings out different ways of improvising.'

When I last talked to Getz he was suffering from a broken foot and other injuries, also recovering from pneumonia. All this was clearly behind him I observed. He laughed and agreed he was fine now.

'The William Morris Agency is at present trying to book a tour over here for Dizzy Gillespie and myself. Yes, I'd like to do that with Diz again.'

Before bidding him good night and letting his daughter, Beverly (who is sixteen and plays guitar), take him off home, I asked how he saw his future here.

'It might be for a few years, and again it might not. I don't know; I can't plan that far ahead. Life carries you. You don't carry it. But I think I'll spend summer in Spain — that's where I keep in shape with my swimming and my tennis. Lovely.

'You're right, I am in shape. I've had no alcohol in a year and sixteen months. Not a blast has touched my lips in that time. No, I don't even take any wine with meals. I'm the kind that has to give up, otherwise I drink heavy.'

And was I right in my surmise that he wasn't personally hit in the struggle said to be facing jazz musicians today? He assured me that the situation didn't affect him so far as his own career was concerned.

'That doesn't bother me. I can always work,' he stated with Getzian confidence. 'When you can draw people you can work.'

Point taken.

For me, the most revealing talk with Stan Getz came later that same year when he looked back with affection at some of the jazz masters he encountered on the climb to the peak. (Melody Maker 9 October 1971.)

I was a bit late calling on Stan Getz, which in itself seemed what betting men used to call a turn-up for the books. But I had an explanation, having come from Apple Corps farther up Savile Row where the new basement studios were being suitably celebrated.

'I don't want to sound like a name-dropper,' I said in making my excuses, 'but I was delayed talking to George Harrison.'

He admits to subscribing to the Hindemith doctrine that the ear is the first and last court of appeal in music. If, say, a jazz-rock amalgam doesn't satisfy his ear, his musical taste, then he cannot embrace it. Likewise a 'free' jazz style which we can remember him taking several steps towards a few visits ago. When I asked about this 'freedom' attempt, he beamed quite amiably. 'You mean when I made a fool of myself,' was his comment. I had used the term avant-garde, and this caused Getz to snap forward in his chair.

'Why do they call all that shit avant-garde?' he wished to know. 'Why is it, if anybody comes along that plays anything different from the accepted, logical way of playing, that immediately becomes the avant-garde?

'That's not avant-garde, it's an artificial affectation of avant-garde, a false reaching out. New styles in music have to evolve from the old.

'Once every twenty, thirty, maybe fifty years a guy will come along like Charlie Parker that's really avant-garde. When he played, people said "That makes sense and it's new." And what he created opened up avenues still being explored today. In TV programmes you can hear his things. That won't be the case with the ... cacophony shall I say ... being served up in the "avant-garde movement" by some players now.'

Getz went on to assure me he understood these efforts on the edge of atonality, that he knew how to play in a free style and also in a traditional style.

'Like I say, you should be able to play Dixieland. You don't have to, but you find it a big help. In any case you should have all the rudiments, have mastered the basic techniques of the instrument before you call yourself a saxophone player.

'Truthfully, I can get these "freedom" guys in the back room and play rings round them.'

We talked a little about the search for individuality, and Getz said the tenor was an instrument which encouraged it to come out.

'On the tenor the tone is completely individual for each man, once he can play. Haven't you noticed how many different styles there are, and have been, on tenor saxophone?'

I said it brought up the ancient subject of Getz and his idol, Lester Young. Stan was a self-confessed disciple of Pres, but his own identifying sound soon emerged and influenced scores of young players. His face glowed when speaking of Young and he said how, once you loved a player's style, you remained faithful to that love.

'For instance, I always admired Hawkins and Webster so greatly. You know, I just love Ben to death. But Lester ... there must have been something about his sound that appealed to my mind at once. And until the day he died we had a good feeling about each other.

'I'll tell you something about Pres. In the old days on 52nd Street, in the Forties somewhere, I used to listen to the great musicians there: Ben Webster's quartet in one place, Erroll Garner in another, Parker in this club and Billie Holiday in that.

'I was with Benny Goodman's band at that time, and I wanted to get in with this exciting music on 52nd Street. But no one would let me sit-in. No one except Ben, that is, a beautiful guy.

'He knew I was keen and some nights he'd say: "All right, kid, get your horn." And I would blow with the quartet and enjoy that.

'And then one night, after I'd played with Ben, there was Lester Young backstage. Pres, you know, had heard me and you can guess how I felt; I was eighteen years old at that time.

'We met for the first time and I mumbled about what a great pleasure it was. You know Lester spoke in a language of his own? Well, he said to me: "Nice eyes, Pres. Carry on." He called me Pres; I'll never forget that.'

The reference to Goodman was timely, as Benny was playing that night at Brighton and, in fact, I was lunching with him at Decca House the next day. Name-dropping again, and Stan responded warmly to it.

'Now take Benny — he knows what's good in music, and who's good. I've got respect for that man. Like I told you, I was in his band at eighteen, a fresh kid, and to watch him rehearse a band was something. His ears and musical knowledge, his taste at picking tempos, and choosing guys with good sounds for his band. So wonderful.

'How do I rate a guy like that? Like I rate Jack Teagarden. Benny and Tea were my first major influences. Teagarden, now there was a man with a beautiful tone, a full and human sound.

'Yes, I worked with Jack's band when I was sixteen. We'd play *Struttin' With Some Barbecue* and *That's A-Plenty*. I liked them, and I was in fact weaned on Dixieland. I think everyone should be weaned on it.

'And big bands ... I love the sound of them. I did play in the Teagarden big band in '43, and the sextet out of that band. I'll never forget those days, either. We did maybe 260 jobs in the year, more or less one every day, and we drove two or three hundred miles to each in Jack's big Chrysler convertible. That was some training.'

Johnny Griffin

I sat down between sets at Ronnie Scott's in June 1974 for a drink with tenorman Johnny Griffin. The bassist Lloyd Thompson raised his glass and said we'd down one together to Duke Ellington. No sooner proposed than done.

The name of Paul Gonsalves was raised, and I mentioned that these were tragic losses. Griffin said they'd not really gone. 'Just the body got tired but the spirit, the music will go on.' Then he went on to lament the passing of so many great jazz players, saying: 'All the good musicians are dying and all the sad ones are living like crazy. Man, all those sad ones on that macrobiotic diet, they're living on.' He laughed briefly and added: 'And I'm healthier than ever. No chance for me to die; I've got too much suffering to do.'

Not everything the Little Giant says in the late hours is to be taken seriously, though he's very serious about jazz-playing which he believes is another way of speaking. He remarked on the quality of the rhythm team working with him at the club — Mike Pyne (piano), Ron Mathewson (bass) and Spike Wells (drums) — and their habit of breaking back to half-tempo, a peculiarly British thing, he thinks. This was not just a praise for the sake of politeness because 'Griff' — who has been inspired by our rhythm sections before now — said he would like to make a record with them ('Oh, I really would, given the opportunity'). I wondered whether he might get the opportunity, or was he tied by contract to this label or that? 'I'm under exclusive contract to myself.'

He went on stage and interpreted *When We Were One*, a romantic ballad of his own creation which can be found on *Tough Tenors Again 'n' Again* on the MPS label, and *You Are My Heart's Delight* in a manner which affirmed that he has a lot of melody in his head. Afterwards we talked about his move from France to Holland, which had taken place since our previous meeting at the Dunkirk Festival the year before. Griffin said he had been living in Holland off and on since June of '73 but only let his French apartment go (it was in a Paris suburb) that September.

'If I'd stayed in France I would have moved to the countryside anyway. I was a tourist in Paris for ten years — never settled down. I'm from another planet. Then I got this good deal to purchase a property there in Bergambacht, about 16 or 17 miles from Rotterdam. So I'm all set in Holland and like it very much.'

Whenever I interview the tough tenorman I seem to touch at some time on the subject of a return to the United States, even of a visit to sweet home, Chicago. Was Johnny still contemplating such a journey? The man of property shook his head and declared that he couldn't look that far ahead with certainty.

'I really don't know. I feel like a free spirit right now, living in Europe, and I don't see that I'll be leaving too soon. But maybe I will go and visit America. I had planned to go sometime.

'I don't know. Maybe, presented with a nice opportunity for something that I'd like, where I could feel that I'd develop more, I would go back.'

Asked if the nice opportunity would involve leading his own regular group, Griffin said that it could do, that he would like to have a group.

'With a steady group you can do so much more. You know, when musicians play all the time together they have an empathy for each other. It means you can really expand; you can take a theme and play for an hour with the one theme, if you really know each other. Whereas playing with different groups, most of the time you must be careful, you must stay more on the surface of things; you cannot delve down into the core of the music.'

Johnny has been a resident in Europe for eleven years; well, it was exactly eleven years on 27 May. Has he been home at all in all that time? A look of surprise switches on at the word 'home', and the saxophonist repeats it with mock surprise. 'Home? Home is where I've got my saxophone.' A laugh, and he states that he hasn't been to America at all since he left there in '63. When pressed on the matter of reasons for not returning to his place of origin, he retreated into Griffinesque humour about the American way of life, then instructed me not to 'put that in' in case he wanted to return.

'No, I've done such terrible things that I can't go back there. But I'm sure, with all the suffering I've done, they'll call me back.'

He broke off for a bout of brandying and bantering reminiscence with Lloyd Thompson. Names like Rene Thomas, Benoit Quersin and Barney Wilen came and went. 'Griff' claimed that he admired Wilen's tenor work. We talked on about Europe, and the musician's life over here. Musicians are different from other people, Griffin pointed out. They live differently and their work is different. So what is it like for them?

'It's difficult at best for a jazz musician because the music itself is not subsidised and it's not pop music, although you can hear the essence of jazz in almost all commercial music on the air, I mean on programmes like detective stories, things like that. But for the real hard-core jazz musician, making a good living is very difficult. For me, though, it's been very nice in Europe. That's why I've stayed.

'I've learned how to relax in Europe ... to relax in my life, because it seems to me that Europeans relax more than Americans. The work drive is not so strong here; the people tend to vacation more in Europe than in America.'

And what of the argument that an American musician may well run out of inspiration after a long stay in Europe? What is the effect of all that relaxing? Some people say that without the intense competition met with in the USA, where there's always a competitor breathing down your neck, a jazz musician is liable to become complacent or perhaps lazy. Griffin agreed about the competition but didn't know if it had any relevance to the argument about running out of musical steam.

'You know, I think that after a certain point in your life as a musician you have acquired enough experience to keep on feeding you. I left America when I was thirty-four or thirty-five years old and I feel that I had enough of the roots embedded in me, in my soul, in my life, to not have to worry about roots any more. I want to blossom; want to grow above the earth now.

'To me it's more a matter of developing your mental outlook, and broadening yourself spiritually by meeting new souls and looking for new horizons.'

And the European free-jazz scene, which turns more and more to European music — classical and mainly avant-garde — for inspiration. How did he feel about that? Not too concerned, it appeared. Johnny said the 'so-called avant-garde jazz' had its roots in European music rather than among the jazz roots. 'For me, jazz has its roots in African rhythms, the feeling of African rhythms, you know. It's a different motion. That's why when you find jazz musicians reading a phrase and classical musicians reading the same phrase you get a different concept. And, well, I have the feeling that free jazz or so-called avant-garde music has adopted a lot of European concepts.'

Griffin has visited Britain on numerous occasions since 1963. Several times he came to town with the Clarke-Boland Big Band, and I said how sorry I was that the orchestra had died. Did he like playing in the band? He aahed and oohed for a moment and said he wasn't actually a big-band musician although he had played in them now and then, mainly with Lionel Hampton (an amused lifting of the eyebrows) in the '45 to '47 period and the lamented CBBB.

'You see, it is necessary to have organisation in a big band, but playing the same things night after night becomes kind of boring for me, although there are times when a big band is playing something very exciting that you really get carried away with the music.

'How good was the band? Not being a big-band player I can't really make comparisons, can't compare it with anything other than Lionel Hampton, so I won't compare it with other bands. But for me as an experience, well, it was one of the most fantastic experiences I've ever had in my life, and for a variety of reasons. The musicianship in the band was of such a high level to begin with. And the ambience of that band, the spirit among the musicians themselves, it was beautiful, you know? Then there was the music Francy wrote; it was different, totally different, from anything I was used to. Yes, it was some experience.'

'Chips' of the Scott club came up to acquaint Griffin with the time, which was the time for his last set. The tenorman looked at his impressive gold watch, then took it off and showed me the back. On it was engraved 'To Griff from Jaws'. It is an alarm watch, presented to Griffin so that he could get to work on time in the days of the Eddie Davis-Johnny Griffin Quintet.

'He used to set it 45 minutes before we hit, which should have given me time to get across town and on the stand. But I was usually late.'

I said he hadn't better be late for Ronnie's and he got up, stretched himself and smiled enigmatically. Someone requested *There's No Place Like Home*, which Johnny plays sensitively, and the smile broadened. It turned out that he had been playing in the Club Montmartre in Copenhagen on New Year's Eve, and the owner had asked him to be sure to go into *Auld Lang Syne* at midnight. On the stroke of midnight eyes were turned bandwards. After a moment's silence Johnny struck up *There's No Place Like Home*. He doesn't know why. But he remembers everyone stood there looking at him.

Coleman Hawkins

During December 1967, Coleman Hawkins was appearing at Ronnie Scott's club in London when this piece was written. Although I saw Hawk in Britain in 1934, '38 and '39, got to know him a little in '49 and better on subsequent visits, this was my only interview with him.

Last week I called on Coleman Hawkins at the Piccadilly Hotel. It was a little after 3 pm and the Hawk was trying out reeds, lightly but elegantly clad in shrimp pink pure silk pyjamas and slippers, with a beige sax sling hanging from his neck.

'I've got to get me another,' he explained, sorting through a box of Rico V3s. 'I had a good one but it got a bit soft and I changed it. I'm afraid the new one isn't quite right — I couldn't get my high G real good last night. It's a little too stiff.

'It might get all right and start playing well tonight, but it's hard waiting on that. I need one that's going to play in front. It might be the next one I try, and it might take the whole box. You never can tell with reeds.'

I heard later that Coleman found a good one at about 10.45 that same evening.

Hawkins, an old friend of Britain's, is enjoying being here for a decent length of time again. He says he intends to start coming over more regularly.

'I'm going to make different arrangements in the States so I can get over here more often. At the moment I want to get home because my business isn't straight, but I have a lot of places to go to first. And you know what? They want me to do another tour here, and there's something about an extra week at Scott's.

'I've always had it in mind to spend half my time at home and half in Europe, and I'd like to do it. I played all over the Continent before the war. I could do it again, starting out with Amsterdam.'

There was a time long ago, before he first crossed the Atlantic, when Hawkins doubled on clarinet for a record session. I haven't heard of him playing one since, but in these days of double, treble, quadruple-instrumentalists it might have served his public image well had he done so. But Coleman has no wish to double and very little desire even to talk about it. 'Clarinet? No-o-oh,' he said with a long 'O', 'I've never wanted to — can't be bothered with none of that jive. I don't fool with anything but tenor. One instrument, that's all you can hope to master. And I'm still learning.'

Listening and learning are acts frequently referred to by Hawkins in conversation. He listens, or has listened, to almost every kind of music, and throughout the day his ears are alert for interesting themes, or bits of melody, which may crop up.

'That's all I've done in my life is sit up and listen. I even listen to people talk. What other way are you going to learn? It's the only way I know of. While I've been over here I've found something I'm going to use. I heard it on TV. Just a riff out of a certain piece, but I'm gonna use it, tonight I think.'

Obviously, Hawk's taste in gramophone records would be liberal. A friend in Goody's shop in New York tells me Coleman often comes in to buy recordings of symphony or chamber music, sometimes opera, but seldom jazz. Hawk agreed he didn't buy many jazz records these days, though his admiration for Ellington, Benny Carter, Teddy Wilson and such masters is as great as ever.

'Of course I don't need to buy jazz records,' he said, laughing. 'They send me those. But I don't listen to too much jazz. I'm a classics man, but then I started like that. That's where I got myself from, and I keep it up.

'You should see my record collection, it's terrific. Everybody and everything you can think of. When I'm not listening to records I sit and listen to the TV. That's where you hear a lot of music today. Most of it's crap but I learn a lot from it and I love to learn. It's never too late to learn, you know.'

The subject reminded him of some of the younger saxophonists who in his opinion have not learned to play correctly. Hawk stood up and did his best to explain to me how deeply he breathed and how he achieved power and breath control when playing. 'The lungs come right down here, and that's where the power comes from,' he said, patting the lower part of his belly. 'They need to study all of this, some of these boys coming up. But it's no use telling 'em because they can't get with this shit.They'll never learn it unless I teach 'em, and I ain't gonna teach 'em'. Coleman smiled to himself. 'No I'm not, because they're smart enough already.'

After a time he relented a bit about teaching, mentioning younger players who came to listen to him and ask him questions.

'There's a lot of things I've still to do, and maybe I should teach. There's these newspaper cats up in Sweden who want to get me a school. But I don't know. Some kind of way I've got to start teaching, got to teach these boys how to play. Someone's got to do it, no question about that, and it shouldn't be too difficult.'

I wondered if any of the young avant-garde saxophonists appealed to Hawkins, or seemed important to him. He thought, and shook his head.

'I don't think they're ready yet. Not those I've heard. I mean, I don't hear anything in what they're playing, just noise and crap.'

Allowing that he doesn't like the 'new thing', does Hawkins concede that its exponents are adding a dimension to jazz?

'No, goodness no. There is nothing to do but play the horn whether you're talking about jazz or classical music. If you don't do that well, you can't do anything else. It's all you have.

'It makes no difference what music you're playing. Master your horn, that's all you've got to do. And it's hard to do, you better believe that. They have schools, but most of these kids don't use them.

'And that's a terrible thing, because these kids are playing nothing — nothing. Well, nothing that I've heard. So I feel it is something I ought to do eventually, to get around to teaching.'

But what if the up-and-comers don't wish to learn? Coleman brushed the question aside.

'Oh, they want to learn all right, otherwise they wouldn't be in there listening night after night and asking me questions. I'll tell you something: all the musicians who play funny want to learn, because they didn't start right. And when you don't learn right you always want to know how.

'So-and-so,' Hawk mentioned a well-known name he didn't want me to quote, 'has been asking me things because he didn't know.

'My drummer, Eddie Locke, he says about the new kids: "They ain't listening to the shit you listen to. Instead of Bach and Berg and Shostakovitch they listen to all that crazy stuff like they play." I said to Eddie: "As long as they keep bringing the kids up to play like that I can be a millionaire. Why should I bother to help produce players who listen and know everything about their horn? Don't bring up good players. So long as they keep bringing these kids up I've nothing to fear."'

Johnny Hodges

Hodges was the first alto player I listened to on purpose; or if he wasn't the first I heard on records, he tied for first with Jimmy Dorsey. In either case he rapidly became my favourite and was the first great saxophonist I saw in person (though Dorsey had beaten him over the Atlantic by three years — as a member of the Ted Lewis Band). The Duke Ellington Orchestra played a season at the London Palladium in June, 1933, and when the curtain rose on that wondrous, smartly-attired fourteen-man ensemble — with Hodges seated between Harry Carney and Barney Bigard — the sound and spectacle were such as to rob me momentarily of all reason. It was total magic.

At that time I was sixteen, playing tenor and soprano in a semi-pro band. To us, and most real musicians and enthusiasts in Britain, Hodges (not yet twenty-six years old) was already a star. When he played his first masterly solo, on Ring Dem Bells, *the audience roared approval. I had to wait seventeen years to see him again, this time to meet him, too. Duke's band steamed into Le Havre in the spring of 1950 to begin a French tour. Travelling overnight to that port, I gained entrance to the Ile de France and began searching the vast liner for Monsieur or Madame Hodges, soon found Cue and then 'Rabbit' and later the Man. With the permission of Ellington and band manager Al Celley, I joined the troupe for coach rides (and concerts, and receptions,) to Rouen and Paris.*

The acquaintance thus forged was strengthened when the orchestra made its long overdue return to Britain in the autumn of '58, though I nearly blew it by offering car space at the airport to both Hodges and Cootie Williams. Johnny at once started to bale out of the Zodiac, stating crisply: 'You take who you like, young man, but I don't run with Cootie.' We drove Hodges, then and on plenty of subsequent occasions, and struck up a good lasting relationship until the dark day when Ben Webster rang, in May of 1970, and informed me in sad tones: 'You know why I'm calling you ... Rab's gone.' Despite time spent with him over twenty years I never felt I understood the character beneath the sceptical eye and imperturbable expression; nor why he was nicknamed 'Rabbit', though he hinted it was to do with his facial appearance. In this 1964 conversation he was rather less reticent than was his habit.

'Young man,' said Johnny Hodges, holding up a glass of Bourbon and ice in welcoming salute, 'did I tell you about the record I just made?' He moved across the bar and told me. 'It's titled *Everybody Knows — Johnny Hodges*. I had most of the band on four titles, but Sam Woodyard, Chuck Connors and Cootie weren't on it. Britt Woodman and Ray Nance made the date, and I forget who the drummer was.

'It turned out pretty nice. We did *Main Stem* and *The Jeep Is Jumpin'*, and Cat Anderson came in with one of his own things. Then there were two of Billy Strayhorn's tunes, and I made *Everybody Knows* and *Papa Knows*. You connect them? Then I made another album with Paul Gonsalves, along with Ray and Rolf Ericson, Walter Bishop Jr, Osie Johnson and Ernie Shepard. I wrote two originals for that date: *Rapscallion* and *Impulse*.

I asked Hodges if he still wrote many tunes, and if he earned money from the old ones. He said 'Yes, oh yes' to the second part. '*I'm Beginning To See The Light* is apparently doing well. It's a standard now; a lot of people don't know that I wrote it. *It Shouldn't Happen To A Dream* is another of mine which has become a standard. Then there's *Jeep's Blues* and *The Jeep Is Jumping*. And we just recorded *Harmony In Harlem* again.

'I don't write so many tunes, but every time I do a record date I put in two or three of my own. And I try to accommodate a guest who is on the date, like Wild Bill Davis, by using one or two of his. Right now I'm working on a new one, *Twice Daily*. I called it that because we're doing concerts twice daily, but it could mean many things. It will be recorded by Cat with some of the guys when we get back to the States.

'Yes, I like to use titles that mean something to me. What was that pub you took me to? "The Old Spotted Dog"? I might do that on a date ... *The Spotted Dog*, yes.'

People often inquire what Hodges thinks about when he's on stage, what he thinks of the numbers he's playing, and so on, but it isn't easy to find out.

'I don't think about anything special,' he said.

'You mean you may be wondering if you'll get a meal after the show?' someone asked him. 'That might have happened,' Hodges allowed.

And what of his feature numbers?

'I like some better than others,' is all he admitted.

Which ones does he like better? 'Oh, I don't know.'

Another writer observed that the alto-man did not look happy on the stage. 'I've never been the emotional sort and it's too late for me to change now,' was the reply. 'I've never jumped around. I don't think a good showman is necessarily a good player.' Nobody could ever accuse Cornelius Hodges of leaping about on the stand.

As usually happens when collectors talk to Hodges, the name of Sidney Bechet came into the conversation. Bechet helped Hodges to master the soprano saxophone, and he gave Johnny an instrument.

'That soprano was given me in the Twenties, and it's the same one I played right up until the 1940s. I still have it, but I'm about ready to make a lamp out of it now.

'You mention *The Sheik of Araby*, made in 1932, on which I played soprano. Bechet taught the band that. He played that for us, and Tizol put it down.

'Yes, I'll get a new soprano all right and maybe I'll make a record with it. But these things have to be arranged. I was supposed to make a record with Coltrane; I don't know what happend to that.'

Does Hodges like Coltrane's music?

'I don't, but my son does.'

The son is Johnny Hodges the Second, nearly sixteen and a drummer who was playing a gig last week with his own quartet. 'He has tenor, bass and piano with him,' said Hodges, 'and the pianist, a blind boy, is brilliant. My son is taking music lessons. He's a pretty good drummer. I must telephone home and see how he got on.'

Hodges spoke about the band's recent Far Eastern tour and expressed surprise that Ellington had not been sent on other and more satisfactory State Department junkets. 'We were guinea pigs on that tour,' he explained with feeling. 'Almost everywhere we went revolution broke out, or we just missed an incident. Guys were walking the streets with machine guns. And we were on a goodwill mission.

'But I'll tell you this: music has a whole lot to it. It can soothe a lot of pain, and it'll get closer to people than money can. We found out years ago that you can go to the most prejudiced state and they will accept the music you play. And in Europe before the war we found the same sort of thing. Yes, music's a hell of a weapon.'

Normally, I don't ask musicians about record sessions from the distant past. But Hodges has been quoted as remembering a record he made with King Oliver, and Brian Rust is anxious to have the details. Hodges said, Yes, he made one, shortly before he joined Ellington — which would put the date at very early '28.

'I did this thing for Brunswick records, I think, and Luis Russell was on it and Paul Barbarin, also Barney Bigard and Omer Simeon. Oliver was having his teeth fixed at that time; I don't think he played much. It's hard to remember, but I think Jelly Roll Morton had something to do with it; maybe it was one of his tunes we were playing. I used to visit New York from Boston, and made the date on one of those visits.'

What about the future? Will Johnny Hodges lead his own band again?

'It's bound to happen one day. I've been out twice before and I'm bound to do it again eventually. Well, the band can't go on for ever. But I'm in no hurry. No-o-o, too many headaches. But still, I like to try out my ideas every once in a while. Like Lawrence Brown and I got together recently with a rhythm section for a couple of weeks in Boston.

'I like to take a few days off and work out some things to play. And that's the kind of group I'd have ... five or six pieces, not too heavy, three horns and three rhythm at most. I have used four front-line before but not again. Trumpet and alto, alto and tenor, alto-trumpet-trombone — that sort of line-up is ideal. You make a nice sound, and that way you carry no passengers. I've only one other ambition now. I'd like to settle down at home and take time to compose — — really work on writing some tunes. I may just do that.'

Gerry Mulligan

This meeting with Gerry Mulligan took place in November 1968, when he was in England with the Dave Brubeck Quartet.

Gerry Mulligan has the reputation in some quarters of being unco-operative so far as journalists are concerned. He didn't deny having the reputation but said it was unjust. 'I remember Jack Tracy told me he'd been afraid to approach me in his earlier days on *Down Beat*. He'd heard I was unapproachable.

'I don't think there was ever any truth in it. Later on, when he produced some records of mine, we laughed about it.'

Mulligan, in fact, laughs a good deal. He looks amused at most of the vagaries of the jazz world, and is inclined to begin his remarks with 'The funny thing is ...' Even the subject of reviewing, and the reviewing of Brubeck's quartet at that, elicited smiles as well as indignation.

'I know that Dave has suffered, and I don't understand this drive to hurt him. There couldn't be a more considerate or straightforward person, or a stronger personality on the instrument, I dare say.'

Another amusing thought struck Mulligan. 'You know these critics who put Brubeck down for not swinging?' I had to admit that I did. 'Well, do you think it's possible, just possible, that some of them are the same people who embrace the avant-garde so eagerly?' He practically danced with joy, adding: 'Including musicians who don't even try to swing?'

I admitted he had a question. Another I wanted to clear up was about his feelings — as a man who threw the piano out of the bandroom in '52 — now he was in a quartet dominated by piano.

'Oh, I enjoy playing with Dave. You see, people often miss the point when you say or do something. I liked the idea of a group without a piano, but it wasn't new then. I like all kinds of different musical situations, and that includes the present and the past. In Dave's group we've often been able to get a feeling of orchestration between the two of us, though piano is not a horn.

'It's funny, I've always thought of myself as an accompanist more than a soloist. Though I enjoy playing solos, the most important thing to me has always been the ensembles.'

Gerry Mulligan has not spent a great amount of time working with Brubeck. And because of the vicissitudes of touring I imagine he may not spend too much more. He did two weeks with Dave Brubeck's group in the spring, then this present tour. Which hardly adds up to regular work.

'It sure feels regular to me on the road like this,' he said. 'I got sick of it a long time ago, before Dave did. I just feel rotten on the road. I envy the guys that really enjoy it because I love playing. But it's living like this I can't stand. I guess that's why Dave broke up his group before. He's paid a lot of dues on the road.'

Talk of Brubeck and pianos reminded me that Mulligan had learned the instrument as a boy, and plays it sporadically. Was it true, as Art Farmer claimed, that he only played piano 'when he's bugged?' Mulligan didn't know about that, but recalled that he used to play mostly in clubs. 'because it was a way of getting out more composing ideas than was possible on baritone.' He went on to say that the kind of playing he liked most of all was 'a thick, orchestral style, an internal sort of composing,' exemplified by Clarence Profit, Nat Jaffe and 'a third fellow whose name I've forgotten.'

These three were his favourite pianists. 'Everything was moving inside their music. Really it was a form of orchestration. They were the ones I admired, and all of them died within quite a short time.'

Ever since his days in the Claude Thornhill orchestra, Mulligan has been noted for the originality of his arranging. Such pieces as *Jeru* and *Godchild*, for the 1949 *Birth Of The Cool* sessions, have long been accepted as classics of their kind. But lately, few things have come from his pen that have seen the light of performance. Is he still writing as much as he should?

'Well, to some extent it's a matter of demand. I've been doing some commercial writing at home for TV. Film writing? There's a difficulty there, the film centre being in Hollywood. We live in New York.

'When I was living in England during the summer I wrote some jazz things, but I haven't had the opportunity to hear them yet. Two arrangements were for Johnny Dankworth.

'I heard Dankworth's band at Ronnie Scott's and was intrigued by the instrumentation. I began to write some arrangements for it, and two of them we rehearsed last July for the Jazz Centre gala. They were called *Sandy* and *Etude*. Unfortunately I had an appointment and couldn't make the evening performance.

'The bulk of the work I did this summer, which included a couple of long pieces, I'm taking home with me at the end of this tour. Then I'll see what can be done with them. But first I'm off to join my wife in Vancouver.

'In 1967 I did a movie score in Hollywood. But it kept me there three months, and I don't like being separated from Sandy that long.

'I'm interested in the things being done today in popular music. It's got into a new bag that I enjoy very much. In fact I feel left out because no one asks me to do anything in that field, either playing or writing.'

I suggested that people might consider him a bit long in the tooth for involvement in pop music, but he didn't look convinced.

'Why,' he replied, 'do the young think that each new thing grew up full-blown, and that the last generation had nothing to do with it? When Bird came along a lot of people thought he suddenly emerged fully mature, just like that. Yet to me, even as a youngster, the influences were clear, you know.

'And I have to admit to being knocked out by the Beatles' last two albums. Well, some of the stuff in *Revolver* I admired, but *Sgt Pepper* was really the one for putting so many diverse elements together.

'I tried writing something a bit like that for a film, but realised that for it to come out the way I wanted, it would have to be put together like the Beatles do it. You know, that sort of hit and miss approach with tapes and everything. I'd love to find out how to put it together that way. But it's too difficult for film purposes, so I wound up doing it as a big jazz band kind of thing.'

Considering that he has been described by musicians — and who are harder judges? — as a natural bandleader, Mulligan has done precious little leading of late. Some of the reasons are obvious. Bandleading means headaches for some-one, and he isn't partial to headaches; then it means touring at some time or other, and, as we've seen, he's none too enamoured of that.

'It's a lot of work organising a band and running it. For that reason, a band is most fun when you're in rehearsals. When you're working you don't have so much time to enjoy it — you sort of get locked in. So from that point of view, a workshop or rehearsal orchestra is one answer.'

I mentioned that there was also a matter of repertoire. Bands like Ronnie Roullier's New York Jazz Repertory Orchestra set out to preserve and cata-logue the finest compositions and arrangements from the past. Mulligan agreed it was important. He'd given his *Young Blood* Kenton score to the NYJRO, and they also had some of his earlier work for Thornhill.

'It's a shame to think of so much great music lying around in garages,' he added. 'But to return to my own future; I probably will form another band though I have no plans at present. You see, I want to pursue writing and studying.'

Flip Phillips

Like most record collectors of pre-war vintage I was introduced to the soloing of Flip Phillips by various Woody Herman 78s of the middle Forties. Then he became a star turn with 'Jazz at the Philharmonic' and, at that period, I thought his tenor playing, though exciting, less satisfying than it had been with

the First Herd. It was during the JATP's ban-breaking visit to London in '53
that I met Phillips and, on the band's day off, helped him, Oscar Peterson and
Norman Granz to see such sights as Westminster Abbey. Flip was taken with my
MG (TC-model) and volunteered to be photographed behind the wheel. You
can see the result elsewhere in this book. More than a quarter-century later,
expecting to see Flip at the Berne Jazz Festival, I took along a print of the picture
and presented him with it. To my surprise he said: 'Was that your sports car? I
gotta large blow-up of that shot on my wall at home — always wondered
whose MG I was sitting in.' His playing was splendid in Berne, and in London
in 1982 when this article appeared.

In persuading Flip Phillips to come over to England for a couple of weeks at the
Canteen, that Covent Garden eaterie has brought off one of the surprises of
the season. For the Brooklyn-born tenorman is a rarely spotted visitor to these
parts. Like some good wine he doesn't travel well, doesn't wish to go touring
either. The last time I can recall seeing Phillips in London was in March 1953
when he was a member of Norman Granz's Jazz At The Phil troupe at the
Flood Relief concert. I've seen him in Europe once or twice since, but that's all.
And in the Sixties he shared music with a management job in Florida, though
he continued to lead a group of his own in that area.

So far as British jazz buffs are concerned, Flip Phillips remains something of
an enigma; and from my experience he's not over-keen on shedding enlightenment around on the world at large. He consented to a brief after-lunch chat one
day in the Schweizerhof Hotel, Berne (during the run of the jazz festival in that
city) after ducking two previous dates for an interview. Once cornered he
turned out to be companionable enough — an alert, laconic, self-contained,
dark-eyed man with a flickering smile which hinted at intimate knowledge of a
music business he had often found wanting.

As we set the tape spinning for a cautionary check — it was impossible to re-
charge the power-pack via the hotel's electrical outputs — Phillips agreed that
his real name was Joseph Edward Filipelli — thus the nickname Flip. It has
been written that he once excelled on clarinet, and he allowed that it was his
first horn.

'Don't know about excelling, but that was my instrument at the time I
started in music, taught by a cousin named Frank Reda. My cousin was one of
the great saxophone and clarinet players and he bought my first clarinet for
me.' The smile flashed. 'It was all of fifty-four years ago.'

And was the clarinet a Boehm System? Flip said no, an Albert.

'And I still play it, still use the Albert System. You say you never heard me
on clarinet? Well, I didn't stay with it that long; found I preferred the tenor
saxophone. But I played it originally in my career, you know, with Frankie
Newton's Band in 1940 and '41. Later I worked with clarinet leaders, Benny
Goodman and Woody Herman, so I just put it away.'

'A good clarinettist?'

'A good player? Frankie Newton said I was; I don't know. Did you ever
meet Newton?' I said no, he never came over but I knew all his records.

'Good, a fine player I thought and an interesting man. He invented that "buzzer" mute. Like I say, he was a great trumpet player; we worked almost a couple of years together, I guess, and I was on clarinet, no tenor.

'Peter Brown was the alto player — another good musician. Jump style? That's right; Peter would jump you right out of the room. He was a great swinging player.'

What was it triggered off Flip's interest in jazz? Could he pin-point a single episode? He could. It was hearing a certain gramophone record. And that record was one by Frankie Trumbauer's Orchestra.

'Yeah,' he said. 'I can remember which it was — *Singin' The Blues*, that's right. And I still play Trumbauer's chorus on it, the one he put down back in the Twenties, though I do it a little differently.

'Oh, yes, his chorus was exceptional. Well, in those days, you know, most saxophone players were slap-tongueing and all that. He was the first guy I heard using different intervals, pretty notes and everything, so I sort of took to him at once. Yes, that recording, made in 1927, was the first one I really heard.

'I was twelve years old when that record made its mark on me, and that is when it came out.' He laughed at the exactness of his memory. 'It was the year that Lindbergh flew over to Europe.

'Now Trumbauer was something. When Lester Young and I were touring together Prez used to talk about that. He said he used to listen to Tram too, listened to him good.'

Flip, from my first acquaintance with his Herman work of 1944 to '46, had always struck me as being a strong Coleman Hawkins admirer. When I mentioned this, he nodded and conceded that it was so.

'I sort of belonged in that school: Coleman and Webster and Don Byas. They produced good sounds on their horns, all of that school, and that is what I was after. I mean, the most important thing for an instrumentalist is to get a good sound. Do that first, then what a man plays is a matter of personal opinion; if you like it, it's good, you know what I mean.'

'How do you feel about the fashionable lean sound with little vibrato?'

'If it is good, yes, I like it, but perhaps it's not for me. I think the tenor saxophone is the happy medium of all horns. On it you can play, naturally, like a tenor. And you can play like an alto, like a baritone, and like a trumpet sometimes, you know. You can get a lot of sounds out of a tenor saxophone, like I say. You can go any which way you wish, according to what mood you're in. You can shout, you can scream, play soft or, in fact, make it several different horns. The saxophone can do many things.'

The clarinet, I said, was considered to be more difficult to master than the saxophone. All instruments have their problems, he replied. There was no easy instrument. 'There's no man can say that he's mastered the saxophone. If he says so, he's not telling the truth because you never finish with this instrument. There are many combinations of things to study. You can go on and on; there is always more to come.'

Phillips lapsed into silence, contemplating the extent of the problems. 'There's plenty to go yet, for me or anyone else. I don't know anybody who mastered the saxophone. Anyone who says he did is full of shit.'

We shifted the subject to Flip's career and present mode of operations. He went out to Florida long ago and left the jazz centre field. Was he disillusioned like, say, Artie Shaw?

'No, nothin' like that. I just settled down there and didn't go out as much. I felt that way, wanted to live a little bit, too. But I continued to play music and, of course, still do. Now I don't believe I could stand the one-nighters like I used to do. I think we hold the record for that. We did eighty-one one-nighters in a row, without a single night off. And it's pretty hard to endure that. However, I still love to play and all that, you know, but I don't want to kill myself either. That's why I'm down in Florida. If something comes up that I like, I'll take it.'

Things that Flip likes include special events such as Dick Gibson's Colorado Jazz Party and the occasional jazz festival. He goes to a few of these because of the change of scene, saying that they're nice so long as there's not too much travelling involved.

'And I took up the game of golf,' he told me, brightening visibly. 'I'm hitting that little white ball and working my frustrations out that way. Like I said, I want to live a little bit.'

'Do you play very much out there?'

'What, golf?'

'No, jazz.'

'Oh, that. Yeah, I play enough. I don't want to play every night of the week.'

Is he sufficiently well set-up financially, then, to be able to live that way?

'No, but how much can you eat? I eat enough. I eat very good in fact, and I've become a chef, you know, kind of a gourmet cook. So I took up golf, and now I eat good and play golf good. I wish I could play golf as well as I can cook, though.'

And when he plays music, does Flip enjoy it as much as he did with Woody Herman, Lester Young, Charlie Parker, Johnny Hodges, Ben Webster, Benny Carter and such?

'I get a lot of satisfaction from playing,' he answered carefully. 'Because I don't do too much of it.'

Zoot Sims

If ever a person sounded as though he enjoyed playing saxophone, that person was Zoot Sims. He didn't always look happy at work, it wasn't his nature, but the enthusiasm could be felt, as well as the dedication to flowing melodic phrases, whenever he set about making music. Zoot, it seemed to me, was a pure case of talent, unshowy and firmly based; as he progressed in years he improved in jazzcraft, and his sound grew even more personal and beautiful. For my taste the Pablo albums from his later years are outstanding for musical feeling and that extra ingredient we tend to call soul. He sang the songs on his horn, and swung them, and the effect was magical.

John Haley — as I sometimes addressed him, having read Leonard Feather's dictionary — was the first American 'single' to be booked into Ronnie Scott's (in 1961), and he became a regular and popular 'resident' at the club, both old place and new, as a solo attraction and in partnership with Al Cohn. When he wasn't blowing with Cohn, Zoot was often talking about him. In fact, in conversations with me, he mentioned Al more than any other jazz musician. He also spoke of Basie, Ellington, Herman, Wilson and Holiday, Parker, Rollins, Lester Young, Goodman, Getz and Tubby Hayes with variable approval.

Zoot had his own sense of humour as well as his own sax style. One Saturday I came back from Belfast and realised it was Sims' final night at Ronnie's; so down I went to catch him. Backstage between sets I told him I'd just returned from the Belfast Festival. 'Who'd you see?' he asked. I said: 'Mostly Illinois Jacquet.' He grinned. 'Illinois,' he said. 'I can hear him from here.'

At the close of his first season at Ronnie's, in November of '61, Zoot left Britain for Paris. Before he went, I asked for his afterthoughts on the London trip. This, from the Melody Maker *of 2 December, captures the novel nature of these musical 'exchanges' at that period.*

Zoot Sims is not a loquacious man; when he said that what he really wanted to say was how friendly everyone here had been, he clearly meant it — and more.

'To tell you how I feel about this visit. I'd have to think about it and write you a letter,' he explained.

And later: 'Everyone is concerned about jazz over here — about what you're playing and everything, and that's all right. But what has really impressed me about England is the people themselves, as *people.* I can't speak about the British in general, but in our field, those I've met have all been fine and very friendly. To me, that's more important than the other thing, though, of course, I'm delighted if my playing has been enjoyed.'

He broke off after this marathon speech and took a small mouthful of tomato juice — an unusual choice for John Haley Sims ('My family gave all of us the wrong names') and one probably dictated by the previous night's celebrations. After an eventful farewell date at the Marquee — where he played a set with Ronnie Scott's rhythm section and two final numbers with Johnny Dankworth's orchestra — Zoot had been given a send-off party at the Scott Club. There, besides pushing the boat out, Ronnie Scott and Pete King presented Sims with a silver brandy flask. Other musicians gave him a selection of 'Goon' records. Naturally, all this affected him. Zoot told me that he preferred club work to concerts in any event, but this particular club had been nearly everything he could ask for.

'I was comfortable there,' he said. 'I was here before, as you know, with a concert package, but this is a completely different experience,' he went on. 'I don't enjoy playing concerts too much. And *that* show I didn't enjoy at all. So there's no comparison between my two visits.

'The thing about Ronnie's club is that it reminds me of the Half Note. The atmosphere is warm; it's an easy-going place; musicians like it; it has the same kind of management. I feel there's a connection between the clubs already. I've

played them both, and Tubby Hayes has been over and made it at the Half
Note. You know, Tubby — he did it just like that. . . .'

Zoot snapped a finger and thumb to demonstrate the decisive way in which
Hayes won over the American patrons. 'And now,' he said, 'I'd like to see
Ronnie have a try there.

'How would he go over? That depends on the amount of confidence he feels.
I'll tell you this: if he decides to go, everybody there will help all they can to see
that it works out all right.

'I really feel this about the two clubs. Both of them get *going*; there's good
guys work at both, and if there's some way of doing a regular exchange
between them, then it should be done. It can only be to everyone's benefit. I
mean, if the musicians can play and are happy there . . . what else? So let's make
a big thing of it. I'd like to see this club exchange publicised, like to see it grow.'

When Sims has finished his three weeks or so in Paris ('I'll be at the Blue
Note probably') he hopes to revisit London before returning home.

'I plan on looking in for a few days,' he says. 'I open at the Half Note on
Boxing Day with Al Cohn and the quintet. I'd love to come back here with Al
and work the Scott club. I think it could work out. We have a whole book of
tunes and I'm sure Al is well liked in Britain.'

So Zoot Sims takes away a very favourable impression of us. But not more
favourable than the one he leaves behind.

Ronnie Scott summed up the situation: 'My God!' he said. 'What an anti-
climax this week's going to be.'

*One year later Sims was back in Ronnie's and about to be reunited, for his
second week, with sidekick Cohn (they first crossed axes early in 1948). Zoot
spoke more about Al than himself for the* Melody Maker *of 8 December 1962.*

'Well, I hope we'll kill 'em.' The hope was expressed by Zoot Sims, hoping as
much on Al Cohn's behalf as on his own. Sims has already been resident for a
week at Ronnie Scott's club, and he hasn't needed help to keep the place
crammed.

'I'm glad to be back in Ronnie's myself,' he said, 'but I'm especially pleased
about being joined by Al on Friday. It's his first time here, and I think you will
enjoy him.

'Yes, he'll enjoy it, too. He always enjoys playing, and on the social side . . .
he has so many relatives here.

'As for me, I feel Al and I have something more to say musically when we're
together. We have a library, and a lot of things worked out. You know, it's
easier with Al because we have a *band*. There's more we can do. When I'm here
alone, I'm up there thinking of tunes to play, and making things up. Yes, I
know about improvisation and all that, and I like it. But I know so many tunes
I can't think of when I'm on the stage.

'Al and I have the arrangements, and we've played together a lot since — oh,
I guess it was around '57. We met in 1948 in Woody Herman's band, of course,
but it was in '57 we made a couple of record dates and just took it from there.

We used to go on the road and all but we stopped that. We'll still occasionally take something that's not too far from New York, but the Half Note sort of keeps us in town quite a bit. Well, four engagements a year there, and record dates and a few festivals. That takes care of it, and of course Al writes.'

What numbers shall we be hearing from them at Scott's?

'We'll do the things we've recorded,' says Zoot, 'and a whole lot of other numbers we've added. I'm afraid we're going to need an extensive rehearsal for some of them.'

Today, few tenors can escape the warm wind of the bossa nova, and Sims has been bossa-ing in the studios. He says:

'Al and I haven't really been doing bossa novas, but I have an album out in the States and it's doing nicely. Al wrote half the date, and Manny Albam did the other.

'How do I feel about bossa nova? The melodies from Brazil, they're beautiful. And I find the tunes easy to blow on. It's really big in the States now; you know, it's really caught on. And on the Continent ... more than in this country.

'Of course, they're going to run it into the ground, ruin it, but that doesn't take anything away from the original music.'

In 1967 when the Sims–Cohn group was making another return appearance at Ronnie's, now situated in Soho's Frith Street, I asked for joint reactions.

Zoot Sims and Al Cohn are regular visitors to Britain, but this doesn't mean that their familiar duo sound is any less welcome than it was. The warmth, swing and sheer teamsmanship of their current Scott Club offering are as endearing as ever they were, and it is no surprise to see the nation's saxophonists trekking nightly towards Frith Street. ('I've been in every night but one since they opened,' Harry Klein told me.)

Zoot and Al, to coin a phrase, play good together. And that is something to pleasure the ears of club-goers who feel deprived just lately of the basic jazz sustenance.

'It's been a very happy visit this time,' said Zoot. 'We've had good crowds pretty well every night and we're both enjoying it. We haven't played together a great deal recently and this has been a ball. I think I like to play now more than I ever did before.'

Al Cohn confirmed the ball. 'We generally have a good time. You know what a jazz performance is: it can't be top all the while but most of the time we have a ball.

'I suppose six months of the year would be the most we work together. Generally it's a little less. That's why we have fun, I guess, because we're not playing together all the time. So we don't get tired of ourselves.'

When the Sims-Cohn Quintet is laying off, Al devotes much of his time to composing and arranging.

'Mostly I've been working with singers, and I've done the orchestrations for quite a few industrial shows lately. Paul Anka, Steve Lawrence, Tony Bennett and Bobby Vinton are some of the singers I've written for.

'Some of the singers I work for come on with big bands, so that gives me a chance to write for a big orchestra. Yes, I like that field. I like it all, and I've done all different kinds of work in the last couple of years ... but not much jazz as it happens.'

And what about the pop field? Modern hippie groups, as opposed to popular singers?

'Well, I haven't had any call for that so far. What's my opinion of it? It doesn't reach me too much. I like guys who can really play, and I don't think that's what they're trying to do.

'I don't mean to knock these groups. I guess I don't understand what they're trying to do. It's hard for me to judge what's good and what's bad in that music. They tell me some of it is good, but nearly all of it sounds the same to me. I did hear a rock and roll group I liked, though, and it turned out to be the Beach Boys. Very musical stuff, I thought.

'Really it comes down to age, I suppose. If I was that age, maybe I'd be playing that music, too. Except that when I was that age I was practising. In my young days I was trying hard to master an instrument.'

Zoot Sims' attitude to that scene is almost non-commital. 'No, I don't even know about it, the music. But those kids and all those flowers and things. I think it's better than Hell's Angels, however they do it.'

As for Charles Lloyd, often accused of taking the flower path: 'Yes, I like his music. It's a little more advanced than ours. You know, he's working on newer lines.'

I said that I found Al and Zoot's music fully satisfying. 'Good,' Zoot said. 'It sounds kind of mainstream, doesn't it?'

Discussing jazz trends, he expressed a tolerant view about avant-garde music. 'It's something that has to happen. I mean, if you're young you're not going to play like Coleman Hawkins today. It's got to change; it cannot stand still. Take Hawkins ... he doesn't stand still, either.

'Mind you, I'm not one of the changers. I know a couple of musicians I grew up with who changed their styles overnight almost, playing this free form. But they can't do it. It isn't like pressing a button. You can't play it if it isn't in you.'

What does Sims listen to for pleasure these days?

'Well, I still like all my old favourites but I don't have to listen to them so much now. Mostly I go for guitar music. Oh, Segovia ... that's what I like to hear when I get home. I have to get away from jazz sometimes.

'But you know what makes very relaxing listening? Old Billie Holiday records. There was something about those records ... they used popular songs of the day, Billie and Teddy Wilson, but they picked the best of them.'

Before we started talking Zoot was practising flute, the one Harold McNair gave him. I wondered how the new craft was progressing, and whether he'd blown the instrument in public.

'No,' Zoot said firmly. 'I'm not ready for it. I don't want to play it until I've learnt it properly. I still crack notes once in a while. You know, the embouchure is hard on a flute; you can't leak any air.'

A letter on the back page of last week's *MM* caught my attention: 'Jazz — the word and the cult — is dead as far as young people are concerned,' it said. I asked Zoot if he thought the demise was imminent. He said he didn't think so, though he had to admit audiences were going down a little.

'But that's in the clubs. That last Jazz At The Phil concert tour attracted big crowds, and they were more enthusiastic than I expected. I always say one thing: jazz has been dying for seventy years and it's going to last a lot longer than the record we're making now.'

During early 1971 the ever-rewarding tenorman shone his light on the Frith Street jazz room at the head of a quartet. This interview dates from the Melody Maker *of 6 February 1971.*

It is always something to see and hear Zoot Sims in action at Ronnie Scott's — blowing solidly, creating melody, swinging as if his life depended on it and looking meantime modestly pleased to be there. Without fuss or pretentiousness he offers a steady supply of consistently good and inventive tenor jazz. In a way I suppose he is the perfect jazz pro, getting on with the business of making original music as though it was the easiest thing in the world. And when you talk to him you might get the impression that he thinks it is.

For someone of my jazz tastes, the sound and style of his playing are reassuring factors in a world in which tone quality and logical construction of solos count for less and less. Among other things, he represents a tradition; more than one really, but in any event a tradition which had Lester Young at its fountainhead. And in these days of experimental jazz breaking out on all sides, that traditional discipline and firm way of swinging are virtues to be fostered.

I asked Zoot if, as a musician, he felt he was in a tradition — if he even agreed that such talk, much favoured by the writing brigade, made any sense. He nodded, in half agreement at least.

'Well, there are certain slots you can put the music in. Wild Bill Davison is in a tradition, isn't he? Now Miles Davis is in one, a different one than it was. That's freedom music, isn't it? The last time I saw him on TV it was the freedom thing.'

Zoot is quite definitely not in that bag, nor heading for it.

'No,' he insists, 'I couldn't do it any kind of way; I'd feel a fool if I tried. I just don't lean to it, can't do it anyway. Which doesn't mean that I can't appreciate it. But when I think about trying to play that way . . . ' he shook his head and poured a little whisky from a flask into his empty glass. 'I've been playing for twenty-five years, longer, and I can't just press a button and be someone else. It wouldn't be real.

'I've changed my playing but very slowly. I can't really pinpoint it. I just take a tune and play it the only way I can. That's it. I don't really dwell on it very much. Some people probably do. I can only say I play it the way I feel it.

'One thing I do feel is this: I should add a lot of new material to my repertoire. It would be good for me, very satisfying, if I could get around to doing it. And I want to.

'Yes, I listen to everything I can. You've got to, and I think there's a lot of great things coming out of the last ten years. Look at the tunes that have been written, like Bacharach and the Beatles. I like many of them, yeah.'

Zoot's attitude to most things musical is tolerant. When we talked about the power drumming of many percussionists in free or 'open' groups, his comment was that a drummer of that type wouldn't work with his group.

'I do like loose drummers, but I feel that some of them get the idea people came in just to hear them, and that wouldn't fit my style at all.'

As for electric pianos, so well in today: 'I don't think I'd mind one; it's kind of a pretty sound. But I'm not going out looking for one. Certainly I don't need it with the things I play. I'd like to keep electricity out of my group. The neon wouldn't fit.'

On the subject of playing with strings, he had this to say: 'Yes, it can be nice. I recorded with strings for Gary McFarland; it was great. And Stan Getz's *Focus* album is a favourite of mine. Stan plays marvellously on that record. Eddie Sauter left plenty of freedom for him on that.

'I had the chance to play that music when they did two or three college concerts in New York. Eddie is up there near where I'm living. It was the same thing, with me in Stan's place, but unfortunately there wasn't the budget to have all the instruments that are on the album.

'Yes, *Focus* — it was quite a challenge, an experience for me. I'll tell you, after I played it I went back and listened to Stan's record and appreciated what he did on it even more so.'

Back-tracking to his remark about modifying his way of playing, slowly, I mentioned an aggressive, hard-toned passage with which he'd ended one of his numbers at Ronnie's the previous night. It was, I thought, almost out of character as set in the known Sims mould.

The tenorman admitted he thought he had changed quite a lot through the years. 'Of course I hear myself every time I play. Maybe it's too subtle for most listeners. When I hear an old record of mine, that's when I really notice it.

'But I don't believe it's important to alter your style that much. If you're Johnny Hodges, why change? The only thing I noticed specially on Johnny's later records was that he just played a little harder. What do people want? They couldn't expect Johnny to jump up and down on stage.'

Zoot and Al Cohn are still in partnership whenever there is work for the two-tenor group. They played in Toronto last year, and thrice in Los Angeles during '69 and '70. As Zoot says: 'It's so easy to get it together. In fact we don't even need to rehearse.'

Lucky Thompson

'This is to inform you that I am leaving the States for Paris, November 11, by way of London.' An air letter from Belleville, Michigan, dated November 5 1958, was the first information I received about Lucky Thompson's impending visit. After notifying me of flight number and so on, the letter continued: 'My

plans are to spend a few days in London and I would like for you, if possible, to meet me at the Airfield. This will be my first visit to London and of course I don't know my way around. Here's looking forward to my pleasure at seeing you again soon.' The tenorman signed-off with a typical flourish: 'Authentically Yours, "Lucky".'

Having derived great pleasure from his rich and inventive playing since the heady experience of the 1948 Festival International du Jazz in Nice — where he appeared as a 'single' with the bands of Jean Leclere and Francis Burger, and enjoyed plenty of apres-fest sitting-in — I looked forward eagerly to further encounters with a man of forthright views and considerable unsung talent.

We spent the days agreeably, doing the rounds and listening to music, and of course discussing the evils which beset the jazz business. Fate seems to have cast Thompson in the role of 'difficult customer,' and he played it quite well. However, throughout our many meetings in London and Paris I could seldom have said to him with conviction that he was wrong in what he preached, merely unwise now and again. Humphrey Lyttelton, who enjoyed Lucky at the '48 Nice at least as much as I did, once wrote of him as an independent spirit whose uncompromising attitude understandably 'failed to endear him to the big-time showbiz dictators.' Thompson was then (1960) living in Paris and working around Europe. 'Last time I saw him,' Humph went on, 'he was addressing an impromptu meeting on the subject of the atom bomb in the gents' lavatory in Essen.' I don't know what effect that report would have on the jazz establishment, but it endears Eli Thompson to me.

I am setting down some of the articles I wrote about him (or with him, or aided by our man in Paris, Henry Kahn) during his sojourns in Europe; and adding a few thoughts in Q and A form. First, then, in the sequence is a story, dated 22 November 1958, in which he soon has something to say about the exploitation of musicians.

After his three-day introduction to London, American saxophonist Lucky Thompson departed last Saturday on the four o'clock Paris plane.

He was unable, then, to say precisely what he would be doing in Paris. But when I telephoned him at his Rue St. Benoit hotel on Wednesday, he told me he was opening that night at the Blue Note Club.

For the first week, he said, he would be working with a French rhythm section. After that, he understood that the quartet would consist of Thompson, Oscar Pettiford, Kenny Clarke and French pianist Martial Solal. This should be an effective team.

Thompson has been to Europe three times before. The duration of his stay is uncertain, depending on what materialises in the States, but Lucky says it 'looks very doubtful' if he'll be home this year. Home — for Thompson, his wife, Thelma, and children, Jade and Darrell — is now a 35-acre farm in Belleville, Michigan.

'We got it this year,' says Lucky with understandable enthusiasm, 'and so far I've devoted the year to running it ... you know, growing fruit and vegetables, and we're going to have poultry. I've never had so much fun.'

'Of course, I've been writing as well, also practising and studying — I always study to make myself as well equipped as I can.

'What do I write? Oh, songs and instrumental things, jazz and orchestral. Yes, I've recorded a few, and Sarah Vaughan did a song of mine once for Columbia, *While You Are Gone*.

'But I've had no luck with publishing, so at the moment I'm storing up material. Meanwhile, I've loved working outside, spraying trees and so on, cultivating a new slant.'

The farm is a major protective move on Thompson's part. He has a low opinion of the business side of the music business, and he doesn't keep it to himself.

He reckons he was frozen out of New York club work for five years on account of word getting around that he was 'difficult'. But he is still determined to stand up for his convictions. The farm offers the security that nourishes his independence.

It would take this whole page even to summarise Thompson's objections to the set-up. But among the things he most dislikes are the hastily thrown-together session (concert or recording) which allows the musicians no time to build up a group feeling; the manager or club owner who tells you whom to hire for your band; and the recording official who tells you how you should play.

'These vultures will do anything to tie you up — even pay you double money to bait the trap. When they have you, they tell you what to do, what to play, what to say, maybe.

'If you buck them over anything, they'll leave you on the shelf. Yes, they'll try to starve you. You have to be ready to take a beating for what you believe in.

'Another reason I like Europe is that I have the opportunity to study composition. I feel I can study better over here, be more free to express myself. And then there are the audiences, an improvement on those in the States which seem to have too many preconceived ideas, and don't give the artist a chance. In Paris I find them better, and the people in Sweden, Germany and Holland will also give you a chance to be heard. If you come through hard enough you can capture them.'

And the vulture situation? Is that less serious than in the USA?

Says Lucky: 'They have them here, too, but if you find them out, they don't resent it so much. Back home, when you protect yourself by pulling the covers off one, he sets the machinery in motion to hurt you. In France, you can catch a vulture and still operate.'

The second Thompson progress report was dated September 1959, and in it he had a go at white supremacists as well as those moved simply by the profit motive.

It must be nine months since I introduced Lucky Thompson and his vultures in this column.

Since then, accounts have come in from various Continental countries of Thompson at work and pursuing his one-man campaign against the exploitation of jazz and jazzmen.

Now Lucky writes from Paris to say that after an up-and-down Fall and Spring he is in good spirits. 'This contentment,' he writes, 'is due to the wife and children, who are now with me here.'

He has been approached concerning a possible tour of Britain, but has come to no agreement yet. He sounds this cautionary note, however.

'On several occasions, here in Europe, I have been involved with business situations of the lowest degree. The American influence, businesswise, is certainly catching on in a big way.'

Henry Kahn visited Lucky, at his home in Rue des Patures, to bring me a fuller interpretation of Thompson's jazz philosophy.

Lucky thinks that too many jazzmen look on jazz as a day-to-day art.

They never trouble to ask themselves: 'Where we are going and where do we stand right now?'

Both questions should be asked regularly, Lucky believes, 'because the musician who thinks for himself is no friend of the vultures.'

'I know Europe also has its share of vultures, with exactly the same motives as the American variety. In fact, the vultures of both continents are now working hand in hand.

'The name vulture applies to anyone who lives dishonestly by exploiting the talents of others.

'If the European public and musicians are not careful, they'll find themselves exposed to the stifling conditions which have practically destroyed so many musicians in the States.

'Music must be free if it is to be sincere. All jazz, whatever its style, must free itself from the grip of the vultures who are more concerned with turning jazz into cash than giving the public good music.

'Jazz is acknowledged to be America's most original contribution to the field of music,' Lucky Thompson said.

'But now it has been reduced to a kind of fad, with one fad after another taking the place of a once healthy, inspiring and beautiful art. These fads are better known as the Modern, West Coast and Cool schools.

'The desperate attempt of many critics — supported by booking agents, publishers and recording companies — to inject a form of white supremacy into jazz is partly responsible for these fads.'

Lucky believes the wide boys eventually saw commercial possibilities in the new jazz idiom, but says that 'Dizzy, Charlie and Monk were made to beat the sidewalks until the boys were ready to do something about it. These three, and a few others, paid a dear price to maintain their own personalities.

'The scheme was to try and prevent the coloured musicians in America receiving all the credit for creating this new idiom.

'Controversy and distrust grew, friendships between musicians were broken, and jazz suffered by it. Jazzmen must learn once more to love, trust and respect each other, and the way to save the art of jazz.'

On the subject of rock-'n'-roll, Lucky said it had unfortunately been accepted as a form of jazz, whereas most of it should be classified as an 'act'.

'At one time, the vultures were more than happy to type it "Race Music," meaning segregated music performed by and for people of colour.

'To us, it was just a form of blues. The birth of rock-'n'-roll was the result of an effort to inject "white supremacy" in this field of traditional blues.'

Thompson spoke of Armstrong, Basie, Ellington and Lunceford as 'the planets' whose music will live for ever.

'No one can hope, and no intelligent person would try, to pattern his music entirely along the lines drawn by these great artists,' he said, 'or any other great artist for that matter.

'And each man is entitled to his own way of playing; that is what being a free musician means.'

In the summer of '62 Thompson played a season at Ronnie Scott's in Soho, London. Not for the first time, he complained about the shortcomings of many European rhythm sections (while not doubting their enthusiasm); so vehemently on this occasion that I refused to convey all his strictures direct to Melody Maker readers for fear they might affect certain musicians' employment prospects. Lucky was incensed but not for long. Soon I was chauffeuring him about town again. Noticing an empty whisky bottle on the back seat of my Ford, he made a jokey remark about early tastes. Lucky was himself extremely choosy in matters of fluid intake, eschewing even tea and coffee, never mind alcohol, and when he stayed with us I remember him mostly drinking milk. Though an abstainer he was no spoilsport, viewing my fondness for liquor with a tolerant eye. I reassured him that morning by saying it was yesterday's bottle. At once Thompson echoed: '"Yesterday's Bottle", I'll write a tune of that name and dedicate it to you when I record it.' I don't know if he ever kept his promise. Anyway, here he is talking about the pros and cons of working in Europe. Date: 23 June 1962.

'To begin with, I'm very grateful to Europe for having made it possible for me to extend my musical life these past four years. Heaven only knows what new types of isolation I might have had to endure if I had remained in America. And being here has not, I feel, stifled my growth in any way, because I'm fortunate to possess a certain initiative which continues to flourish even under chaotic conditions.

'Naturally, working as a single performer in Europe presents problems — such as not finding the facilities I'm used to. Principally, this means not being exposed to the type of musicians I'm accustomed to working with in the States. This is in no way the fault of the musicians in Europe. I'm happy to say that in most instances they are willing to give their best — and you cannot ask more than that.

'One of the biggest disadvantages, I would say, is the fact that many people, including a lot of the critics here in Europe, expect a man to perform his best under any conditions. This could be expected from a robot, but should not be expected from a highly trained artist.

'In so far as my first playing visit to this country is concerned, I'm very pleased to have the privilege of playing England at last, even though the conditions under which I've had to work are not to my satisfaction. I am unhappy about this, because the situation has made it impossible for me to give my very best. I have done the best that's been possible in the circumstances, if that's any consolation.

'As it seems to me, the main difficulty lies in the fact that there are such vast differences in conception in the rhythm section itself. This makes it impossible to establish the type of impulse to which I could respond most fully.

'A situation of this kind naturally doesn't create a very pleasant atmosphere for everyone concerned. I'm truly sorry about that, and wish the circumstances had been different. But these are the kind of circumstances a "single" performer must expect. Having experienced so many of them, over the past few years, I've come to this conclusion. Either I must call it a day and retire at the end of the year, as I had planned to do, or I must work consistently with a formation of my own choice.

'Why haven't I done this already? Because, first of all, it has been difficult for me to keep operating as an individual, let alone keep a group going. And this is primarily because of the position I am faced with on account of the views I hold pertaining to the improper exploitation of musicians. My convictions won't change, so in order for me to accomplish this I must appeal to the people who want to hear me to help. That's the only way it's going to happen.

'One last point, about my style on tenor having undergone some change, as people have said. ... I feel I'm always growing. I don't feel that I've nearly reached my peak. If someone says I don't sound like I did on one of my records, made years ago, that's a compliment to me. Because I wouldn't want to sound like I did ten years ago. It's not that I'm looking around for a new sound or being different for the sake of being different.

'I'm not an eccentric.

'It is all a question of development, and this is naturally something a non-performer has difficulty in understanding.'

Pensées

On Louis: Well, Louis Armstrong is, as I put it, one of the planets. I came over on the same plane as Louis and his band to France back in 1948 for that Nice festival, but didn't work with him then, of course. I saw a lot of him in the studio during the recording of tunes for that Musical Autobiography set; I played tenor on many of the titles recorded late in 1956. Yes, he was friendly with me, always called me 'Face' or 'Old Face.' That guy's crazy, I'm telling you. That 'Face' is one of his *words*, and he has a number of them. Only Louis could tell you what he means by them.

On Lucky: I guess I came by the name as a kid when I used to wear a jersey with the word 'Lucky' across it. The name suited me; I was lucky. Nowadays some people think it doesn't apply, most of them say I haven't been lucky. But they judge by what they believe is important, like being active and making a lot of money. I tell you I have been fortunate because I still hold my convictions and am free to express them, and to express myself musically. And I don't have a string of vultures round my neck.

On Instruments, 1958: As you can see I'm carrying a tenor and soprano, both French instruments. I added the soprano last year in Paris. Yes, they are all Selmers. Maurice Selmer made five instruments for me last year: bass clarinet, ordinary clarinet, tenor (Mark 7), alto and the soprano. This tenor, a Mark 6, is the one he made the year before. He believes in a musician being adaptable, and so do I.

Ben Webster

One of the all-time tenor titans, Ben Webster figures in most older followers' lists of favourite jazz 'voices' and larger-than-life characters. In his years of European residency, from 1964, he built on his (to us) legendary reputation as drinker, sociable companion, prankster, dangerous adversary, music lover, sensuous balladist and forceful swinger. He made many friends and gained a legion of admirers; enemies too, no doubt, for his moods could be quick-changing and unpredictable, not to say alarming.

I saw much of Ben over the years. He took to the Jones family and we spent a fair amount of time driving him about and trying to keep him approximately upright for the evening gig. One night we had difficulty getting him out of the bath, dressed and ready, out of his White House apartment (London has a block of that name) into the car, and thence to Ronnie Scott's in time to hit. He went on late, far from sober, and after two sad numbers Ronnie bravely removed him from the stand. 'I shall be completing this set for Ben,' Ronnie announced. 'I'm not such a good tenor player but I haven't been celebrating Christmas as early as he has.' A deflated Big Ben looked suitably dejected, almost docile, and some of the customers were far from pleased.

Underneath it all, Webster appeared hell-bent on spreading bonhomie around his ample presence, despite aggressive and self-destructive urges, until a certain level of intoxication brought out the dark side of the moon. The militancy could last a long while, as I realised when calling around lunchtime at the White House for a stimulating chat about stride piano and the like. On the way up, the housekeeper complained that my friend in 802 (an amusing coincidence) had kept some of her people up all night, boozing and otherwise partying. In truth, 'Frog' was lurching a bit and waxing quarrelsome about a lady visitor, but a few references to Tatum and Donald Lambert soon had him laughing and shouting. Indeed, he came up swinging. After a fond enquiry about Betsy's welfare, he assured me: 'Anybody mess with your madam'll have this to reckon with!' In his hefty grasp was a large knife, produced from some part of his clothing. Up till then Ben had been making no sudden movements, so the speed of this one impressed me. I was touched by the intended compliment, though disturbed by the menace.

Tiresome oddities aside, what's important is that Ben played impassioned, breathily melodic music whenever he was able; at times he was unable, but he never sold out willingly, for fame or gold. Among other things, he left behind in Europe the Ben Webster Foundation of Copenhagen, which holds 'Webster Nights' and makes a 'Ben Webster Award'. During a 1967 stay in Britain by Ben, Buck Clayton and Bill Coleman, plans were made to record the trio with a local rhythm team. Buck was taken ill a few days before the studio date and had to miss out. Thus Swingin' In London *was cut for Black Lion with just two front-liners and no new version of 'B.C.&B.C.'. It did, though, include a C & W original titled* For Max. *So glad it was a swinger.*

Webster and Jones 'chewed the fat' over many a glass, and sometimes over the telephone, too. Some names — Hawkins, Carter, Tatum, Jefferson, Ellington, Hodges, Henderson, Pop Smith among them — cropped up again and again, as will be evident from the write-ups which follow. Although the pieces have been edited, I thought the emphases on the chosen few were permissible because they help to clarify Ben's influences and loyalties, and suggest consistency in a contradictory nature. In the past I wrote that Ben had a tone as big as a house and a remarkable gift for ballad interpretation. As soon as I could, I asked how the style was born. This is what he said:

'I was largely self-taught but of course was helped by various people along the way. In the first place I learned violin and piano, and was playing piano in Amarillo, Texas, when I took up the saxophone. In the band I was with, Dutch Campbell's, were the Johnson brothers, Keg and Budd, and we became great friends. To this day I hang out with Keg — Keg and Milt Hinton. And when I hang out with them, before long I'll usually say: "Where's Budd?" Budd showed me the way to play horn. He showed me the tenor in Amarillo, showed me the scale, taught me the way to play. Others helped after that, and I listened to records and studied everything that was happening. I first heard Hawkins in 1924, with Fletcher's band, and knew all his records. I always had a lot of power, but it wasn't until I joined Henderson that I really worked on my tone. It was a fellow named Russell Smith, "Pops," trumpet man with Fletcher and brother of Joe Smith, who made me tone-conscious.'

The Kaycee tenorman reaffirmed his debt to Russell 'Pops' Smith later. Meantime, he had a talk about the Rex Stewart he knew. Stewart died in September of 1967 and in the *Melody Maker* of 23 September 1967 Webster memorialised him thus:–

'It was quite a shock to me to hear of Rex's passing,' said Ben Webster when I visited him in his hotel off Russell Square. 'Yes quite a shock. He was a pretty good friend of mine. I used to see him in California, you know, before I came over to live in Europe. I was living in Los Angeles with my mother and great aunt, and Rex used to visit our house quite often — he knew my people well.

'Rex had a Mercury then, I remember. I didn't have a car at the time and if I called him about something that was happening he was always ready to take me there in his car.'

Webster joined Duke Ellington properly, as you might say, late in 1939. But he first worked with the band in the summer of '35 when Rex was already installed in the trumpet section.

'I don't think I'd ever met Rex until I joined Duke for those three weeks,' Ben remembers now. 'But I'd seen him before. In fact a long time before.

'The first time I heard him I was still at school at Wilberforce in Xenia, Ohio. It was my last year there and we were interested in the music. Horace Henderson, Fletcher's younger brother, had a band at college which included Freddy Jenkins on trumpet, Castor McCord on tenor, his brother on alto and Henry Hicks, trombone.

'Anyway, Fletcher's band was playing a dance in Cincinatti, just over 50 miles from Xenia, and some of the fellows at school had a car and I went with them to catch the band.

'I'd never heard Smack but always wanted to. You see, I was interested in piano then. This must have been early in 1926, when I was just seventeen. I know Pop Smith was on trumpet, and I think Joe Smith, too, and Rex Stewart was in the band. If I'm not mistaken, he was playing a silver trumpet then. Also I remember Hawkins was there, and Don Redman. Big Green was on trombone and Kaiser Marshall, drums. But I went to hear Fletcher, and I don't think I even listened to Hawkins or Rex or anybody else. I wanted to be a piano player so I concentrated on Fletcher.

'Later, of course, I joined Smack's band but Rex, who'd been in the band for two or three spells, had left a long while before. So I didn't meet him until later.

'It was funny how I got into the Henderson band. Hawkins left to come to Europe and Lester Young went in on tenor. But they didn't like Prez much. The musicians were used to Bean's big sound, and Prez didn't play that big tone.

'I believe it was Claude Jones, the trombone player, who told Fletcher: "You've overlooked the fellow who's always admired Hawk and tries to play like him all the way." That was me, and I got the job. But I never could have made that band at the time without the help of guys in the band like Russell Procope who went out of their way to help me. Because I'd only been playing tenor about five years and they had some of the hardest music I've ever seen. In that band you'd play from B flat, B natural up the scale, every key on the keyboard. And all those guys were master readers. As we say, they could see round the corner.

'And you had no rehearsal. When you joined, Fletcher told you to come to work that night. I imagine he thought if you had the nerve to join that band you could make it.

'So I know Rex must have been a good musician to sit up there with Pops and those guys. You had to be pretty fast to keep up with those Henderson musicians.'

It was 1939 before Webster became on friendly terms with Stewart. 'In '35,' says Ben, 'Barney Bigard took two or three weeks off and I got to work in his place. The band was doing one-nighters and maybe some theatre dates. About that time I made a few sides with the band — *Truckin'* was one of the titles — and Rex was in the section with Cootie. Four years later, when I joined the band, Rex was still there, with Wallace Jones and Cootie on trumpets. After a little time I got to know him good.

'The way it is in a band, sometimes you come to work not feeling much like playing. Rex and I were friendly, and if he knew I was down that particular day he'd talk to me on the horn, you know, call me dirty names and all like that, and I'd turn round and wave my finger at him. Then when my solo came up, and if I'd stumble upon something new, some little riff or something, I'd turn to him again. And when he got his turn, he'd try for something new and look at me. You know, he would help to perk me up and this would kind of spark up everybody else. He was a lot of fun, Rex.'

And how about his playing? What impression did that leave with Webster?

'Well, first of all, Rex had his own way of playing — a unique cornet style I should say, because of course he was playing cornet when I first met him in Duke's band. Then, too, he could be fast. He acquired that speed, I guess, in the old days with Fletcher.'

Would Ellington have had much of an effect on Stewart's playing?

'I imagine so; I think Rex really developed that cocked-valve style while he was in the band. If you were fortunate enough to join Duke and be able to stay there, that was a band that could make you.

'It's a positive thing that Duke will write compositions for you, around you, that help to develop you musically. Rex had quite a few of these specialities — *Boy Meets Horn* and *Tootin' Through The Roof* with Cootie, to name just two — and became a noted figure in the band.

'I should think this period would definitely have been the highlight of Rex's career. As I've said before, Duke makes a star of everyone because he's the greatest judge of musicians I've ever come across. Within a very short time of joining the band he'll know your musical abilities, and he'll know the man. Next thing you'll have a concerto to play, and that way you begin to get famous, or more famous than you were before.

'So that's how it must have been with Rex. And that was a very fine period for the band. Blanton was there, Tricky Sam, all the great players. I used to kid with Tricky and Rex all the while, and truthfully it was a ball to go to work. Sometimes I could hardly wait to get to work, there was so much inspiration in that band.

'Rex had his special sound, and Duke knew exactly how to use it. According to the effect he wanted, he knew where to put that melody. When he wanted Rex's sound, Rex had the melody.

'Another thing I remember was a tune he used to do with Ivie Anderson. She'd come to that stand and Rex would call her by name, on his cornet the way he used to do it with the valves. Then they had a little dialogue before she would sing the number.

'Oh, that was a big success every show. He could say a lot of words on cornet. I never knew anyone else do that; that's why I thought it must be rather complicated.

'Yes, Rex sure had a unique style. His death is a great loss, because I'm sure he knew some things about the trumpet that maybe no one else will ever know.'

One of the features Melody Maker *ran regularly during the 1970s was a reaction test — something like a 'Tennis-elbow-foot Game' of instant reactions to the mention of people, places or things. Ben was the subject in May 1971. He had, by then, been resident in Europe for some years, and the interview took place at the end of one of his (by then) fairly regular visits to Scott's club. I have restored a couple of items omitted at the time.*

LONDON: Peter King and Ronnie brought me over here in '64 and I've been coming over ever since. So many friends here now, you know. I always go down to Dobell's in Charing Cross Road every day to hear some good music and see Doug and Don and John and Henry — that's the team.

IKE QUEBEC: Yes, he had a good feeling on tenor, a different feeling from most guys. Quebec could really blow. And he played good piano. He wasn't guessing, he knew where he was. Of course, everyone then listened to Bean (Coleman Hawkins), but Quebec had his own thing going.

SOPRANO SAX: A very difficult instrument to play. Bechet played the instrument well — he played everything well — and I did love the way Johnny (Hodges) played it. In tune ... oh, he always did play in tune, and that's a hard instrument to play in tune.

KANSAS CITY: My home ... I think about the Sunset, on 12th Street and Woodland, and Pete Johnson the pianist, and bartender Joe Turner singing blues. That could be 1932 or '33 and the band would be Pete and Merle Johnson on drums, Mouse Randolph on trumpet and me. I lived down the block from the sunset then. They had a mike on the bandstand and one of the speakers was out in the street. If the joint was empty, Piney Brown would say: 'Better call 'em, Joe.' Then we'd blue the blues for 45 minutes and Joe would sing 'em. The place filled up and then Piney would say: 'Cut it back, Joe', so he could serve some drinks. Yes, to me the boss. And those days Joe would depend on tips. One day somebody asked him for *Trees,* you know that ballad, and Joe wanted the tip. Well, I heard Joe Turner sing *Trees,* and believe me that was the *Trees Blues* ... the funniest shit I ever heard in my life. Oh, but that was funny. I swear Mouse cried.

ELECTRIC MUSIC: Don't want to rub anyone wrong, but no. A friend told me to get one of those things you put on your mouthpiece, and an amplifier. 'Fill it out,' he said. So I said maybe he was right at that. He's a good friend of mine, wouldn't want to hurt his feelings. But here I am, playing horn since nineteen-twenty-something. Why stick some electronics on it now? Because when I started, singers sang through megaphones without any mikes. I remember Rush with the Blue Devils and George E. Lee — didn't need no microphone. And Joe Turner, when he was way out in back serving drinks, if he sang you heard him.

COPENHAGEN: Well, I've been there two years in June and I like living there . . . got a lot of friends. Yes, I'll stay as long as they let me. Funny place, though. I went to the rehearsal of a friend of mine, Maddie Peters, and she was carrying on and I was kind of encouraging her privately, you know, with shouts of 'Move your arse, you . . .' Well, you know how it is at rehearsals. But they taped the rehearsal and broadcast it. Another friend told me I'd better listen to this *Madeline Peters Show*. 'You're on it,' he said. And I was. A hell of a thing . . . they repeated it three times.

BENNY CARTER: I call him King. You know why? Because he knows more than anybody. Besides alto, he plays the piano, trumpet, clarinet, drums, tenor, and writes . . . Goddam he is king. He's a perfectionist, that's why. Did you ever taste his cooking? This man can bake a cake. And he's fast with these (Webster demonstrated with his fists). Yes, he's the king.

FLETCHER HENDERSON: Like I always say, the only band I was really afraid to join as I'd heard they played in every key on the keyboard. That's right, they did, back in 1934. No, there was no rehearsal for me there. Fletcher thought if you had nerve enough to join his band you could play his music. First number might start in B flat just as nice as you like, then that next chorus — you'd be looking at a gang of sharps or maybe five flats and break out into a cold sweat. Scuffling? If it hadn't been for Buster Bailey, Russell Procope, Pops Smith and Hilton Jefferson, I don't think I would have made that job. I mean, they were so far advanced. Procope said for me to take my book home — I was living at Fletcher's house at that time — and he'd show me how that stuff went. And he did. Anyone else's band was like kindergarten after Smack's band — until you got to Duke. That was something different. One thing I must say; Pops Smith, the lead trumpet with Henderson, made me tone conscious. 'You got a pretty nice little tone there,' he told me one day. 'You want to study that. Let those other fellows play sixty thousand notes, you play just three with tone. That makes the difference.' I took notice of that.

DUKE ELLINGTON: You're not going to get me talking about the Duke, are you? Well, a funny thing was that when I joined him I didn't have any music. He hadn't written any parts for me. I guess I'd been in the band about three months and still no music. I was added to the saxophones, you see, and I was trying to find that fifth part. Barney Bigard used to give me his parts sometimes — he hated tenor — and I'd try to look at Johnny Hodges' music and transpose to tenor. So after a while I asked Duke: 'When are you going to write me some parts?' And he said: 'You're doing all right.' He was having fun at me trying to work out that fifth part. So finally, when he started to get me some parts, Tizol — who sat right behind me — noticed that certain notes I played struck him as soft. He asked why I didn't blow those notes out, and I told him some of them didn't sound right to me. That's why I blew them softer. He told me: 'Blow them out, that's the way he wants them.' So I did then. You talk about sound . . . Carney was at one end of that saxophone team and I was at the other. And I tried to blend with him. We used to run Duke mad, me and Harry Carney. Duke would say: 'Cut it out fellers, I can't hear anyone else.' I say Pops made me tone-conscious and that section did the rest. Because Johnny, he sounded like a tenor on that horn of his. I warned you I'd go on about Duke. One more story ... I thought once I'd go to Juilliard for some theory, and I told Duke. He was fixing his bow tie, I remember, and he just said: 'Ben, you'll only learn what you already know and it will mess you up.' I was mad at that, you know, and later I told Jimmy Jones what Duke had said. I thought he didn't want me to learn nothing. Jimmy Jones, he say to me: 'Frog, he told you right.'

BARITONES: I never played baritone, bass sax either. Sometimes I used to ask Carney could I play his horn, and sometimes he'd let me. But he was frightened to death I'd mess up his reed or something. But I never played one in a band — started on violin as a boy, wanted to play piano always. First horn was alto — Lester's father taught me the notes — then I went on tenor. And I've had a clarinet. In fact I bought a new one in Paris three, four years ago. If you don't feel like taking your horn out, it's nice to take that up and blow around a bit, keep your chops up. But not in public.

RECORDS: That's the first thing I do in the morning; I turn on Donald Lambert, Art Tatum and Fats. First thing I listen to in the morning, last thing when I go to bed. I have records I play when people come round, and others I play for myself. Other records I wake up to are *Time After Time* by Joe Turner and some things by J. B. Lenoir. But when cats come to the house I don't play those. And I don't play my classical records or own records — unless someone asks specially for one. Among the best records I have is Stravinsky's *Firebird*. I thought of that when I read of his death. This man, he knew so much. I'd like to get some more of his records. *Petrouchka*, that's one I want.

LOUIS: I never did play with Louis. Well, I didn't get started until 1929, down in Texas there, and Armstrong was already in New York. When he was with Henderson, I was fifteen (in 1924) and going to school, but we used to go to dances at night. Of course I listened to his records later on. This man had fantastic creative ability in the Twenties, superb feeling, too. He must have had incredible ears and an original mind because nobody was playing like that. And I never heard anybody who got such a fantastic sound out of the trumpet; when he played, you knew it was him. Know him? Yes, I got to know him quite well.

EUROPEAN LIFE: As I say, I'm happy in Denmark and I was happy in Amsterdam before that. The tempo over here is slower than in New York. Europe's a place I can relax in. There are some fine players here and I've been fortunate in the people I've worked with. No, I've no plans to return home soon. Of course you miss your old friends, though I've managed to see quite a few over here. I don't believe I miss the musical inspiration of the American scene. You see, I only try to play one way. If you try all different styles that are in vogue, I think you con yourself. Me, I just stick by my guns; I don't want to play out of another man's bag.

THREE

Brass

Red Allen

Red Allen was a remarkable figure in trumpet jazz: a sort of traditional superman whose wayward improvisations were repeatedly surprising on account of their modern character. He created an impression of up-to-dateness (on his mid-Sixties solo tours in Britain with the Alex Welsh Band) on such evergreens as St Louis Blues or Ballin' The Jack. And while his tone was not akin to that of most modernists, it would fluctuate from whisper to blast, from the cool to the vibrant.

Red died in April 1967, just over a year after his last visit to Europe. Alex Welsh, recalling him for me as 'one of the finest trumpet players of all time' said:

'You couldn't help liking him. I don't think I ever heard anybody say a bad word about him.

'As everyone noticed who knew him, Red was pretty ill on his last visit. He must have known how sick he was, and it's a great tribute to his professionalism that he should have chosen to fulfil a tour like that, and done so well. And he was still playing lovely little things, interesting ideas I assure you. He kept well up-to-date on happenings and could still bring up some surprises for us after all the shows we'd done together.

'We had some hard journeys that last tour, but not a murmur of complaint from Red. And you know the sad thing was, when he said goodbye he gave me a funny look out of the side of his eyes. We all said: "See you next year then," but we were certain we wouldn't see him here again.'

Never again shall we hear the cry of 'My man!' or 'Make him happy!' rapped out in Red's distinctive voice. Never again shall we see that big frame bounding on stage and announcing 'Look out! St Louis!' — or whatever the tune happened to be. No more the drawn-out 'Nice!', which was his all-purpose comment or verdict, even when accompanied by a frown of enormous and rutted proportions.

I talked to Red during his second tour as a 'single'. He had visited with Kid

Ory's band in 1959, and again as a solo in 1964. This is what I wrote in February 1966.

It is pleasant indeed to see once more the tall, bulky figure of Henry Red Allen striding the streets and hotel corridors of Kensington, sampling the bitter and passing his customary verdict: 'Nice, nice.' As usual, he sounds delighted to be in Britain. And this time he looks forward with keen pleasure to meeting such old friends as Pops Foster, Jimmy Archey and Alvin Alcorn. 'Of course I've known George Foster and his brother since they were longshoremen in New Orleans. I left home with Foster the first time in 1927. We went to meet King Oliver in St Louis. I didn't like it away from home too well at first, so I came back and left again in '29.'

At most of his jobs these days Red works with a quartet. When he's completed his British tour, he takes one into the Theatrical Restaurant in Cleveland.

'Quartets are pretty good for travelling use,' he explains. 'You have your regular rhythm section, and you can play along with them without offending anyone. Then they're good for financial reasons. Clubs won't pay for bigger bands — if they could cut you down to a single they'd be happy. Musically, a couple more horns would help. You know, someone like Buster Bailey — we understand each other — would make it more of a band. But you have to study the financial side. When I was coming up, it didn't matter; I didn't mind if I didn't get paid. When I began in New Orleans, I didn't think it would ever be my living. To my way of thinking, if I was a millionaire I'd still be playing.

'And I guess I would at that. I can see the point of people like Louis who want to go on playing. My father, Henry Allen Sr, used to play a few parades right up until a little bit before he passed, in 1952, at the age of seventy-five.

'Of course, I was in my dad's band from eight years old, ever since I was old enough to march, and I used to pass the music out on parades. We used to carry the parts in little sacks, and I had those on my shoulder. In those days, bands kept the names of the tunes they played secret, and my father cut the titles off all the music and numbered it instead.'

It is always tempting, in conversation with a New Orleans jazzman of Allen's experience, to try and add fragments of information to the legends of Crescent City history. Recently, I talked to Pops Foster about Buddy Bolden, and now I was interested to see what Red knew of him.

'Well, I never heard him, of course. He blew his top just before I was born, according to my dad. I knew about him, though, because he'd played with my father's brass band. And I met him once — at the Louisiana State Hospital where he was detained. I wanted to go and see him, and I went after I'd been in New York a while. I left New Orleans for the second time in '29, so I guess it was between 1930 and 1931. I went into a kind of yard where there were a lot of people talking or walking about, and asked someone for Charles Bolden. They said he was over there and I went up and spoke to him.

'Aside from Bolden, I heard most of the old bands like Jack Carey. And I had a chance to play with a great many of them. I was considered to have a keen ear and flexible mind, and I kept up with what was happening. Great trumpet players like Guy Kelly and Kid Rena, they didn't need me to play, but they used to add me to the band sometimes because I knew what was popular on records, and they weren't interested in it. They played the way they played. But I listened to everyone.'

Another temptation for interviewers is to find out which musician, past or present, is held in highest esteem by the man being interviewed. I put the 'greatest ever' question to Allen.

'I never think in terms of great players,' he said after a while. I have different feelings for different players. Some guys can play an awful lot, and others play less but are friends of mine, which evens things up. But I must say that when he's in shape, a guy like J. C. Higginbotham is a rough man to beat. Higgy, in his form, he's a most flexible player. He had everything: power, excitement, flexibility.'

Ruby Braff

Growing-up in jazz during the Thirties I was nourished by the full-toned, singing, swinging trumpet sounds of Armstrong, Lips Page, Allen, Cootie, Berigan, Ladnier, Eldridge, Rex Stewart, Bill Coleman and other warriors who saw action with the big bands. Years later I often yearned for the re-emergence of those kinds of traditional horn styles — still kept alive by some over-40s and older men — and so the coming forth of young Ruby Braff in the Fifties was a godsend to me, and something of a miracle. He has remained, to my ears, among the most moving of players. I agree with Paul Sampson who wrote of Ruby in Down Beat *that his 'rich tone and soaring romanticisms are a constant joy'. And with Nat Hentoff's: 'Ruby is a jazzman who swims so confidently and creatively in the main stream that it is difficult to pin a period-label on him.'*

In my experience, which goes back to an introduction in April of 1961, it is difficult to pin anything on Braff. He was then with George Wein's group in Paris, and I have since interviewed him a number of times, finding him as enthusiastic a talker as a player. The best approach to this heap of material is for me to present some of Ruby's heretical conversations, more or less in the order I heard them. First it should be explained that he uses a cornet because he prefers it to the trumpet as an instrument for solo performance. 'A trumpet is more of an orchestral instrument,' Braff said. 'Cornet has a softer, mellow tone.' And, he added later: 'Most musicians play too loud anyway; they believe they have to because everyone else is playing loud.'

If the outspoken man from Riverdale is not quite the quiet American — too much fire and fury in him for that — he produces a great deal of quietly melodic music (he is another who dislikes the name 'jazz' and, though he cannot avoid it, uses it as seldom as he can), and if justice existed in the music business he'd be richer and more famous than the late Liberace was. About 15 years ago Eddie Condon wrote: 'Ruby has a facility for turning down work but always has

expensive cars. I don't think he is a car thief because he never leaves his house.
He's a particular guy, though, when it comes to what and where he plays.'

   Nothing much has changed except that Ruby claims the work offers are not
coming in. He is a friend of ours who 'phones now and then from home without,
he thinks, revealing his identity. Last time it was: 'This is Scotland Yard here.' A
photo of him at a nightclub table with Jack Lesberg and others is captioned in
ink: 'The Last Supper.' And a letter is signed: 'Love ... Your Father.'

   So, over to Ruby: In 1965, on tour in Britain, he had this to say about the
saleability of jazz.

'You see, people all use phrases. One is: "You can't give the public good music;
it won't sell." They learn it from each other. "Nobody likes good music." The
truth is that nearly everybody likes good music except them.

   'Take the George Wein band I'm doing the festivals with, we've played all
over the place, to audiences of all ages, and we've never come up against these
people who don't like it. Usually, the only complaint is: "Why can't we hear
more normal music like this?"

   'In my opinion it's your A&R men, disc jockeys, critics and your characters
who don't like lovely music and push something different. These people keep
repeating that good music won't sell, but you have Tony Bennett, for instance,
who does nothing but beautiful songs and old standards with good arrangements behind them, and sells millions. So what have the record companies to
say to that?

   'I've never heard one pop group that plays great. People who say they do are
reading into them things that don't exist. It is not for people who've had more
experience of listening, and whose tastes are cultivated, to lower themselves to
the tastes of foolish children. It's for children to come up to the tastes of mature
people. Very often the parents, who've played such a weak and incompetent
part in bringing up their children, think the only way they can make up for this
incompetence is to sink to the child's level in matters like music, dancing and
the arts. Really they are seeking child acceptance, see? It is their way of buying
off their children for not being able to teach them about life and cultivate their
minds properly.'

   And what, I wondered, about the musicians who seem to favour modern
pop.

   'Most of the musicians I've heard speak well of this music are those who have
to make a living, or part of their living, recording in the studio with this kind of
thing. And many of them feel so miserable and guilty about having to do it that
they talk themselves into thinking it's good music. This is the danger of people
of musicality becoming involved with this rubbish. They begin to believe in it.
Just as this happens to fine musicians, so it can happen to a whole public. Their
taste becomes corroded. It is very sad, because it makes me think that a lot of
these people never really loved and appreciated the things they paid lip service
to for many years — the recognised great works.

   'Now there's nothing wrong, so far as I'm concerned, with record companies
producing this rubbish for people who don't know, or with musicians record-

ing the same in order to earn their livelihood. But they mustn't get to believe in it.

'The important thing is this: those who've lost their way had better renew their faith in things they once knew were wonderful and valid before they end up with the same immaturity and indecision and sickness as so many young people are featuring in their philosophy.

'In any case, the idea of trying to stay young by acting young and dressing up young is wrong. One way to stay young is by becoming wise and being constantly busy studying, learning and accomplishing something. Love for something that you do well, that helps to keep you young.'

You can never take Braff's opinions for granted, not for long anyway; like many of us he thinks differently now — as I write and read his latest contentious letter — from the way he thought back then. But you can count on him to hold strong opinions and express them fearlessly. At this encounter, in March 1975, he was feeling appreciative of the response the Ruby Braff–George Barnes Quartet had got at Ronnie Scott's night spot, the group's first European club engagement. This is from a report I wrote for the Melody Maker *of 15 March 1975.*

Many of us who have been revelling in the joyful, intelligently constructed music of the Braff–Barnes Quartet this past fortnight can count ourselves very fortunate. We're lucky to hear a band as good as this any time, any place; and we're extra lucky to have had the band standing for so long, as you might say, at the platform in Frith Street, London.

Ruby Braff, the blowing member of this chamber-jazz group, has always held firm and precise views about the kind of work he wishes to do and the music he wants to play. He has never, for instance, wanted to be in a big-band brass section, and never considered becoming a studio musician, though he admires people who do these jobs well. 'I respect anyone who does any work properly,' he says. 'It's just that those jobs have nothing to do with my life and never did. I'm not a service musician. If I were here just to service people with what they want, well, I'd open up a club date business.' He laughs quietly and adds: 'But that's not my racket, you know. My racket is to take lovely music and to express it as well as I can so that people know what I'm saying and understand me'

Yes, Braff believes in audiences and the need to communicate with them. 'I didn't learn the instrument in order to play in my bedroom,' he says.

He likes to play in places which aren't too noisy because the quartet itself is not noisy. 'That's why it's easy to play in this group, you see, because there isn't noise. So there's dynamics and a feeling of ease. Nobody makes you work very hard, in that sense, you know. You're not fighting noisy drums or many horns or that sort of thing.

'You say we look as though we're taking it easy, and I think that's the way you're supposed to look on the stage. You're not supposed to look as though you're struggling or throwing up while you're playing. You should look nice. Of course, if you know what you're doing it makes it easier.'

This is not revivalist music, and nostalgia is not involved in it at all so far as the cornettist is concerned.

'There's no nostalgia in anything we perform,' he says firmly. 'We're just playing good compositions. There's no nostalgia about playing Mozart or Chopin or Ellington, is there? You're simply playing good music, and that's our idea.

'As for a revival — it's a revival of nothing because there's no other group which plays like that. In order for that to have happened the four of us would have to have been in it.'

He's not been the most contented record-maker I've met, not always been satisfied with what company men term the product. 'That's for sure, that's true,' he agrees. So how much satisfaction is he feeling nowadays?

'Oh, I have a whole lot of satisfaction from this group, and it's very pleasurable to play with it. I enjoy it.' Asked if he would continue to record outside the quartet, Braff says he will, so far as he knows now. RCA Victor expect George Barnes and him to record with a quartet, and he feels that if he wants to record other things he is free to do so.

'I think the group could have tremendous commercial potential, because we've never seen anyone from five to 90 who actually disliked our music. And I don't know too many other types of music of which you could say that.'

So far as repertoire goes, Braff and Barnes look among the finest popular songwriters for most of their material. Among what Ruby calls 'the best guys', like Harold Arlen, George Gershwin, Richard Rodgers, Van Heusen, Berlin, Kern, Ellington and Cole Porter.

'George loves all those good tunes, as I do. Most musicians eventually get tired of hearing little original bullshit numbers that some person wrote for the band, rather than something written by the masters, let's face it.

'Yes, those people are the masters. And not to play them is to be robbed of not only an opportunity to play beautiful music but of an education.'

In the following year, Ruby was back in Britain without the quartet, appearing as a single and ready to voice his views on the best singer on the scene and sundry other topics. This piece was printed, not quite in this form, in the Melody Maker *of 28 August 1976.*

'There were two things I enjoyed very much. The gig at Fairfield Hall — a tribute to Louis Armstrong or something — that was very pleasant, nice and cool. And the other was the Palladium when I went to see Bing.

'It was such a thrill. A friend got me tickets somehow and I sat in a box right over the stage, a few feet away from Bing. It was a wild thing. I'd never seen Crosby in person before. Naturally he's a great performer, and then he's so casual. Jesus, he looks wonderful out there carrying on. You know Bing has wonderful time, the most incredible time in the world, and he has everything else. He 'plays' better than all the horn players that you think are the greatest. They're not one eighth as good as him. He's good at everything.'

Ruby's enthusiasm seemed boundless, and it was interesting to hear him on this subject. So many people feel that Crosby is a good popular singer and not much more, and I started to say this.

'Let's not get into a hassle about what people think of him.' Braff sounded impatient. 'He's one of the greatest musicians in the world. That's what makes him better than anyone else. Also he was born, luckily, with a tremendous voice — an instrument. You're born with those beautiful pipes or you're not. The rest can be learned, and of course he has that great gift of music as well. He has unusual artistry. There is that casualness he invented that's him. It's so marvellous to sit and look at this relaxed guy doing all these things. I couldn't believe it.'

It has been said, and frequently, that Ruby is not only a blunt speaker but a difficult person to get along with at times. I asked if he considered himself to be too outspoken. He didn't feel that he was.

'I look on those as derogatory remarks.' he replied forcefully. 'I never speak to anyone unless they speak to me, and I don't believe I ever tell anybody anything unless they ask me. When they do, well, if the answer doesn't agree with them and they want to put labels on me, then I say fuck them. If they don't like it, tell 'em not to ask me questions. That's my outlook on that subject.' It seems a fair point of view to me.

The last time I spoke to Braff, prior to this visit, was when he was here in early 1975 with the Braff–Barnes Quartet. Then he claimed to be enjoying his work with that remarkable group but said he looked forward to the day when a more settled existence would afford him leisure for practising, studying and writing music. Was this the reason he discontinued playing in the quartet with George Barnes? If not, why did the group split up?

'There wasn't enough work for it, we had nobody to manage it and take care of us. Every time we worked I had to book the date, and I can't do that and worry about everything and play. Either get somebody else to do that or forget it, you know?'

The quartet had looked to me like a very fair commercial proposition considering all the favourable mention it received. Ruby said:

'I don't see any reason why it couldn't have been. And it was nice so far as the playing was concerned. But I had a few problems; as I've said I had to work with this guy whom I don't like at all, and we couldn't get along and finally it got pretty ridiculous. Well, eventually, he came up and said "Look I have a letter from my doctor saying I have a bad heart." And I said. "OK George, I'll see you later." And that was that.'

The trumpeter laughed merrily, but stopped abruptly when I suggested (only half-seriously) he might have teamed up with another guitarist.

'Might have done what?' His voice rose on an incredulous note. 'I don't want another guitar player. I hate guitars. I don't ever want to hear any guitars again. I want a screaming rhythm section with drums and noise. I don't want to hear anything quiet. It makes me nervous.' He dissolved into more laughter, while I pointed out some of the merits of the quartet's finely constructed music.

'Yes, OK well, I'd like to have a group which did all of that, which could play soft and also play ... I don't mean loud, but with more force and drive, you know. I'd like to have it all. If I had my way I'd use 20 musicians so we could do all kinds of things.'

Meanwhile, said Ruby, he was getting by and working with certain musicians for whom he felt the greatest respect. And when the time was right he would put something good together. Who were some of these players he'd like to have in a group?

'Whenever I have a chance to do anything, I always try to use Connie Kay. I'm so fond of his drumming; he plays so perfectly and with such taste and time. He's like the Sid Catlett of today.

'There are two drummers I really enjoy working with, Connie and Jake Hanna. Out on the Coast I like to play with Jake, and in New York I get Connie. He does a lot of work with Benny, works in Condon's a lot of times; he does a lot of things. Now a funny part of all this is, with the way I work, sort of freelancing you know, if I have good people playing with me I really don't have to rehearse anything. I find the way it works out best is to just do anything I want, and have guys with me that are ready to do it. That's the way I made a record recently, and it turned out wonderful. I mean the idea was wonderful, not that I was.

'We went into the studio, and I had such people as Connie, Bill Crow on bass, Jimmy Rowles, piano, and I had Vic Dickenson too, as a matter of fact, and I said that all I was going to tell them was the tune.

'No such thing as who's going to take what choruses. All they had to do was look at me, because I said I might stop them in the middle of a tune and go into something else. "What," they said, "on a record date?"'

'I says, "Yup, right. There'll be no re-takes. That's it. What goes out is the way it's going to be." And, you know, everything worked just about perfectly. I told 'em what one tune would be, anyway, and I stopped them in the middle of things ... the guys in the control room were close to nervous breakdowns, didn't know what was happening. But it worked and we played some great tunes; did the whole album in, like, about three hours. Now that's the way I like to play. I can't go on a bandstand and start wondering if he knows this tune or that guy knows the other. By the time I get through scratching my ass and talking to each musician, I don't feel like playing that tune any more.

'No, I don't want to work that way, don't want to go through this kind of crap. I find I play best when I play what comes to my mind. And the only way to do it is to have some fine musicians and give them a few ground rules as to how it works.

'That's for me. Like an old saloon player. If I want to go into something weird, I can do it. Of course, when you work a while with a pianist you come to know his repertoire and he knows what songs you know, so it's never too difficult to jump into this or that. I really enjoy playing that way.

'But you have to know the people you're working with. I mean, one of the guys I had over here, he'd say yes to anything. No matter what tune I suggested. "Yeah, I know it." Then we'd play it and I'd think. "Christ, how do I get out of this?"'

I gathered from all this that Ruby had misgivings about the type of 'all star' jam sessions assembled, for example, at the Nice Jazz Festival. He did, and said that he couldn't make 'that Nice thing' any more.

'It's a holocaust of jam sessions there,' said Ruby. 'I love jam sessions if the people in them fit. But in a lot of those sessions, the people seem mismatched, and it doesn't make any sense to me. So you're likely to make a damn fool of yourself. So what's accomplished? I like to leave knowing that I played well. What's the point of my playing if I'm not going to play good? It's stupid. For Chrissakes, my reputation has been ruined in this country from playing with weird people on this tour. If I'd been in the audience, I'd have walked out after hearing some of the things I heard. It was terrible.'

On his last night in Britain, playing at the Pizza Express in Dean Street, Soho, Braff had an audience which included many musicians — Jake Hanna, Joe Bushkin, guitarist Johnny Smith, Aubrey Frank, Ron Rubin, Mike McKenzie, Keith Ingham and Susannah McCorkle among them. It was one session he enjoyed immensely, especially when he called Hanna up on drums for a second set which went on long beyond the normal span of Braff sessions.

'I played deliberately for an hour and a half last night,' he said, 'because I didn't want to stop. It was so good and I was afraid if I did, something would happen that would interrupt that situation; if I stopped something would go wrong or somebody would be missing. You know what I mean?

'I told myself I owed it to me to have a good time on my final night. So I says to Jake after a long while: "Do you want to run off or do you want to stay on?" He says: "Let's stay on." So I said: "Great." So we played on until one in the morning.'

At the end of his next working trip to London, the cornettist was in a happy frame of mind. This is from an article of August 1978.

It was a contented Ruby Braff that left Britain the other week for New York and home after a stay — mostly at the Pizza Express in Soho — in which he loosed off some of the most graceful and finely wrought improvisations I've yet heard emerge from his cornet. Musicians went night after night to hear him, and trumpet players especially — from Alex Welsh and Digby Fairweather to John McLevy and Leon Calvert — flocked to the small restaurant downstairs to savour Ruby's approach to a superb repertoire of worthwhile melodies. Often there was standing room only and I remember Leon Calvert bending over the stair-rail between levels for most of one set, listening hard and smiling. Afterwards he came by and said, in effect, that it was how jazz trumpet should sound but seldom did. No grumbles were reported from Braff, and when he agreed to an interview I said that, after some of the rough comments, it was pleasant to know he had something nice to say about Britain.

'No, no, no,' he corrected at once. 'Just a minute. That is quite untrue. I never had anything rough to say about Britain. I like Britain. I've had something rough to say about some people that have tried to fuck me up here. And I think you know who they are. But there's a big difference.'

The point was conceded and I remarked that this visit appeared to have been a happy one for him. He said with fervour that it had been the happiest one, not just a happy one

'I don't habitually complain about anything unless there's something to complain about. I told you before what a good time I had with Eddie Thompson, didn't I? And this time it's been marvellous. And there are two very nice people playing with us: Len Skeat and Russ Bryant, they're both wonderful too, you know. And, of course, last night at the Pizza on the Park I worked with just Eddie. I really enjoyed that.'

Cornet–piano duets are something of a speciality for Reuben Braff, whose *Two Part Inventions* with Ellis Larkins have knocked out many a musician and jazz collector over the last twenty years. Would he agree that this format, with the demands it makes on both players, exposes a musician — and would he pardon the expression? Ruby grinned at the thought.

'Yeah, you're both standing there pretty naked, you know. So you gotta make something come off.' He sat back in his corner and laughed delightedly. He likes to joke almost as much as he likes to play.

One of the benefits of two-man bands is that either member can play as softly as he wishes without being drowned by a loud rhythm section or obtrusive riff 'background'. Braff isn't given to much loud playing, and I guessed he liked this aspect of the duo performance. At the Pizza On The Park, it was observed by one spectator, you could have heard an olive drop while Ruby and Eddie were swopping musical ideas. Oddly, perhaps, the cornet ace did not call for deferential silence, but says he is accustomed to the sound of talking.

'I don't believe they come to a nightclub to be in a concentration camp. You can't ask people to come into your club and sit there and hardly breathe. I won't go to a place that does that. I mean if somebody was shrieking insanely that would be different, but normal talking in a nightclub is expected. I don't really notice it, 'cos I'm busy playing.

'Look, Duke Ellington and Louis Armstrong liked to hear the sound of people in a place where they were playing. Duke told me himself that it was the reason he took that gig in the Rainbow Grill every summer. He said: "I like it. People dance around and come up and sit down on the stool with me, and tickle the piano and everything." he says: "That's what I came from: I'm a saloon player." It doesn't really mean that a saloon player or singer can't play in a concert hall. But there are very few people who really are saloon players. I get it from listening to all those old singers who could handle it, and, you know, people like Frank Sinatra who know how to handle it in a club.

'With all the noise there may be in this club, we can play very softly. Once in a while I play a little loud, then a little soft, and they shush down a bit. They know when to talk and when not to talk. You don't have to tell them anything.'

I took it that Ruby didn't play very differently during this engagement from how he usually plays at home. He said yes, he did play differently. He played much better.

'And I played better because this is the best place I've ever worked in. It's been the most enjoyable gig I've had in my life — ever, anywhere. The best gig

I've worked in 40 years, I'm telling you. There were no hassles at all.' Ruby believes in brevity, unless something of unusual musical consequence needs to be stated, and this precludes the routine handing out of solos in each number to one and all.

'It will get boring if you do that,' he declared vehemently. 'Numbers must be short so that you want to hear more. It's always better to do less than too much; that extra bit can be bad. We play a lot of tunes and we keep mixing it. We keep it moving. People listen to hear what we're doing, and if the music suddenly changes, goes quiet or something, they think: What's happening? Then I make a noise again to catch their attention.'

How much does a taste for drama colour his presentation of music? 'I am not thinking of drama. To me, that should be the magic of it. I want the audience to feel nice, and not feel like they're looking at people labouring. It should all be fun and light-hearted, you know what I mean?

'I think Duke Ellington had a great sense of drama, Louis Armstrong, too. That's what made them so great and wonderful to see, and that's why they never overdid things. They always acted nice and kept everything beautiful. Yes, they were naturals in a theatre. They were showmen; we're all in entertainment, whether you like it or not. And I think if guys like Duke and Louis didn't mind people in a nightclub having fun, then I don't believe anyone else should mind very much.

'Personally I love it, and I realise that in a club you can't demand quiet. If you ask people to be quiet they're going to leave. I know I'm going to leave. I played at a place in Boston where the MC got up before the set and announced that, due to the nature of this music, we had to have quiet, no talking and no serving of drinks. As soon as he got through I went up to the mike and told them to forget about what he just said. "I must have noise; there's got to be serving of drinks and clinking of glasses, and talk." I says: "I'm not George Shearing . . ." He used to do this with George every night, see. But I don't need that.'

When I suggested that singers did need the crowd noise turned down at times, Ruby looked unimpressed. Wasn't it funny, he pointed out, that the greatest singer in the world, Louis Armstrong, never told anyone in the audience to keep quiet — unless perhaps it was a heckler? And people managed to listen to Louis didn't they?

So Ruby is a most happy fella right now. Which is good because his exceptional musicianship should bring him satisfaction as well as recognition from musicians and critics. Recognition he has had from the start, as I recall, but it has been reported frequently that he has felt disillusioned with the music business from time to time. Ruby said yes, with the business, never with the music.

'You see, the music business is often a very seedy thing because you have to deal with people you don't like, and they can even spoil the music for you with this atmosphere. It's a difficult thing to separate one from the other and keep aloof from it. You try, and you may do it successfully until some person goes and does something that's exasperating, you know, or frustrating, and sometimes you just don't know how to deal with it.

'About the recognition or acceptance you speak of, I'll say this: I've never had bad criticisms and I've never had a bad audience. The whole thing with me wasn't ever a problem of audiences or criticism, because anywhere I played they liked it. Really it was a question of not being exposed to enough things, and to this day it remains a problem. There are many places I haven't played in this world that people do play. I haven't been invited, for whatever reasons, to places or events that I would like to do and where, if I did play, I think the people would like it too.'

Buck Clayton

In 1958, we learnt that Buck Clayton, one of my very favourite trumpet players, was to go on the road with a small swing band, playing the kind of relaxed mainstream music which owed much to the Basie influence. In the following years I frequently saw Buck on all his British visits and also in the Paris Olympia in April '61, and he once spent much of a fortnight at our home — a signal occasion. He had a long series of medical problems in the Seventies, during which I kept readers abreast of the latest crisis or recovery, and Buck's indomitable and optimistic outlook. Buck has now written about much of this himself, so rather than duplicate that, I went back to a flying visit from Buck in 1958, after his Brussels appearance with Sidney Bechet and Vic Dickenson. In 1961 he was nice enough to name Mr Melody Maker *after me on a US Columbia LP.*

When you speak to Buck Clayton you find that the music he plays is the music he believes in, not an uncommon state of affairs among jazzmen of real merit. He is concerned, above all, with melodic ideas and the technical command that enables you to perform them faultlessly with a swinging beat. Something of a perfectionist, he is tough in his judgment of bass players and drummers, hard on himself and the records he has made. Of his latest album, for example, he remarked: 'I don't particularly care for anything about that record. Nothing went right; even the studio we normally use was occupied, and the room we used gave the music a dead sound.'

He is not an admirer of the bop or cool schools and doesn't pretend to be. When George Wein asked him, after a Lyttelton Club session, how he had enjoyed the band, and observed that 'they looked as though they enjoyed the music,' Buck smiled in agreement and added: 'They sure don't play no bebop.'

I got the impression that Clayton was meticulous in his approach to any engagement. He assured me that the band he was bringing over was carefully picked and would be well rehearsed.

'Believe me, we're not going to put on a jam session,' he said. 'That's an impractical thing to do with five horns, anyway, and truthfully I prefer the sound of music which has been in some way prepared or organised. I'm going to write arrangements for the entire concert.

'Of course, with these men I have in mind, the odd number can be jammed safely because they have all graduated through the big bands — they all know the ropes, have what I call musical discipline.'

This matter of big-band training is close to Clayton's heart. Time and again he referred to musicians who had 'come up through the bands,' and he seemed to feel sympathy for the young player who lacked this necessary upbringing.

'In my day,' he said, 'you couldn't make a name except with a good band. You went through the mill, building up your lip, technique and ear. It gave you a background, and a sense of proportion. You didn't expect to be a star overnight; you mastered your instrument, and by the time you made a name you knew how to handle any situation.'

This is what he means by big-band training, the sort of experience that will tell when we hear him in company with Emmett Berry, Dicky Wells, Earle Warren and Buddy Tate — all graduates of Basie bands. And it is the sort of experience, no doubt, called on by Clayton when he worked with Sidney Bechet and Vic Dickenson at Brussels two or three weeks ago.

Somebody asked Buck how he got on with Bechet, suggesting that he probably ran into trouble. Clayton gave the question proper consideration and said, quite gravely: 'I enjoyed working with Sidney.' He enlarged on it: 'You know, two or three guys told me I might find it hard going. But I went out prepared to work with Bechet to the best of my ability. When he played lead, I played a third below. I saved my ideas for the trumpet solo, and there were plenty of spots. You get plenty of solos with Sidney — he's not one of those guys who won't let anyone solo but him — and I thought he was a good leader. You know what struck me right off about him? He's *serious* about his music. I like that. I'm kind of serious myself. I mean, I take my music seriously — always do the best I'm capable of. Do you know what I mean by that? If I'm playing a date in an empty ballroom, then I play for myself, and I'm hard to please.'

Billie Holiday, in her book and in private conversation, spoke of the favourable impression made on her by Clayton when she worked with Basie twenty years ago. It is easy enough to understand her enthusiasm. To match his handsome appearance, Buck possesses an agreeable, almost imperturbable, nature which, together with his musical talents, could hardly fail to charm any lady interested in good jazz.

Five years later, after several encounters in London and Paris, I caught up with Buck again, after a very successful appearance at the Manchester Festival

Anyone who has read much about Buck Clayton will have come across the story that he was taught to play trumpet by Papa Mutt Carey in California about 1930 or so. One or two people — Ken Colyer among them — mentioned Carey to Buck during the Manchester Festival, and were perhaps surprised by his reaction.

'I was certainly around Mutt at that time,' said Buck, 'but the only advice he gave me was: "If you can't outblow a man, at least you can hit him alongside the head with your trumpet."'

Before he left for Paris last week, Clayton spoke to me about his formative years, saying he would like to explode this Papa Mutt myth once and for all.

'I think it must have started with Hugues Panassié,' he said. 'I talked to him about Mutt probably, but I don't know why he ever said Mutt taught me anything. Mutt never did, though he told me many stories about the older New Orleans trumpet players — such as the guy who used to cover his fingers with a handkerchief in order to prevent anyone seeing what notes he was making. And I did like to listen to Mutt play as well as talk.'

If Carey didn't teach Buck, who did?

'My father must take credit for that. He taught me piano, then trumpet. I didn't take up the horn until my late teens, then I ran away from home — you know, to Hollywood to find fame and see the world. So I was already playing when I ran into Mutt. I had a lot to learn, and I wasn't professional, but I'd played second in my father's church orchestra. After a time in California, I went back home and finished school.'

I asked Clayton to name the players he thought had influenced him most. As I expected, he began with Armstrong.

'In my younger days, everyone listened to Louis and I guess we all were influenced. At one time, people tried to play like him note for note. I know when I started I used to play a lot like Louis.

'As I say, the younger men were all listening to Louis. I know you had Nat Gonella over here doing the same thing. Eldridge? I guess so, though he used to deny it. Roy would always tell me: "Rex was my man."'

I suggested that the influence could have travelled via Rex Stewart, since he too was in part inspired by Armstrong. Buck was resistant.

'Rex, I know that he played quite a few of Louis' things, but he wasn't influenced by Louis when he was learning. When Louis came to New York, remember, Rex was already there.

'Another man I did listen to was Joe Smith, and I used to play quite a bit like him. I heard him with McKinney's Cotton Pickers. *I Want A Little Girl*, played with mute of course, was one of my favourites that he did.

'Who else? Well, I used to sound a lot like Bill Coleman. People told me that, and I know it's true. But believe me, I'd never seen him then and didn't even know there was a Bill Coleman in this world. One day John Hammond played me a record with Bill on it, and as I listened to the trumpet I was thinking: When did I make that one? Yes, I love Bill's playing; those records he made with Django and Dicky Wells were very good records.

'I'll tell you how it is with "influences". For a guy who was learning when I was coming up, the music got right in you. And you may sound like this musician or that one even when you're not thinking about it.'

Clayton is known to be a man whose playing largely transcends hard-and-fast styles. Could he sum-up his feelings about jazz?

'It's not easy,' he said, 'but I like music which comes from the emotions, in which the chief aim is to create beauty. I'm not against progress, you know. I don't want jazz to stand still, and I'm interested in most of what goes on. But when beauty departs — beauty of tone and continuity of ideas — I'm ready to quit. A lot of modern jazz sounds kind of machine-like ... you can count it. The more notes played, the more jazz, seems to be the idea. It leaves you cold ... no soul at all, no feeling.'

Lee Collins

In November 1951 I travelled to Paris with Betsy expressly to report on the concert tour by Milton (Mezz) Mezzrow's band. It was a combination which included Lee Collins, trumpet, Zutty Singleton, drums, and Guy Lafitte, tenor, clarinet, and promised much. On a personal level my interest had been whetted by the chance to meet Papa Lee, a man I latched on to, musically speaking, some ten years earlier through my friend, Albert McCarthy, who had converted me by regular helpings of the four sides of aromatic New Orleans music by the Jones and Collins Astoria Hot Eight. He owned the pair of Bluebird 78s, and I did not, but he generously shared playing time and his enthusiasm with me.

Collins and his wife Mary turned out to be agreeable, friendly people, and he was as choice a trumpet player as I could have wished for. We spent a good deal of time together, and within a day or two I realised that Lee was not well. He seemed in some ways frail for a man of fifty. After he returned to Chicago (prematurely because of ill-health) he wrote several times to us and also sent photographs. One featured him with his hero, Bunk Johnson. Subsequently, when Lee was dead, Mary Collins wrote to request the return of that particular picture. I looked in the Melody Maker files, where I had placed it, but the print had vanished. Not for the first time I cursed the picture vultures; at least I would have copied this historic shot and then returned the original.

Because of inter-Union disputes I could do little to help Collins fulfil his wish to play in Britain. By the time the ban was lifted it was too late. Papa Lee was recovering from a stroke, and unfit to play. What follows is what I wrote about him on my return from France.

The first time I heard Lee Collins in person was at the rehearsal for the Mezzrow concert. Backstage at the Salle Pleyel he warmed up with a few scalar runs, then stood silently at one end of the stage while Mezz, Hugues Panassié and the French musicians discussed routines, lighting and so on, in alternate French and English. Throughout the rehearsal, I thought, Collins seemed remote from the fuss and talk. Nobody asked his advice and he offered none. But when the music started he straightened up, blew air through the trumpet, wiped his mouth on the back of his hand, and shot an anxious look at Mezz who was having trouble with his second clarinettist (Guy Lafitte) and the harmony of *Really The Blues*. Time for the trumpet solo came, and Collins was waved up to the mike by Mezzrow. It needed only three or four bars to tell that here was the real thing in New Orleans trumpet.

The tone was hot and pretty big, with a kind of crackling vibrato on the long notes that I had noticed with Armstrong and Bechet when hearing them in person. The feeling was right, too, and there was the dragged timing and off-the-beat swing of Armstrong's blues playing. Later numbers confirmed that Lee Collins was like Louis, not in a piecemeal fashion but in an organic musical way. Armstrong, I am told, allows that Lee plays more like him than anyone else does.

Lee's blues choruses recall *Muggles* and also *Please Stop Playing Those Blues*; in addition there is some of the blues quality of the last Ladnier performances – – and here and there a run in the Henry Allen tradition. Collins himself swears allegiance to Bunk Johnson.

'Bunk was my idol when I was a boy,' he says. 'And when I was coming up, he was my inspiration. Louis and I grew up together, always played in that way. I guess it came from Bolden: through Bunk to Buddy Petit, Louis and me.'

From four hours of conversation with him I got the impression he spent little time listening to records — Armstrong's or any others — and it was certain he had not often been able to hear Louis in person since the early days. It was hard to believe this when he started playing even though the style was so obviously personal and deeply felt, for we are conditioned to discern Armstrong in-fluences in so much trumpet work. The truth may be that Louis was influenced in part by Collins, and that both stemmed from the same school of jazz trumpet. One thing I know: Collins is a fine jazz player still; a man who missed earlier fame by some chance that kept him from the recording studios except on three or four occasions. As Denis Preston said in his BBC broadcast report: 'Unlike Bunk, Lee Collins never stopped playing — never lost touch with his technique. He has, in fact, been in constant work since he first came into the music business over thirty years ago.'

Unfortunately, his work has been largely unheard outside the Chicago area all these years. Rudi Blesh recorded him with 'Chippie' Hill in 1946, and his blues playing is adequately captured on those Circle sides. Robert Stendahl also cut good Collins (on Century), with Little Brother's Quintet. Otherwise there were only the Spivey and Morton records, and the four excellent Jones-Collins Astoria Hot Eight titles, as examples of this trumpet — until he came to Europe.

Now, it looks as though Panassié — who did a great deal towards Europe's 'discovery' of jazz as an art before the Americans honoured it at home — is helping to bring recognition to another neglected jazzman. In October, Lee Collins celebrated his 50th birthday. The half-century should see him gain a belated place in the European sun. What follows is Lee's own story.

'I was born on 17 October 1901, in a house on Delachaise street and Robertson, in the uptown neighbourhood. My mother was born in the same house, which was my grandmother's. We had musicians in the family, namely, my father — who played trumpet out on road shows — and my uncle, Oscar Collins, who travelled with Lorenzo Tio, Sr (the clarinettist) in a brass band.

'I began on cornet at eleven, picked it up pretty fast and came out pro-fessional in 1916. My first job was at the Zulus Club; that was a very proud day, I remember. After that, I played dances and parades with many of the bands of the day — with Papa Celestin and the Tuxedo: with Manuel Manetta (piano, saxophones and most other instruments: he was a real musician); with Tig Chambers and the Columbia Band; and with Jack Carey, the *Tiger Rag* man who was uncle of Mutt Carey.

'Right up until 1924 I worked in New Orleans. Then in that year King Oliver sent down for me from Chicago. Louis Armstrong had left the band, and I replaced him at Lincoln Gardens. I stayed about six months, but by then was feeling homesick, so I went back to New Orleans. I guess the St Louis man, Bob Shoffner, came in after me.

'I didn't make any records with Joe Oliver — which I'm sorry about now — but around that same summer time, 1924, I did record with Jelly Roll Morton in Chicago. They were the first I ever made. That was a picked-up band with Roy Palmer on trombone, and an old guy named 'Balls' Ball on clarinet. Roy is still in Chicago, doing a little teaching, but Ball is dead. He'd be about seventy-five today if he was living. I didn't know of him as a musician before those records, and didn't see anything of him afterwards. I just don't know where Jelly got him from. But he played *High Society*, and at that time when you heard a clarinet play *High Society* you didn't ask him where he was from. You knew he was from New Orleans. As a kid I found bands playing the tune, and it was the first standard I learnt. Creoles wouldn't come to a dance then unless you could perform *High Society*.

'Another tune we made that day was *Fish Tail Blues*. I remember that one because it was my tune, though Morton put his name to it. Those days they were all doing the *Fish Tail*. I played it over once or twice and Roy Palmer made a lead sheet. Palmer was a good musician who taught Al Wynn, Preston Jackson and some other fellows. No, I didn't record with Jelly again, though I believe he wanted me.

'Back in New Orleans I went to work at the Entertainers with a four-piece. I could read some by that time, but there was no music on that job. We stayed two years and then took a band down to Dallas, Texas, on a tour led by Sherman Cook, an MC and dancer who originated the Lindy Hop. We carried on through Mexico, then headed back to New Orleans where I formed my own band in 1926 for the Club Lavida on Burgundy Street in the French Quarter. With me I had Big Eye Louis Nelson on clarinet, Earl Humphrey (brother of Percy) on trombone, Joe Robichaux on piano, and John and Simon Marrero on guitar and bass. These were two of the Marrero brothers; there was a large family of Marreros, all playing one stringed instrument or another. If I remember right, we closed there in 1928 and I went in with David Jones – a fine mellophone player and one of the most underrated musicians in the world. He played tenor sax with me: he was a man who could go through the band, all instruments, nobody like him. I knew him all my days, and got early training from him.

'I don't know the direct place he was from, but he was playing mellophone in parades in New Orleans in my youth. Sometimes he played street parades with Louis and me. And for years he was on the boats with Fate Marable, who liked to use mellophone. We took a group into the Astoria Gardens on Gravier

Street, near Rampart, and were billed as David Jones and his Band — featuring Lee Collins, the Cornet Wizard. That was the band made those Jones-Collins records in 1929. We had Theo Purnell, who played alto and clarinet; Davey Jones, tenor and cornet; Al Morgan, who played with Fate Marable, on bass; Joe Robichaux and some more rhythm. The band was good, and one day Mr Pierre of Victor came looking for us. We were supposed to make the records in a music store on Canal Street, but something went wrong and they took us downtown to Esplanade to the Italian Hall, strictly an Italian dance place where they used to give parties. The trombonist Nat Story, who also played on the boats, was expected to make this date but didn't show up. Sidney Arodin was not in the regular band. I picked him specially for the date — always did like his clarinet.

'It was simple to name the tunes we made that day. It was raining, I remember, so we called one of them *Damp Weather*. *Astoria Strut* was clearly titled after the place we played at. *Duet Stomp* was because the saxophone players made the breaks together, and *Tip Easy Blues* got named after Theo Purnell who used to beat his feet when he was really tippin'. "Theo's tippin' easy," we used to say. That's how that one came about. The Jones-Collins Hot Eight was my last band in New Orleans.

'In 1930 I started playing excursions to Chicago, and by the latter part of that year was working with Luis Russell's band in New York. I couldn't stay long with Russell because I was a transfer member of Local 802 and you had to be in town a year before you were accepted. So I had to leave that band, and once again didn't make any records. After finishing with Luis Russell I went in with Dave Peyton at the Regal Theatre on Chicago's South Side. A tour brought me to the Lafayette Theatre, New York, and then I closed with Peyton and went back on my own. It was 1931. I opened at King Tut's Tomb, 47th and Michigan in Chicago, with five pieces, all Chicago boys. It was an after-hours spot for musicians, started at twelve and stayed on till six or seven in the morning in those days.

'From that time, I worked practically all over Chicago; and out in the suburbs, at the Hi-Ho Club in Cicero, with Danny Barker on guitar. For a while I played in Zutty's band (I was once with him in New Orleans back in the Twenties) at the Three Deuces, where Art Tatum was the pianist between sets. And that was a cold winter in Chicago, it really was. Other places I played were the 29 Club, with Baby and Johnny Dodds; the Bee Hive, with Miff Mole's Band; and at Calumet City where I had my own group, until 1938 or '39, with a good piano player named Henry Simmons. Also, I made a lot of records with blues singers Lil Johnson, Victoria Spivey and Lil Green.

'In '39 I opened the Ship's Cafe on Clark Street and Ontario. This was the most notorious place in the world, and a great success for me, with all the kids coming in from the colleges. William Flakes was on piano and Bucket Crosby on drums. Later I moved further down Clark Street, to a cabaret called the Firehouse, with a combination that had drummer Jimmy Bertrand, Little Brother Montgomery on piano, and on tenor sax was Jeep Robinson (he never recorded, but he really would kill you). So I went on playing one or two pieces with Little Brother in the early Forties, and doing some concerts with him too, for the Chicago Hot Club — also with Baby Dodds and Albert Wynn.

'For five or six years now I've been at the Victory Club at Clark and Erie in Chicago. I guess I made that place famous, for most nights you couldn't get through the door for kids from Northwestern and Chicago Universities. I was working there right up until I came over to France, and on 17 October last, the boss, Willie Catenese, gave a party for my 50th birthday.

'Bunk Johnson came in to see me at the Victory, and I played a concert with him in Chicago in 1947. Now I've already told how Bunk inspired me very much when I was a boy. He was the greatest jazzman when I first came up — greater even than Oliver around 1912, when I was a little kid. There were others who could blow a lot of horn in their different ways, but when it came to jazz — I mean hot phrasing and not just trick tone and effects — Bunk was ahead. He was recognised by the younger men to be the hottest, and it was believed he took his style from Buddy Bolden. Now I never did hear Bolden, so I'm not saying anything about him except that it was understood the line of hot playing — this particular style — passed from Bolden to Bunk to Buddy Petit, Louis Armstrong and myself. Of course I cannot speak for others and so I'll say what I know; that Bunk was my idol. But I did not like to hear him play as an old man. I appreciated him too much when he was on top. To tell the truth it was like when I saw Joe fall. I'd seen him great and I saw him pitiful. I guess Bunk was discovered too late.

'Another real Creole player was Buddy Petit; he came up with Bechet, a little ahead of Louis and me. He took after Bunk with melody and great drive. Manuel Perez was more sweet, more straight; not so much of a jazz player as Bunk Johnson was. Kid Shots (Louis Madison) I knew too. He was sound, always considered a very good second horn. Now Oscar Celestin, he was what I'd call a mixed man — played a lot of music but not the hottest style like Louis Armstrong. He played it hot but different and was a good brass-band leader. Kid Howard was another good man. I knew him well and he played for me once on drums when he was a boy.

'If you're talking about strict jazz players, well, Freddy Keppard was the man. You never heard him if you only heard his records, because Keppard never really *played* on records. He never wanted to make them, was afraid people would pick up his tricks too easily. So he would just sit there and play as little as he could. Those are not stories I'm telling you. It is what I *know*. Joe Oliver, always a great cornettist, was another that you never heard *playing* on phonograph records. I guess he sounded all right on some, but it never did sound like Joe to me. He used some mutes when he was down in New Orleans, but his best playing was open. Mutt Carey, now, was always a mute man. He was a lighter player; not so hot a man as Joe. I came up behind Mutt. Why, he was blowing cornet before I could blow my nose.

'I found Tommy Ladnier outside New Orleans, in Mandeville I think. I don't believe Tommy worked in New Orleans, and I didn't know him well. He played fine, though, really great. So did Herb Morand, who also came up with me in my hometown. Herb is a brother of Lizzie Miles, the singer, you know. I'm afraid he was pretty sick when I last had news of him*.

'Of the present trumpet men I like Roy Eldridge. I'm not limited in my taste to the old players or tunes; in fact I believe those set tunes like *Muskrat Ramble* are ruining jazz. In my day we used to play new and old alike, and they all sounded like jazz. Did you know I played with Dizzy Gillespie in Chicago? It was on a tribute to Jimmy Yancey, with my band, Miff Mole's, Art Hodes and Don Ewell. Dizzy came in on second trumpet, played *High Society* and filled in along with it, believe me.

'In 1947 I went to New York to play a Carnegie Hall concert with Kid Ory's Band, along with Little Brother. It was a very good band, strictly relaxed music; that's what I call real jazz. Before that, the last time I had played with Ory was back in New Orleans around 1981. Ed Ory came from outside town, from La Place, Louisiana. La Place was one of those Creole places, and going there was the same as getting off in Paris, I can tell you. If you couldn't talk French you could hardly be understood. And the ones that spoke English had such an accent you thought they were talking French as well.

'My grandmother had English and French blood mixed in her; my grandfather had some Spanish too, and my father came from downtown French section. But I wasn't able to get on with that language then, and I can't now I'm in France. I want to say how I felt right at home with this Claude Luter Band over here. When I walked in, those cats fell right into the music as though they'd been born to it. They took me back to Ory's band, when they came down the bayou from La Place and took New Orleans by storm, playing together then — like Luter's boys today. Now, there is just one place old Papa Lee wants to see. That's England.'

Harry 'Sweets' Edison

Harry Edison, smart and smiling trumpet swinger with years of big-band experience behind him (Alphonso Trent, Jeter-Pillars, Lucky Millinder and Count Basie during the Thirties and Forties), has excelled in many fields. We in Britain have been able to enjoy a wide variety of in-person performances by 'Sweets' since 1964, when he blew in with a JATP unit. For me, as for many of my generation, he is indelibly linked in the mind with a sequence of fervent solos he produced while a pillar of the Basie brass establishment. In this first conversation we talked of a 1967 reunion with the Count.

Musicians, unlike murderers, don't often return to the scene of their greatest successes. It was with some surprise, therefore, that I greeted the news of Harry Edison's return to the Count Basie ranks. Edison worked with the band from late '37 until its break-up in 1950, and during that time he made an

*Morand died three months later, on 23 February 1952 in New Orleans

international reputation and first became an influential voice on the trumpet scene. Now he is in Britain with the band, winning praise for the excellence of his solos. I called on him this week to ask what had persuaded him back into harness after seventeen years of liberty.

'In one word, Basie. I wouldn't have gone out with anyone else,' he explained. 'That was about seven months ago. Basie needed someone and asked me to join him again.

'He had a lot of spots that trumpet needed to fill, and he thought I could do the job. I was complimented, of course, and anyway, after knowing a man thirty-one years you can't really refuse him a favour.'

How does it feel, being back in the fold?

'Well, first of all it's been a change. I haven't been out with a big band since 1950. That is to say, it's my first big jazz band since I left Bill Basie last time.

'And I'm enjoying it all. It's quite a kick playing with Basie; he has the sort of band musicians like playing in. It's nice to work in a big band as good as Basie's because he knows just how to spot you. Then, too, I feel right at home. Being with Basie and Freddie Green is like being with brothers, knowing each other so long. And all the fellows in the band are marvellous to work with.'

Does Edison expect to stay long with Basie's orchestra?

'I'll stay with Basie as long as he needs me. I just turned down the Joey Bishop TV show to remain with the band. Then, when I do leave, I anticipate going back to California and the studios.

'Apart from that, I'm trying to get a deal worked out where I can come back to this country and work Ronnie Scott's club. I want to spend some more time here, and I'd like to work with your musicians. I hear the rhythm sections are good. We've negotiated once or twice but so far it hasn't come to anything.

'I went down to the club a couple of times last week and enjoyed Johnny Dankworth very much. And that girl singer is tremendous; just out of sight. Tony Coe? I've heard about him of course, but he didn't get a chance to play while I was there.'

For a time, Edison led his own quintet on club and recording dates. In the early Sixties his group accompanied singer Joe Williams on tour. I wondered what caused him to give up the quintet.

'Really because I got interested in studio work again, and because I was playing in and managing a club in Los Angeles named Memory Lane. For about two years I had my own quartet there in the evenings, and I could still do my studio work in the day. It was a nice arrangement; if I was late, my trio would play until I arrived.

'The club is owned by Larry Hearn, a friend of mine for, oh, twenty-five years, and I still do a lot of talent scouting for the place. As I say, I wouldn't have left there for anybody but Count Basie.'

Speaking of Basie again, had Edison run into any other of his old team-mates lately?

'Yeah, Jimmy Rushing. I had dinner with Rush my last Sunday in New York. He's been ill, you know, and had to go on a diet and lose 50lb. That's a lot to take off. But he's quite well now and getting around much better. He asked to be remembered to all his friends over here.'

Has Sweets made any new recordings?

'Yes, I did an album with a big group — fiddles, singers, reeds and rhythm section. It's called *When Lights Are Low* and it's been out on Liberty in the States seven or eight months now. I had a good band on that: Bud Shank (alto and flute), Bob Cooper (tenor and oboe), Bill Hood (baritone), Bill Perkins (tenor), Ray Brown (bass), Herb Ellis (guitar), Earl Palmer (drums) and Lou Levy (piano). And I had an Australian fellow, Julian Lee, to do all the arranging. He's fantastic. In fact, it's one of the few albums I have enjoyed making.'

Finally, what about the old association with Frank Sinatra? Does that still exist?

'Oh yes, I've been with Sinatra fourteen years on records and it still goes on. And since he now owns an interest in Warner Brothers I do quite a bit of film work. I just did a soundtrack for his movie, *Walk Don't Run*, with Quincy Jones. He did all that music and it was very nice. Solos? Yes, I have a few solo bits and so does Ray Brown. I think you'll like that soundtrack when the movie gets here.'

The second piece moves us ahead three years, to another reappearance with 'The Chief'.

Periodically, Harry Sweets Edison pays us a visit. Each time he makes it clear that he has continued to keep his lip in shape and his technique well shone. On this visit, just concluded, he was if anything playing better than on his first trip with Basie in '67. He works regularly and it shows.

With a cup of coffee and a meal in front of him on the coffee room bar at the Strand Palace Hotel, he told me about his return to the band in which he came to prominence in the late Thirties.

'Well, at this time of year it gets a little slow in the business. So when Basie called me last month and asked if I'd like to go over to Europe for six weeks, it just fitted in with my plans. My family are enjoying a weekly pay check, which is wonderful, and I'm definitely enjoying myself with this band. Of course, after being friends with guys like Basie and Freddie Green for more than thirty years, it's bound to feel like home.'

Sweets said that Basie made sure he carried a few arrangements, such as *Willow Weep*, which gave the trumpet man stretching room. Edison approved of this, but conceded that a bit of effort was involved.

'Basie, he works me hard. Every night I take two or three solo features and a wind instrument is harder on you than a piano, naturally.'

Does he still get a kick out of visiting Europe?

'Oh yes, it still gives me a kick. I love Europe and have quite a few friends over here. It seems like if I don't return to brother Basie every so often I just don't get to see my English friends.'

Though Edison has been away from the Basie ranks since '67 he has not entirely lacked big-band jazz experience. Some he has gained from Louis Bellson when he's at home in Los Angeles that is.

'Every Wednesday night at Dante's in LA Louis has a fine band: just four trumpets, four trombones, five saxophones and five rhythm — he uses an extra percussionist. It's a big band through and through and a very popular band on the West Coast. For us studio musicians it is a great idea because it gives us a chance to play something different — to emote your own sentiments.'

Speaking of sentiments, how does Sweets feel about the modern developments in jazz, I asked? It seemed he was very reasonable in his views.

'Oh, I like a lot of the things the youngsters are doing. I believe you have to take a little of theirs and a little of yours and try to make the evening interesting for everyone. You don't have to go to extremes in my opinion. There's good things in most styles. I say, listen and take some of the good things, mix them in and make your music interesting . . . for yourself as well as for your audience.'

What is the most exciting band Edison has worked in since he left Basie in '67?

'The greatest band I played with since Basie was the big band behind Della Reese, under Pete Myers' direction, on her TV show. We worked five days a week and the show closed in March this year. I was with it ten months. It was the best show on TV to me, musically. I like Della. She has a beat. And we had a hell of a band, as I say.

'Bobby Bryant, Bob Brookmeyer, Herb Ellis, Ray Brown and Earl Palmer were some of the men in it with me. Oh, Buddy Childers was on trumpet too, and we had Bill Perkins, Jack Nimitz and Don Menza. Yes, and we had some good guest singers. Carmen McRae, Sarah Vaughan and Tony Bennett were all on that show.'

I wondered whether Sweets got as much satisfaction out of his career as he used to in the older and wilder days.

'In fact I get more now. I look forward to playing. Of course I've been fortunate in playing with some great studio orchestras. There's no greater thing than freelancing like I do mostly.

'You get to play under all sorts of people, and you get the satisfaction of performing music by men like Quincy Jones, Benny Carter, Nelson Riddle, Bill Holman, Jack Elliott and so many more. You make the movie scores and so forth, and in general it keeps you contented.

'And being contented makes you play better and keeps you playing longer.' Sweets smiled at this piece of philosophising. 'Yes, I've been blessed.'

The third of these pieces was run in the Melody Maker *of 18 April 1981. The former Basie sideman threw more light on some favourite things, past and present.*

Rap as you may with Harry Edison — the sharp, smooth-talking trumpet veteran known everywhere as 'Sweets' — you're liable to find the conversation harking back often to the Chief. Edison enjoys talking about Count Basie. Most bandleaders have feet of clay, not to mention other parts, in the estimation of their employees; Basie is an exception. Edison, like many alumni, speaks of him with fond regard. The Basie band was his jazz university. It was a wonderful teacher, and Sweets reckons he was a keen learner. As for the old man himself, he was something of a father-figure.

'You see, when I went to join Basie I was still a young man. Bill was born in Jersey and knew all the guys I'd longed to meet. He was close friends like with James P. Johnson; he was a close friend of Benny Carter, and he'd known Duke Ellington for years around New York. He took me around and opened doors, introduced me to Duke and Benny and all these people.'

The subject of Basie is hard to avoid, as things have turned out. From time to time, since the mid-Sixties, Sweets has gone back to the band. It was the first big-band touring he'd done since he left Basie in 1950, and he told me he wouldn't have gone out with any other. In addition he has worked with 'Basie Alumni' groups and, most notably, in partnership with Eddie Lockjaw Davis, with whom he was teamed at Ronnie Scott's recently. 'Jaws' tenored with Basie, off and on, from 1952 till quite lately.

Even when he might expect to be away from it all, as in Japan last year, Sweets is forcefully reminded of his 'old school'. Jazz is very big in Japan, he said, and 'you can hear an orchestra and not see who's playing and it will sound very much like Basie's band'.

The Japanese have a tremendous enthusiasm for jazz, and respect for its artists, and these things lead to first-class conditions for visiting musicians. 'Oh, you get such a royal treatment,' said Edison wistfully as he nibbled limp toast at our brunch meeting in Bloomsbury.

'In Japan they give you the due respect that you should have because you are contributing something to the culture. They really are avid fans. I enjoyed it enormously. I went over with Benny Carter in August; he had Teddy Wilson, Milt Hinton, Shelly Manne and myself. It was a big concert. They had Benny Goodman and his big band, Dizzy Gillespie, Freddie Hubbard, Illinois Jacquet, Jaws [Eddie Davis], the Brecker Brothers, Joe Henderson, George Duke and Helen Humes.

'A fantastic concert, and the first time I've ever played to 40,000 people — that just doesn't happen to jazz any more. And it was 20 dollars a person to get in. It was done by Toshiba, the electronic people. Yes, I think Japan is coming to the rescue of jazz and jazz artists.'

Rubbing his chin and looking thoughtful, Edison explained that when he said he absolutely loved the Japanese visit, this did not mean he failed to enjoy professional visits to other places. Whether it was Denmark, France, Britain or for that matter Istanbul or South America, he continued to derive pleasure from the playing and the people he met, and enrichment from the opportunities to see the beauty each country had to offer.

'I look forward to coming to Europe, and especially London where I see old friends and friends associated with old friends of mine such as Coleman Hawkins who had travelled to England back in the mid-thirties. You know, Coleman and I were friends so it became that I would ride with him on little gigs we would do after Basie's band broke up in 1950, and I would ask him about his years in Europe and all the people he knew there. So one result of this was that I looked forward to meeting certain people and seeing certain things when I eventually came over here in the Sixties.

'In the past ten years, travelling has become more interesting to me because I have opened my eyes more to the history and culture around me. I've been to Europe with a friend who is an English teacher in Los Angeles and with her visited the Louvre, Notre Dame Cathedral and places like that. I'd been coming to Paris since 1965 and had previously had no desire to see points of interest in the way of architecture, art galleries, museums and so forth. But the first thing she wants to do is go sightseeing.

'So, you see, music has given me the chance to travel widely and broaden my views, musically and historically too; given me the freedom to enjoy some of the things in different parts of the world that I'd read about. And these new interests, and the happiness in your life, they affect your music. These things show in your playing, you know, and I don't have to tell you how much I enjoy playing.'

True, he did not. It should be evident to a child of ten that Edison gets a charge from applying lips to mouthpiece and letting loose a series of distinctive, often wrily humorous brass sounds. But is playing the pure source of joy it was in the dear, departed days of the Basie class of '38? Sweets smiled in a manner which lent some credence to his nickname, and replied that so far as he was able to judge such a matter, it was.

'I love it still, I really do. 'Course it grows a little more difficult the older you get, physically harder I mean, but in other ways it becomes easier. Because things that used to be hard, I can improvise more easily now. Like they say: "Fools rush in." But now you know how to do it and you've learned to pace yourself.'

Given his time over again he would, I guessed, opt for being 'just a jazz player'.

Sweets agreed: 'Do the same thing all over again. I wouldn't change a thing; not one minute of my life over, if I had it to do again. I'd live the same life because I wouldn't know any other. And I wouldn't wish to, because I've met the most interesting people I could ever have hoped to meet and I've achieved a great deal of artistic satisfaction.

'I'm not the greatest of trumpet players, and don't profess to be, and I haven't made a lot of money. But I have enjoyed what I've done ... enjoyed it to the fullest, believe me. What little bit I've tried to give to the jazz world has been honest, been my own, and I've always been happy to contribute. Well, at least, I hope I've made some sort of contribution to jazz.

'Now I've said this so many times before, but it's nonetheless true for that: the days in the pre-war Basie band, those were some of the most precious days of my life. We had so much fun in that band. And I was making 6 dollars a night, and he was only making 15. But they were just marvellous, thrilling times. When I start talking about them everything recurs in my mind quite vividly: all the incidents, the humour, the friendships, the fun we had, the music we made night after night. They had to be enjoyable days because the band was so great, and I mean the whole band.

'Sure, we had Lester Young; everybody knows about him. But you must remember that Lester was just a part of it. We had a rhythm section that anybody could play with. Jo Jones was at his height; Freddie Green, unequalled as a rhythm-guitar player; Basie of course; and then Walter Page ... uh! To not swing with them behind you, you had to be dead.

'Now Walter was a fantastic man to keep a band together. He wasn't what you'd call a soloist, but his tempo and the notes he picked. Gee whiz ... Walter Page was the first to go up that high on bass, and as most of the bass players couldn't do it, they had a five-string instrument made so other players could get that note Walter got on a regular bass. He was a professor from the University of Kansas, you know.'

Page didn't need to take long solos because the wonderfully solid but subtle rhythm quartet played its own part in the Basie routines: a sort of soloing section which did much to redefine conceptions of swing in the later Thirties.

'The only soloist we had in the rhythm section was the drummer, Jo Jones,' Edison further explained. 'Freddie could have been a fine soloist, and was a good soloist at one time, when it became fashionable for guitarists to play solos. Of course Charlie Christian and he were very close friends, and Christian gave him an amplifier. But whenever Freddie would lay out of the band to take his solo, the whole rhythm section used to fall apart. So it got to the point where we had to do something about it. So one night I would remove the plug from Freddie's amplifier and it wouldn't work. Next night Prez would take the plug out, you know, and Freddie would have it fixed. Next night Herschel Evans would break a wire in it so it wouldn't play. And that was how we did it. I mean, the band wasn't swinging.

'At that time we had a group in the band called the Vigilantes. If there was something in the band we didn't like, we would get rid of it quick. So finally we took all the guts out of the amplifier. Freddie got ready to play one night and there was nothing there but a box. Naturally he got furious but nobody paid him any attention.

'"Did you do this," he asked. "No." So he reached the point where he said: "Well, to hell with it; I won't play any more solos." That rang a bell with us. "Great," you know. So that's the reason he's not a soloist today. He probably could have been one of the best at that time, but we had to sacrifice him for the good of the band.'

But what of the horn soloists, those the bandsmen did want to hear? Did they get much chance to stretch out? 'Did they?' Edison threw the question back.

'Basie's was the first band to start letting the men play extended solos. You could play for as long as you wanted, because we had no music, just used head arrangements. At a dance you could play four, five or six choruses, whatever you wanted to take. See, that was the only band that really allowed soloists to improvise for as long as they wished. Like with Fletcher Henderson or Jimmie Lunceford, you would generally have a chorus and then the band would play. You had all written arrangements. But Basie had a band in which he'd set a riff behind, say, Prez for one chorus, then he'd go for himself.

'And of course we had the other tenor player, Herschel Evans ... a fantastic sound and he just *swung*. Well, the whole band used to swing like nothin' you ever heard. And Herschel influenced many tenor players: Don Byas, Illinois Jacquet and quite a few more, even Buddy Tate.

'Of course Basie's band was full of individualists and together they made up the original Basie style, which changed as different musicians came and went. When I joined, I think I contributed a little to what Basie was playing. My concept changed the brass section around a bit because I had a different approach, and I believe I added something to the band. I didn't contribute as much as Lester because he was one of a kind, you know, the only one, but whenever a new guy would come in the band there would be another whole concept brought in. Of course he had to be able to say something, to match up to players such as Buck Clayton, Benny Morton and, a little later on, Dicky Wells.

'I know when I came in, about the beginning of 1938, I was scared to death. But the guys were nice; Buck and I became roommates, and Basie was always very good to me. Fortunately the band seemed to like my playing, but Prez had the reputation of being a very stern critic, so it was kind of a tough test.' The memory could be laughed at now, and was.

'Yes, Prez was a great critic. He had a bell he would ring, and when he rang his little bell it told Basie this wasn't it. And if a guy really wasn't making it, the bell told him he wasn't going to be there long. And if Freddie Green had that disapproving look, the guy was on his notice then.

'But Prez was obvious with his disapproval 'cos when you stood up to play, if after a couple of choruses you didn't really start some fire back there, then he'd take up the bell and ring it. That told you, and it cued Bill Basie.'

And was this ringing criticism heard in a public performance? 'Any place,' Harry confirmed. 'Any place we happened to be playing. Lester had many ways of expressing disapproval, and in no uncertain manner. Like that famous time in the Strand Theatre on Broadway. I'll never forget it. But I've told that story a number of times; it's a classic.'

I had heard it already and, in fact, read an account in Stanley Dance's *The World Of Count Basie*, but still laughed at it. Tell it again Sweets!

'Well, it was our first trip into the Strand and Basie wanted a big production number in the show. You know, all the bands featured a production number then. So he got this idea of a big arrangement of the song, *I Struck A Match In The Dark*, with Earle Warren doing the vocal. Smiley Warren was the ballad vocalist in the band.

'Basie said he wanted the stage completely blacked out for the song, and he says: "When Earle starts singing I want everyone in the band to strike a match on the stage." It was to be a striking effect as you might say. Remember this was our debut on Broadway in a theatre, and we all had on our uniforms and were sharp and everything.

'Now Prez, he didn't like the sound of this. The only male singer he liked was Jimmy Rushing, 'cos Rush had fire when he sang the blues, and he never had no eyes for Earle Warren's voice. I mean Earle had quality and he wanted to sing the love songs, and Prez wasn't a love type, you know, not in that way. He loved Billie Holiday's singing, of course.

'Anyway, at the first show, we got out this big arrangement and Earle stood up front there and the stage was completely black. When he sang "I struck a match in the dark", we struck our matches and suddenly we saw all this fire. Prez had held his music up and put his match to that, set the arrangement on fire in the theatre,'

Sweets, laughing, repeated that he'd never forget *I Struck A Match* or Lester Young. Prez's way of expressing emotion, he added, was something different from Warren's. But then Prez was a one-off type.

'Lester named him Smiley, and he didn't have no eyes for his singing. Prez, now he could interpret a love song; but he could play anything. I was over to a friend's house last night and he played me Prez on *I Guess I'll Have To Change My Plans*. Oh, he had such a tone and so much feeling; a feeling for love.'

Mention of 'Smiley' triggered thoughts of John Le Carre, then back to 'Cat Eyes' (Lester's name for Buck Clayton), 'Rev' for Emmett Berry, and 'Rabbitt' for Snooky Young, among many band nicknames bestowed by Lester. 'Sweets', too, was laid on Harry by the hiply spoken tenorman, two or three months after Edison signed on.

'Yeah, Prez started calling me "Sweetie-Pie", then Basie used to call me "Sweetie-Pie," and they cut it short and began calling me "Sweets". When Lester gave you a name it was liable to be one that would hang for ever. He re-named Billie Holiday "Lady", of course, and at times everybody was called "Lady'. It was "Lady Basie" and "Lady Duke", you know, and so Billie was "Lady Day". Then he nicknamed Freddie Green "Pepper".'

'Why? Because he came from Charleston, South Carolina. Sure, I was tight with Lady Day, but not as tight as Prez used to be. We were close, though, and when she made those last records in 1959 she insisted on having me play trumpet on them, wouldn't cut them till I came off tour.

'I guess you could say Lester spoke pretty much a language of his own, and he's remembered by friends for that as well as for his music. Basie, now, we had several names for him but Prez laid a special one on him that stuck: the Holy Main. That came from Basie being the holy man, which he was, especially on pay days, and also the main man. Because he *was* the main man, you see, so Prez put the "holy" on it and shortened it to Holy Main. But in spite of him being the man, we used to pull jokes on him.

'I remember on our way to Los Angeles during the war, in '42, Basie would charter a train. We had a Pullman, you know, and they used to sidetrack the train at different cities, and that was the epitome of travelling — the joy of living then, to have your own coach and cars to take you to the dance hall and back. And after the job that Pullman would be absolutely bulging with food and drink and girls would be running up and down, falling over you, and we'd have so much fun. Very unpopular of course in some places, because they thought we were living too good, having our own Pullman.

'But anyway, at one place, when our next stop was Los Angeles, Basie had the valet to buy him two or three orders of fried chicken, sandwiches, some bananas and so on, and lay them in his room. Naturally he had the drawing-room on the Pullman.

'Well, about two o'clock in the morning, I and somebody else — I forget who — got hungry. So we got out of our berths to see if we could find something to eat. When we opened Basie's door, he was fast asleep and we saw all this chicken and everything. So we sat and feasted on Basie's chicken while he slept. We ate it all up, the chicken and the fruit, and placed what we'd left back in the sacks just like it was, even the banana peel, so that it looked just right. And when he woke up, I guess around 4 o'clock, he felt hungry. So he put on the light, put his robe on, got out the bags to feast, and found the remains.

'He came out of his room, woke everybody up and called them — you know what — "All you mothers are fired; I don't give a damn who did it. This is my room and you had no business coming in, eatin' up the chicken and all my fruit. You could have saved me a banana".

'Everyone looked surprised because Basie's a guy that's hard to make angry. Max, if you'd been on that train that night you would have died. No, nobody gave us away 'cos no one knew who had done it. I'd eaten so much until I was barely awake: I was just lying there smiling.

'Why didn't we have our own chicken? Well, in the first place we didn't have a valet. That valet would go anywhere for Basie, but he wouldn't go anyplace for us.'

Bobby Hackett

Cornettist Bobby Hackett, once described as 'the most graceful jazz musician alive', has always been something of a so-called musicians' musician and, for collectors, a special and subtle taste. I acquired the taste some time in the late Thirties and early war years, through records by Condon and others, and a few broadcasts, but was beginning to think I'd never set eyes on him when he turned up here with someone I already knew, Tony Bennett.

Later on, through Dick Sudhalter's good offices, we had the pleasure of a long visit by this fine player one Sunday in the September of 1974. He was set to play the Camden Jazz Festival in London, and his admirer and fellow cornettist, accompanied by his wife, brought him over to the house after rehearsal. Among other things, such as having a good memory and workmanlike manner, Hackett struck me as being self-assured but not self-important. Like his playing he seemed to be unflashy and on the modest side. He was a musician with a desire to be capable of playing anything good, inside or outside jazz, and he contemplated a few 'giants' in awe. In this respect he differed from such men as Bechet or Armstrong who were convinced that everything they played was important, a music which transcended jazz and was good by any standards. It may be that this contrast in egos and personalities is one explanation for the difference between very good and great, given that all the parties had secure techniques. But hold on ... I'm beginning to sound like a critic. It is time, as they say over there, to hack it.

'When Duke died and when Louis died, I felt that maybe a little bit of me went with them. Maybe I'm wrong; it's a crazy theory but I can't help suspecting it might be true. All of those guys like Louis, they were part of my history and upbringing and so a little of you goes with 'em each time; you can't help but feel that, and deal with it. They're part of my sensitivity. Right?'

Bobby Hackett looked thoughtful. Great original jazzmen were in his view absolutely indispensable. 'There are good players, fine, but not like those. And it's not going to happen any more, either, not in our lifetime or anybody else's. Nobody's going to come along and play like Louis Armstrong. It can only happen once. You'll find great talent, sure, but it's different. And jazz playing, real good playing, has nothing to do with time; nothing to do with dates, only excellence.

'I think it's like fine painting. Who painted better than those old masters yet? Nobody has. But people can be stupid enough to say, well, this is contemporary, as if that means it's better. If it is better, OK. But if it isn't as good, I don't know what you would call it.

'Me, I'll take who's a great painter — period. It doesn't matter when it happened; if it happened strong enough, it's there for ever. No good looking at something inferior and saying that it's modern. I mean, don't lie about it and say it's this neck of the woods or that one ... hell.'

The New Englander lapsed into silence, his expression showing clear distaste for such evasions. Sudhalter suggested that most musicians were not without regard for the traditions of their art. Hackett's neatly groomed head nodded agreement though his tone was sceptical.

'The good ones, they're respectful ... Right? They have respect for tradition and for the melody. A straight melody, that's the most difficult thing to play well; that's where Louis was so superior. A lot of musicians, asked to play a song, they play like wild men. I mean guys who don't know. It's like a fighter, really; if he goes wild the other guy's going to win.

'Yeah, Louis Armstrong once told me, he said: "I just play the melody, Bobby." You see? Such a special guy. Asked for a song, he'd play the song, which is so hard to do right. It's a little like being a writer — you edit as you get older, don't waste words. You don't need to say a hundred words sometimes to make an impact. Same thing with music, one or two notes might be better. It is a way of maturing; but try and do it, it's not easy. You gotta have an idea in your mind just how the music should go.

'And then, being typed as a jazz player can be dangerous too. I don't want to be considered as just a jazz something — whatever! I shoot for versatility. If I had my way I'd be able to play in a symphony or any other ensemble, under all circumstances, and I believe that's what every musician should aim at. You should be able to handle any kind of music ... if you're a musician. That's the way I look at it.'

This, I was told, had always been Hackett's doctrine, and on his first visit to Britain (with Tony Bennett in 1965) he stated his liking for any type of good music, and his dislike of being associated with one style. 'I never did agree with categorising it as modern jazz, Dixieland and so on,' he said. 'I don't believe in naming it — I'd rather listen. To me, everything we play with Tony is jazz. ... I like all of it as long as it's well played. That qualification is very important.'

He went on to say that he loved Louis but also liked Bunny Berigan, Miles Davis and Wild Bill Davison 'with no trouble', adding that there was no reason why you shouldn't enjoy, say, Dizzy and the Kenny Ball Band — which he had lately heard — at the same time. Now, nearly a decade afterwards, he was reaffirming these beliefs.

'Every musician should be ... broad-minded might be the best expression. I mean, what is jazz? It's a freedom of interpretation, and it is a personal thing. If I hear a song, I know how I want it to play. I kind of make it a rule that if it's by a good composer, I'll aim for a faithful interpretation, not change too much 'cos he knew more about writing it than I ever will.

'So a soloist to me is an interpreter. How did the writer wish the song to sound? That's the way I try to make it sound. If I'm playing a Cole Porter tune I don't want it to sound like Birdland — that would be a misinterpretation, and I won't do it. And the better a song is, the harder it is to play. Say you're Porter or Gershwin, Berlin, Ellington — and there's no better example — well, you did all that thinking before putting the song down on paper. So we had better play it the way you conceived it, unless we're sure we can improve it. I'm not capable of improving on Duke Ellington, and any guys who think they are, well, they must be very vain people.

'Now I'm talking about change for the sake of changing it. I mean you can embellish a melody but this has to be relevant to what the composer intended — if he's a good composer. I know they talk about substitute chords and all that; there are no substitute chords if they don't make music with the original chords, which the composer knew more about than I do, or Archie Shepp or anybody like that. They are not really composers, they're players, and supposed to play a song ... faithfully could be the word. An instrument should be an extension of a voice, a kind of amplifier.'

Robert Leo Hackett, who was born in Providence, Rhode Island, on 31 January 1915, was always by his own admission, a Louis admirer. Armstrong was his idol, and the reason he became 'hooked on trumpet', despite which he was written-up as 'the second Bix' during the early years of his career. It is probable that Hackett drew on the inspiration of Beiderbecke and others when the chance first came for him to play cornet, in addition to violin and guitar, but I never heard him refer to Bix as a significant influence. At any moment, though, he was inclined to speak of old friend, Louis. On the initial trip to Europe, for instance, he remarked that Bennett had picked up a copy of the *Armstrong Town Hall Concert* album. The event had been set up by Ernie Anderson, whose first action, after signing Louis, was to appoint Hackett as MD. Bobby said simply: 'I had a lot to do with that date, and I tell you I was scared to death. It's like playing in front of God.' The concert was, he remembered, a big turning point in Louis' career. 'He never made any real money until then. It was rags to riches, and it was Ernie Anderson's brainstorm.'

But how did the buzz about him being 'the New Bix' get started? I remember it, but don't know how it came into being. I wondered if he knew.

'No, I don't know. Coincidence? I just played the way I felt like; I never tried to copy anybody. At the beginning I guess you do, instinctively, but you

soon find out that's not it. Now don't get me wrong, I appreciated Bix
Beiderbecke probably more than anybody, but Louis outplayed him. Maybe I
could say Bix was the greatest of all cornet players, and Pops was the greatest
trumpet player. Beiderbecke was a genius, there's no doubt about it.'

Bix also spoke often of loving Armstrong, didn't he?

'Oh, they learned from each other, of course. I can show you old records of
Pops on which he sounds a little like Beiderbecke — when Louis was playing
cornet, actually. But this business of tying me in with Bix, well, I was highly
complimented but I never did try to play like him. What would be the point?
Nobody could ever be as good as the original ... in anything. Almost every
jazz trumpet player in the world at one time started out trying to sound like
Louis Armstrong. Then you find out shortly that he's inimitable. Find another
way because it can't be done. You mention Ruby Braff: I think Ruby is like me,
we learn something from everybody, then find something of our own. He's got
his own style, and anybody that you can recognise I have a lot of admiration
for; that's why I dig Miles Davis. You hear him and say: "That's Miles." I give
him a lot of credit for that.'

We know that Armstrong and Hackett constituted a mutual admiration
society. How did his friendship with Louis begin?

Bobby smiled and shook his head. 'Jesus, you're going so far back,' he
complained. 'He was always like God to me, I never got over that. But the way
we got to be close friends goes back to the time when I started to get any
publicity at all. Those were the days when Ray Anthony, Harry James and all
those guys were being written up and interviewed, and usually they'd get the
conversation goin' to where they're the greatest. Right? Now I began to get
busy and was on radio programmes, things like that, and my opening line was
set. The guy asked who was the best trumpet player in the world, and I said:
'Louis Armstrong.' Then I would get into why: he invented everything and
was absolutely the king of the music business. 'I'd give him the whole show,' I
used to say. And word reached him I was doin' that, and it put me in like
Flynn.'

Talk of the great man over coffee and drinks (black coffee only for Hackett)
reminded Bobby of many occasions — funny, nostalgic, uplifting or otherwise
rewarding.

'That thing you mentioned, the tribute concert from the 'Newport in New
Orleans' festival, let me tell you about supreme compliments that really hit you
when they happen. We had about six fine trumpet players there and I was jazz
maestro again. So we had a quick rehearsal in the afternoon, and it paid off at
night because that was a very, very good show; everything went smooth, you
had to be there to know.

'Well, as Pops is singing I'm playing everything behind him with the mute,
and after two or three numbers I started to feel funny and I went over to
George Wein and says: "Hey, George, every one of these trumpet players is
dying to play with Pops when he sings." And he said "Oh no, Pops gave me
strict orders; you're the only guy can play when he sings." And, you know, we
had musicians like Wallace Davenport, Jimmy Owens, Wild Bill and so on.

During rehearsals I'm asking Wallace — he's a wonderful player, strong you know — when I got stuck somewhere: "What do you do there?" I wanted to play it note for note the way Pops did it. At one spot I stopped and asked "What the hell happens here? I forgot", and Wallace sang if for me. so I said: "Why don't you play this number, let me do something else?" He said: "No-o-oh, no." Nobody wanted to do it.

'Let me tell you something else: Punch Miller, man, he knocked me out! Boy, did that guy play. Yeah, at the time of that film he was getting very sick but when he came out there rompin' and stompin' he reminded me very much of Pops, but different you know. He had the authentic New Orleans swing. Yes, Kid Punch, when he started blowing he'd got that magic.'

The matter of Armstrong and his reputation, *vis-à-vis* other remarkable contemporaries, has long been the subject of rum speculation about management's hand in the affairs of trumpet rivals. We recalled how Punch Miller claimed he could, with luck, have been where Louis was, and vice versa. Hackett acknowledged doubtfully that it could have been so. And then there was the extravagantly talented Hot Lips Page, who was removed from the Basie band to become star material and never was blessed with more than a few whiffs of big-time oil.

'Yeah, they had no use for poor Lips,' Bobby agreed. 'It was tragic. Some evil guy got in the middle there and kept him down.' I intimated that, since Joe Glaser booked Armstrong and Page, he could have manipulated their popularity charts.

It could have happended, Bobby allowed, though he didn't know the facts. 'See, Joe was like that. He'd make believe he's representing you, any trumpet player, but it's strictly to keep you out of Pops' way. You'd never get any place.'

I derived a great deal of pleasure from my few meetings with the 'quiet man' of the cornet. He had become for me, over three decades of hearing him on record and hearing about him, a sort of secondary legend. By the time I first saw him, Bobby was fifty years old and as slight and tidy a figure as I had expected. He displayed a polite amiablility which cloaked, I am sure, an underlying toughness of outlook, also those touches of regret that he was unable to drink any alcohol (because of a diabetic condition which had put him on the critical list a few years previously). He retained a sense of humour about everything to do with the jazz life — even the booze — and was frequently moved to exclaim: 'I got to tell you this', or 'This is a funny story'. Thus, at the mention by Sudhalter of some bandleading situation concerning Armstrong, Hackett smiled in anticipation and said: 'Hey, Louis had answer to anything you would think of,' before launching into another of his funnies.

'Let me tell you of the time we were doing a rehearsal, see? And Louis had stopped the band to correct a note from the third trumpet. So he looked at the guy and told him in the third bar there it was an A flat, not A natural, or something like that. So this kid stood up in front of all the rest of the band and said: "Well, you know Pops things change, man; nothin' ever stays the same." You know, he's trying to put Louis down and of course Pops has to come up with an answer, but quick. Now Louis comes up to him and he looks at him kinda strong, and he says: "Man, I'll tell you one thing that'll never change." And the kid says: "What's that?" And Pops says: "You'll always be a spade." After a break for laughter, Bobby came back with a reasonable imitation of the Armstrong pipes: "You can bet on that", he says. "That ain't gonna *change*!"

'Oh, Louis was always nice to me. One of those Timex things came up, and they got Louis and Jack Teagarden on it, and then they got me; and you know they needed me like a hole in the head. It was one of those answer things, and there's no place to play a note without bumping into somebody. You can picture, they got me standing between them like an idiot — I've got a mute in — and Pops is going: "Old rockin' chair's got me" and so on, and I kept breaking off. So I says: "Don't make me do this. Please, there's no way I can play anything that makes sense. You can't." But they insisted: "Don't be afraid; get in there, Herb Alpert." And I said: "Come on, let me out. Jesus, this thing is complete. It's impossible." So I go to Pops and ask him: "Tell me what to do. You know I don't belong there." He said: "Play whole notes." The perfect answer, but how would it ever occur to me? You know you're thinking, and trying to make good, and he says "Play whole notes." The only thing that could make sense, which was what I did and got away with it. But he had the answer to anything you could think of ... I found that out.'

The importance of race in jazz, and of colour prejudice in particular, bedevil many an argument, it was agreed. Bobby usually kept his comments on this topic to a minimum, except when telling stories, but in matters of biased opinion hoped he had a good reputation 'because I believe it is the only fair way to think'.

Louis, I mentioned, had always enjoyed working with Teagarden, and his All Stars were a 'mixed' combo from their offical start in 1947. Hackett nodded but said his opinion was that the idea misfired somewhere along the track.

'You know, some bass player once told me he was in line for the job but didn't get it because he was black. Yeah, it's ironic but there's a big point there; the group had to be mixed. You show up with an all-black band, you're lucky to get maybe $1500. Throw in a whitey or two and you're liable to be paid $2500. That's the way people think.'

Mrs Sudhalter hinted at a correction. 'That's the way Joe Glaser thought people will think.'

Hackett said no, that was not absolutely true. 'It was business with him but maybe he'd spotted a trend. You know, the old racial thing has been changing for a long time; I guess it's all diferent now. In some cases today it's a handicap being white.'

Not all jazz musicians, it should hardly need saying, are as debonair as Bobby Hackett was then; not all of them laugh as much or, especially, accept competition as readily. The great Armstrong-Goodman combat of '53 kept swimming into mind, and I guessed Bobby could throw light on the event. Breath-taking reports of the feud, which developed rapidly on their shared tour, had been made to me by Joe Bushkin, Trummy Young, Ernie Anderson and others, all of whom placed the blame firmly on Goodman. Even Teddy

1. Regents Park 1934: (left to right) Bert Houston (reeds), 'Ronnie' (Max) Jones (tenor and soprano saxophone), Dinah and Connie (both were later to become wives of members of the band)

2. The *Melody Maker* office: (left to right) Max Jones, Charles Delaunay and Stephane Grappelli

3. A lecture recital by Max Jones (*c*1945–6). The saxophonist Buddy Featherston-haugh is among the musicians (centre) on the left (*photo courtesy Melody Maker*).

4. Left: Bob Wilber (*photo courtesy Hans Harzheim*)

5. Below: Max with Albert Nicholas

6. Left: Paul Barnes (*photo courtesy Val Wilmer/Format*)

7. Below: Paris 1955: (left to right) Edmond Hall, Max, Winnie Hall

8. Johnny Hodges (with Paul Gonsalves) (*photo courtesy Bob Thiele, Impulse Records*)

9. Lucky Thompson (photo courtesy Flair Photography)
10. Left: Zoot Sims (photo courtesy Melody Maker)

11. Westminster Abbey 1953: Flip Phillips at the wheel of Max's famous MG TC (numberplate MMM 192) overlooked by Oscar Peterson and Norman Granz

12. Left: Stan Getz (*photo courtesy Hans Harzheim*)

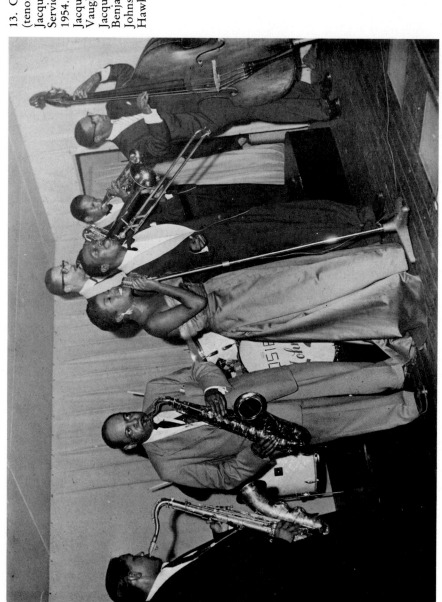

13. Coleman Hawkins (tenor) with Illinois Jacquet's Band at a US Service Base in Britain in 1954. The group includes Jacquet (tenor), Sarah Vaughan (vocal), Russell Jacquet (trumpet) and Joe Benjamin (bass). Osie Johnson (drums) is behind Hawk.

Wilson, unwilling to go into details, told me it was largely Benny's doing. From what I'd heard, trouble hit the fan from Day One when B.G. commandeered as of right the star dressing-room. Other informants claimed the hostility was rooted in Twenties Chicago, when Louis fancied he was insulted by the younger white musician. One day, as it transpired, I found myself seated next to B.G. at a Decca lunch given in his honour. Between courses, while Benny seemed disposed to comment on past achievements, I asked about the true cause of the dispute. After assuring me he had never disagreed seriously with Armstrong in his life, the Master studied his wine glass fastidiously and enquired: "Are you familiar with Californian champagne at all, Mr Jones? We have some pretty good vintages."

There was no equivocation on Hackett's part, however. He said he felt things were a bit taut when he tried to attend the B.G. band's pre-tour rehearsal.

'Do you know what? Benny threw me out; he didn't want anybody at that rehearsal. Nobody but the band was allowed in there. I understood, of course, and I said it was okay. But I did make it clear to Benny that I went there to see old Pops. I don't know exactly what happened then, the dressing-room stuff, though I heard Louis was expected to use the same room as his guys. All I know is that Benny started to lay down the law to Louis Armstrong. "This is my package and you'll do this and you'll do that, and you won't do this." Can you imagine? Pops said: "We-ell ..." Right away he wanted to kill Benny, see?

'Now a man like Pops wasn't hard to understand. He was convinced he was the king of swing. That had been his life; he proved it, and he was. So when Whitey comes along and claims he's the king of swing, well, it ain't necessarily so! (Laughter) No, Pops is dead serious about this, and I'm thinking: "Whoa, what's he going to do to Benny Goodman?" Anyhow, they all got it together for opening, and I'm wondering ... hard to tell why, but I could feel it. Hell, I could read Pops' mind.

'You should realise this was no small deal. The tour was sold out, and it was like a month or a month and a half. They had maybe a million dollars cash sales in advance. I think Joe Glaser and John Hammond were crazy to ever think of putting a package like that together. But of course it had appeal, and now they had to try to rescue it. I'll have to skip a little 'cos it's a long story. But let me say that Louis had an all-time band with him: Cozy Cole, Trummy, Joe Bushkin, Bigard I think, and a good bass player. I went to catch them at Carnegie Hall when they played New York. It was a week or two after they went out, and already I was getting reports that Goodman was sick.

'So they begin the programme with Goodman's band, and Benny sounded like Sol Yaged with scarlet fever. Oh, did he sound terrible? Just couldn't do anything. It was embarrassing. Jesus, if I'd been able to do so I'd have stopped the show already. He sounded like someone first learning the instrument, you know, practising.

'And then Pops came on and shook that place ... oh, I never heard him play like that; well, I have, but you know what I mean. Was he angry? He was out to get Benny Goodman. And they tell me there was a scene backstage, and I believe it, like you never heard. Peanuts Hucko came there one night — you know he still worships Benny, and I wish he'd get over it, but he never has — and he wanted to be with Goodman and Benny was so sick from tangling with Pops that he fluffed Peanuts off, wouldn't talk to him. And Pops went up to him when he saw that, and told him: "You no-good mother, who do you think you are, to hurt a kid like that?" He said to Benny: "You're nothin'!" It's a fact.

'So when I go back-stage in between I say to Pops that maybe it would be better if his band went on first. "We tried it last night," he says, "and it was worse. Benny Goodman is sick." And sure enough he goes into the hospital a few days later, up in Boston. The tour? Oh, Gene Krupa jumped in but it was a failure. I'm tellin' you it was a terrible thing; Pops came close to killing him (Goodman) without touching him, just playing.

'And the first time I ran into him after the tour had dissolved, he was recording up at Decca. I got nothin' to do, so I'm there, you know, and I looked at him and I say: "How's the TKO artist today?" He growls back: "Man, I didn't do anything." I says: "No? You know you stuck that up. It's me you're talking to, Pops." As I say, Louis blew him right out of the place. I says: "You know you stuck that up a little." What could he say? He just laughed. We were talking the truth by then.

'The best that can be said is that Benny believed he was the boss. And Pops didn't take that, as you know. Benny tried it on him, and Pops was so mad at that guy, man. I don't remember all the details but Lucille told me when Benny was up in New Jersey he wanted Louis to come and have dinner with him, wanted them to try and make contact of some kind with each other. Louis wouldn't go, said to her: "Are you crazy? I don't want to have dinner with that m.f."

'I've become pretty well acquainted with Benny lately, been doin' a lot of concerts with him, here and there, and I must admit I got to like the guy. If you understand him, he's like an absent-minded professor; and he's a genius when he is really playing, when things are right all around him. I was supposed to be with him tomorrow night, actually, somewhere in Switzerland. He's there, and I believe he has Chris Griffin on trumpet. Anyhow, I get on with Benny well enough — I make him laugh and don't let him get too serious. He's eccentric, but he's got a lot of good qualities.

'I say he's absent-minded, see? Because twenty-four hours a day he's not thinking or dreaming of anything but the clarinet; he's either practising physically or mentally. So when somebody says something to him he's liable not to hear it, and he'll give you an answer that has nothin' to do with what you asked . . . and five minutes later. But that's the reason. He can't get that clarinet out of his mind. And there are times when it pays. I mean I've heard that man play things . . . times when nobody could come near him.

'To tell the truth I'd spent all my life avoiding him because everyone told me he's hard to get along with, so I just thought, "You go your way and I'll go mine." Then out of a clear sky he calls me up one day to say he's got a tour coming up. "I think it might be interesting and I wonder of you'd like to do it with me," he says. "Well, tell me more," I reply. "You know I'm not looking to rough it these days." I want to let him know he's got to pay me heavy, see?

And he says: "Don't worry, Bobby, neither am I." So I agreed and it wound up being a three-week tour in which we played like four nights one week, three nights another ... very easy, made to order.

'So the first night out we're on a bus and we all get in and we've got a hell of a band. You know he's always got the best players possible. Well, we pull over to eat at a diner some place and we go in and sit down and we all eat. Now the other guys are scared to death of him, and he means nothing special to me, honest; I respect him but he doesn't scare me. In fact I tried to keep a distance then, because I want to know him better before he's my buddy. So the waitress comes with the check and everyone's wondering what we do now, because according to his reputation everybody will have to pay his own bill. I look at the waitress and tell her: "Give him the check; he's got all the money and we're all broke. So give it to Mr Goodman. He won't mind." She hands it to Benny and he pays it. Thanks! Oh, there were a lot of funny scenes with that band.

'I have to jump around a little though. To begin with we must have rehearsed twenty hours at least. Every day we went to a studio to rehearse, and that's all right. Guys are bringing in arrangements; everything has to be correct. So we play the first night out, at Orchestra Hall in Philadelphia, and all of us are in tuxedos and proper white evening shirts, and we've got the arrangements off and all that. But when we get out in the hall and we're under fire ... it's time to hit ... he asks: "What do we play?" Forget all that rehearsal. That was only 'cos he wanted to practise and he figured it's good for everybody. Right?

'He keeps on mumbling, "What do we play," and I says to play this, or play that. Okay, but the first chorus he played on the first tune — a little like Sol Yaged. I can tell he's nervous. Talking of Sol, that was really just a joke between us. You know Benny was Sol's idol. He once asked Benny what size shoes he wore, then went out and got a pair. Once in a while I'd throw that on him, when he'd played something and he's looking for encouragement, I'd say: "Sound a little like Sol today." And he'd laugh; he knew what I was thinking.

'Anyway, towards the end of the first chorus things are beginning to jell. We've got a hell of a group with John Bunch on piano, Steve Swallow playing bass ... Benny's not happy with it, he's never happy with any rhythm section but never mind ... and at the end of the chorus I looked at him and shouted: "Play another one, Benny." You're not supposed to do that in a concert hall, but it jolted him and got him loosened up and *playing*.

'These concerts were so easy I loved doing 'em, to tell you the truth; you worked about ten minutes out of the hour, or fifteen at the most. Because then he'd go on with the quartet, while we'd go out and take a smoke or a rest. Then he finishes up with the *Sunrise* which is a *tour de force*, right? Standing ovation and everything. Now he picks on me, and makes play. And he calls a tune, *Lazy Afternoon* which you can never play unless you have Dave McKenna at the piano because nobody knows how to play it. I used to struggle through that thing. The guys never did learn it properly; how can they learn unless you get the music and show 'em it? It's a hard piece. If you've got Dave you play it well. But we were getting a good response, a nice reaction although I'm struggling.

'Now, after a few months, I'm still featured on this damn thing and can't make it sound right because everybody's composing behind me. No one knows the theme. Then we open in Basin Street East in New York, a wonderful itinerary which included two weeks there and three in Mexico. One night I go in to see Benny and ask if I can play a different song. Did he mind? I always gave him the respect, see? You've got to do what he says; he's paying you well and he's entitled to that. So he says: "Well, what?" And I tell him there's a little tune called *The Good Life* that's nice, and I'd like to play it.

'Well, he agrees to that and I do it, and it's just one of those things: the applause wouldn't stop and it's becoming embarrassing. It must have gone on for three or four minutes and I'm thinking: "Get me out of this!" Anyhow, we finished that show and when we're about to go on for the second show — we did two a night — as we're walking on to the stage, Benny says to me: "I think you'd better go back to the other one." Isn't that funny?'

A lover of pretty songs and correct harmonies, Bobby Hackett often had piano players on his mind. When he thought them good he liked them very, very, much. One he esteemed most highly was Dave McKenna.

'Now Dave, you have to hear him in person. On records, you haven't heard him. I wouldn't like you to print this in case I lose a lot of friends but really, I've worked with every good piano player ever — practically every one — and you believe me when I tell you that, if you could be exposed to this guy's playing for three or four nights, you'd realise he's the best jazz piano player that ever lived. Max, I'm tellin' you, Joe Sullivan, Jess Stacy, Joe Bushkin, Art Tatum (well, Tatum I have to keep by himself, the greatest of all) ... there's nobody to beat Dave.

'Then, you see, a lot of the guys are just a bunch of soloists, whereas Dave's playing is right at all times; he plays every song exactly right. I can only say you gotta hear him.'

Why did Hackett think McKenna had been under-recognised?

'Why? Oh, he's a shy sort of guy, he's got a funny outlook, and he'd rather live on Cape Cod and play in a neighbourhood saloon. He doesn't want to get anywhere, doesn't like New York. Well, he's playing there now but he'd prefer to be home every night. I've got to send you some home-made tapes of Dave to show the way he plays, because on records he sounds different. Dave is right up to the minute, musically, but he didn't start yesterday. He started like Jelly Roll and Fats Waller and includes Tatum; he's got 'em all in one piece: everything!'

Another player Bobby held in highest regard was Coleman Hawkins, and at the drop of a 'Hawk' he was off on 'a lovely story' concerning jazz photographer-enthusiast-promoter Jack Bradley, who was organising a session at New York's Town Hall.

'Jack was trying get this thing together for a Saturday afternoon, but there was no money involved. Everybody wanted to do it for fifty dollars or something like that, which ordinarily would have been five hundred, a thousand, anything if you could get it. So anyway, I said I'd do it. I'd be practising in any case, might as well pick up fifty dollars. Jack told me he'd called Hawkins and Hawk says he's not interested in things like that. But, he says, "If Bobby Hackett's going to be there, I'll do it." Wasn't that some compliment? Yeah!

'Another time I was booked for a wonderful affair in Austin, Texas, and Hawk and I made the plane trip from New York together. So we're sitting next to each other and the stewardess comes over, and I said to her: "Miss, I want you to know that this gentleman here is the world's greatest saxophonist; if there's anything he wants, see that he gets it." He had brandy every fifteen minutes. I don't know how he ever managed it, because he'd stay on his feet and he was a gentleman, and everything. He was killing himself but he did what he wanted to.

'But it was a great concert, racewise too. On the stage and in the audience it was mixed fifty-fifty and everybody was so happy, no problems. I'd gone as a solo artist, so I asked who I'd be with and wound up working with Pete Fountain. Behind the stage, waiting to go on, I said to Pete: "What'll we play?" He says: "Wanna play *Georgia On My Mind*?" I says: "Do you want to get me killed?" It was something else, Jesus, but I thought it was funny.

'So it was a good scene there, reminiscing with all the musicians. Someone was talking about Lester Young, who'd asked him to do some little gig, and this guy asked: "What does it pay?" And Lester said "Twenty cent", which means twenty dollars. The guy said: "Oh, I don't know if I can make that, gettin' there and everything. It's not enough bread." And Lester tells him: "That's the trouble with you greys; you don't save up your money so you can play with Prez."

'And they told me a very good one about Jo Jones, who we know and love. Jo gets a gig in Boston, and he takes a quartet — piano, bass and something else ... it doesn't matter. They never rehearse or anything and when they get on the stage nothing's been set. So Jo starts playing the drums, he's got a tempo goin', the lights are up and people are wondering what they're going to do. So the piano player leans over and says: "Hey Jo, what are we going to play?" Jo says: "Don't you dig?" You're supposed to know.

'And this is funny, too, while I'm with Tony Bennett he gets a wire from Jo one time, and it says: "Tony, I need five hundred dollars in a hurry. It's a crisis. Would appreciate it", words to that effect. Tony says he would have sent him the money right away but he lost the wire and didn't know how to reach him. So a couple of weeks go by and he gets another wire from Jo, and it says: "Dear Tony, thanks for making me a father."

'Another time, I did an affair at the Louis Armstrong Stadium. They'd re-named it that and Lucille wanted me to do it. I'd forgotten about it, to tell you the truth, until I get a call from this guy Honi Coles, a dancer who had been stage manager of the Apollo for about forty years, great showman and every-thing. Well, it's outdoors in Flushing, and there is Redd Foxx and all the oldtimers, you know, a high-powered cast, and Sweets Edison who is Redd's conductor. I'm the only one who's a non-brother. So I ask Sweets: 'What do we do now?' We started warming up, and he says: "Let's play *Song of the Islands*." And the band's got Billy Taylor on piano, see, and he don't know *Song of the Islands* and when we come to play it he's got somethin' else going.

Anyway, we get on with it and the band's great; it's in the open air and the pit band's in front of us — Billy with the grin, and he's playing *Firebird* or something, it doesn't have anything to do with *Song of the Islands*. Funny, but anyhow Sweets gets on the microphone and this is like the Yankee Stadium, everythings's magnified, and he looks across at me (I'm on the other side of the stage) and he says: "You know, Bob, running around with you is gettin' me in trouble. People are asking me what I am doing with Whitey." I wanted to say something back, but I figured: "Don't say anything, keep quiet." What I wanted to say was, like: "You're not foolin' me with that tokenism." However, everyone laughed and I decided not to continue the game.

'Now let me tell you a couple of stories about Max Kaminsky,' Bobby continued. 'I do a lot of work for Bob Thiele back home, and he's got a lot of integrity for a record producer and company executive. He had just moved in with RCA and that was nice for me because anything I want to do, he lets me do it. So this time he had a thing going in the studio and there was Maxie on the date — Pee Wee Erwin, Maxie and myself, I think that was the trumpet section. Now the recording was going to go into overtime and Maxie started to pack his horn, and Bob says: "Hey, where you goin', we've got to finish the date." And Maxie says: "No, I gotta be somewhere else at five o'clock," and he just went. He played it by the book. I know it's hard to explain how funny it was.

'And then another time, we got a very big thing together for television; a good job, and we had to put the whole thing together musically, so we all showed up at nine o'clock in the morning. Even Benny Goodman was there, and Dave Brubeck, super-market you know, and Max and I were included. Well, it got to be around eleven in the morning and Maxie told me he'd got to run. I asked how he was going to leave when nothing was properly together. Maxie said: "I don't care; we booked a Jewish wedding, and I'm going to play it." Said he'd come back later, you know. When the laughter died down, Dick Sudhalter said: "No comment."'

Mention of several prestigious TV programmes reminded Bobby he wasn't wild about large, organised prestige events of any type, on or off TV, though he participated naturally enough in a TV tribute to Armstrong, after Louis' death (Dizzy, Hines, Budd Johnson and Peggy Lee were others featured).

'But I always try to avoid those funeral scenes if I can. It's not that I'm a coward, just that I often think I won't be able to stand it. It repels me that the wrong people go and for the wrong reasons, some of them I mean. They go for the publicity.'

Switching topics, as a man will do in the company of dedicated jazz characters, the cornettist told how he was meant to do a tour with the Dutch Swing College Band, but the reply to his invitation went astray. After some months passed, he went to Holland for a week, when the misunderstanding was sorted out. The invitation was repeated and it was explained that the tour would be less tough than it sounded.

'All the jumps were short and everything would be comfortable. So I almost went and did it but then I got home and changed my mind. The money was good, too, but I thought: thirty-one days, I don't feel up to it. I suggested that

Billy Butterfield do it because he's stronger than me, and I knew he'd like it and everything. To sum it up, he went.

'Now the guys are asking me again. See, the week I did in Holland, we got together. Peter Schilperoort came over and we had an afternoon at his place — in a fishing village or somewhere, oh, nice. And it turned out he's a recording nut, an engineer but a good one. So I spent Sunday afternoon there and all of the cornet players showed up. You know, the band changed personnel from time to time; as a guy got older they brought in a young cat, and then guys came back, and it's just a happy family. So we'd all play and run the tape machine, and it was a joyous day, wonderful.

'Yes, the band's very competent but what I'd like to say is that there's something better over here in the way of group feeling. You can't get that today in New York when you have a bunch of stars because they're all trying to trip each other. It's not the same. It's hard to explain to you, but the feeling is not the same and it just never could be, no matter how well the guys play. They're too much individuals.'

Speaking of individuals, brought drummers into focus. Bobby said he liked a good drummer, 'but there aren't too many good ones around any more. Buddy Rich spoiled 'em — they all want to be stars.'

Another hour passed, more food and coffee was consumed, and the Sudhalters warned it was time to leave. Hackett said just time for one more story, right? Artie Shaw and Benny Goodman were the subjects.

'I had never realised they were, like, arch rivals. They think they're competing with each other, and Artie Shaw — great as he is — well, he's not Benny Goodman on the clarinet. Sorry! So one night not long ago Artie comes into where I'm working and I'm sitting with, I think it was John Hammond and some other people. Well, he sits down and I says to Artie — not knowing how he thought of Benny, like they'd always been enemies and I didn't know that — I says: "Artie, I've been doing some things with Goodman lately and I gotta tell you as one musician to another that guy is just the greatest clarinet player. I wish you could have heard him."

'"Oh, I've heard him play," he says. Then, after a few moments of silence: "He can't play, can he?". I says: "Artie, I can only tell you the truth. That guy's a complete genius of the clarinet." I said: "If you heard him the way I heard him you wouldn't have any choice, you'd have to agree with me." I've got him solemn now, right? And I like the guy; he's a real person, crazy but he's all right.

'So another five minutes goes by and I have to get up to play. I say: "Excuse me, I've got to make some noise, you know." Artie tells me: "When you see Benny next, give him my regards." And I said: "That's more like it; don't close your ears." And then I told Benny this story and it tickled him. Well, they're friends now, and it never would have happened if I didn't stick my neck out.

'As I say, I get on okay with Benny. It was Louis that was the matter with him. As soon as Benny called himself King of Swing his days were numbered. Pops wanted him to *know* who was the King. By the way, have you seen some new stuff they're pushing on TV, called "The King of Swing"? I think it's a book about Babe Ruth. Ha-ha, now Babe Ruth's the King of Swing! That's really funny.'

Preston Jackson

*Until 1974, when he came to Britain with The New Orleans Joymakers,
trombonist Preston Jackson had been a remote, colourful figure who stalked the
pages of New Orleans jazz history, recorded with such nobles as Armstrong and
Noone, and wrote in* Hot News *and* Jazz Hot *during the Thirties about the
golden years in New Orleans and Chicago. I knew he was still playing in the
Seventies but hardly expected to meet him. When I did, it was some experience.
On this particular afternoon I had been invited to take my borrowed BBC
recorder to Jackson's hotel room and I went armed also with John Chilton (co-
author of the book,* Louis*) as jazz guru. Our immediate purpose was to get
'quotations' for a series of ten broadcasts on Armstrong, then in the pipeline, plus
additional information for the revised edition of* Louis *(which came out in
1975).*

*In the event, we popped only a few questions and let the historian in Jackson
take over. As the following pages make clear, his mind and memory were soon
in top gear; the occasional inaccuracies have not been corrected. People came
and went, and the heating radiators and the telephone often interrupted his
story — thus some of the breaks in continuity — but he always returned happily
to act out the narrative of a decade of jazz. If we had asked other questions I
feel sure his response would have shown a similar grasp of names, personalities
and period. Suddenly reminded of Jelly Roll, because of Andrew Hilaire,
Preston recited the personnel of the first Victor Red Hot Peppers — 'all New
Orleans boys except Little Mitch on cornet, he died quite recently' — and added
that later Jelly had Quinn Wilson from Chicago on bass horn.*

*'Now, about Jelly Roll: he did a lot of talking but Jelly Roll really could
produce. He bragged on himself, you know, and he had diamonds in his teeth.
Jelly Roll had been alleged to've been a fast man, a pimp I'd say, playing for
Lulu White and places like that. And he'd always have an audience, ten or
fifteen guys with him in the middle talking about this town and that, mostly
about himself. He was quite a character.'*

*The following reminiscences are printed with the permission of, and
acknowledgments to, John Chilton.*

Four tracks by Young's Creole Jazz Band, cut in Chicago in 1923 with Happy
Caldwell on clarinet, are the first records made by Preston Jackson. Among the
best-known early recordings featuring his trombone are those by Arthur Sims'
Creole Roof Orchestra, made in Chicago in June 1926 and released in the UK
on the purple Parlophone label. Bernie Young was the cornet player on all
these, and Cassino Simpson the pianist on the Sims session. Would Preston tell
us about Young?

'Well, Oscar Bernie Young had a cornet in New Orleans but didn't do
anything particular down there. So I happened to meet him in Chicago one
day; I had my horn with me, so I met him and he had his horn. And he told me,
says "I'm forming a band and I want you to play trombone with me." Well, I
agreed. I mean I was just a beginner and he was a little further advanced.

'Then he began to get in contact with other members such as Kenneth Anderson, who at that time was playing trumpet though he is a saxophonist and a pianist. A little later on we got hold of Jimmy McKendrick, who was a drummer. And young Jimmy, every job we played, his mother would come on the job and take him right straight home after we'd finished. To begin with, a girl named Thelma Clark played piano; her father, Professor Clark, he ran a dance school and what they call Society Dances.

'So after we got together with Jimmy McKendrick, then came the Simeon brothers, Omer and Al. And when this girl, Thelma, she quit the band, we got Simeon's brother-in-law. A little later, as things began to change, we had a fellow called Edward Temple playing drums with us. And I'll say that a little later we had a guy they called Sheik — I never did know his right name – who played bass violin. And finally Dominique came into the picture, Natty Dominique that is, and then Richard M. Jones, Myknee Jones, he came in on piano. And also in that particular band were Stompy Evans and Happy Caldwell. So I'd say that's when we made *Dearborn Street Blues* and those things with Bernie Young. As things went on, we had changed piano again and had Lil Richardson, she played piano, and then we got Cassino Simpson — he worked with us for a long time.'

JOHN CHILTON: Where did he come from, Cassino Simpson? Chicago?

PRESTON JACKSON: I guess so. You see he was way ahead of us. He had been playing with Celestin's Tuxedo Band. Anyway, he was with us on those records we made for Paramount. But it was always one of those things where guys were in and out of the band and we finally split up as the fellows began to hit a little better, and naturally got better opportunities.

Now there used to be a business agent by the name of Monroe — he was about 6ft 7in, I recall. At that time all of us was non-Union, what the communists called scab, and this Monroe just about ran us into the Union. So he run us in, and according to our qualifications we began to get jobs, you know, with other bands. The late Clarence Jones, a pianist, I remember he gave us our examination. He put an orchestration up there, and we could all read pretty good because we'd been studying under Roy Palmer. He taught me and he taught Bernie Young.

Sometimes a fellow couldn't read too well (like Cass Simpson) but be outstanding as a musician. So in certain instances they'd be given a membership card. So, getting back to this Clarence Jones, he had a wonderful band at the Howard Theatre, about ten pieces. See, at that time the theatres mostly had good bands, like the State Theatre, and as you know Erskine Tate had his orchestra in the Vendome Theatre.

During this time the young Lionel Hampton was to be seen every day; he always carried his snare drum under his arm. Lionel was crazy about Teddy Weatherford, followed him around everywhere he went — this was at the time Weatherford was playing piano with Jimmy Wade's band. At about this time I had branched out a little and went with Eli Rice and his Dixie Cotton Pickers, worked with him fourteen months. We toured Wisconsin, Michigan and Minnesota and also worked in Milwaukee. Finally, Arthur Sims, he got the band up in Milwaukee at the Wisconsin Roof. Charles Elgar had been up there and it seems like his contract ran out and Sims went in, and I joined his band.

But to get back to Clarence Jones, fellows like that, they didn't play no one type of music. Clarence was an accomplished musician and that band could handle most any kind of music. You see a lot of musicians there were playing in theatres. Musicians came into different categories. Some were just good for brass bands and there were some just good for buffet flats — you know, they'd play around those places where the guy would take in enough people to make five or six hundred dollars, then have 'em lock all the doors, let nobody in. That's where Pinetop would play, and all them fellers in that same category. That's what they did because they wasn't good enough to play with the real musicians; Pinetop Smith, Yancey and all those guys, they didn't see good. That's what we called it; means they didn't read any too well. So them flats and saloons, places like that, that was far as they could go. They just couldn't play with legitimate musicians that was reading, and legitimate musicians couldn't play with them 'cos for most of them F sharp, C sharp didn't mean a darn thing. They was only fakin' anyhow. You sit down with them guys and there ain't no tellin' what key he's playing in because it doesn't affect him. One key's the same as another; whatever he learned the tune, that's it, whatever it was.

JC: I remember Louis Armstrong telling us that when Johnny Dunn came into town once he wanted to read the parts Louis had. Well, Louis said the particular piece was in five sharps, and Dunn looked at the music and it caught him unawares, you know.

PJ: Yes, Louis was right about that, and I may add something else about the two. You see Johnny Dunn, he was pretty high during that time, I think with Mamie Smith and some other singers. Louis had been to New York and played one year with Fletcher Henderson and then he left Fletcher because Lil had a job at the Dreamland Café. I heard she told Louis 'either you come back to Chicago now or forget about it'. Anyhow he did return because everyone was saying 'Well, Louis's back!' And one night Johnny Dunn strolled into the Dreamland and asked for Louis's horn. So Louis gave it to him, and when he got it back he just blew Dunn out of the place. He did the same thing with Jabbo Smith; 'course it was a little closer with Jabbo than with Johnny Dunn.

MAX JONES: When did you move from New Orleans to Chicago?

PJ: I arrived in 1917 during World War One. There I came in contact with Roy Palmer, which I proudly state because he was one of my teachers. He and Honore Dutrey were really very nice to me and I attribute my success on the trombone to these two people. More to Roy Palmer because he used to room with us and I didn't like to see him move. At that time he was playing with Doc Watson's Band, and in that band were Franks, a drummer from Iowa, Willie Hightower on trumpet, and we had Wilson Townes clarinet, Roy Palmer on trombone, Horace Eubanks, saxophone, and Watson on piano.

Now Townes, he left soon afterwards and went abroad to Paris. Later on he died, never did come back. Eubanks, he lived in France for a long time and worked in Europe several years before coming back to St Louis — that was his home. I don't think he lived long after that. Willie Hightower was a very good trumpet player, a little different from the average New Orleans player. I'll say he was more on the order of Manuel Perez; he had a nice swing but he had a delicate tone, a mixture of jazz and the sweetness. So I wouldn't put him in the same category as Joe Oliver or Tommy Ladnier because he didn't sound as rough as those fellows, and he wasn't as strong as Louis. He was on the order of Buddy Petit. You see Buddy Petit's range was just a little over the staff — he wasn't very strong in the high register, neither was Bunk [Johnson] — but he made so many pretty changes. There's people will tell you now that Petit was better than Louis.

And then we had Henry Rena; he was a little fellow, too, but he was stout. He could stay above the staff. And at that time in New Orleans (the early Twenties) we still had Chris Kelly, Sam Morgan, Petit and others I've mentioned, and that boy who died not so long ago — yes, Punch Miller, he had returned there from the army. We had so many good horn players in New Orleans.

Now Chris Kelly, he could play the blues better than any of those fellows but he wasn't much known outside the city. I'm going to deviate a bit, as these things come back to me, and say that New Orleans was like a reservoir during that period. Joe Oliver could reach down there whenever he needed a trumpet player, reach down and come up with a player as good as the one he'd lost. Oh, there were solid trumpet men in Chicago, but many they had there had already come up from New Orleans. And there were a lot of fellows didn't want to come north. I mean, Papa Celestin was still around naturally, never did come north until much later. And then Kid Rena and Petit wouldn't leave New Orleans to come north.

MJ: Can you tell us why you left New Orleans?

PJ: Well, that was my mother. Her name was Murrit [sounds like he says Merrit but he spells it out M-u-r-r-i-t] until she married a Robert McDonald. I want to mention this because you might see in my passport it says McDonald, though I've been known as Preston Jackson for years; that's due to the fact that when my mother re-married she married Charles Jackson, a brick mason, and I took that name.

My mother taught school in New Orleans and finally decided to leave the city due to the brutality of the people there, particularly of the police. There was no defence against them. See, whenever a black got shot he just was shot. All the police had to say was 'This nigger, he threatened me', and the law would take his word. So one day a dear friend of our family had a fight with some guy, a fist fight, and this fellow brought a policeman to his house, and as he walked in the door, unarmed, he was shot in the stomach and killed. My mother never did get over that, said then that she'd leave New Orleans and she did. With my stepfather and me she moved to Chicago. That was 1917, and it was in Chicago I got my first trombone.

I met my real father, too, Robert McDonald, in Chicago, hadn't seen him since I was just a little fellow. Well, I didn't recognise him. Oh, he came back one time and I'll always remember he gave me a little green suit. I was only a child, I'll say about nine years old.

MJ: Speaking of Chicago, how did it compare with New Orleans for civil rights?

PJ: Yes it was tough as far as brutalities, and I was told just today by a very responsible man that the brutality is still there, but nowhere as bad as it has been. There's a lot of difference in New Orleans, too, today; I was surprised. There's more blacks in responsible positions. They're allowed to go into the average hotel, most hotels, and they're served, and there are many other things. It's much better now. Seems like the South's going to make the first break-through so far as equality is concerned.

So anyhow, getting back to my mother, we all had a tough time when we got to Chicago — tough enough to make the average person give up and return where they came from. My mother couldn't get a job teaching school due to this college she graduated from, Southern University, not being accredited. My stepfather was a brick mason, and he laid most of those streets, like Annunciation Street, you know, he and others, and he was said to be a pretty good bricklayer. But the Union wouldn't issue him a card so it wasn't easy for him. My mother had to wind up doing day work, washing and ironing; said she'd rather do that than go back.

But now I'll return to New Orleans and my early days. My public school was Thumy Lafon, and I'm coming to Louis Armstrong. I'm coming to something that I'll say is closely associated with my trip here to Europe. It have to be because I attribute my success to a great extent to Louis. So I saw him though I didn't know who he was during this time. There was a large lot there, a square, full of debris and a lot of stuff, so they decided to fill it up and make a playground, which they did.

Now here comes Louis, here's where I see Louis Armstrong. I didn't know his name but he was outstanding then. He was in this little band from Jones's — you might have saw the pictures, the Waifs' Home band. Now if anybody had told me that this particular boy standing up there — there was about two years difference in our ages — that some day I'd be playing trombone in his band I'd have told 'em they were crazy, because I wasn't interested in music. Only way I'd been interested was usually at commencement, you know, at elementary school, Celestin used to play there and play this tune, *Liza Jane*, and the drummer Henry Zeno had a solo in it. I did a lot of whistlin' and that was it, I guess.

At this time, Clifford 'Snags' Jones, who used to live on Jackson Avenue, he was starting out on the drums. And as I afore stated, Oscar Bernie Young had a cornet. So it must have been about 1914 when I saw Louis. And just seven or eight years later I happened to be sitting on the stand at the Lincoln Gardens behind Dutrey — I hounded those fellows, you know, because by now I'd become interested — and I heard Joe Oliver say: 'Well, Dip is coming with me here tomorrow.' See, they called him Dip at that time, or Dippermouth. That's where the *Dippermouth Blues* came from.

I should explain, I now became really interested and at night I was usually sitting behind Dutrey at the Royal Garden [this was re-named the Lincoln Gardens Café in 1922 — MJ]. Well, Dutrey was afflicted. Dutrey was a gentleman and a fine man. He was in the navy during World War One and was locked up in that magazine, the powder magazine, and it affected his lungs. So whenever he begin to have trouble breathing he'd look back and say: 'Pardner, you want to play a little for me?' Well, I'd have paid him for the pleasure. So there was a long curtain from one end of the stage to the other, and he'd go behind and I'd hear pss, pss, pss as he'd squirt something in his nostrils and throat, see? Then in about 15 minutes he'd come back and be as good as new.

Now this would have to have been 1922 because during 1921 I had returned to New Orleans, and by that time I'm playing pretty good. So I went down into the village there and sat in with this band, playing at a hall they called Sans Souci. Well, I stayed there one month. Nice band with Henry Rena, Joe Rena, Maurice French on trombone, and they had Simon Marrero on bass, and one of his brothers also. They were two of that great family of musicians, the Marreros, in that band. So, as I said, I played around about a month with Rena's band.

So it was one night in '22 when Oliver says 'Dip's coming with me tomorrow'. And, as true as his word, I was sittin' on the stand and Louis walked in. He had on a brown suit, tan suit, a sailor straw hat and tan shoes. It seem like he weighed about a couple of hundred pounds, or a little better. I was introduced to him and had the honour to introduce him to the musicians, many of which he knew. You may know the personnel, but I'll repeat it. There was Bill Johnson, who brought the first band north in 1911; he was on double bass. And there was Dutrey, trombone, Baby Dodds on drums, his brother Johnny on clarinet, and they had Lil Hardin on piano.

MJ: Was it Lil Hardin for certain that night when Louis arrived? Lil herself told me she was out of the band then, and that Bertha Gonsoulin [Gonzales according to Lil] was playing piano.

PJ: Now, when you mention Bertha ... she did play in Joe's band one time. It seems that the band was on Pantages time and she worked with Joe out there, and when Joe came back east to Chicago she came along with him. He had Lottie Taylor too, and during this period there were three lady pianists working with him at different intervals. But this particular time, Lil was playing with the band. She had previously been playing at the Deluxe Café with Sugar Johnny, Roy Palmer, Lawrence Duhé (the leader of the band), Wellman Braud and Tubby Hall, see? But now she's with Joe Oliver.

As I afore said, the reason Joe used to dip down in New Orleans for replacements was because he'd hear about these fellows, how they was advancing and how much they was playing. But the Chicago musicians was clannish and there was bad blood, bad feelin', between them and the New Orleans musicians. This bad blood was due to the fact that in New Orleans musicians had most of the work locked up, all except the theatres. There was the Deluxe, and right across the street Joe Oliver played the Dreamland. Then he'd leave the Dreamland and go on to the Pekin Cabaret at 26th Street, see? Now Jimmie Noone, he was in the band at the Royal Gardens when it was Bill Johnson's, before Oliver had it. And in that band — and I'm going back to about 1919 — was Paul Barbarin, Eddie Vinson, Manuel Perez and later Freddie Keppard, Bill Johnson and Lottie Taylor. They stayed there about six months, I'd say, and finally broke up. Barbarin left Chicago and Perez went back to New Orleans; Eddie Vinson stuck around a while then disappeared, never did know what became of him.

So then Joe Oliver come in and taken over (at Lincoln Garden in mid-1922) and soon after Louis Armstrong joined him. And these musicians started coming into the Gardens — about the first ten rows was nothin' but musicians. During this time Paul Mares and the New Orleans Rhythm Kings arrived in Chicago, and a Dixieland band from Memphis, the Memphis Five, and a couple of other white bands had arrived. And at the Gardens you could see people such as the Dorsey brothers, the Teagardens, Muggsy Spanier, also the fellows from this particular school band in Chicago: George Wettling, Teschemacher, all that bunch. Well, all those was young, even some of Oliver's fellows was young, and they used to come over and listen.

Now I'm not going to be prejudiced and say they didn't have any good white musicians 'cos Teschemacher was good, very good, and in fact he was ahead of Benny Goodman. The first time I saw Goodman play he was in knee pants, just put on long pants in order to play the gig, at the Fiume, a place on 35th and State — right in the Black Belt, if I may say so. So these fellows could play. And when Paul Mares came up they became famous, in clubs and on records. They recorded originally for Gennett, and Joe Oliver's band was recording too for Gennett at about that time.

As you've no doubt read it was the breaks Joe and Louis played together that had the musicians wondering. Whenever Joe made a break, Louis would be right there with the second to it, and he never missed. And people couldn't understand that. But Louis Armstrong was a genius. You see, Louis — when he played with Fate Marable on the Streckfus boats — had the first part put on him one day when the first trumpet player was taken sick. And that's when they found out he couldn't read music, because he had been fakin' the second part all that while. When I worked with Louis I said he had a photographic mind; he'd just play something one time, then turn it over. He had it, see? The man was a genius.

Anyway, getting back to Joe, Louis finally left him to go with Fletcher Henderson, and Lil was the cause of that by telling him he'd never amount to anything playing second. So that's history. By now it is late in '24, and for Joe Oliver here comes a new breed. He sent for Albert Nicholas, Barney Bigard, Paul Barbarin and Luis Russell. They worked there a while with Joe but the place caught on fire on Christmas Eve, and that put 'em out of a job. But Joe was a good hustler, good businessman, and I don't understand how he went down. It just escapes me how he didn't do better in later life. Only thing I can attribute it to is that he didn't leave Chicago early enough. He was the type of fellow that if he didn't have a job he'd take him one; he didn't stay idle for long. So at this time he went to work with Dave Peyton's band, and it wasn't long before he was leader of this band. Then he takes this band into the Plantation Café. Besides the Plantation you had the Sunset like here, and the Nest right across the street. And now I'll have to bring in Doctor Cooke's band and mention Charles Elgar, at places such as the Riverview Park, where they used large bands, fifteen pieces and so on. Doc Cooke, he had a big band at Harmon's Dreamland, and in this band, from New Orleans or nearby, was Freddie Keppard, Joe Poston, Jimmie Noone and Andrew Hilaire. You probably never heard Hilaire but he was one of the best drummers that ever lived. He played vibraharp, everything. Good musician. As for Jimmie Noone, whenever he got off work at 12 o'clock he'd go over to the Nest. And you could go on down the line. So, anyhow, it just show you the hold the New Orleans musicians had.

MJ: Was there some other cause for antagonism?

PJ: Yes, there was a little hostility. However, everything went along nice until the New Orleans musicians began to fight among themselves, which I'll say the Chicago musicians welcomed. As far as theatres went, the work was safe for Chicago musicians, as I've said. It was just the cabarets, cafés and probably the dances that we had sewn-up. Otherwise it was safe for them.

MJ: What were working conditions like for you at that time?

PJ: It depended on where you were working but generally it was hard, especially when you had a show to play. Joe Oliver always hired him a man who was good enough, as we called it, to cut that show. That floor show would be an hour-and-a-half long, and by the time them chorus girls come on and take a bow and come back and dance an encore, you've played maybe about twenty-five more choruses.

So Bob Shoffner, he'd come up to Joe's band behind Louis, something happened to his lip after a year or two and he went to St Louis and had it operated on. But his tone was never the same again; which it was good but much smaller. And then Tick Gray, he ran in there. He was nothing but a kid, and something happened to him; so he got that he couldn't play above the staff. With Louis it had been different, it wasn't as hard a work because they wasn't playing for shows; they was just playing for dancing. When you was playing shows you had to, what we called, pound plenty. I mean you'd play that first section, then you'd play a dance, have a short intermission, then show time and you're right up there again to play another section. So when you played both sections, there's no way to go but start over and play that first section again. And durin' that time there were fellows working from 9 o'clock until five, like I worked with Carroll Dickerson at the Grand Terrace; we went to work at ten and got off at five. It's so much better now ... five days a week and they have off-night bands play them other two nights, and they still get paid for seven. But in those days we went into that place in the evening and when we came out it was daybreak. And a lot of times we'd be very fortunate if we didn't have a rehearsal too, because the producer thought there was something wrong with the show.

MJ: Can we turn to the subject of Armstrong the bandleader, in the Sunset and on records with the Hot Five? And his success with *Heebie Jeebies* which was reported to have sold 40,000 copies within a few weeks of release on OKeh. Kid Ory said it was Louis's scatting that made the disc a hit. [At this point, Preston broke into a spirited rendering of that vocal.]

PJ: Yeah, *Heebie Jeebies* ... They were makin' the record, see? And the music fell and he didn't have time to pick it up. I wasn't there in the studio but it was told to me that he had the lyrics up on the music rack, and they dropped, you know, and so he just went on. He had to do a vocal, and that was the next thing he could think of. So that was the beginning of the scat.

JC: You never heard him scat before that? Or sing with Oliver's band?

PJ: No, never did, no. But in Joe's band he played one of those slide whistles, played it very well too. Now, to the Sunset Café. Louis went in there with Carroll Dickerson's big band, 1926, and Joe Glaser was manager of the place; in fact his mother owned the building. After a time Joe and Dickerson agreed to disagree. It seems like a certain movie star went to the ladies' room, and naturally the men's room and the women's room was adjacent to one another, and the wall between them, it didn't quite reach to the ceiling.

So Carroll was in there and he threw what we call a grenade in this profession — that's a note — over the wall and the wrong person got hold to it. This was a movie star and she told her husband about it, and he told Joe. It ended up in a fight between the two, and he fired Carroll and gave the band to Louis. That's the first beginning of Louis Armstrong being a bandleader.

And now, at the Sunset, we begin to see Miff Mole, Red Nichols and others of the Five Pennies, Bing Crosby . . . oh, many of the top flights. Some of them used to make the trip to Chicago just to hear him. Louis began then to gather momentum, you understand what I'm talkin' about, *as* Louis Armstrong. And his records on the OKeh was speaking for him too. So Louis stayed there quite a while, through most of 1927 I'll say, while continuing to work with people such as Erskine Tate and Clarence Jones. Meanwhile they're building the Regal Theatre and the Savoy Ballroom in Chicago, and right across the street was the Metropolitan. Tate has moved from the Vendome to the Metropolitan.

The Regal opened up, and Charles Elgar opens up at the Savoy and he does what the others been doing; he reached down in New Orleans and brought Perez up, and another — a saxophone player by the name of Eddie Cherie. About this time, Earl Hines, Louis and Zutty Singleton decided to go into business and have their own band at their own club. And the first dance they put on happened to be the same night as the opening of the Savoy Ballroom, so you can imagine what happened. Everybody wanted to go to the new place. That ended the business with Earl and Zutty, and Louis went with Dickerson in the Savoy. As I heard it, Carroll some time or another saw the management of the Savoy and they agreed to hire him for a matinée. Well, they went in on that matinée and blew Charlie Elgar out of the hall.

Now we're coming near the end of the Chicago story. They got a new mayor, you may remember — I don't know whether I should call his name — and he began to put pressure on. It was alleged the man was shootin' at President Roosevelt but no one believes that, because when them gangsters get ready to get you they get you; they hire some people to get you, pay 'em to do that, so we never thought he was trying to kill Roosevelt. Anyhow, they put the lid on the place and this started the jazz migration to New York. This mayor, as you might have read, was assassinated in Florida.

I know you all read about Louis in New York. Things finally got bad in

Chicago, attendances fell off, and that's when Louis and Dickerson, Zutty and all made their move. Loaded all their instruments and things into those old cars — you may have heard of Louis's old jalopy — and they made their move to New York.

Now I want to come up to 1930 and my own involvement with Louis. In the meantime I'd been with Weatherford, played in Milwaukee, been at the Michigan with Erskine Tate and the Regal with Dave Peyton. Now I'm playing at the Savoy, one night only, and at intermission I'm standing up against the wall, meditating I'd say. I happen to look up and there's Louis Armstrong. He say: 'Hi, Nosey.' He called me Nosey all the time and I'd call him Nosey. I'd do like that [a gesture], and he'd do like this to me. So we talk and he says: 'I just left Connie's Inn and I'm going out to Sebastian's in Hollywood to front Les Hite's band. I'll be back in three months and you're my man.'

So I didn't think any more about it. I was happy to hear him say that because I'd really advanced. I'd been in the theatre and also rehearsed with this band of World War One veterans every Sunday for two years. We had four trombones, you know, and all this brass-band music, it came in handy. So within a few months Louis was back and looking for me — for two weeks. There's people at the Union knew my address, but due to the jealousy of some people he had difficulty contacting me. Finally Charlie Alexander, the pianist, located me for him; I lived right around the corner.

We rehearsed about two weeks and then opened up at the Showboat, where we stayed about a month, broadcasting every night. And that was a terrible place; that's when Louis had some trouble. You see that man had a whole lot of trouble, of different natures. Now ... we're there, and Louis had left Tommy Rockwell — he's with John Collins now, see? When he left the Connie's Inn he had some kind of dispute about management. Now he gets a phone call one night from New York, and as he enters the booth a gangster puts a gun in his stomach and tells him he's going back to New York. Louis told him he wasn't. Well, he didn't shoot Louis. But thereafter, a squad brought Louis to work, and they brought him home.

After a little while we were approached by the manager of the Suburban Gardens in New Orleans to play a residency. We left Chicago and picked up Zilner Randolph, another trumpet player and the writer of *Ole Man Mose*. He was an arranger, you know, and in charge of the band during the absence of Louis. We did one-nighters in Michigan, in Ohio and Kentucky; we was filling in until the time to go on this job, you understand, and we was drawing nice crowds. Finally we left Louisville, Kentucky, for New Orleans on the L and N, and that's the time all those bands met us at the station — it was a regular parade. As you know, musicians in New Orleans love parades; the people there always was crazy about music. Now we're due to open at the Suburban Gardens but before that this Rockwell, he's on Louis — Louis has broken a contract. So we're called down to the local Union and questioned. There wasn't anything done about it but then they's making announcements over the air about 'the niggers comin' down to New Orleans and taking the white musicians' jobs', and then we were followed every night by a car with three or four guys in it. .

While we were up there at the Suburban something else happened. I've already related how Zilner Randolph had charge of the band while Louis was upstairs resting. So Zilner was leading us on a waltz and this woman kept dancing past us — she was intoxicated, I'd say — and finally she grabbed Randolph by the hand. He kept trying to get his hand loose, and this frightened us, particularly me. We were right up on the levee, where the Suburban was situated, and we could hear the water. All the coloured people was out there on the protection levee because they couldn't come in. Well, there was some 'passed' that came in, because we recognised 'em, but they had to be light-skinned. But the rest was on the levee to hear what they could through the windows; we could hear them, and this water splashing.

They'd had trouble there before, and we didn't know how these people would take it, and it frightened me — I know because my teeth began to chatter, although I was born in that section. But it still was the South and people came into this particular place from Florida, Arkansas and all adjacent states. However, they take it good-naturedly. It had taken Randolph about a minute to get his hand loose, and that's a long time in a situation like that. But it seem like it was fun to them. They knew that he was frightened and they knew it wasn't his fault, and then we went from that waltz into something different. I don't remember what it was but Tubby [Hall] went into a faster tempo and we played out the set — don't know what I was playin' or what the other fellers was playin', we all was scared, but anyway we ended and got in line and went upstairs. Louis ask what's the matter and I say 'Man, a white woman not only grab Randolph by the hand but wouldn't turn him loose'. Then the manager follows up and says: 'It's all right, boys. Everybody knows it wasn't none of Randolph's fault.' But it seems we're beginning to have trouble.

MJ: And what of the first night when, according to Louis, the station announcer said he hadn't the heart to announce him on the radio?

PJ: If Louis said that, it's true. Well, the guy says he wasn't going to announce no nigger, and he didn't. So Louis did his own announcing from then on. Anyhow, after three months there John Collins decided to give a dance with our band, and that would have been some dance, believe me. But it never came off. That night, Rampart Street and neighbouring streets was loaded with people in carts and flivvers, running all up and down the street, the whole area just crowded, you know. Now he'd rented a big warehouse for this farewell dance and when the time came for it to start, the governor wouldn't let him in. The doors was locked.

MJ: This was Southern politics?

PJ: Yes, and what makes me think it was political; there was a fellow by the name of Beansy, he had what you call a hotel — a hotel and gambling establishment, with also a bit of prostitution combined — and I heard he was trying to hire the band for a dance, and he was refused. So now there's trouble facing us.

When we leave New Orleans we go to Texas, we play six weeks there and cross over into Tulsa, Oklahoma, and we play Oklahoma City. Then we doubles right back over the same territory — and that's when we ran into Joe

Oliver and his band, down on the bay. Now Mrs Collins was in the bus with us, and at different intervals they'd switch the lights on to see what was goin' on between Louis and Mrs Collins — they must have thought they was sweethearts or somethin' you know — and so that went on all the way to Memphis.

It was somewhere around 7.30 or 8 o'clock when we hit Memphis, and there this superintendant told us: 'Well, get them niggers out of here because I have to put them in another bus.' Now the other bus was much smaller and more inconvenient, so Mrs Collins told them she'd paid 50 dollars difference in these buses so the boys could enjoy themselves. After a hassle of about ten minutes he told the driver to drive the bus on round to the terminal, which he did. And it looked like half the Memphis police force met us there.

'All right you niggers, get out here,' they said. 'You're in Memphis now, and we need some cotton-pickers, too.' So they put us all in jail except Mike McKendrick, I don't know where he got out of the bus, and all them boys had pistols which they shedded, got rid of the pistols 'cos they didn't want to be caught with 'em. On Rampart Street at that time you could buy a pistol just as easy as a loaf of bread. So they put us all in the jailhouse; I was first in line and something told me not to tell these people I was from Chicago because it would probably go extra hard with me. So they said: 'What's your name' and I told them. 'Where you live?' 'New Orleans.' So then everybody followed suit.

And after the desk sergeant had taken all the names, this Zilner Randolph was standing around and one policeman said: 'I'm going to tell you right now, you niggers, you ain't gonna come down to Memphis and try to run the city. We'll kill all you niggers.' But he'd had a call and was leaving, and we was glad he was leaving. So Zilner went over and looked out of the window, and this police said: 'Get away from that window, nigger,' and reached for his gun and Randolph walked on away.

They put us all in one big cell, and a guy came through, say: 'Louis, I heard you fellers over in Houston last week.' Well, we didn't care where he heard us; we wanted to get out of jail and make Little Rock. Now we'd doubled back to play the Palace Theatre in Memphis, so we were bailed out by the Palace management and made the train and arrived in Little Rock at 11 o'clock. We played there from eleven until two, then they held the train up for us and we went on back to Memphis and broadcast that morning from the hotel.

I know you heard about that programme when he dedicated a song to the police. Some of the policemen was there, that I'd seen the day before, and finally Louis said: 'Ladies and gentlemen, I'm now goin' to dedicate this tune to the Memphis Police Force: *I'll Be Glad When You're Dead You Rascal You*.' Now whether Louis meant well by it or meant it as a slur, I don't know. We did play the song and after the broadcast they all made a dash towards us, 'bout ten or twelve of them. There was nowhere for us to run or we would have ran, you know. But they told us, says: 'You're the first band that ever dedicated a tune to the Memphis Police.' So we got out of that and finished the tour.

JC: And in New York you finally disbanded?

PJ: Right. The beginning of the end is coming now. Here comes one of the greatest battles I ever saw. We plays the Metropolitan in Boston, and I'll say it's early in '32, or the Christmas of 1931. And afterwards we played a battle of music against Fletcher Henderson's Band and the Casa Loma Band.

Now the Casa Loma, I believe in giving credit where it's due, these boys had been in an accident: one had his head all tied up and another had hurt his leg, and so on. But that didn't stop them from playing, and do you know people still talk about that battle of jazz after all these years? Those guys battled and the people, a large crowd, I thought they'd go crazy. And finally Louis played the *Tiger Rag* and he had us count 300 high Cs, then hit that altissimo F up there, and that was it.

But, as far as the band, we were no match for Fletcher Henderson, he was a band. And these Casa Lomas, they had hold of McKinney's in Philadelphia and turned them every way but loose, and McKinney's with Don Redman, Claude Jones . . . they had a band, so you can imagine. You see, the band Louis had was just a band to back him, that's what we did — played the riffs and things behind him. We had arrangements, too, but we wasn't like the average band.

So eventually we came back into New York and that's when we made that cartoon short on Long Island Astoria. We were there all day long with those hot lights shining on us. Now we didn't see Collins for two weeks past, and we got about six, seven hundred dollars coming, due to recordings and makin' this film. On about the third week he showed up and paid us. Now the people wanted us back at the Suburban Gardens and wanted us in place of Les Hite's Band, but these things never came off and the band broke up.

The reason, I believe, is that Louis was an easy-going fellow who left everything to his manager, accountin' and everything, and I don't think that was right. Now in Texas, in Houston the first night, we played to 12,000 people. Louis always taken his manager's word; I'm not sayin' Collins was cheating him, either, but it was foolish of him not to check. I remember, too, when we was staying at the hotel in New Orleans at 6 o'clock he wouldn't let anybody bother him until then, he'd come out of the rooms and there's a queue of people half a block long on both sides of the hallway, and he's passin' out money just like that. That happened the whole three months we was there. He bought 'em baseball suits and caps, bought 'em radios, and he bought radios and things for the Waifs' Home where he'd been one time, and they named a cigar after him, the Louis Armstrong Special or some Special. That's how he was.

JC: Did you sit-in with any bands while you were there, or meet any of your old friends?

PJ: Yeah, yeah. I remember Paul Mares one night, he invited us back to his home. He had some nice home brew, and he had some gumbo; we had a real good time back there. I mean, there's some Southerners like that; it have to be some man that don't give a damn — excuse my expression — who'll go to bat for you. You understand what I'm talking about?

MJ: We've heard a lot about Armstrong, how he appears to have impressed you when you were a kid and obviously not very interested in jazz. Do you know why that was?

PJ: Well, after thinking about it, I guess I didn't pay too much attention, but the thing that impressed me perhaps more than the music was his bearing. I had to be impressed in this manner, because he was outstanding; there was the way he carried himself, like somebody bragging and all, and saying 'Look, I am good'. If you see the old pictures, that's the way I first saw him. So naturally, when I heard of him again, the boys was comin' up to Chicago from New Orleans and talkin' about Louis Armstrong this and Louis Armstrong that. See, after Joe left, Louis'd taken his place with Ory's band. So I'd be telling 'em about Joe, how he was blowin', and they'd say: 'Oh, but he can't play with Louis Armstrong.' And I'd have an argument, say there ain't anybody in New Orleans could play as much as Joe Oliver. But I found out better. 'Course they had different styles. Joe had large hands, he was a large man, and that little mute — he made it do all kinds of things. He made it cry like a baby. There was a tune they called *Eccentric* and they was taking breaks in there. Bill Johnson did the talking, and the baby would go something like 'wah-wow, ah-wow', you know. So that was the baby figuring on jus' when he was going to cry. So finally he would cry, yow-ow-ow, one of those things, and Bill would say: 'Hush, baby, hush baby.' Joe was great with that mute. Louis was great with the open horn.

Now Freddie Keppard, a big man, was very powerful too. You see, this Harmon's Dreamland was a large place and the elevated trains ran right over it. That's why they needed a 26-piece band, needed that volume, and Keppard — you could hear him for about a mile — he was awful strong, and one of the best trumpet players in my opinion.

MJ: Looking back now, over a long life in jazz, how would you rate Armstrong as a player and an original? How high overall?

PJ: I may be a bit prejudiced 'cos as I afore said, that man was the cause of my bein' in Europe today. I made other records of course but those recordings with him, I'd say, made my reputation almost entirely and are the cause of my being here with this band. I could of been here with Armstrong's band, of course, but I was in the Prudence business and couldn't clear things up in time to join him, so I didn't join him. And I never played with him again. So, in answer to your question, I think Louis is the greatest trumpet player that ever lived.

Now I never heard Buddy Bolden, but I'm sure he wasn't in the same category as Louis. 'Cos Louis, the ideas that came forth from him, well, you can hardly find a good player that doesn't play some part of what Armstrong had already done. Now another good friend of mine, Roy Eldridge, I've read where he as good as said he didn't get anything from Louis, that he always did play fast like a saxophone. Roy do have his own distinctive style, same as Dizzy has, but it's hard to believe that he, or any other trumpet player, hasn't used something, some phrase, some time or another, that was originated by Louis Armstrong.

Thomas Jefferson

The New Orleans trumpet star Thomas Jefferson paid his first visit to Britain in the winter of 1973/4. He came back since, of course, frequently with Sammy Rimington the clarinet and alto player. In January 1974, Jefferson played a session at London's 100 Club with a local band, denying (as he left the band stand) that he was any kind of star: 'I'm a band man — just aim to fit right in with them. And they played right alongside me. I'm no star; don't want to show off.'

His relaxed, disciplined, often stomping lead part illustrated clearly what he meant by being a band player. He got round the instrument well but without exhibition. His singing, too, was to the point and devoid of ingratiating show-manship. As I had expected from records, his style showed the effects of his early immersion in the music of Louis Armstrong. But neither the trumpet nor vocalising was directly in the Louis manner, though it reflected an almighty admiration.

In conversation, Jefferson touched early upon the subject of Satch, saying he'd found that people expected a New Orleans trumpeter such as he to sing like Armstrong. So he had obliged on various sessions but now wished to sing like himself. The results of a recording he made on Wednesday last week confirm that he does sound like himself, with a bow to God.

'Did you know that I'm a cousin of Louis Armstrong? 'he asked. He speaks with a strong Southern accent, so that a quick reference to *Milenburg Joys*, say, may have you asking him to repeat the name, and calls his idol "Lewis".

'Yeah, a cousin; he was related on my mother's side. And like him I spent part of my early life in the Jones Home for Waifs, taken in by a policeman who didn't like me.'

Why was he sent to the Colored Waifs' Home? The same reason, he said, that so many youngsters were arrested and sent to reform school. 'You know, we used to go swimming in the Basin and this particular policeman on a horse would catch you and send you up there.'

Jefferson's stay 'back o' Jones' would have been in the early Thirties, nearly twenty years after Louis was sentenced to an indefinite term in the Home for Boys. But he was coached on French horn and trumpet by the same warden, Professor Peter Davis, that taught Louis to play snare drum and bugle and finally cornet. Jefferson didn't get his musical start there, however. He learned music from singing in the Baptist Church, and thinks he might have remained a churchman and choir singer had it not been for his wayward temperament.

'Oh yes, I was the singin'est boy in church but I put some tacks on the choirgirls' seats and when they sat down they all cried out in unison. They put me out of the church for that.'

The trumpeter laughed as though it had been worth the expulsion, even allowing for the walloping he got.

'When those girls cried out all at the same time, 'course I really laughed. The deacon grabbed me by the hair and took me outside and slapped me. Good and proper.

'Do you know, I met him in San Francisco when I was up there with Kid Ory in the late Fifties. But after he'd slapped me I couldn't stand him.

'Of course, I was genuinely mischievous in those days, used to shout back at the preacher. He was the Reverend Thornton, I remember. He's dead now.

'Anyway they put me out for those tacks, and people at home still laugh about that — still ask me when I'm coming back to church. So that's how I went out into the world and got into music professionally.'

To clear up the matter of Jefferson's age: reference books give his birth date as 1923 but he told me he was born in Chicago on 21 June 1921, 'three years after World War One ended'. He is from New Orleans but his family was in Chicago at the time. He first became interested in the bugle at St Mark's Fourth Baptist Church, and used to blow bugle in scout Troop 121. That in turn led to an ambition to play cornet. But how to acquire one?

'My mother wouldn't buy me one for a long time, thought I was too puny to play it. I was so skinny then. So I used Raymond Randolph's cornet. He couldn't play it but had one. And I could play it.

'Eventually my mama got me one from the store. I cried for that instrument, you know. Right in that store. I could cry, too. I always had long wind.

'You see, although my mother had bought it she didn't take it out of the store that day, wanted to surprise me. I thought she wasn't going to get it, so I fell on the floor crying. Oh, cried so much that the owner's son, he still remembers that.

'How much do you think that cornet cost? Sixty-five dollars, a lot of money at that time when things were so bad. But she paid for it, anyhow, and I got my cornet.

'And I could play. As I say, I was blowing any kind of trumpet I could lay hands on. I was a head player, you know, played by ear, and where did I learn? Right in the back yard.

'I went in all the Baptist churches, playing cornet solos, and they got my picture there at St Mark's when I was a boy. They keep all those things, like all our sports trophies.'

Another of Jefferson's ambitions was to be an athlete, and he assured me he showed much promise — at baseball, football, basket-ball and track games.

'I used to run the hundred yards, also hurdle, and I was a pitcher and star basket-ball player. I was fast, an A.1. athlete. Maybe that's why I got so much wind.

'And then basket-ball, all that stretching. It sounds funny, but maybe that helped me get so tall. I was skinny and cunning and those boys had a job catching me. They called me the Fox, and the Rabbit sometimes.

'You know the bullies, they'd often run you after a game and they could be rough. I used to say "Catch me," and I was gone. That's all they saw of me. I was smart. I met one of those bullies later and he said: "Man, you was the runningest cat I ever saw."'

Thomas Jefferson's first real jazz job came during the Mardi Gras celebrations — of 1934 he thought.

'Dee Dee Pierce was ill that Mardi Gras Day and I got the gig. He had a lingering sickness all his life, poor Dee Dee, and then he used to drink a lot. But he was there in a chair and he'd pass the kitty, which was a cigar box, and it was over-filled with tips. We'd take it back and divide the money, then pass it out again. When we finished I had more money that Carnival Day than I'd ever had before. I remember the job was 5 dollars apiece and your tips, which was good money anyhow. And we took about 45 bucks apiece. That was at the Kingfish Bar. One of the jazz places not mentioned in the histories.

'They had me in kind of regularly after that. I was a little boy still and Billie Pierce was mad about me. I had a little, light voice but I could sing. And play all right. They put me up on beer boxes because I was so young.'

By the time he was sixteen, Thomas (who is the younger brother of drummer-vocalist Andrew Jefferson) was a regular member of Papa Celestin's band. He worked with the Lafon Brass Band and later in a dance orchestra led by Sidney Desvigne. He was with Desvigne on the riverboat *S.S. President,* also on the boat with Piron's band. This was followed by work with Jimmy Davis, Jump Jackson and John Casimer, also some TV dates. From the late Forties on, Jefferson has been resident at the Paddock bar at 309 Bourbon Street. After touring with a band such as George Lewis's or Ory's he returned home to the Paddock, and that's where he went back to when he left here on Monday.

'This May coming will be twenty-seven years I've been there. I'd have been there thirty-seven years or something if I hadn't taken time off. I replaced Kid Howard in the Lewis band in 1956 and stayed about two years, recording with him and touring extensively. Then I went with Ory and visited Europe for the first time.'

He mentioned the youthful-looking photograph of him we published in our 5 January issue, and commented:

'That picture was taken at the Beverly Cavern right on Beverly Boulevard, Yeah, fine engagement that, packed and jammed every night for George's band. Did I tell you Lewis was in that band of Dee Dee's I played with on that 1934 Mardi Gras?'

It seems that Jefferson played trumpet with Ory for some two years and more, but for reasons not known to me did not record with him. He said he worked with the trombonist at his San Francisco club, On The Levee, and did the European tour with the band.

'That was beautiful. I was on that package with Louis and the All Stars, also Dizzy Gillespie. Velma Middleton was on that, which was the last time I saw that girl before she died. After leaving Ory I went back to New Orleans and worked at the Paddock.'

Today, Thomas is enthusiastic about his job at the Paddock Lounge. It is regular work six nights of the week before a crowd well seasoned with tourists. The band is called Thomas Jefferson's Creole Dixieland Jazz Band, and what it's called is what it plays.

'It's a Dixieland place and we feature typical numbers in that style: *Wolverine Blues, Tishomingo, Milenburg* and *Muskrat Ramble.*

'The line-up is trumpet, alto doubling clarinet, piano drums and bass, and the most business is tourists, you know, like the conventions in town. Officially there's no dancing but they sneak and do it between the tables. Say, they have to dance some when I play; they can't sit down.'

As you can perhaps imagine, this bearer of an illustrious Virginian name has innumerable tales to tell — of working with Preston Jackson and Franz Jackson at the Red Arrow in Chicago, of playing alongside Sammy Rimington in Europe and on a London record date, of being the first black outfit to play the Famous Door in Chicago. Well, I'd heard that Miles Davis, of all people, replaced Jefferson in one band. Is that true? Jefferson nodded and said he had to have an operation during 1944 and went home for it.

'The band hired Miles around August that year. Oh, I knew him. I met him in Springfield, Illinois and that's why they hired him. He was playing a lot of trumpet. And Miles liked the way I played, too. He told me so.'

I don't see that I can follow that.

Jonah Jones

When I met Jonah Jones in June 1971, it wasn't the first time he had been to Britain. He had passed through the country for five days the previous year, with his wife Elizabeth, in the course of the European vacation. But on that occasion he hadn't got in touch with anyone 'in the business'. As he said, 'Louis Armstrong told me to get in touch with Melody Maker *but I didn't think you people would want to be bothered with me.' He was wrong, of course, as he found out on his second visit, with many British enthusiasts wanting to be bothered with one of the great names of trumpet jazz.*

At the time I spoke to him he was leading a quintet, although one that functioned in the same way as the Jones quartet that brought him fame and fortune in the mid Fifties. In his band were pianist Lannie Scott, bassist John Brown, guitarist Jerome Darr and drummer Cozy Cole. Jonah described it as a tight swinging little group. All the men except Scott (who replaced Sonny White who had recently died) had been with him since 1968, and Brown, the original bassist with the group, since before that.

At the beginning of his new career with a 'muted jazz' quartet, which he formed in the latter part of 1955, Jonah's band played long residencies in New York, and had a featured TV spot on NBC's Fred Astaire Show. *By the time I talked to him things had changed somewhat.*

'Over the past two years we've been getting around more,' said Jonah. 'We got to Honolulu in January of 1970 and after six weeks there we went on to Bangkok to work a new hotel! We do a lot of work for Western International Hotels, and they sent us out there. In Honolulu, of course, we saw Trummy Young who was next door to us at the Hilton. He was sure playing some rock with that group he's got. Also we met Kid Ory, a pleasure for me.

'It seems that Western don't have a hotel here, which is a pity. I'd like to come over since I've never worked in Britain and always heard so much about it from musicians like Hawkins and Louis. Hawk would tell me about coming over here in the Thirties and playing with Jack Hylton's band. He used to say he only had to do a couple of numbers in the first half of the show and maybe two in the second.

'I was brought up on England, you know, from talking to fellows like that and musicians who'd been over. If I ever arranged to play here I'd want to bring my own group. You see, we're like an act. Cozy and his drum spots and Jerome, he's a very good guitar player. Yes, he's the only guitar I've had in the group. Everyone's using guitar so I thought I would too.

'We're not strictly a jazz group. We swing, we have some very fine soloists, but we don't go too far out. We have a kind of formula, and people know us by that. Like the shuffle rhythm on certain tunes.'

It was, I suggested, basically dance music. Jonah agreed, adding that it was for dancing, listening or even not listening: "just having a good time to." At fiirst, when he went into the soft-swinging style so well suited to the Embers in New York, he was disconcerted if people didn't listen. But he got used to it, and continued to blow soft. His manager and mentor, Sam Berg, who looks after his goodwill with rare dedication, taught him that he should concentrate on playing whatever he was playing to the utmost of his ability at all times. Jonah learned the lesson well, got long-term contracts at the Embers and with Capitol Records, and notched up an audience of millions for his TV appearances. The necessity for mutes at the Embers troubled him most.

'I always prided myself on my tone, that big open sound, and I felt it was stupid to put mutes in all the time. I used seven different mutes at one time, and soon got used to playing that way.

'What I say is, we go in as a show group — that's our job. There's no dancing at the Embers, so we play shows there. We do the popular numbers and they like us. You know, snap your fingers and pat your foot. It's okay. At the Rainbow Grill, where we often play, we do a slightly different thing for a little dancing. But there's not much dancing where we work.'

And the singing, how did that come about? Jonah grinned and said it was accidental.

'I didn't want to sing on those Capitol records; it was Dave Cavanaugh's idea. I used to do the odd vocal, like with Stuff Smith in the Onyx Club days, but I didn't count that. You know, in Stuff's band you might have done anything. Anyway, I'd try something like *St James Infirmary* and Dave would put one or two on the records. The critics didn't like it much but Dave told me: "The singing's not too bad."'

I guessed that Jonah's sudden success had surprised him. 'You never can say which way things are going in this business. Like myself, I had no idea it was going to happen for me.' He shook his head incredulously. 'With bebop on the scene and people turning to rock-and-roll I couldn't have made it no way, wouldn't have bet ten cents on it. But here it come.

'Truthfully, things got so rough I was thinking of giving up music and getting a day job. Then Sammy Berg came to me and said I was crazy to think of quitting. He's a nice cat. He said: "Get you a rhythm section and let's see what I can do for you." He started working and came up with one night at the

Embers. I went in there with John Brown, Harold Austin, drums (a swinger) and a pianist named Bill Austin, used to be with Louis Jordan. One thing led to another, and we worked at the Embers off and on about nine years.

'So I've worked hard for sixteen years with that mute in, but the dues are good. It's made up for everything I missed out on. I didn't know there was this much money in the business, not until we started making those hit albums.'

Certainly the money was good. Instead of the hundred bucks or so a man might make in a big band Jonah began to earn hefty royalties from hit singles like *On The Street Where You Live* and *Baubles, Bangles and Beads* and record albums such as *Jonah Jumps Again* and *Swingin' At The Cinema*. In the spring of 1959, three of the top ten jazz LPs in the US charts were by the Jones Quartet. Figures in the region of £2,000 a night were asked in Europe that same year for the group. Jonah became a business corporation with the indefatigable Berg at the helm, and the former Lunceford–Stuff Smith–Carter–Henderson–Calloway bandsman continued to rack up earnings by the hundred thousand instead of the straight hundred dollars.

'I like to travel and my wife does, too. Previously she couldn't get around so much because of the children, but now I can bring her along.

'Music changes, as we know, and I like to listen to what the kids are playing. I made this album where they put me with the Motown sound and I kinda like it. I found everyone was very nice. What they wanted me to do, I said: "Put it on the paper and I'll play it." So then I put that down with the rhythm section and they added whatever else they liked afterwards.'

Listening to Jonah Jones on records by Teddy Wilson, Stuff Smith and others in the Thirties, I realised he was at least partly inspired by Armstrong, and in fact his conversation turns often to the man he idolised as a boy. Talking of his present-day show, for example, he said at one point: 'Then I sing a few — *Mack The Knife* and *Blueberry Hill* maybe. And you know that's influenced by Pops. Well, loving him so much I try to do everything like him.

'Louis could do no wrong. That guy was like God to me. He had everything: tone, technique, feeling. But that tone he had, all of us tried to duplicate it, everyone coming up then, but not one of us could get that.'

Max Kaminsky

I first heard Max Kaminsky in the Boston-bred flesh when he was over in England with the Earl Hines–Jack Teagarden band. He caused a certain amount of eyebrow-lifting by proving himself able to sound more like Louis Armstrong than most of us had expected. Often in those days Maxie spoke about Louis, and when I met him twelve years later at London's Dorchester Hotel in March 1970 — during a brief holiday in Britain with his wife — the subject soon cropped up. Louis had been into Jimmy Ryan's to hear Kaminsky's band; Max said how well he had looked and how alert he had seemed.

'I've been listening to this guy since I started playing, you know, and he has always been very nice to me. Of course, you had to admire Louis if you took up that instrument. Any trumpet player who plays well has to take something from Armstrong.

'Sure, he is famous now. But I still don't think he's got the appreciation he deserves. Maybe in a hundred or two years from now they'll know how great he really was. That purity that came out of him, that great classical playing; how many could have done that. It's pure genius. And he has such a genius that he can play with anybody, always could play in any company, and make it come out great. I'll tell you, without him I don't think jazz would ever have been popular.

'Yes, Louis and Bix, the two that inspired me most. Bix is the only one I heard, after Louis, that had that gift. You know what I'm talking about? Who were really that exceptional.'

'The reason I got that job with Teagarden, which brought me here in '57, was because Louis recommended me. It seems that Tea was going through some names with Joe Glaser, deciding what trumpet player to use. They mentioned Wingy, you know, and two or three more, then my name came up and Louis said: "Get him." Naturally I was flattered.'

Max remembered the time when he knew Louis was listening and pulled out all his best Armstrong stuff. Afterwards Louis stopped by. 'Very similar,' he pronounced. As it happens, I had heard from Ernie Anderson (Armstrong publicist of the time) that when Maxie's band was playing the first half of the show in Washington, Louis used to sit in his dressing room with the speaker turned up, listening attentively.

Nowadays, Kaminsky is a regular at Jimmy Ryan's where he has led a Dixieland group for some years. He appears to be contented with a job on which he can play as he feels.

'I like to play,' he explained, 'more now perhaps, than ever before. I just feel better about playing. Sometimes I even like what comes out. Really I've worked pretty steadily since I saw you last. Did some touring for the State Department and led bands at various places, including the Metropole and Condon's and at the World's Fair and various festivals.

'A good thing about the job at Ryan's is that we play well, the kind of music I like in the right sort of surroundings. There's no other club in New York featuring that kind of music regularly. Ryan's is a jazz club pure and simple. They don't serve any food or anything. People come in and have a whisky and listen to the band. They want to have a drink and hear that kind of jazz, so we don't have to play any stuff like *By The Time I Get To Phoenix*. Maybe proper jazz isn't all that popular now. I don't worry much about that, because it never was really popular. Certainly not when I started playing it. I had to work in society bands to keep going. But I always did like to play it and I'm still very interested. So I keep working on playing and that satisfies me. I just let it go at that.'

Although he has worked with a large number of New Orleans or Chicago style groups, and is thought of by many collectors as a small-band lead man,

Kaminsky has had quite a bit of big-band experience. And enjoyed much of it, especially spells with the mid-Thirties Tommy Dorsey and Artie Shaw orchestras. Today, Maxie looks back on the big-band era as a healthy period in music. A time when swing music, on the whole, was good and had a reasonably large following.

'People often ask me why there aren't the big bands now like there used to be.' He pointed out, as an aside, that he was excepting Ellington and Basie who looked like going on for ever. He was talking about popular big bands all the way from Goodman to Glenn Miller. 'I say it's because there aren't any great player-leaders like Artie Shaw, Benny Goodman, Tommy Dorsey to catch the public's imagination. I certainly enjoyed playing in that old Shaw band — I was in the Navy band, too — and I used to get kicks out of Artie's clarinet.'

I had often been told that T.D., excellent player though he was, never regarded himself as a real jazz soloist and looked upon men like Bunny Berigan with a sort of wonderment. Kaminsky half agreed, saying that whoever else Dorsey admired he sure as hell admired Teagarden.

'Years ago they told the story of when Tommy first came to New York. It would be the later Twenties and the guys used to drink at a place they had on 53rd Street called Jimmy Plunkett's.

'Well, the story goes that they were drinking there one day and a fellow said to Tommy: "I want you to hear a trombone player just came into town." They went up to a nearby apartment and there was Jack Teagarden, sitting on the floor playing trombone. They all listened, and afterwards Tommy is supposed to have shaken his head and said: "I never heard anyone play like that." I believe that feeling stuck with him. I know he was crazy about Jack's playing, also about Bud Freeman and Dave Tough.'

I asked Max about plans and present interests. Would he like to play again in Britain? 'Sure,' he answered. 'The only reason I've not been back is because no one asked me. I'd like to come and work with Alex Welsh. Bud and Wild Bill and poor old Red Allen told me he's got a good band. Yes, I've heard some of his records. I'd have no problems playing with them, but if I had the offer I'd get here a week before the opening in order to get properly acquainted.'

Wingy Manone

Wingy Manone looked out of his apartment in London and indicated that the natives were none too friendly. It was towards the end of his first visit to Britain, and the 62-year-old trumpet player was summing up the experience.

'I always wanted to come over, because I knew a lot of people from England. I've enjoyed the playing and the clubs; there's been more enthusiasm than I expected from the jazz crowd. And that Alan Elsdon band is very good. Outside of the jazz people things are different. All I'll say is that I don't dig the restrictions at all, and I don't think the British are very hospitable or friendly. If you speak to them they look at you as if you're a freak or something.'

I suggested that it had something to do with British reserve and politeness. Wingy practically snorted. 'Shoot,' he said (or a word to that effect). 'Sure they're all polite. Too polite to be honest if you ask me.' When we'd done with the British character, I mentioned to Manone that many musicians and fans here had been agreeably surprised by his singing. Wingy was delighted.

'I never tried to sing, you know, but after playing a tune for chorus after chorus we also liked to sing it, to break the monotony. Then we found we could explain the song more by singing than playing. My first vocal on record was *Up The Country*, I think, back in 1927. Do you know that Jack Teagarden didn't sing until he saw me doing it? He was afraid to try — but when he heard me he said: "Shoot, if you got guts enough, why shouldn't I?" I said: "Go ahead, I don't care what you do." And he did.'

I remember that Wingy and Teagarden were associated in a South-western band during the mid-Twenties. Was this about the time they first met?

'Yeah. You'd never have heard of Jack Teagarden but for me. He came out of the desert. Around 1924 I brought him out to the Coast on a train from Albuquerque, New Mexico, and I had to shanghai him to get him on the train. How it happened was that I was out there playing the presentation in a picture house, and I heard there was a good big band around there — Doc Ross and his Cowboy Band — working in a ballroom eight miles out of town. After I'd finished, I went to the ballroom, Silver's, to hear the band, which included Teagarden and clarinettist Bob McCracken. When they found out I was in the ballroom they jumped off the bandstand, came down and threw their arms around me. I sat in and we had a great time. When I was ready to leave, I persuaded Jack to come with me. I took him to Los Angeles, eight hundred miles away, and put him in the band on second trombone. We became good friends.

'What did I think of his playing? I thought he was great, a beautiful player but limited in that he always played the same things. He was not so creative as Miff Mole. I think Miff was the boss; but he used to drink too much. To tell the truth, nearly all those guys in the days I'm talking about used to drink too much. Eventually it hurt their playing. If you want to know who I consider the greatest trombonist playing right now, the answer is: Lou McGarity.'

The arguments over which were the first bands to play jazz, and over the right of the Original Dixieland Jazz Band to bill themselves as 'The Creators Of Jazz', have gone on for three decades already and no doubt will continue for many years to come. In his old age, Nick LaRocca — leader and cornet player — forcefully advanced the claims of his band, the ODJB, as the rightful originators of the new music which resembled ragtime but was something different and distinctive. So far as recorded jazz is concerned, LaRocca's claim to be first is acknowledged and thoroughly authenticated. But what of the less fully charted scene outside the studios? Manone was only twelve or thirteen when the Dixielanders first recorded in 1917. But he was already playing trumpet, and he (like the young Louis Armstrong) interested himself in the wild new music developing around him. The strongest impression he carries of early New Orleans music is, rather surprisingly, one of racial integration or, at any rate, non-segregation.

'It was all mixed up there. Buddy Petit, Sidney Bechet, Freddie Keppard, Bunk Johnson, Nick LaRocca, the Bigards ... we were all in one area. The musicians listened to each other, and sometimes played together in parades. They had to — there weren't enough horn players to go round. The young jazz musicians listened to everyone who came up who could play, white or coloured. I listened to Nick LaRocca before I heard Louis Armstrong. As I say, there was a mixture down there in New Orleans then. And today, black or white don't make no difference to me. I go for the truth or nothing.'

Did Wingy hear much of LaRocca and his band? 'Not so much. I was in short pants, you see, and had to put on long pants to get into places they played — honky tonks and whore houses in the district. They didn't make their name in New Orleans; they didn't even make it in Chicago or New York. They made their name here in London. Then they returned and went to Coney Island. I remember this: Nick had a good tone, and he knew how to swing that lead without getting lost. I got some of the records at home. I'll tell you another thing, the Dixieland Band created all those tunes themselves. You know where from? From operas. Nick took all those different strains from operas and then the band jazzed them up. They were the ones who started it all, if you want to know. Yes, started jazz. I know it, because we heard them before anyone else.'

What about the uptown Negro bands? 'Oh, there were Negro bands. Mostly they played ragtime or spirituals. They listened to *Tiger Rag* or *Lazy Daddy* or those other compositions and put a spiritual touch to them. Then someone like Buddy Petit, Freddie Keppard or Kid Rena would come up with something new and swinging. Every now and then a new trumpet man came up. When he did, everyone knew about it and we'd all go out and hear him. And when the Dixielanders played, the coloured guys would go and hear them. There wasn't any prejudice if you could play. All you had to do, if you were coloured, was take your hat off. When you took your hat off you had respect for white people.'

And the ragtime bands? 'They were different kind of bands. People like Yellow Nunez had ragtime bands, but they were not quite the same thing.'

If old New Orleans exercises some fascination still for Manone, the same cannot be said of the city today. In fact a reading of his book, *Trumpet On The Wing*, reveals that once this son of the Crescent City left home, he took care not to return too often or for too long a period. A story of his which always amused me concerns the time, during his Chicago days, when he wrote to his parents saying he intended to pay them a visit. His father replied telling him, in effect, not to bother. 'Just send the money you would spend on transportation,' he said. 'We got your picture.'

I asked Wingy if that really happened. 'Yes,' he roared, 'it's quite true. The old man's attitude was why spend all that money.' Wingy's mother and father are dead now, but he still has 'lots of family down there', some of whom he sees occasionally. 'I got two sisters and two brothers left and a hundred aunts and uncles. I get to see 'em from time to time when I go there on a visit, and that's all. I don't like New Orleans, you understand. The town stinks. There's nothing in New Orleans to take up my time.

'Another thing, that's too much animosity for me down there. They're jealous people, inclined to envy us who got away and made good. And you can't make no money there; the clubs don't want to pay you. No, they're ignoramus people, and I've got to say I know of better cities to live in. Most New Orleans musicians don't go back. I don't; Louis Armstrong neither. We go back and see our folks, but we wouldn't stay there. The best two things in New Orleans are a good meal and a train leaving out. That's what George Brunis says: "Eat and get out, man."

'But of course I've visited New Orleans in recent years. I happened to be there when Papa Bue was there. Oh, that's a good band with a nice lead trumpet. I heard them at some event, but I was on the train the next day.' So much for the city, but what of the music? Will the New Orleans style die out?

'No, it never will go out 'cos they'll always return to it — they've got plenty of bands to follow us. All those other jazz and rock-and-roll styles come and go but not the New Orleans music. Ours is happy music — unique and gay and colourful. Millions of bands tried to change it and they couldn't do it. I believe there are still more Dixieland bands in the States than rock-and-rollers. Billy Maxsted, he's got the best Dixieland band in the States; Peanuts Hucko had a good band at Condon's, Yank Lawson's got one, and Preacher Rollo is going strong around Seattle, Washington. That's a great Dixieland spot, and so are Tucson and Phoenix. Pete Daily, he's another who's still playing real jazz in Arizona. Another coming up right now is Jackie Coon. He's a trumpet player from Los Angeles who can play just like a native of New Orleans. Frank Assunto plays good trumpet, too, and I used to like that George Girard with the Basin Street Six. He was the only one ever upset Louis Armstrong.

'Of course, I always admired Louis, and I liked Billy Butterfield and Bunny Berigan. Well, I got Bunny his first break, when he was at college in Madison, Wisconsin. I told Paul Whiteman "He's good; get him!" Johnny Best still plays great, and Bobby Hackett — oh yes, he's beautiful.'

What is Manone's opinion of the Revival and its music? 'You mean trad, with the banjo and everything? No, we might play one number in an evening — *Liza Jane* or something — but not much. I guess I made just one record using banjo and tuba.

'What we're trying to do now is all those ballads. Would you believe it, all us New Orleans musicians like pretty music: you know, play the tune pretty and swing it right afterwards — in other words, kick it. One time in LA, at the Casa Manana, Louis played the *Star Spangled Banner*. That was the end. We all grabbed our hats and coats and flew out of the place.'

Looking back now, how does Wingy feel about the jazz life?

'I've had no regrets and I've done everything in life I wanted to do. It's all been great, and especially the five years with Bing Crosby on the *Kraft Music Show*. I worked with all the big stars on that show and they got a kick out of me because I wrecked the English language. So if I go out today or tomorrow it doesn't make no difference. But while I'm alive I want to go on playing. I like to play, and if I couldn't I'd be a miserable old man. Right from the start I've been satisfying myself that I could please myself and the people, and not just playing out of a wallet.

'In the old days, a lot of guys would see us New Orleans musicians up there and ask "What?" and "Why?" and "Where you get it from?" We couldn't explain that. It can't be taught; you can only soak it up. I know this: you gotta have it to go in the first place, and you never lose it. The guys who can't play are the ones that never had it. You've got to be born with it, to live it. It's been my life, and when I'm on the bandstand, that's when I'm really living. That's what jazz has meant to me.'

Jimmy McPartland

When you think about old jazz professionals you include James Dougald (Jimmy) McPartland, still unretired as I write this note. On 15 March 1987 he reached the nicely rounded age of eighty and notched up sixty-four years of professional playing. I have been acquainted with his trumpet/cornet work since Liza *and* Sugar *by McKenzie and Condon's Chicagoans were released in Britain, but first got to speak to him in 1945 when Marian (Turner) McPartland brought him to my office with some news. Both were working in a USO unit when they married in Germany in March '45, and both wore fetching uniforms on their visit to the MM. From that time on I met Jimmy in Europe now and then, Marian much more often as she returns 'home' every year or so and plays a few European festivals.*

This life story of Jimmy, originally titled 'My Thirty Years in Jazz', was taped in two or three sessions during 1954 at our house in Primrose Hill. It appeared in his own words over a number of weeks and was the longest running series about a trumpeter that I ever did for the paper. Indeed those were the days.

'I suppose everyone who has read about the jazz of the Twenties knows the name Austin High School Gang. I was one of that group of youngsters who took up jazz very seriously at Austin, a school situated near Washington Boulevard and Central Avenue in Chicago. It was lucky for me I got in with that gang, because as a boy down there on the West Side I might easily have been mixed up with a different kind of mob. So for me, and perhaps other Austin guys that got the music bug, jazz supplied the excitement we might otherwise have looked for among the illegal activities which flourished then in the neighbourhood.

I'll tell you how I got in with the Austin mob and how we became interested in jazz in the first place. Every day after school, Frank Teschemacher and Bud Freeman, Jim Lannigan, my brother Dick, myself and a few others used to go to a little place called the Spoon And Straw. It was just an ice-cream parlour where you'd get a malted milk, soda, shakes and all that stuff. But they had a Victrola there, and we used to sit around listening to the bunch of records laid on the table. They were Paul Whiteman and Art Hickman records and so forth. And Ted Lewis, he was supposed to be the hot thing but he didn't do anything to us somehow.

This went along for two or three months: we'd go in there every day, and one day they had some new Gennett records on the table and we put them on. They were by the New Orleans Rhythm Kings and I believe the first tune we played was *Farewell Blues*. Boy, when we heard that — I'll tell you we went out of our mind. Everybody flipped. It was wonderful. So we put the others on, *Tiger Rag, Discontented, Tin Roof Blues, Bugle Call* and such titles. We stayed there from about three in the afternoon until eight at night, just listening to those records one after another, over and over again. Right then and there we decided we would get a band and try to play like these guys.

So we all picked out our instruments. Tesch said he was going to buy a clarinet, Freeman plumped for a saxophone, Lannigan picked the bass tuba, my brother said he'd play the banjo, and I chose cornet, the loudest instrument. Anything loud — that's for me! For the next week we scrambled around finding money to buy them. My brother and I were lucky because my father was a music teacher. He gave Richard a banjo and I got a cornet. Then he sold Bud Freeman a C-Melody sax. Of course, Bud didn't pay him for a long time. We were all short of dough then, and Bud's a rough man with a buck.

One way and another we all got instruments and that was the nucleus of the Austin band. Every day we used to go to one of our houses or apartments, a different one each day because people got tired of us in a hurry. I mean we had to change flats, otherwise the people downstairs did.

What we used to do was put the record on — one of the Rhythm Kings, naturally — play a few bars and then all get our notes. We'd have to tune our instruments up to the record machine to the pitch, and go ahead with a few notes. Then stop! A few more bars of the record, each guy would pick out his notes and boom! we would go on and play it. Two bars or four bars or eight — we would get in on each phrase and then all play it. But you can imagine it was hard at first. Just starting, as most of us were, we'd make so many mistakes that it was horrible on people's ears. So as I say, we had to move around because neighbours couldn't stand it too long.

It was a funny way to learn, but in three or four weeks we could finally play one tune all the way through — *Farewell Blues*. Boy, that was our tune. After getting that one down straight, we worked on another, and so on. Within a few months we could play nine or ten tunes creditably.

Thinking of it after all these years, it seems surprising to me how fast we did pick it up. One reason for that was the enthusiasm — it couldn't have been any better — and another was that most of us had some musical training. My brother and I had learned violin from my father since we were five. Tesch was a violinist too. And Jim Lannigan was the most accomplished violinist of us all. Bud Freeman was the only guy that had not had any training, consequently he was slow picking up the music. In fact it was murder those first weeks. Tesch used to get disgusted with him and say: 'Let's throw that bum out.' But I said 'No, no, no, don't. He's coming on, he's playing.'

There was one thing I could recognise in Bud then: he had a terrific beat. He still has. He began by just playing rhythm, getting on one note and holding it; I mean swinging on it, just that one note. He didn't change the harmony or anything, and we used to get so mad at him, you know. We'd yell at him: 'Change the note.' Still, as I remember, he played with a great beat.

So in this way we built up our repertoire. Now, when we finished at Austin High around three, we would go on to a jam session up until dinner time, have dinner, then go to somebody else's home and play from, say, 8.30 till eleven or twelve at night. Every day we'd do that. So naturally that was our practice and our tuition. We all built our embouchures, built for tone, developed our ears. The method stayed the same: play a few bars of the record, then everybody would grab his notes and build up the tune. The New Orleans Rhythm Kings, that was our model.

It finally got that we would go and play at charity meetings and different fraternities around high school, until one time we played a social in the gymnasium at Austin. Somebody said there was a kid there who could play drums. He was from Oak Park High School, which was just the next suburb, and the kid's name was Davie Tough. He got some drums from somewhere and came in and, man, that was it! He just was great. That beat, he had it right then. He told us he patterned himself on Baby Dodds, who used to be with the King Oliver band at Lincoln Gardens.

And that was the Austin High School Gang. Oh yes, plus a guy named Dave North. I guess few people in Britain ever heard of him, because he didn't record. But he used to play piano, and he stayed with us quite a while. Me being the loudest, and all that, it fell in that I was the leader. So I used to stomp off.

Of course, we had to give the band a name: the Blue Friars. It was my brother's idea, and he got it from the Friars Inn, downtown, in the Loop, where the NORK were playing. On records, they called the Rhythm Kings the Friars Society Orchestra. What a society orchestra! Hello! Gone! We were too young to get into Friars Inn, so the only way we could get to hear the Rhythm Kings was to go down and stand in the doorway and listen. It was great when someone opened the door and we could hear it louder.

Paul Mares and the Rhythm Kings, then, were our earliest inspiration. But we listened to everything we could. We sometimes went down to a Chinese restaurant, the Golden Pheasant, where there was a band by the name of Al Haid. They played pretty good, a semi-commercial brand of jazz, so we used to go down and eat chop suey and listen to this orchestra. It wasn't as good as the NORK — but we listened. The musicians used to come over and talk to us, and one night I heard them ask Tesch if he knew of a cornet player.

Said Frank: 'There's Jimmy there plays cornet fine.' They asked me if I would sit in and audition for a job, and I said 'Surely.' Next night, I came in with my cornet and sat in. All the guys were there to hear me audition. Of course, Haid had to play the tunes that I knew, and I naturally picked *Farewell Blues*, *Tin Roof* and others I had down pat. Everything went fine, and I got the job: 35 dollars a week, room and board. This would have been 1923, and I was sixteen. All that summer I worked up at Fox Lake with the Haid band. To me, it was a big deal.

The next thing I recall, after returning from my first professional job, with Al Haid's band at Fox Lake, was a couple of weeks on the excursion boats from Chicago to Benton Harbour, just across Lake Michigan. As soon as I started, I was told about a band playing on another boat, which had Bix Beiderbecke on cornet and a youngster named Benny Goodman on clarinet. Everyone was saying how terrific the music was on this other boat, and rumour had it that Beiderbecke was the greatest yet. As a matter of fact, I had heard of the newcomer from Davenport but hadn't heard him play. And I didn't get to hear him now, because he only worked with this band for five or six days — and when we were going across the lake they were coming back!

As for Goodman, I had never heard of his name at that time. I first met him when I was working with Frisco Hasse. After the boat job I went back to Austin High School in the fall and for a bit we continued our gang sessions. Then I picked up a steady job over at a place called Eddie Tancil's in Cicero, Illinois. The band was Hasse's and the job was good. It paid 65 bucks a week, good money for a kid turning sixteen-seventeen, in those days, or any others.

Frisco was a drummer, and he played in this nightclub. It was during Prohibition, and he used to sell liquor on the side. So I went to work there at Tancil's, and the guy says, 'I got a little kid clarinet player coming out to-morrow night to sit in with the band. He's too young to hire.' Well, it developed that the kid was Benny Goodman — aged thirteen at most. And I thought to myself: 'This little punk play clarinet? He's too small to blow it.' The little punk climbed up on the stand and got his horn ready. Then he played *Rose Of The Rio Grande*, which is a hard tune — I mean the changes for those days were difficult. This little monkey played about sixteen choruses of *Rose* and I just sat there with my mouth open.

Benny blew the hell out of that clarinet and I almost died hearing him do it. So I latched on to him immediately, and said: 'You gotta come to our sessions over at Austin High.' He was most happy to, he said. 'Glad, sure!' And he came out there and sat in with the Austin gang.

Meanwhile the job at Tancil's kept on. Eddie himself used to be a boxer and was a tough guy. He was what you'd call a rough-neck — and needed to be! Al Capone and his mob were just moving into Cicero and naturally they wanted to clean out all this rough element so they could take over. Of course I didn't realise it at the time, or I'd have been less happy there. One night a bunch of tough guys came in and started turning tables over to introduce themselves. Then they picked up bottles and began hitting the bartenders with them, also with blackjacks and brass-knuckles. It was just terrible. To us they said 'You boys keep playing if you don't want to get hurt. That's all.'

And you know who kept playing.

The thugs tore the place apart, beat up all the waiters and barmen and Tancil too. Eddie was fighting them and he was good, could beat the heck out of any two of those strong-arms. But when they brought out the 'billies' he was outclassed. All over the place people were gashed and bleeding. The mobsters would break a bottle over some guy's head, then jab it in his face, then maybe kick him. They made mincemeat of people. I never saw such a horrible thing in my life. But we kept playing — period.

A couple more nights of work and they came and did it again, much worse. That was the finish. Tancil got rid of the band, and two days later we found out he had been shot dead. That was the beginning of the mobs moving in on nightclub business.

Now, during this time, Goodman began working with a guy by the name of Podolsky. Podolsky played piano with Chuck Walker (guitar), Johnny Carsella (trombone), Harry McCall (drums), and some other fellows. On one job it was Walker's band, on another Podolsky's. The band became short of a trumpet lead, and Benny got me with 'Murph'. 'Murph' was Podolsky. His real name was Charles but for some reason — because he was a Jewish guy, I guess — we called him Murphy.

Benny and I worked around for a while with Murphy and did quite well. Guys from the University of Chicago and North-western University would call up one of us for a band, and we came to be quite a team around these different dances in Chicago. Both Benny and I would earn from 80 to 100 dollars a week and still go to school. They paid good money, those college boys.

In those days I had just started to play golf. I remember Benny used to come out and play golf with me — still in short pants at that time! He was fifteen, as I say, only a year or so younger than me but a deal smaller than I was. Then one day, he asked if I'd go with him shopping to buy some new clothes. I took his hand crossing State Street because he looked such a little kid. And Benny was scared to cross in front of all the traffic down there. It isn't important really but I just happened to think of it. I mean, those stories of Benny playing in short pants are true, I know.

And while we were going with those University students, they used to take Benny and me over to hear Louis Armstrong, Lil Hardin and the Dodds brothers playing with King Oliver. This was just one thrill on top of another, hearing Louis and King and those New Orleans guys.

Along about this time, I can't say exactly when, there came out some new records on Gennett by the Wolverines. When we heard Bix on these we did another flip. How could it be so good? To me, Bix ... well, that was it. What beautiful tone, sense of melody, great drive, poise, everything! He just played lovely jazz, and he knew how to lead a band.

Bix Beiderbecke ... he had just about everything that I looked for in a musician. And when he came up on those Wolverines records, why, me and the rest of the gang — we just wore the records out! We copied off the little arrangements, and what was going on in the ensembles. One thing was definite that we would never do; copy any solo exactly. We didn't believe in copying anything outside of the arrangement. An introduction, ending, a first ending or an interlude, we would copy those, naturally. But never a solo. For instance, if Bix would take a solo, I wouldn't copy that. I would just play the way I felt. But I was tremendously influenced by Bix, and hearing the Wolverines was a step forward for all of the gang. We got their numbers off, and added them to our repertoire.

While Benny and I were getting these college jobs, Jim Lannigan used to come in on some of them, and sometimes Tough or Freeman or Dick would get in too. We didn't get many dates with all the Austin gang together, but we managed to keep in touch with each other.

When it came summer again, I went up to Lost Lake in Northern Wisconsin with a band called the Maroon Five from the University of Chicago. It was a resort engagement, one of those room and board things. We only worked one night a week there, then went out to book other dances for ourselves. We worked up there the whole summer — I guess it was the summer of '24 — and I then came back to Chicago and Austin High. My brother had found a job for the band with Tesch, Bud, Lannigan, Dave North and no cornet, at radio station WGN. They called the band the Blue Flyers, and they were doing great.

I was going to join the Flyers when I received a wire one fateful day from Dick Voynow, pianist and manager of the Wolverines. It read:

CAN YOU JOIN WOLVERINES IN NEW YORK REPLACING BIX BEIDERBECKE AT SALARY OF EIGHTY-SEVEN DOLLARS FIFTY PER WEEK QUERYMARK STOP ANSWER IMMEDIATELY STOP

Of course, I showed this wire to everybody. Though I patted myself on the back, I was feeling doubtful. Was it a gag? Was someone playing a joke on me? All the guys said: 'No, you're crazy! Sure, it's real. Take it: it's the greatest honour in the world.' So I said I would. They advised me to wire right back, and I did: SEND TRANSPORTATION. I ACCEPT THE JOB. — MCPARTLAND.

The rail fare was 32 dollars and 50 cents from Chicago to New York: that was third-class coach, no Pullman or anything. And that was exactly the sum Voynow sent me. Dick Voynow was handling all their business, and he said to leave immediately.

Well, I left that same night ... with just my bag and my little beaten-up cornet. It was beat-up, too, and getting worse and worse. As I pressed the valves it would go clank, clank, clank. Gee! A noisy affair! Anyhow, I went down to the station, bought a ticket and asked what time the next train was to New York. They said it left in about half an hour. I waited there and a whole gang of the guys came down to see me off — even Murphy Podolsky was there. Then I got on a day coach. Wow! I had caught the plain milk train — the slow train to New York — I didn't know any better; had never been on a train ride that long before. It took me two days to get to New York, but I had plenty to think about.

Taking Bix's place was the biggest thing that had happened to me. The Wolverines were *the* jazz band in the country, so far as we were concerned. And Bix — as I say, I had never met him, but just hearing him play was enough. I've heard many great trumpeters since those days, but I haven't heard another like Bix. Somehow or other his style, the cleanliness and feeling, was lovely. Let's call him the master and leave it at that.

I finally got into New York about six in the morning. It was the first time I'd been there in my life, and a beautiful hour to arrive. From the station I called up Dick Voynow, who said: 'Hop in a cab and come to the Somerset Hotel.' I got over there and started talking to Voynow. He 'phoned Bix, who was just coming in, pretty high.

So I met Bix.

The Wolverines were rehearsing that afternoon, and by the time I got there I was very nervous. Of course I had memorised all the arrangements from the band's records, and when Dick asked what I wanted to play, I said: 'Anything ... *Jazz Me Blues, Farewell, Riverboat Shuffle, Big Boy*. Anything.'

They said: 'Do you know all those tunes?'

I said: 'Sure.'

So Voynow said: 'Okay, let's go!' And he beat off and I just started right in. I knew all Bix's lead parts — so BOOM! I must have surprised those guys: their chins dropped, and everything else. I played their routine, took my solo where Bix used to take his. And when the number was finished they patted me on the back and said, 'Great, kid,' and all that stuff. It made me feel good; I was no more nervous — got my cockiness back. We went through some more tunes and I was in, right then and there.

Now Bix, from the first, had been very reticent. He didn't say anything until the rehearsal was over. Then he came over. 'Kid,' he said, 'I'll tell you what you do. You'll move in with me. I like you.' That was what he said. So I moved in with Bix. It was to be a week or two before he joined the Jean Goldkette orchestra, and while he was still around he stayed with the Wolverines to help break me in properly. As we roomed together, he was able to show me the different tunes and arrangments the band had, coach me in certain little figures he used in his playing. Then, at night, we would go to the job — the Wolverines were working at the Cinderella Ballroom on 48th and Broadway — and play the tunes together. Yes, for about five nights we both played in the band. First Bix would take the lead, then he'd play second in with me to break me in. He was an enormous help and encouragement, and I got to admire the man as much as the musician.

I must tell you about his generosity to me, a complete stranger to him until I took his place in the Wolverines. After a few days he asked me: 'How can you blow a horn like that? It's a terrible thing.' I've told you that my cornet was beat, had leaks in it and everything. But I had not realised how horrible it was until Bix took me over. At that time, he was using a horn called the Conn Victor cornet — a long model cornet and a beautiful thing. He had me blow it and it sounded great. Said Bix: 'You need a horn like this, Jimmy, come on out with me.' Out we went to see Voynow, who gave Beiderbecke some dough. Then we went over to the Conn company, where Bix picked up four or five horns and tried them out. Finally he said: 'This is the one, Jim, for you.' He just gave me the cornet — period. So that I would have a good instrument to play. I remember him saying: 'I like you, kid, because you sound like I do but you don't copy me. You play your own stuff; you're a good guy.'

That was nice, you know, coming from him. I had patterned my playing after his, but had tried to develop my own self at the same time. That was what we believed in the Austin gang in Chicago: play the way you feel, yourself!

But to finish this particular episode: Bix then joined Goldkette who was playing there at the Roseland Ballroom, just down the street a little way. That was the reason he quit the Wolverines, to go with Goldkette for more loot. So I lived with the man all the time he was in New York. After five weeks or so, he left to go on the road. Then I had a room of my own.

It was 1925. For several months I worked with the Wolverines, and while we were at the Cinderella Ballroom many of the coming jazzmen — like Red Nichols and the Dorseys — fell in and took a turn with the band. Though the music was considered wonderful, the place did not do consistently good business. Around the end of that year we left New York for a job down in Florida, at a place known as Oklahoma Bob's Roundup, on Biscayne Bay in Miami. Unfortunately, the day we were to open they had closed the joint up. Prohibition agents shut it for violation of the Volstead Act — they were selling whiskey there — so no job.

It was a bad start to Florida. Actually, I went three days with nothing to eat but an O Henry bar. I tried to get work in a railroad gang but the foreman said I was too young. Next I sent home for some money, and then Vic Moore (drummer in the band by this time) picked up some gigs which took us to Palm Beach.

For a while we worked at the Everglades Club, and it was there that Jascha Heifetz visited one night and complimented the band. How well we played, he said, without violins. The Wolverines broke up down in Florida. Clarinettist Jimmy Hartwell, bass saxist Min Leibrook and Vic Moore left us when the season ended. Dick Voynow, Bob Gillette, George Johnson and myself went back to Chicago and picked up Jimmy Lord on clarinet, Ralph Snyder on drums and a guy by the name of Arkey Morgenthaler from Cincinatti on bass. With this band we got a job at the Valentino Inn, and later we played the Casino Gardens and the Montmartre up on the North side. It was during this time that Jimmy Lord was replaced by Rosy McHargue. Also at this time I met my friend Squirrel Ashcraft, the Chicago lawyer and jazz lover. We worked till four in the morning at these joints, and afterwards Squirrel and I used to go out playing golf — right from the job.

So, anyway, this combo then disbanded. All that was left were Voynow and myself. I saw the chance now to get the Austin High School mob in. I got Tesch, Davey Tough, my brother, Bud Freeman, Jim Lannigan, and we played a while with some vaudeville acts. Finally, we augmented with a trombone, Floyd O'Brien. We hadn't used a trombone much up to then, and I've heard it said that the 'Chicagoans' preferred a tenor sax in their groups. Believe me, the reason the Chicago bands used that kind of line-up — didn't have a trombone — was because there were no trombone players around! Outside of George Brunis who blew real solid trombone, the first guy I heard play anything was Floyd. So we got him.

We scuffled around vaudeville and different one-nighters, and Dick Voynow started to get very commercial. I was called upon to sing songs like *She's Got This,*

She's Got That, She's Got ... well, you know, the stage department. Bill Robinson even taught me a few Charleston steps, and I'd get out there and sell it! We didn't really like it, though. We were young and we were keen; we wanted to play jazz, that's all: didn't want that commercial deal. I guess we worked with Dick like that for six weeks, then threw in the hat. 'We're leaving,' I told him. 'The whole band's leaving. Goodbye, we'll see you.' Voynow got mad and everything like that, but he found himself a job with Brunswick records and said I could use the name of the Wolverines. He was kind enough to do that.

So we brought Dave North, who we had started with in Chicago, back on piano: and through a sharp-talking agent called Husk O'Hare got a job up in Des Moines, Iowa, where we stayed practically the whole summer. This was a darned good job too. The guys were pulling in 90 dollars a week and the leader made near to 170. I was the leader — and about eighteen years old then. Truthfully we did have a good band and we just played jazz — just blew! The people all came to dance to us, the kids used to holler, and everything was great. But we never recorded. I wish we had.

When we got back to Chicago, O'Hare had work lined up for us at the White City Ballroom. There the band sounded better than ever. On opening night we didn't want to get off the bandstand; it sounded so good to us that we kept playing, right through intermission. We were supposed to break for half an hour, but we played continuously, wouldn't stop. 'What's the matter with you guys?' the manager asked. 'Don't you want a break?' We said no. He said: 'I'm telling you fellers you're going to have to, 'cos we want the dancers to stop and order refreshments and so forth. It's hurting our business.'

On two nights a week they had a second band at the White City: Sig Meyer's band, with Rosy McHargue, Muggsy Spanier, Jess Stacy and, I think, George Wettling.

George had played with the Voynow outfit when Tough quit for a little while, so I knew him already. But it was the first time I had ever heard Muggsy and I enjoyed it.

But to get back to my band: I should explain that I was the leader of this thing. Husk used to call it Husk O'Hare's Wolverines — under the direction of Jimmy McPartland. Hooray! It was quite a combo and everybody came around to hear us ... especially Louis Armstrong. Louis was playing then over at the Sunset Cafe which started later than us and went on till 4 a.m. or so. He came over two or three evenings a week and sat in back of the band, listening to us and chuckling all over the place. He was about twenty-five then.

Pee Wee Russell, Bix and Frankie Trumbauer were working down at Hudson Lake about 80 miles south in Indiana. Every Monday, their night off, they would come up to hear us. When we had finished, we would all go off together to catch Louis or Jimmy Noone — another of our favourites. Sometimes we sat in with Louis at the Sunset, or with Noone at the Apex. The Apex Club was one of our regular stops.

And that was about the last of the Wolverines. We worked at White City until the job finally petered out. That was when Art Kassel stepped into the picture.

He had a job up in Detroit, Michigan, and he wanted to take over the band intact. His offer was pretty good, so we let him.

Under Kassel's name, and augmented with a couple of instruments, we opened at the Graystone Ballroom in Detroit. There we played opposite Fletcher Henderson's orchestra, which had Coleman Hawkins, Rex Stewart, Joe Smith and Buster Bailey. That's where I first met Buster. We used to go out on jam sessions with Fletcher's guys and really had a good time. Bud Freeman was knocked over by Hawkins, while I was particularly impressed by Joe Smith. He was a lovely trumpet player, and exceptionally good with the plunger mute.

Anyway, when we got to Detroit we found that Kassel wanted to play real commercial music: he had some horrible commercial tunes for us to play. It was no good, we couldn't stand that. So during the course of the evening he called some corny tune, *Jingle Bells* or some stupid thing, and the guys looked at me as much as to say, 'Impossible can't do it.' I told Art: 'Sorry, Art, can't play the tune.' Then Dave Tough muttered. 'Come on, *Shimme-Sha-Wabble*'. And I started off ... 'One, two ...' and we went into '*Shimme-Sha-*'. Well, we kept that up, and had a lot of fun. We played more or less what we wanted to play, and Art would stand there and make a face, as if to say, 'What can I do with these guys?'

The job finished and we came back to Chicago, and everyone started splitting up. Together with bassist Lannigan I was offered work down at Friar's Inn with Bill Paley's band — 115 bucks a week, as I recall. We took it: Jim Lannigan by this time had a bass fiddle as well as tuba and he played both.

Now Friars Inn was the place where the gangsters used to hang out, the big boys. One night, real late, there were only a few customers left. They were these tough blokes, as you say. I knew the gang it was, the Northside mob, which later on did the St Valentine massacre — when they slaughtered all those monkeys against a wall. So it was late this night, and we were off the bandstand and sitting in the back, when all of a sudden — bang, boom, bang! Somebody was shooting a gun. Mike Fritzel was the boss there, and Mike says: 'Play, play, fellers'. We weren't all that keen, but the shooting had ceased so we got up on the stand to play, and there was the bass fiddle all shot to pieces. One of these guys had shot it into splinters just for target practice! Jim Lannigan was sore, but he was the retiring type, and I wasn't. I said: 'What the hell is the idea, Mike, this guy busting up my brother-in-law's bass?' Mike said not to worry about it, the guy would make good the damage, and I said: 'That's a different thing — if he'll pay for it.'

Mike asked how much Jim had paid for the bass. I happened to know he had laid down 225 dollars for it, but I said 850. Believe it or not, in five minutes Mike came over with 850 in cash. The torpedo just peeled it off a roll: you know these Prohibition guys were loaded with loot. So Jim got 850 bucks and he'd never said a word! With the dough he bought himself a new instrument, a beautiful thing. And he kept the remains and had them fixed up, then sold the old bass.

Jim and I stayed at the Inn about four or five months, after that back to

Kassel. Benny Pollack was leaving the Southmoor Hotel in Chicago, and Art had been booked in his place. He wanted Lannigan and me to rejoin him. This time we asked first what kind of music he was going to play. 'The kind you want to play,' Art answered. He also said he would pay 140 dollars each a week. So we let him hire us. It was big money, and in those days there was no tax, nothing like that. But a clause in the contract said that we would play so much jazz. I wouldn't take the job otherwise.

During these months with Kassel some interesting events took place. The Mound City Blue Blowers came to town, and one night Red McKenzie came into the Southmoor saying that his guitarist had quit him. I said, 'Well, get my brother on guitar.' So Red hired him right off the bat, and Richard went into the Blue Blowers on guitar (by this time he was playing guitar instead of banjo). While I was still with Kassel, McKenzie got together with Eddie Condon and they secured a recording date from Tommy Rockwell of Okeh. These were the records, put out as by McKenzie and Condon's Chicagoans, which created something of a stir in the Windy City in 1927–8. I'll tell you how we made them.

Red and Condon got together some of the Austin High School gang to talk about the date, and a rehearsal was fixed. The four tunes were decided and Teschemacher agreed to write out a few introductions and interludes and so on, which he did. He got up three-part harmonies, for us: you can tell which are the parts on the records. The day before the recording we ran through them and got them for timing. Then the next day we went down and recorded. All the guys were there — Mezzrow and all the hang-arounds — and the band consisted of me, Tesch, Freeman, Lannigan, Condon, Joe Sullivan and Gene Krupa. As you know Tough was our drummer, and a lot of the ideas we used were his. The reason he was not on these records is that he had recently left for Europe to join up with Danny Polo. I do not know where Wettling was. He was the next drummer, but he couldn't have been around. So they got Krupa for the date.

Gene was really the comer. Tough and Wettling were already established, but Krupa was a couple of years younger. And in those days it made a lot of difference. This was, in fact, the first time I ever played with Krupa. And it was the first recording session on which any of our guys had seen a bass drum used. We came into the studio there, and Gene set up his bass drum, tom-toms — the whole set. Then we made a take to see how it sounded, and immediately the recording manager, Mr Ring, ran out saying: 'You can't use all those drums, throw those drums out; just use sticks, cymbals, wood blocks and so forth.' After some protests they finally worked the thing out by laying down rugs that took up the vibration. The vibration was the thing they worried about mostly. So they let Gene play the drums, and he beat the heck out of them all the way through the set, which was fine for us, because it gave us a good solid background.

They say that we got our particular style down well on that session. Of course, we didn't have a name for it or anything, it was simply the way we used to play. We had names for certain devices though, like the 'explosion'. That was in the middle of a chorus. We would build up to an explosion, then go down soft, 'way down, we would say. Like, for instance, that final chorus in *Nobody's Sweetheart*. Then at the end, the last eight or sixteen bars, we used to break out and ride. We called that the 'ride out'. These things were largely Davey Tough's ideas. *China Boy* features something similar. *Sugar* and *Liza* were the quieter tunes. Very few people know this particular *Liza* which was written by a guy named George Rubens. He was just a guy that liked jazz, and he was a friend of Condon's.

Another thing happened on that date: we had a vocal trio. The trio was Condon, Freeman and myself, and we had rehearsed a couple of songs before the date. One was *Mean To Me*. I knew that. And I know we recorded it: but not until the end of the date. And by the end of that date, everyone was knocked out — or shall I say intoxicated? — from all the stuff, that singing became a thing of chance. Mercifully, that side was not put out! But all the rest came out, and they were a big hit overnight. For their time they sold very well. And I guess they helped to bring renewed offers from Ben Pollack, the Chicago drummer.

Soon after Benny formed his band at the Southmoor, I had been invited to join him. Now he was at the Blackhawk Restaurant and he and Gil Rodin and Benny Goodman came out to the hotel one night to persuade me. I said I wouldn't leave unless it was okay with Kassel. Art said: 'All right' and Pollack said he'd also want to take Bud Freeman. That made it better for me because Bud was my pal from the Austin High mob. So we decided 'Fine!' and went with Pollack to the Blackhawk.

Ben Pollack ... now there was a drummer: one of the finest that ever lived! He used to be with the New Orleans Rhythm Kings, and he produced as good a beat as I've heard. When he got behind you, he'd really make you go: yes, he'd send you. And he had a marvellous band at the Blackhawk, with Benny Goodman, his brother Harry on bass, Vic Breidis (piano), Gil Rodin (alto), Dick Morgan (guitar), Glenn Miller (trombone), and, a little later on, Bud Freeman. Glenn was making arrangements as well as playing, and Fud Livingston also arranged. Both were terrific.

That band really swung. We didn't play all jazz, naturally: had to play popular tunes of the day for the customers. But everything we did was musical. The intonation was fine, the band had tonal quality. It was a ten-piece outfit, and it played nice, danceable music.

So that was the band I joined at the Blackhawk in Chicago. The Blackhawk was a very high-class restaurant and it had good acoustics — a beautiful place to play in. The man I replaced was Harry Greenberg. I know that because I ran into Harry in New York not long ago.

We stayed there at the Blackhawk a few months and recorded a couple of titles in Chicago for Victor. Then came an offer from a place called the Little Club, on 44th Street, New York. In New York we all moved into nice places to live and spent our money fast. Bud and I put up at the Mayflower Hotel: then suddenly Pollack quit over an argument about the show. So we were out of a job. It was a tough lay-off: no work, nothing saved up, of course. But there were always the cocktail parties. This was 1928 before the Stock Market crashed, and there was plenty of money floating around — though we didn't have any of it for the time being. A lot of people gave a lot of parties, and often we would be invited. You could get all you wanted to drink but nothing to eat. Just the same, it was better than nothing at all.

We couldn't pay the rent, though, so after a couple of weeks we moved into the Whitby apartments where Gil Rodin, Dick Morgan, Benny Goodman and Glenn Miller had a suite. We all moved into that, practically the whole band, with the exception of Pollack, sleeping on chairs, couches, the floor, anywhere. The number of that apartment was 1411. And that is how that title came up: *Room 1411* by Benny Goodman's Boys. We had been out of work about five weeks when Benny came home and said: 'I've got a recording date with Brunswick. We can get some money, buy some food, eat!'

We made that date. Goodman, Miller, myself and two or three more, playing different kinds of numbers like *Blue* and *Jungle Blues* and this one we named *Room 1411*. After the session was just about over, we started kidding around and playing corny. Out comes the recording manager from his booth, and he says: 'That's it! That's what we want, just what you're playing there!' We were playing as corny as possible. As a matter of fact, Tommy Dorsey had come up and was standing listening to us, and he picked up a trombone and started playing, kidding around too. The manager said: 'You gotta do that.' That is what he wanted. So we sort of used the 'St Louis' chord progressions and blew all this cod Dixie, and we called the number *Shirt Tail Stomp*. It sold more than any of the others; or I should say that it sold the rest of the sides because it was corny. It shows the taste of people: still the same, I guess, the world over.

This was not the first time I recorded under Goodman's name. After we made those Victor records with Pollack that I mentioned, Benny got a date with Brunswick for a small band. There were just the Goodmans, Miller, Breidis, Morgan, myself and drummer Bob Conselman, and I think we made only two titles: *Jazz Holiday* and *Wolverine Blues*. Anyway to get back to the lay-off: at that time, Bix was in New York with Paul Whiteman's orchestra. One night we were invited to a cocktail party on Park Avenue and Bix was there with Trumbauer, Bing Crosby and the Dorsey brothers. I was drinking in a corner with Bix and telling him how murderous it was being out of work, with no money and nobody who would buy you a meal. Right away he asked: 'Do you need some money, kid?' and I told him I would appreciate 10 or 20 bucks in order to eat, which I would repay the moment we started work again. Bix brought out his wallet, and from a bunch of cheques and notes picked out two 100-dollar bills. 'Take this,' he said. I explained that I didn't want so much, just 20 bucks or so to save myself from starving, but he insisted. It was another typical example of Beiderbecke's generosity towards me.

A week or two later we went to work again, with short engagements in Atlantic City, Syracuse and so forth. Back in New York I was having a couple of drinks with Bud Freeman and Pee Wee Russell one evening in a little speakeasy on 51st Street when Pee Wee began talking about a trombone player, the greatest thing he had heard in his life. We said we would have to hear the guy, and Pee Wee said, right, he'd just pop over and get him. Two drinks later, Pee Wee was back with the guy who was wearing a horrible looking cap and overcoat and carrying a trombone in a case under his arm. Pee Wee introduced us. He was Jack Teagarden, from Texas, and looked it. 'Fine,' we said. 'We've been hearing a lot about you, would sure like to hear you play.' The guy says 'all right', gets his horn out, puts it together, blows a couple of warm-up notes and starts to play *Diane*. No accompaniment, just neat: he played it solo, and I'm telling you he knocked us out. He really blew it. And when he'd done with that he started on the blues, still by himself.

We had to agree with Pee Wee, we'd never heard anyone play trombone like that. We were flabbergasted. They were going to a jam session later, up on 48th Street where Jack lived, so we went back and told Gil Rodin and a couple of the others how wonderful Teagarden was. The other guys scoffed, but Rodin didn't. He came with us on the session that night, and when he heard Jack he reported back to Pollack and the whole band, and next night they all came up to hear the new trombonist. Glenn Miller was among them, and he was gracious enough to bow to a real jazz player like that. It was the greatest he had ever heard, too. Until then Miff Mole had been Glenn's idol, the person he'd patterned himself on. When Glenn raved, that was it so far as everybody was concerned. Teagarden was earmarked for the Ben Pollack band.

We have arrived at 1928, to the point where Jack Teagarden came into Ben Pollack's band. After a short time, Glenn Miller relinquished the trombone chair in favour of Tea. Glenn still wrote for the band but did not play in it any more. Soon we got a terrific job at the Park Central Hotel. This, I think, was the time we got Ruby Weinstein on first trumpet in place of Al Harris. We had Benny Goodman, Bud Freeman and Gil Rodin on reeds, and when Bud left we got Larry Binyon in on tenor (he had been with the band before). Breidis, Morgan and Harry Goodman were still in the rhythm section, and — because this was a swank hotel job — Pollack thought he should add strings. He got himself Eddie Bergman (a fine violinist from New York) and Al Beller (Benny's cousin from Chicago) on fiddles and a guy named Bill Schumann on cello. Then Pollack got himself a manager, Bernie Foyer. Bernie was a cigar-smoking New Yorker who knew that Rudy Vallee was a very big thing around town. Somehow or other Bernie persuaded Pollack to quit drums, just to lead the band and sing, no less. In came Ray Bauduc on drums. And that was the set-up. Jack Teagarden used to play vibraphone too, during this time: not hot vibes, just on pretty things a few chords, here and there, and it sounded real nice.

We stayed at the Park Central more than a year, 1928–9, and the band was a sensation. We made all kinds of records and doubled into a show called *Hello Daddy*. It meant starting at the hotel at 6.30, doing a broadcast and playing until 8.0, then going to the show from 8.30 to 11. After that, back to the hotel where we finished around 1.30. That was our routine, with records and some-times pictures in the daytime.

So we were doing fine. I was making between five and seven hundred dollars a week, and Goodman was pulling in about the same. The show ran for at least nine months: the money was tax free too, so it began to pile up in the bank.

Then came the vaudeville circuit around New York, and one week we were in a place called the Fox Theatre in Brooklyn. The Goodmans, Gil Rodin and I used to play a lot of handball together on the beaches or any spot where we saw a chance, and this particular afternoon Benny and I were playing ball against a wall on the roof of the Fox. We used to have cute black and white shoes for our uniform those days, and naturally our shoes got a little dirty. Suddenly it was time for the next show. There was no chance to clean up, just time to run downstairs, grab our instruments and hurry on stage. During the act, why, I would get up a couple of times and do a solo out front. When I got back to my seat Pollack began hollering about my shoes. As soon as the curtain rang down he went off into a tirade, was going to give me my two weeks' notice. Up steps Benny Goodman to say: 'If you give Jimmy his notice you're going to give me mine, too.' Pollack gets real mad then, and says: 'All right, he's got his two weeks' notice.' So Benny comes back mildly: 'Well, you got mine.' And that was it.

It so happened that the whole band was pretty much fed-up at that time. Pollack had changed lately from being one of the boys, shall we say, to acting like a real leader, and the thing developed so that all the boys got together and were going to have Pollack's band without Pollack. We would have put Rodin in charge, because he was the one that more or less handled the band anyway. Gil was the diplomat who smoothed things over, and he didn't have the leader complex. We had a lot of fun talking about it but nothing materialised. They sent for Matty Matlock on clarinet and Teagarden's brother Charlie to fill the trumpet spot. They couldn't have made a better choice, for in my books Charlie is a wonderful musician.

So the band moved on and Benny and I rented an apartment together. Benny got a job over at the Paramount Theatre — with Rubinoff, his Violin and Orchestra (Benny Goodman, first saxophone and clarinet) — while I went to work in a club with Arnold Johnson. I was playing there one night when Goodman and Manny Klein came over. Manny had turned down an offer to go with *Sons O' Guns*, and asked if I wanted the job. I said 'Heck! Yes,' and was with the show for about a year, through 1930.

Right around this time I got married to Dorothy Williams, one of the famous Williams sisters, and then I worked in the pit of Billy Rose's *Sweet And Low* for another year.

At this time, 1931, Bix had been out on the road with Whiteman and I hadn't seen him for a long time. Then he came back to New York. I ran into him one evening on the street close to Jimmy Plunkett's, a very fabulous speakeasy where all the musicians hung out. Naturally we went in, and this was the first chance I had to pay Bix the money I owed him. I gave it back in one lump. I was married, as I say, and by now we had a baby. So I didn't get out as much as I used to. But I saw Bix a few times after that, mostly when I dropped in Plunkett's to have a drink and say hello to everybody. The last time was two nights before he died. It was the summer of '31 and I was working this Billy Rose show. On my way home from the theatre I stopped by at Plunkett's and

Bix was there, looking bad. He was all run down and miserable, had been drinking excessively and not eating much. We talked about it, I remember, and he said he didn't feel like eating anything. I told him he should at least swallow some silver fizzes to get something nutritious inside him.

Fizzes were concocted out of gin and the whites of eggs and they sure set you up. So we both had about six of these, with a little sugar, and I gave Bix some dough because he was clean out. It felt good to be able to repay him in some measure for his kindness to me. And it made him happy too.

Not long before, Bix had been home to Davenport, Iowa, where Paul Whiteman had sent him to get his health straight. He came back looking quite fit, then he started in again and had to leave Whiteman. Things didn't go right after that. He wasn't doing well, and this night I'm speaking of I could see his condition was poor. Anyhow, two days later I was told Bix had died. It was a terrible shock. I actually cried, because I loved the guy — not only for his music but personally you know. Take it from me, Bix was a lovely guy.

The depression and the repeal of Prohibition pretty well put paid to jazz as a living. Because of this, and a variety of personal reasons, I left New York after the Billy Rose show closed and made some cruises with a little band to South America. Up till now I had always played cornet, always used a number three Bach mouthpiece. But the first trumpet man in the show had asked why I didn't get a trumpet. 'You'll have a better range,' he assured me. 'And it will blend better with the section.' I didn't mind, so he had me change. But after blowing for a couple of days on this new mouthpiece, the whole structure of my embouchure seemed to go flooey. Really, I had a horrible time, struggling through the last couple of months of that show.

My lip was so out of order that I went back to my old horn and mouthpiece. Even then I had a heck of a time getting it back in shape. It seemed everything was sort of piling on me about now. My wife had gone to live with her sister, and somehow or other a millionaire came on the scene and she wanted to marry him. She asked for a divorce, so that was it.

I suppose I was twenty-five then, and in the dumps. With all these problems I said: 'To heck with everything!' I played these ships to South America, and even stayed down there for a while — because I had some insurance money I'd drawn out. I came back pretty much busted up, and after about six months of doing nothing I got a wire from my brother inviting me to Chicago. He had a little outfit called the Embassy Four, and I joined them at the Palmer House Hotel. By now, as I say, Prohibition had been repealed. In Chicago, drinks were flowing like mad. So was I. We played opposite Ted Weems, also Shep Fields and a couple more 'Mickey Mouse' bands, then went to St Louis, Kansas City, New Orleans and down around there. I did this for a year and a half before deciding to have a change.

During this time, around 1935 and 1936, I was seeing a lot of Squirrel Ashcraft. Now Squirrel came from a family of lawyers — barristers I guess you would call them. His father, and grandfather before him, built up a great law firm, Ashcraft, Ashcraft and Ashcraft. So Squirrel was flush with money then — I don't know how he's doing now — but that didn't affect him. He was a swell guy, he loved jazz and I would call him one of the best friends I ever had. Squirrel played piano, string bass and accordion, and he was darn good on that accordion. I used to go up to his house all the time and tell him my problems. He knew I was busted up, and he often helped me. He brought me out of my shell to a degree, and I would like to pay him a tribute on that score. Squirrel said to me: 'You want to play jazz, Jimmy. Why don't you get a band together and start off with a recording date?' It was a little commercial for me with the Embassy Four, so I set out on my own again.

Benny Goodman was in Chicago at the Congress Hotel with his first great swing band — Krupa and all those guys — so I got his trombone player, Joe Harris, and the tenor saxophonist, Dick Clark. My brother was on guitar, Rosy McHargue on clarinet, Jack Gardner on piano, George Wettling at the drums, and Country Washburn — out of the Weems band — on bass. Ashcraft booked the recording date at Brunswick, and we made four titles: *Eccentric, Panama, Original Dixieland Onestep* and the *Mason Dixon Line* thing. It wasn't quite like the original Chicago mob, of course. That gang had all split up, and though you met other players you liked, they didn't seem to have the drive of the originals. That Chicago mob! Every one had a beat, and when we got them all together, they spelled ... 'Mother' shall we say?

Anyway, I had got started, and after a while I secured a job at the Three Deuces. *Down Beat* had a guy by the name of Carl Conns: he opened this place and helped get the men together. I know Joe Rushton was there on bass sax, and George Barnes, who was seventeen then, came over for an audition. He had an amplified guitar. I had never heard one of them before, and thought it would be horrible. But when he started to play, it was really something. This was the same George Barnes I had on the recent Bix album, and he was a wonderful addition to the band. Floyd Bean came in on piano, Pat Pattison was on bass, and we had Anita O'Day doing the vocals.

I worked there for several months, then had an offer to go to the Sherman Hotel as the alternate band to all the big names that went in there. We took Gene Krupa's place for a week — and stayed about a year and a half. Came 1939 and I was still in Chicago. One day I got a letter from George Avakian, with Decca in New York, asking me to round up certain men for a Chicago Jazz album. All were to be Chicago-born and raised. Avakian more or less picked them — Boyce Brown, Bud Jacobson, Floyd Bean, Jim Lannigan, Hank Isaacs and the two McPartlands. Boyce was a great artist on alto, even then hinting at the modern style. He was full of fire and enthusiasm, wrote poetry also. He is a monk now, I am told, living in a monastery.

But as I remember the date, it was rough. When I woke up that morning I couldn't open my mouth; had an infected wisdom tooth, and my jaws were all swollen. When Bud came in he said: 'We'll get some brandy down you and see if we can loosen it up.' I kept sipping on this brandy till I'd drunk about a pint. My mouth began to open, and boy! I felt good. Then I tried playing. It sounded okay, so we did the date. I think we did very well on those four sides. *The World Is Waiting For The Sunrise* was named by *Down Beat* the jazz record of the year. It still swings!

Indirectly, it was Glenn Miller who brought me back from Chicago to New York. You see, Bobby Hackett was leading at Nick's when he was called to go with Glenn's orchestra. Nick Rongetti and Eddie Condon got together and sent for me. So I took over the band, which included Eddie, Pee Wee and pianist Mel Powell. I was up on West 10th Street for maybe nine months, then took the band from Nick's to the Brass Rail in Chicago — all except Mel, that is, who went with Benny Goodman. After about six weeks, Jack Teagarden came through town and asked me to join him for old time's sake. He told me brother Charlie was going to come on the band, that we would have a wonderful time together. That was enough, I said, 'I'm sold!' The band was terrific, and I enjoyed playing in it until suddenly, in the latter part of 1942, I got very patriotic.

When the war came on, people tried to duck the services. 'How are you going to win a war,' I asked myself, 'if nobody joins the army?' There was one answer for me. I went in with an automatic weapons outfit. Army bands wanted me, but I wouldn't go. I was in for rough training for a year and went down from 195 to 165 lb. That's a lot of weight to lose but I had it to lose, because there had been a great deal of eating and drinking with Teagarden. After that year, we sailed for Europe, landing in Scotland.

We had had a few drinks, and coming in on the tender the guys shouted: 'Hey Mac get out your horn and blow.' I played *Bluebells Of Scotland*, the first tune my mother ever taught me, starting off sweet and then swinging a chorus. You could hear it all around the bay; it was a very dramatic thing really.

Up came a colonel to ask who had played the trumpet. I said: 'I did. Cpl. McPartland.'

'Very good, Corporal, very good for relations,' says the colonel.

I'll skip over the war, except to say that after the invasion in Normandy I eventually got in a US camp show called *Band-wagon*, and in that show was a girl called Marian Page. I knew her about four weeks, liked her very much, thought she played piano very well. I proposed, she accepted me, but we had to postpone our marriage, because of the war, until February 3, 1945. We got our own show together, and came to England for a while. After returning to America we had six months' vacation, then went to work on the South Side of Chicago — Marian, myself and a rhythm section.

Then the fellows from the Brass Rail asked me to come in there. I said that if I went in, I wanted to play jazz. They said that was what they wanted me to do. After we'd been there about three months, doing very well, *Time* magazine gave me and the band a heck of a good write-up. It made business real good, and we stayed in the Rail a year and a half.

Dave Tough came to Chicago with JATP during that time, so we naturally got together, and he came over to hear our outfit. Marian was making the arrangements, and they leaned towards the modern side. I didn't mind them, though, because they allowed us to swing. And so long as the music swings, what's the difference? I asked Dave to come back with me. He said he would, after he had straightened a few things out. He could see we weren't playing real old-fashioned, and he liked the music. Then I got a letter from him saying he had just been in hospital. We'd talked over the drinking problem, which we both had, and agreed to give it up. I was just writing to ask him exactly when he would be joining me, when I got word that Davey Tough was dead.

To me, and to a whole lot of jazz musicians, Tough was the best drummer in the world to play with. He laid down a tremendous beat, a good steady rhythm. And he'd let you play all the time, would complement your playing and feed you with rhythm. He wouldn't throw 'bombs' and a lot of things that didn't add anything to the music. He saw it as his job to keep that rhythm going, and his beat was constant, flowing — in the groove, as we say. The reason why we didn't hear so much talk about Tough is that he was a band drummer — for the band instead of for himself. Dave used to make a band GO. What more can you say? George Wettling probably comes next on my list for that kind of drumming, by the way. And both were interesting men. Davey wrote exceptionally well, did a lot of reading and writing. Wettling is the artist. He paints, does impressionist things.

I'd like to end this series, which I have really enjoyed doing, by telling you my own philosophy as far as jazz is concerned. I believe in the wedding of modern and traditional music so long as the jazz swings and flows and has feeling. Naturally the fundamentals must be right: intonation, phrasing and instrumental facility. Then if a person plays with swing and feeling, that is all I ask, whether the style be jazz or progressive, or whatever you wish to call it. I don't go so much with bands playing the real old-time jazz such as ragtime. It's a matter of opinion, of course, but I think it has to progress. I want to impress upon *Melody Maker* readers that when they discuss jazz they shouldn't put a thing down unless they've heard it enough to form an opinion — and let's hope it's an honest opionion. Please don't be swayed by a clique into saying 'This is good and nothing but this is good!' I certainly want to keep my mind open. If it's good music, enjoy it, no matter what facet of jazz it may be.

As for recreating the past, I don't wish to do it, unless for a special purpose, like the Bix tribute. Jazz has progressed, and what I like about the modern phase is that it has brought in beautiful harmonies. I love that, and I am sure it is one thing modern jazz has contributed to standard jazz. Of course there are differences in the styles. I've noticed that the kind of jazz I play is more of a 'let yourself go' thing. Some of the modernists like Miles Davis seem afraid to do that — they hold themselves in check, and that seems drab to me. But others can let themselves go, and when the music's swinging it's good. All you can say is that genuine progress is a slow process. Meanwhile I love to listen to Louis Armstrong, and Billy Butterfield, and Bobby Hackett. And then I'll take Bud Freeman any time. He swings.

You can't always sound great — remember that. So just play your best, forget about factions, and do your darn'dest to swing. Maybe 70 per cent of the time it'll be there.

Good Luck.

Sy Oliver

*For a good many years Sy Oliver was something of a musicians' musician, an
inside name respected in the trade but only familiar to younger jazz collectors,
when known at all, as musical director of an assortment of record sessions. In
earlier decades, though, his was a Great Name. Sy Oliver was the man popu-
larly supposed to have created the Jimmie Lunceford sound; then he overhauled
the Tommy Dorsey band and cemented his standing as one of jazz and swing
music's most original orchestrators.*

*Now, seen in Europe quite frequently over the past few years, Sy has been
breaking fresh ground as a 'personality' leader who sings, blows trumpet, chats
up the audience and bandsmen and features many of his own tunes and scores.*

*I spoke to Sy in April 1974, after a tour by Warren Covington and the Dorsey
orchestra, and this piece dates from that conversation, and one a year earlier
when he led his own band at the Dunkirk Festival.*

Oliver's name — or rather his nickname (he was born Melvin James Oliver) —
has been bandied about by veteran collectors for so many years that the 'Sy'
sounds perfectly natural, though it obviously has nothing to do with his first or
second names. His favourite story of how he came by it is that he was 'so
sagacious as a boy that people started calling him "Psychology".' But that isn't
entirely true, he says crisply. 'The truth of the matter was that I was playing
with a bunch of idiots that didn't understand anybody that spoke English. And
they used to follow me around and tease me. I was a kid, you know. So one of
them nicknamed me "Psychology" for no reason except that it was a big word
and sounded ridiculous.'

He laughs uproariously and adds that of course he is basically a very fine
psychologist, which comes from years of 'training in self-denial'.

It is one of the remarkable facts about Oliver, as I always understood it, that
though both his parents were excellent musicians, and his father was a professional teacher too, he received no formal musical training. He agrees he had
little beyond basic music tuition, even on trumpet. 'I came up in a musical
atmosphere. My mother was a fine piano player, my father played several
instruments, and both of them were teachers actually. But I didn't want to learn
piano.'

Did his father teach him trumpet? Not really, he says. 'He showed me how
to run a scale. But almost immediately afterwards he became quite seriously
ill and never recovered. By then, however, my interest in music had been
awakened and it seemed natural to me to be in music.

'To be truthful, my interest was stimulated by a friend I had named Al Sears
— you probably know him as a tenor player. Well, Al and I grew up together;
he played in the local orchestra and I followed that. At that time I had to be
home at dark, and my one interest in being in that orchestra was so I could stay
out with Al. And they needed a trumpet player. So I got involved with
trumpet, and learned quickly.

'After dad got sick I started playing with the orchestra, while I was in my teens. And I was still at high school when I joined a band called Cliff Barnett's Club Royal Serenaders. There were two trumpets in the band and I was one of them.'

At the age of about seventeen, Oliver left Ohio to work with Zack Whyte's band, after which he joined Alphonso Trent for a few months and then returned to Whyte's Chocolate Beau Brummels. In the summer of 1933 Sy became a trumpet player, singer and arranger for the Jimmie Lunceford band, and it was then the jazz world at large got to hear about him. He had written scores for the Zack Whyte band, and recalls that his arrangement of *Nobody's Sweetheart* was one of their popular numbers, and was probably the first arrangement he had done entirely on his own.

'I had written saxophone choruses, trumpet and brass choruses, little ensemble choruses, but I think *Nobody's Sweetheart* was the first thing I did completely. And I worked on it from Maine to Florida — a month. Well, I said I did the arrangment but there were no rhythm parts; there was just the front line, I didn't know anything about chords.'

Among the bands and arrangers from whom he derived early inspiration, Oliver mentions Ellington, Henderson, Don Redman, Jelly Roll Morton and McKinney's Cotton Pickers.

'I listened to Fletcher's records. He was becoming quite prominent then; in fact he was prominent, with records like *Hot Mustard*, *The Stampede* and *Clarinet Marmalade*. And of course I was quite close to the Cotton Pickers, at the time they started. They were from Springfield, Ohio, and used to play in my home town. And I heard them before Don Redman joined them. But they were already basically the band that they were to become. Yes, John Nesbitt was with them then, also Dave Wilborn, Cuba Austin; all the guys were there.

'Fact is, I copied a lot of the things they played. You remember the record they did on *Baby Won't You Please Come Home* with the long-metre chorus? Fathead Thomas sang it. Well, we do that now.

'Oh, I listened to them a lot and you can imagine the influence. Many of those things I copied literally and, as I say, we're still doing that long-metre chorus.'

After his casual apprenticeship to the arranging craft, Oliver — without a single lesson in theory behind him — knew that writing was for him. And he wasn't all that knocked-out about being a trumpet player.

'I wasn't nearly as interested in the trumpet as I was in writing — that was what appealed to me most, and that was what I decided to follow.'

Sy was heard during 1933 by Lunceford, to whom he submitted a few scores. As a result he was asked to join that band in the early summer of '33. For Lunceford, he made his reputation with a series of distinctive arrangements. *Four Or Five Times*, *My Blue Heaven*, *Stomp It Off*, *Dream Of You*, *Since My Best Girl Turned Me Down*, *Swanee River*, *Organ Grinder's Swing*, *For Dancers Only*, *Annie Laurie*, *Margie*, *Cheatin' On Me*, *'Tain't What You Do* and *Ain't She Sweet* are some of the better known. There were many more which went on to records, and I ask what percentage of the arranging he did. Was it the bulk of the book? Oliver looks quizzical and says he doesn't know.

'I never thought about it, actually. Eddie Wilcox, the pianist, and I did most of the writing. He wrote quite a few, and was excellent. All that beautiful saxophone scoring like *Sleepy Time Gal, Sophisticated Lady* ... Wilcox wrote those things.

'I'd say the work was equally divided but more of my arrangements got recorded because I did all the vocal quartet and trio numbers, the vocal things. *Hittin' The Bottle*, now that was by Eddie Durham, and he did quite a few arrangments, too. But that sterling vocal on *Hittin' The Bottle*, that was me. How it came about, they allowed me to sing it because nobody else wanted to be bothered with the song.'

Lunceford's was a disciplined ensemble and, former members have told me, a close-knit community with its own rules. Oliver is on record as saying that 'the guys played so well that anybody could have written for the band.' But did he not experience some difficulties in the beginning?

'Well, the only problem I ever had with the fellows was the one I've had all my life. I used to be very impatient with the musicians about getting things played. But other than that, no problems. At that point in life I just expected too much of people. Not that I wrote difficult arrangements. But the thing people don't understand about music is that it's more difficult to play simple music, which requires interpretation, than to play technical stuff. Anybody with technique can play lots of notes. When you play something like *Swanee River* it's nothing but footholds where you have to supply whatever spirit is to be in it.'

Were there other difficulties, though, with Lunceford and later Tommy Dorsey, in the way of musical resistance to ideas he had, to his conception of a successful jazz score? He says not in the sense I mean, because he never worked for a leader who told him what to write.

'The only difficulty I ever had was in that many of the things, back in those days with the Lunceford band, that I attempted to do were innovative and the fellows didn't understand them. I remember once getting into a hassle, and I questioned Jimmie's attitude and asked him why he was siding with the fellows. And he said: "Well, Sy, the fellows need me to side with them. Furthermore you've got to understand that if they thought and felt exactly as you do, I wouldn't need you. They'd all be Sy Olivers. Give 'em a chance."'

One or two musicians I have spoken to had less than unmixed admiration for Lunceford as musician and bandleader. How much, in Sy's view, did he contribute to that band. Well, says Oliver, he will put it this way: if there hadn't been a Jimmie Lunceford there wouldn't have been any Jimmie Lunceford band. Quite so, but will he elucidate? Gladly.

'People don't understand what actually creates a band, an organisation like that. They don't understand why Lunceford's was different from any other band that ever existed. It was different because of Lunceford. If he hadn't contributed a thing musically it wouldn't have made a bit of difference. It was his influence that counted. Until I met Jimmie I'd never met anybody of whom I felt any intellectual fear. I'd never met anyone who impressed me as much.

'The musicians don't all realise it, but that man raised them. He changed their lives. They may resent him for any number of reasons, but there's not one of 'em whose life is not better for having known Jimmie Lunceford. You could not be around him without learning — about life, that's something he taught us. There was a certain *esprit de corps* existed in that band, and he achieved the whole thing by saying absolutely nothing.'

Talking further about the Lunceford 'Express' in its heyday, Oliver ventures to suggest there were two outstanding qualities which made the band unique: first, the showmanship-with-musicianship; and second, the individuality of its style.

'Never before, to my knowledge, had there been a band which was an excellent show band but also was immensely musical. And the other thing was the sound, as unique in its fashion as Ellington's was in his. But there was an important difference. Ellington, Basie, any fine band of established character has a certain sameness about anything they play. Darn near every number Lunceford did was different from the one which preceded it and the one which followed.

'Now musicians are a funny group of people. They don't usually attempt to please the public who pay the bill; they attempt to please other musicians. So the guys in the band sometimes used to say: "Gee, Sy, why don't you fix such-and-such a number like so and so's playing?" I'd say: "What? I could do that, but you just remember that this year we had five hit records and you're making a whole lot of money. And they're still playing at the Savoy. Which way do you want it?"

'But on the other hand, those same musicians would come and hear our band and say it was the greatest thing they'd ever heard.'

Mention of the Savoy brings to mind the jumping Savoy Sultans which once used to give a hard time to even the most illustrious rivals who did their stuff at the Lennox Avenue dance hall. Smiling cheerfully at the memory, Sy gives a carefully weighed opinion that the Sultans were ideal for the place where they were playing and the people they were working to.

'They were there for the dancers. That place used to be called the House of Happy Feet, and that's exactly the music they played.'

In 1938 Oliver quit Lunceford — wanting more money for his arrangements was one of the causes — and before long became staff writer (and occasional singer) for Tommy Dorsey. Again, did he run into difficulties over the matter of interpretation?

'What happened there,' he says, 'is that when I joined the band it was of a Dixieland persuasion and couldn't literally play my arrangements. I knew they couldn't, and Tommy knew they couldn't. In fact, we'd discussed it before I joined, and he assured me he'd get musicians who could play in that fashion, because he wanted a band that could swing. However, I heard them broadcast one night from the Astor Roof, and I got out of bed, went down there and up to the bandstand, pulled Tommy's trouser leg and said: "Later, daddy." He caught me before I got out of the hotel and told me at that time: "Now Sy, we both know these guys don't play the style, but I will get men who can." A year later there were two men in the band that were in it when I joined it. And the band we wound up with was the one with Buddy Rich, Don Lodice and those guys. And that was a swinging band — one of the best I ever worked with.'

Dorsey himself was a man of imagination, then? He was a man bordering on genius, according to Sy.

'He was a great man on the points of leadership, concept, musicianship and understanding. He also was highly intolerant of incompetence, and because he was himself such a tremendous player he expected everybody to do what he did, and everybody couldn't.'

What about his alleged intolerance in general? And the fighting streak so generously publicised by press and film? Sy's bearded face nods in half-agreement. 'Tommy was very physical,' he allows. 'But while we're on that subject, people tend to talk about that part of Tommy's character but never talk about the other side, the things he did like taking care of Davie Tough, the drummer, from the day he got sick to the day he died. And when Bunny Berigan was at the point of drinking himself to death and finding it hard to get a job, who gave him a job? Tommy. And when Gene Krupa had the rap, who gave him a job? Tommy. People don't know about these things he did that were never publicised, and which he never talked about.'

Time's late, and we've not said much about Sy's trumpet playing. I know that his initial enthusiasm for trumpet began to wane towards the end of his stay with Lunceford, but in the mid Thirties he was rated by some critics among the foremost exponents of the muted growl style. He explains why he took to specialising in growl playing.

'I decided to play that style because it was really the only thing left open to me. Steve Stevenson and later Paul Webster had the high-register work; and Eddie Tompkins was quite fluent, and played very well on solos as well as lead parts. So the only thing left for me to do was play the growl style, which was different from what the others were doing. Now I was very impressed with Duke Ellington, of course, and liked many of the pieces he did using growl trumpet. In fact, early on, when I first heard his record of *East St Louis Toodle-O*, in 1926 or '27 (I think *Birmingham Breakdown* was on the other side), it actually changed my life. Life was never the same after those records. It sounds almost too simplistic but it's true.'

Ex-Luncefordians have been known to smile about Sy's horn prowess, and I tell him this. Fortunately he smiles too, and tells a couple of stories against himself. Trummy Young often referred to him as being 'good in the middle register', and Sy receives the information with the remark, 'I'll have to speak to Trummy about that, tell him to stop destroying the myth.'

Well, he continues, one day while he was playing a solo of something like *Stardust*, very quiet and tender, Moses Allen suddenly piped up in his high tenor voice: 'He's the low-register man in the band.'

Much laughter before Sy concludes with the statement that he stopped trumpet playing in 1939 when he left Lunceford. And when he started his new band in 1970 he got out his horn and played with the band.

'I had retired, you know, and my wife — to whom I'd been married nearly thirty years then — had never heard me play trumpet because I'd never even taken it out of the case at home. Anyway, I was sitting one day writing the book, with TV on of course, and then I took up the horn and just started to blow a little. And she listened to me and told me: "That sounds good." But later she told me she went into the next room and closed the door and said: "He'll never make it."'

Jim Robinson and Kid Howard

From time to time I have interviewed more than one musician together. One of the most memorable discussions took place in January 1959 when the George Lewis Band of New Orleans visited Britain. Here is the piece I wrote.

For the past five days the staid Imperial Hotel in Bloomsbury has housed a group of players from the pages of New Orleans history. Their names are George Lewis, Kid Howard, Jim Robinson, Joe Robichaux, Slow Drag Pavageau and Joe Watkins. They arrived in Liverpool last Saturday afternoon to a stirring reception, and visited the local jazz clubs the same night. On Sunday they steamed (rather late) into London, and at Euston Station walked bewildered into the most spirited welcome I have yet seen given to visiting jazzmen. Understandably they had no complaints. As Jim Robinson remarked, when I called on him next day: 'It was a wonderful greeting. After I got off the train and saw what was happening, I knew the people's hearts were in the right place.'

Said Avery (Kid) Howard, his companion in the brass section: 'George had told me about the English people, but I wasn't prepared for that welcome. Though I was carrying my horn, a case and some other things, that band of Ken Colyer's had me dancing a few steps as I walked up the platform.'

I asked these two brassmen, who came before the public eye as a result of the mid-Forties resurgence of interest in New Orleans jazz, what effect the revival had had on them.

'Musically, it made little difference to me,' said Robinson, who is a tall, good-natured man, not at all grey-haired despite his sixty-six years.

'I never changed my style ... can't play no other way. I like all trombone players but I continue to play my way. I blow a little easier today — don't exert myself too much — but basically it's the same music I always played.

'I make more money now, because in the old days in New Orleans the music was good but you didn't earn much money. And then there's the appreciation ... that makes me *feel* good. If you enjoy my music, well, I'll try to play more.

'Sometimes it's a hard shift, even now. But it's better to be a professional man than a worker, you know what I mean? Shifting them rocks, man, that's *real* tough.'

Kid Howard, shorter and younger than Robinson but equally good-humoured, agreed about the appreciation.

'When you're playing and your soul's in there, then, if nobody pays no mind to what you're doing, it kills you. That recognition is good for the soul.

'As for things being easier, that depends where you're working. We have some easier jobs now, and since the revival I made more money. But if you take out a pencil and figure it, it comes out about the same as it used to. When I worked at 308 Bourbon Street, The Tavern, we had four pieces. I started with the band at a dollar a night — I'm talking about the Thirties — but the proprietor liked me and raised me to two. Finally I made four, seven nights a week (that was before the Union got strong), which was 28 dollars. We didn't have no tax to pay, and the people would often leave 10 or 15 dollars apiece in the kitty for the members of the band.

'The cost of living was lower; you know, rent was cheap. . . .' Here, with a flash of gold teeth, Jim Robinson interrupted to remind him: 'Pork chops were cheap, liver was cheap, so was liquor.'

'So you see,' Howard concluded, 'you were doing as good really. Because now, when you make money, Uncle's got to have some and the Union's got to have some, so when all that's taken out and you go get a steak, man, you're into real money.'

Kid Howard, who started in jazz as a drummer, has broad tastes in trumpet playing and music generally.

'From the beginning,' he says, 'I played with a lot of trumpet men, while I was on drums, and I'm for *all* good trumpet men — that's for sure. I make one exception . . . that is Louis Armstrong. He's truly my favourite.' Howard quite often speaks of Louis, pronouncing the name 'Lewis', as many Americans do.

'Let me straighten you on this subject: you know the type of jazz we play — that's what I play. But when I'm at home, listening to the radio, I like bop or classical music or any type of music . . . and every type of trumpet player.

'You asked me about some of the New Orleans men. Well, Joe Oliver, I never knew Joe. . . . I'll be fifty-one this April. Freddy Keppard? No, that's out of my jurisdiction, too, though I know his brother, Louis. He's still very much alive, right around the corner from me on North Villere Street.

'Mutt Carey I never worked with, but I did work in parades with Kid Shots Madison, a fine man. Bunk Johnson I heard when he was in New York, and he was good then.'

So far as influences go, Howard was ready to acknowledge a debt to Chris Kelly.

'The man that gave me my first lesson in the major scale was Chris,' he says. 'Chris was wonderful. He wasn't a man to go upstairs, wasn't a high-note man or anything like that, but he could use a mute and play low. I still have my mute exactly like Chris Kelly's.

'Now Buddy Petit, he played like Chris, and played a lot of horn. He died in 1931 and I played in the funeral procession. Louis Armstrong, who was in New Orleans at the Suburban Gardens, was a pall-bearer.'

One obvious question to ask was why the nickname Kid. Howard explained: 'I gave myself the name when I started out on cornet. I took it up from Kid Rena, Kid Shots, Kid Punch and the others. By the way, did you know Punch Miller was back in New Orleans, playing occasionally?'

Robinson and Howard have enjoyed a long association. In the early Thirties they worked together at the La Vida dance hall, and also in Kid Howard's Brass Band.

'The La Vida was what we call a jitney joint,' Jim remembers, 'in the middle of Iberville, between Rampart and Burgundy. We played 8 o'clock till three in the morning. The band would never stop playing, but you could leave the stand, one guy at a time.

'They were short numbers, just two choruses; the dancers paid a nickel and grabbed a chick. Well, it was a nickel when we started. Later it went up to a dime.'

That was in the old days, but hard work is still done by musicians in New Orleans.

'On Bourbon Street, at the Paddock or anywhere, now that's a tough job,' says Jim. 'Tough, tough, tough. You work six hours, and those six look like twelve.'

Does Robinson ever get tired of music?

'No,' he says, 'I love it. I enjoy playing trombone and when I'm not playing I like listening. I have the TV at home, the radio and the music box. Sometimes I'm just putting some records on when my wife says: "From the TV to the radio to the phonograph ... when you going to eat?"'

FOUR

Rhythm Section

Piano

Mary Lou Williams

Between April and June 1954, Melody Maker ran the life story of Mary Lou Williams. It ran to eleven instalments, was based on three weeks of interviews and was entirely Mary Lou's own words. All but the final section is reprinted here. Through '53 and '54 Mary became a greatly valued friend, and after her return to the USA she kept in contact. She visited us again in 1969 and I last saw her in Nice a few years ago. A lovely woman.

I have been tied up with music for about as long as I can remember. By the time I was four I was picking out little tunes my mother played on the reed organ in the living-room. We lived in a big, timber-framed building: what we called a shotgun house, because if you fired through the front door the shot passed through all the rooms and out into the back yard, likely ending up in the privy.

Quite a few musicians came to our house. And my ma took me to hear many more, hoping to encourage in me a love of music. But she wouldn't consent to my having music lessons, for she feared I might end up as she had done – unable to play except from paper. Soon I was playing piano around the district, though I was so small I had to sit on someone's lap to reach the keyboard.

There were two children, me and my older sister Mamie. My father I had never seen. A year or two later, the family moved to a neighbourhood in Pittsburgh which brought me my first experience of inter-racial feeling. This entire section was 'white' for five or six blocks, and for a while somebody was throwing bricks through our windows. There was nothing to do but stick it out in silence. Pretty soon the people there were tolerating us.

Then my mother married a man called Fletcher Burley. As a stepfather he was the greatest; and he loved the blues. Fletcher taught me the first blues I ever knew by singing them over to me.

Now it happened he was known as a professional gambler, and he sometimes took me with him at nights – to bring him luck, he said. We had moved again, to Hamilton Boulevard in East Liberty (a suburb of Pittsburgh about six miles from the main drag), and I went with him into a variety of smoke-filled gaming rooms, most of which had an upright against one wall. The game was generally 'skin' – the Georgia skin game – and the players would all be men, for women weren't allowed in these places. I was kind of smuggled in, and before the cards began I used to play a few things on the piano. Often I received as much as 20 dollars in tips, which my stepfather had started rolling by dropping a dollar in his hat. This 'pound' had to be returned to him as soon as we got outside. Still, it was a fair deal.

We also visited Saturday hops and parties given at someone's house to raise money for rent and other bills. These functions were known as house-rent parties or chitterlin' struts. The windows were kept shut and the atmosphere was stagnant, but I was always fascinated by the boogie pianists and shuffling couples dancing on a spot. Sometimes they'd hire me at a dollar an hour for three hours. I would bring out all the blues and boogies Fletcher had taught me. Should I attempt a popular song or light classic, my step-father would ask why didn't I play some music.

I had now been attending Lincoln School for a couple of years, learning music and playing college teas and such. Outside, I had earned a local reputation as 'the gigging piano gal from East Liberty'. I was playing quite a bit of jazz now, and beginning to give it my own interpretation. Of course, my playing was influenced by favourite pianists: principally by Jack Howard, Earl Hines and Jelly Roll Morton. Of all the musicians I met in my childhood, one who stands out: Jack Howard, who played boogie-woogie so forcefully that he used to break up all the pianos. For those days, he was one of the grooviest, but never made the name he deserved. Jelly Roll I dug from records, and his composition, *The Pearls*, was then my number one solo. Many years later I recorded it for Decca at the instigation of John Hammond.

Offers for me to play dances, society parties, even churches, were now coming in regularly. For most dates I was paid the sum of one dollar per hour, and they always tipped me at the end of the night.

And there was usually something worth hearing in town those days, even if Pittsburgh was not one of the jazz centres. One Saturday night I went to a theatre on Frankstown Avenue where all the Negro shows were booked. But I hardly noticed any part of the show, for my attention was focussed on the lady pianist who worked there. She sat cross-legged at the piano, a cigarette in her mouth, writing music with her right hand while accompanying the show with her swinging left! Impressed, I told myself: 'Mary, you'll do that one day.' (And I did, travelling with Andy Kirk's band in the Thirties on one-nighters.)

The lady turned out to be Lovie Austin, who was working with the pit band and making all the orchestrations. It so happened that she was behind time, and hurriedly arranging a number for one of the acts further down the bill.

Another week, the fabulous Ma Rainey came into a little theatre on Wiley Avenue. Some of the older kids and I slipped down-town to hear the woman who had made blues history. Ma was loaded with real diamonds — in her ears, around her neck, in a tiara on her head. Both hands were full of rocks, too; her hair was wild and she had gold teeth. What a sight! To me, as a kid, the whole thing looked and sounded weird. When the engagement ended, and Ma had quit the scene, rumour had it that the jewellery was bought hot and that Ma was picked up and made to disgorge —losing all the loot she had paid for the stuff.

Of our local characters, one of the most famed was Lois Deppe, the popular baritone singer who had been around since 1918 or earlier. His band was the talk of Pennsylvania, and at that time included the great Earl Hines — a local boy from nearby Carnegie — and Vance Dixon on saxophone and clarinet. Wherever Deppe's band appeared, the kids from all around were sure to go — and when Vance started to slap-tongue on that saxophone they really went wild. Numbers I remember the band doing were *Milenberg Joys*, *Isabelle* and *Congaine*. The last two were recorded by Deppe in the early Twenties. *Isabelle* I made as a solo for Columbia around 1935; I once asked Hines about it, thinking he might be the composer, but he did not remember it.

I must have been ten or eleven when I was taken to the Saturday afternoon dances at the Arcadia Ballroom where Deppe was playing. These dances ran from noon until 4 p.m., and shortly before break-up time the biggest fight would invariably commence. Half the kids in Pittsburgh could be seen running from the hall, grabbing the backs of street-cars to get away.

We had groups of kids from the different districts — East Liberty, Soho, the downtown district, and so on — who were considered very tough. If an East Liberty kid was caught in Soho, or downtown, he would either be assaulted or chased back to his own district.

I was at high school when my first big chance came along. *Hits And Bits*, a travelling TOBA show, had just hit town, and the pianist had failed to show up. 'Buzzin'' Harris, the owner, was frantic for a replacement. 'There's a girl in East Liberty could play your show,' he was told. He drove over to investigate, found me playing hopscotch with some kids, and thought a gag had been pulled on him. Reluctantly he agreed to hear me, and I must have proved something, because he started humming the show tunes for me. Within a few hours I had them off, was about ready to play the shows. That night I opened, and during the week Harris was over to the house to talk my mother into letting me leave home.

It was just before the summer vacation, and after a little argument my mother agreed. But she was backstage next day with the public notary, signing papers for me to go with the show for two months. My salary was to be 30 dollars a week, and mother fixed for a friend to go along with me. So I left Pittsburgh with *Hits And Bits* and travelled west to Detroit, Chicago, Cincinnati and St Louis. In the Windy City I again ran into Hines, who introduced me to Louis Armstrong. Both were working at the Vendome Theatre with Erskine Tate's orchestra. In fact, so far as the audience was concerned, they *were* the orchestra. Specialities were played from the pit, and I saw Louis stand up, wipe his mouth in preparation for a solo, and break up the place before he'd blown a note. That's how it was with Satchmo in Chicago then. After the show the boys took me over to the Sunset cabaret — owned by the now famous booking agent, Joe Glaser — to hear King Oliver. I was impressed no end by Oliver's kicking combo, and by his own expressive, tale-telling cornet.

I also looked up Lovie Austin — by now making a name in Chicago — at the Monogram, another house on the TOBA circuit. The initials stand for Theatre Owners' Booking Association — or, to us who had to work it, 'Tough on Black Artists'.

Next stop, St Louis: and there I met Charlie Creath, the river-boat king, who was known all over the Middle West for his crazy growl trumpet playing. Besides being a top jazz performer, Charlie was a most handsome cat.

In St Louis, our show picked up a young blues singer named Irene Scruggs (now in Paris with her daughter, dancer Baby Leazar Scruggs). Irene had not long settled in St Louis, and was starting out to become one of St Louis's finest singers.

Then on to Cleveland, where I met John Williams, later to become my husband. He was working at the theatre where we appeared, leading a five-piece combo known as John Williams and his Syncopators. John played alto, soprano and baritone saxes, also clarinet. Acknowledged to be one of the finest baritone players, he was much in demand. We named him 'Bearcat', on account of him being wild on the big saxophone, and it was this nickname which led in later years to the Kirk instrumental number, *Bearcat Shuffle*.

The Syncopators were strong in all departments. A man called Martin, a friend and schoolmate of Coleman Hawkins from St Joseph, Missouri, played tenor. Shirley Clay, from St Louis, was already blowing good trumpet (we used to call him 'Hoggy'). The drummer, Edward Temple, was a showman, but also a solid, subtle rhythm player. Then they had a banjoist whose name has got away from me. They didn't carry a brass bass. John Williams blew a slap-tongue two beats on baritone, when he wasn't taking a solo, like a bass horn would play. It eliminated the need for a tuba.

I played in the pit with this band, doubling on stage in the second half with a speciality that was slightly sensational. Spreading a sheet over the keys, I did a version of *Milenberg Joys* mostly with my elbows, winding up by taking a break while spinning around on the piano stool. I perpetrated this novelty until an older musician came to me one day and said he had detected something nice in my playing. He explained how ridiculous the clowning was, and there and then I decided to settle down and play seriously.

The piano had done well enough by me, but I wasn't going to be hung up with it without trying some other instruments. And at Westinghouse junior high school the opportunity existed for every pupil to study a variety of instruments. I was back at school after my eight weeks' tour with *Hits And Bits*, having said goodbye to comedian Buzzin' Harris and his wife Arletta, and parted from the show in Pittsburgh.

At Westinghouse we had some of the best music teachers in the world (I guess). Under their guidance, I tried out most of the instruments — last but not least being the violin. Right after the first fiddle lesson I played *Sheik Of Araby* on one string. My teacher advised me to forget it and stick to piano; which I did.

In later years, both Billy Strayhorn and Erroll Garner attended that same school and class, receiving tuition from the master I was with. One day I pinch-hit for a tuning fork the teacher had lost, and it was discovered I possessed perfect pitch. Rumour of this oddity spread throughout the school, and pupils would drop pots, pans and other loud objects, asking: 'What note, Mary?'

At this point in my career a very fine jazz orchestra came to Pittsburgh: McKinney's Cotton Pickers, with Prince Robinson on saxophone and Todd Rhodes at the piano. Todd became a friend and adviser to me, used to take me out jamming, and on one date let me sit in with the band. Some nights we jammed all the way from East Liberty down to Wylie Avenue, then a notorious section of town which was held in dread by so-called decent people. We always wound up in the Subway on Wylie, a hole in the ground to which the cream of the crop came to enjoy the finest in the way of entertainment. For me it was a paradise. Visiting musicians made straight for the place to listen to artists like beautiful Louise Mann, and Baby Hines, Earl's first wife.

Until this time I had paid little attention to singers, but the feeling in Baby's singing made the strongest impression upon me. Baby is still working, I believe, for I saw her in Jersey City in 1952: but she never received the recognition she merits. Those days, when she began a number like *You're An Old Smoothie*, the customers showered tips on her in appreciation — and I've seen 50- and 100-dollar bills among them. Her torch songs brought real tears to their eyes — as you can guess, for that kind of dough!

At this same spot I heard a lot of Prince Robinson, and have never forgotten his excellent tenor. He was one of the outstanding jazz players of the genera-tion. Prince would refuse to jam with inadequate musicians, waiting until he could round up some other out-of-the-ordinary players to make the session inspirational or at least worthwhile.

One way and another I was having a ball — playing gigs, jamming and listening to fine musicians. Then came a crisis at home. My stepfather fell sick, and it meant I had to support the family. Finishing up at high school, I went back to Buzzin' Harris'. John Williams still had the band, which by now included trumpet player Doc Cheatham. Doc came from a long line of medicos, was studying himself when he decided to follow the call of music. He was a very accomplished musician.

For a time the tour went well, taking us to different theatres on the TOBA and Gus Sun circuits. Suddenly we found ourselves stranded in Cincinnati — 350 miles from home and short of gold. Just as we were feeling dragged, Fate stepped in — in the shape of a telegram inviting us to join the celebrated dance team of Seymour and Jeanette to play the Keith-Orpheum theatres. It was practically the rags to riches routine. We were on our way to one of the top theatre circuits direct from TOBA, one of the toughest. At that time, Keith's were booking only one other Negro act besides Seymour and Jeanette (I think it was Bojangles), and we felt justified in saying 'at last!'

Right away John sent to Kansas City for banjoist Joe Williams. On trumpet

14. Bud Freeman and Buck Clayton in England, 1963 *(photo courtesy Melody Maker)*. 15. Left: Harry 'Sweets' Edison *(photo courtesy Nancy Miller Elliott)*

16. Nice, 1975: 'A Tribute to Louis Armstrong': (left to right) Earl Hines, Ruby Braff, Bobby Hackett, Pee Wee Erwin (*photo courtesy Beryl Bryden*)

17. Top: Thomas Jefferson with Sam Lee (tenor) and Joe Watkins (drums) (*photo courtesy Howard Lucraft*). 18. Below: 1945: Max with Jimmy and Marian McPartland

19. Paris, 1954: Lee Collins with Zutty Singleton (drums)
20. Left: Max Kaminsky (*photo Jack Bradley*)

21. Slam Stewart (left) and Major Holley *(photo courtesy Hans Harzheim)*

22. Mary Lou Williams.

23. Left: Joe Bushkin (*photo courtesy Capitol Records, Inc.*)

24. (Left to right) Sarah Vaughan and Billy Eckstine (*photo courtesy Melody Maker*). 25. Left: London, 1959: Dinah Washington (*photo courtesy Beryl Bryden*)

26. 1954: Billie Holiday with Max and Betty Jones at the Jazz Record Retailers Association dinner (*photo courtesy Doug Dobell*)

27. Max and Betty Jones with Billie Holiday, Studio Club, London, 1954 (*photo Louis McKay*)

there was a guy called Max. Doc Cheatham's uncle, a St Louis dentist had reclaimed him for a while. On trombone we had the fabulous Sylvester Briscoe, who could and did play more horn with his foot in the slide than most cats can with their hands.

Seymour and Jeanette had previously worked with pit bands. But Seymour was now a sick man who could no longer dance flat out. He was famed for a wild strut, which he performed with cane, and it was said that the dance had stretched his heart to the size of a saucer, which seemed likely to anyone who had seen him strutting. He needed a supporting attraction, and it was our job to accompany and provide a couple of speciality numbers.

When Seymour saw me seated at the piano at that first rehearsal, he shouted: 'What's that kid doing here? Call your piano player and let's get started.'

'She is it,' replied John, smiling.

'We cannot have a child in this act,' Jeanette put in. 'Especially a female child. We'll have to put pants on her, or something.'

By this time, the boys were falling out. John told the dancers not to worry but just to listen. We ran through one or two of our showiest things and we were in.

The band went over well: so well, in fact, that Seymour kept changing our spot. We thought at any moment we might lose the job because of the way the public was going for our *Tiger Rag*. This featured Briscoe's crazy act of playing trombone with both hands behind his back, the instrument somehow wedged between his mouth and the floor. This may sound impossible, but it is the truth. I never knew how he did it, and never saw anyone who could imitate him.

Tiger Rag was the last number, and needed to be. The applause even stopped the movie that followed us, often a Rin Tin Tin picture. After our show, the house would be blacked, then the dog appeared on the screen. Some nights they had to cut the picture for us to take another encore, and the guys would say: 'Don't look like Rin Tin Tin will bark tonight.'

Seymour's death cut short this engagement, and the group was disbanded while Jeanette looked for another partner. By this time drummer Temple had gone and been replaced by a good but heavy footed Kaycee man named Abie Price. Trombonist Briscoe had also split.

My travels had not taken me to New York until now, when we played the 81st Theatre on Broadway and a few weekend gigs. To someone who lived for music, this was it. Jeanette did a stint at the old Lincoln Theatre, off Lennox Avenue, and not being able to afford five pieces, she just took me in with her. I played the entire show in the pit, then went on stage to accompany her act. That week was the most exciting of my life thus far. I was working with some of the boys from Duke Ellington's Washingtonians — Sonny Greer, Bubber Miley and Tricky Sam Nanton among them, and never had I heard such music before. The two growlers, Bubber and Tricky were the nicest to me. Though they invariably took their jugs into the pit with them, they never got too juiced to play or to respect me. Coming downstairs for the show, I sometimes overheard Bubber warning the guys: 'Be careful now, the kid's coming down.'

I stayed in New York, eyes and ears open to all the attractions Harlem had to offer. Like most other pianists I revered the amazing Fats Waller, who had lately made a splash wailing on organ at the Lincoln. When he quit New York, his admirers wouldn't let anyone follow him on organ, and those frantic kids were likely to throw most anything if you tried. Naturally it was a great day for me when some musicians took me across to Connie's Inn on 7th Avenue to meet Fats, working on a new show. The way Waller worked was anything but slavery. The OAO (one and only) sat overflowing the piano stool, a jug of whisky within easy reach. Leonard Harper, the producer, said: 'Have you anything written for this number, Fats?' And Fats would reply: 'Yeah, go on ahead with the dance, man.' Then he composed his number while the girls were dancing. He must have composed the whole show, with lyrics, while I was sitting there — ears working overtime. Meanwhile, he bubbled over with so many stories and funny remarks that those girls could hardly hoof it for laughing. The girls, 35- to 40-dollar-a-week chorus beauties, were loaded with enough ice around their shapely ankles to sink a battleship, for these were generous days in New York.

After the rehearsal, one of the boys — knowing my memory — bet Fats I could repeat all the tunes he had just written: a bet Waller snapped up at paying odds. Falling apart with nerves at having to play before this big name, I was prodded to the piano, but managed to concentrate and play nearly everything I had heard Fats play. He was knocked out, picking me up and throwing me in the air and roaring like a crazy man.

Not long afterwards, Harper asked me how I'd like to work at Connie's Inn. I would, and I began playing intermission piano while the band was over at the Lafayette Theatre, just up the Avenue near the Tree of Hope, where musicians used to exchange stories and await work. In these later months, I ran into many great artists: luscious Florence Mills, Bill Robinson, Adelaide Hall, comedian Johnny Huggins and Nina Mae McKinney (then about sixteen), who wished me to accompany her.

I was glad of the chance to meet Clarence Williams and Jelly Roll Morton. I had admired Williams's compositions for some time, and I found him a kindly man who seemed to like me, and who was reassuring about the things I played him. I have never seen Clarence again, though he lives in New York to this day.

Mr Jelly Lord was a more frightening proposition. He was considered a big deal then, and he had me scared. When the guys dragged me into his office downtown we were surprised to see him playing duets with an ofay piccolo player. At a convenient break, they introduced me and told Jelly they would like for him to hear me. Indicating that I should park my hips on the stool, Jelly gave over the piano and I got started on my favourite Morton piece, *The Pearls*. Almost immediately I was stopped and reprimanded, told the right way to phrase it. I played it the way Jelly told me, and when I had it to his satisfaction, I slipped in one of my own tunes. This made no difference. I was soon stopped and told: 'Now that passage should be phrased like this.'

Jelly Roll had a mouthful of diamond and spoke with a stammer when he got excited. He was what we call a 'big mouth', and the sound of his voice had me shaking in my boots. Any minute I was expecting to get up off the floor because I had played his *Pearls* wrong. That's how they trained you in those days (half those chorus girls had black eyes!), and Morton had the reputation of being a demanding taskmaster. Musicians — they really have it easy now!

My first real experience of the South came about the year 1927. In my earlier tours I had not crossed the Mason-Dixon line; now, domestic business rather than music took me there. John Williams and I decided to get married, and it meant going to Memphis, Tennessee, to meet his parents. Apparently they had saved for John to go to college and study law, and they didn't approve of his musical career. I could understand their disappointment, because I saw that education meant everything to the Southern Negro then. A teacher, lawyer or doctor was regarded almost as some kind of a god down there, while musicians were more often looked on as undesirables.

We were married very quietly, and decided to spend some time in Memphis. John set about forming a band of local musicians of whom there were a good number, though not many who could read music well. Now John was a smooth talker and a shrewd character. He soon manoeuvred the new combo into clubs and hotels that ordinarily never employed a coloured outfit, and dug up a job at the Pink Rose Ballroom, where we made quite a name. One thing I have to say for John: he knew how to talk up salaries. Memphis musicians were getting a dollar and a half or 2 dollars a night when we went there. John kept working on it, and by the time we left they were making 5 and 7 bucks, and I was making 10.

Through the neighbourhood grapevine we heard one day that a young man was in town looking for work as a teacher. We heard he was shabbily dressed, and that the 'fay' board of education were going to interview him to determine if he was capable. In no time they found out. In fact, he knew more than they did, was answering so fast he had them baffled. The scholastic young man was Jimmy Lunceford, later to take America by storm with a very hard-hitting orchestra, but then an unknown saxophone player out of Denver, Colorado. He became a close friend of John's, and they spent hours playing checkers together. Usually John won the games, but Lunceford used to say he'd get a band and beat John with that. He was for ever kidding about building up a combo that would make ours look sick. Finally he started out to do it – not an easy job because we probably had the pick of the men in Memphis then, yet they were not top class. Still, Jimmy went ahead, and we had to admire the way he taught the young musicians in his school.

Drummer James Crawford was one from the school; perhaps bassist Moses Allen was there, and others whose names I have since forgotten. To begin with, Jimmy had a small group like ours, even to the girl pianist – talented Bobby Jones. Then, unable to get the band sounding right, Jimmy went off to Nashville and returned bragging with pianist Eddie Wilcox and saxophone player Willie Smith. By the time we left Memphis he must have had twelve pieces.

Our leaving was caused by a telegram from Terrence Holder, a bandleader in Oklahoma City, offering good money for John to go out and join him there. John went first, leaving me in charge for the rest of the dates we had contracted.

This made me a bandleader at the age of seventeen. I had no alto player, so had to ask Jimmy Lunceford to play the remainder of the dates with us, which he consented to do.

Though we didn't meet too often while I was on the road with Kirk, I remained friendly with Lunceford. Later, when I lived in New York, he once came to my house at four in the morning, asking if I wanted to fly to Pittsburgh with him. I said: 'What are we going to fly in?' and Jimmy said: 'Didn't you know I had a pilot's licence and my own plane?' I hadn't known, but refused to go anyway, saying: 'It's too foggy there.' Pittsburgh with its hundreds of steel mills makes its own fog. Not for nothing is it called the Smoky City.

To get back to Memphis, though: I worked off the outstanding engagements, then set out to join John in Oklahoma City, 700 hard miles away. He had left our Chevrolet for me to make the journey in, and with John's mother and a friend I hit the highway. The Chev wasn't much of a 'short' to look at. It looked like a red bath-tub in fact, but ran like one of those streamlined trains on the Pennsylvania Railroad, and was the craziest for wear and tear. Unfortunately, we had miles of dirt and turtle-back roads to travel, and these excuses for highways were studded with sharp stones. To top all, it was August and hot as a young girl's doojie. Every 40 or 50 miles we stopped to change tyres or clean out the carburettor. As my passengers were strictly non-drivers and non-fixers, I was in sole command. We got along somehow, and after what seemed like weeks of blow-outs and fuel trouble we fell into Oklahoma City. Considering it was surrounded by every description of oil, well, the place was a beauty spot. But the smell of gas ... wow!

John was anxious to show me off musically, for he was proud of my ability. Though out of my mind from the journey, I went without sleep to make rehearsal the next morning. Holder's boys rehearsed two days a week, beginning 11 a.m.; and I was in the hall by nine. I don't know what Holder's band made of me, but I thought them the handsomest bunch of intellectuals I had seen so far. They looked like collegians, all had beautiful brown complexions and wore sharp beige suits to match. Going out, they sported yellow raincoats with the instrument each man played illustrated on the back. Most came from good families, and their manners were perfect. I could hardly wait to hear the music. As I suspected, it was out of the ordinary. They had a novel arrangement of *Casey Jones* featuring Claude Williams, who was strong on both guitar and violin. Tenorman Lawrence 'Slim' Freeman supplied the show stuff by playing bass clarinet while lying on his back. For the rest, they played jazz numbers and the better commercial things. They were all reading like mad, and I had to admit it was a good and different orchestra: smooth showmanship (minus the 'Tom-ing') coupled with musical ability. No wonder Holder had held this one job for more than two years. And at high money for a no-name band.

As I shall explain, this was to be the basis of the Andy Kirk combo. Kirk was a tuba player with the band, and he also played alto and baritone saxes. Bill Dirvin doubled guitar and piano, and Harry 'Big Jim' Lawson was on trumpet. Holder conducted and didn't play an instrument. I guess he was the most musically ignorant one in the band, but a fast talker and a sportsman who took chances. He liked to gamble, and I was told he had more than once lost the payroll in this way. There was talk about bad management, and one day the boys got together and arranged a change. They put Andy Kirk in charge of the band, incorporated it, and renamed it Andy Kirk's Twelve Clouds of Joy. I reckon the year would be 1928.

We moved to Tulsa, and I went to live over an undertaker's. Apart from natural deaths, there was a killing every other day, with weekends the best for business. I was not working, and to break the monotony I'd got permission to drive for the undertaker. In those days they had to go after work, racing to the scene as soon as a killing was reported. Whoever got there first took the body.

Apart from this, I had no way of passing the time. I couldn't see myself getting ahead in music, and the life was getting me down fast. Then a letter from home said my stepfather had passed away, and this broke me up. Inveigling the fare out of my husband, I made for Pittsburgh — not sorry to escape from the oil fumes of Oklahoma.

While I was at home the Kirk band began to shape up nicely. An offer came for them to go into the Pla-mor Ballroom in Kansas City, Missouri. The Clouds of Joy accepted, were held over several times, and took the first stride towards the nation-wide success they won in the mid-Thirties.

I found Kansas City to be a heavenly city — music everywhere in the Negro section of town, and fifty or more cabarets rocking on 12th and 18th Streets. Kirk's band was drawing them into the handsome Pla-mor Ballroom when my husband, John Williams, had me return to him in Kaycee. This was my first visit to Missouri's jazz metropolis, a city that was to have a big influence on my career.

With two sisters, Lucille and Louise, who knew every speak-easy in town, I began to make the rounds from 'Hell's Kitchen' on 5th Avenue to a club on 18th where I met Sam Price. Sammy was playing an unusual type of blues piano which I thought could hardly be improved on. I had the luck to hear him again when we were both in New York during 1934.

One night, we ran into a place where Ben Pollack had a combo which included Jack Teagarden and, I think, Benny Goodman. The girls introduced me to the Texas trombonist, and right away we felt like friends. After work, he and a couple of the musicians asked us to go out, and we visited most of the speaks downtown. One I remember particularly, because it was decorated to resemble the inside of a penitentiary, with bars on the windows and waiters in striped uniforms like down-South convicts. In these weird surroundings, I played for the boys and Jack got up and sang some blues. I thought he was more than wonderful. While they stayed in Kaycee, Jack and some of Pollack's men came round every night, and I was very happy to see them.

Now at this time, which was still Prohibition, Kansas City was under Tom Pendergast's control. Most of the night spots were run by politicians and hoodlums, and the town was wide open for drinking, gambling and pretty much every form of vice. Naturally, work was plentiful for musicians, though some of the employers were tough people. For instance, when Kirk moved from Pla-mor, the orchestra went to work for a nationally feared gangster. He was real bad: people used to run when you just mentioned his name. At that time, Andy was playing tuba, and the band was conducted by our singer, Billy Massey. Billy was a man not easily scared, and one day at the new job he ran off his mouth to the boss. The hood concluded he was crazy (which was not far wrong), and told all the band to pack and leave — but fast. The rest of the guys were too nice, he said, for him to think about killing Billy.

I heard that Count Basie later worked for the same dracula, and also had a slight misunderstanding. As a result, Basie had to work two weeks without pay.

So for the Clouds of Joy it was more one-nighters. After a few, short trips, we headed east to New York to open in the Roseland Ballroom, that spot made famous by Fletcher Henderson. Kirk was on his way up. By now, I had graduated to composer, arranger and first-class chauffeur for the organisation. I was not playing in the band but was doing their recordings for Brunswick, and sometimes sitting in to try things I had written.

In Kansas City, Kirk had liked my ideas, though I could not set them down on paper. He would sit up as long as 12 hours at a stretch, taking down my ideas for arrangements, and I got so sick of the method that I began putting them down myself. I hadn't studied theory, but asked Kirk about chords and the voicing register. In about 15 minutes I had memorised what I wanted. That's how I started writing. My first attempt, *Messa Stomp*, was beyond the range of half the instruments. But the boys gave me a chance and each time I did better, until I found myself doing five and six arrangements per week. Later on, I learned more theory from people like the great Don Redman, Edgar Sampson, Milton Orent and Will Bradley.

The Clouds of Joy had a long run at the Roseland, playing opposite a bunch named the Vagabonds, then opposite the Casa Loma Band (later led by Glen Gray). From the Roseland, they moved to the celebrated Savoy Ballroom, where they faced Chick Webb's orchestra. The Savoy was a place of tremendous enthusiasm, a home of fantastic dancing. And Webb was acknowledged king of the Savoy. Any visiting band could depend on catching hell from little Chick, for he was a crazy drummer and shrewd to boot. The way I made it out, Chick would wait until the opposition had blown its hottest numbers and then — during a so-so set — would unexpectedly bring his band fresh to the stand and wham into a fine arrangement, like Benny Carter's *Liza*, that was hard to beat. Few visiting bands could stand up to this.

Kirk must have played a couple of months at the Savoy, during which time I often sat in, playing either *Mary's Plea* or *Froggy Bottom*, and doing quite well with the kids who liked a good beat for their dancing. From there, we toured Pennsylvania and the Eastern States, and after what seemed like a year of one-nighters, returned to Kansas City.

Kaycee was really jumping now — so many great bands having sprung up there or moved in from over the river. I should explain that Kansas City, Missouri, wasn't too prejudiced for a Mid-western town. It was a ballin' town, and it attracted musicians from all over the South and South-west, and especially from Kansas.

Kansas City, Kansas, was right across the viaduct, just about 5 or 6 miles distant. But on the Kansas side they were much snootier. A lot of their musicians were from good families who frowned on jazz, so the musicians and kids would come across to Kaycee to blast. In Kaycee, nothing mattered.

I've known musicians so enthused about playing that they would walk all the way from the Kansas side to attend a jam session. Even bass players, caught without street-car fare, would hump their bass on their back and come running. That was how music stood in Kansas City in those years around 1930.

At the head of the bands was Bennie Moten's, led by pianist Bennie, and featuring his brother, Buster, on accordion. Then there was George E. Lee, whose sister, Julia, played piano in George's band and took care of the vocals.

From Oklahoma came Walter Page, with a terrific combo named the Blue Devils. Page, known as 'Big One', was one of the very first to use the string bass as well as tuba, and he also doubled on bass saxophone. For a while he had Bill Basie on piano. Count had come to Kansas City with the Gonzele White touring show, and dropped out of it to join Page. Later, Basie returned to the roadshow, again leaving it in Kaycee to go into Moten's band on second piano.

Singing with Moten then was the lovable Jimmy Rushing, 'Mr Five by Five'. Unlike the run of blues shouters, Jimmy could read music, and he could be heard ten blocks away without a microphone (they used megaphones then, anyway). Jimmy was big brother to me, and some of the other band wives. I remember him playing piano and singing wonderful ballads to us; other times he would keep us laughing with his *risqué* stories, getting a kick out of seeing us blush.

Yes, Kaycee was a place to be enjoyed, even if you were without funds. People would make you a loan without you asking for it, would look at you and tell if you were hungry and put things right. There was the best food to be had: the finest barbecue, crawdads and other seafood. There were the races, and swimming, and the beautiful Swope Park and zoo to amuse you. There were jam sessions all the time, and big dances such as the union dance given every year by our local. As many as ten or twelve bands participated in this event, and you were sure to hear at least eight original styles there, as well as one or two outfits trying to imitate Duke.

For private entertainment we had our hot corn club every Monday, at which the musicians and wives would drink and play bridge, 'tonk' or 'hearts'. At these meetings the boys drank corn whisky and home brew — in fact, most anything with a high alcohol content — and they got laughs out of giving me rough liquor so strong it would almost blow the top of one's head off.

One of the regulars was Herman Walder, brilliant tenor player with Moten and brother of saxophonist Woodie Walder. Herman asked me if I'd like a cool drink one night, and not knowing the taste of corn I gulped down a large glassful. The next thing I remember was people putting cold towels on my head. Being stubborn, I thought: if they can take it, so can I. So each Monday I tried to drink, with much the same result. They boys took to betting that I'd be high within ten minutes of entering — and they always won.

It was in the winter of 1930-31 that the breaks began to happen. Andy Kirk's band had hit the road for another string of one-nighters, leaving me in Kansas City. Then came a wire, telling me to meet the band right away in Chicago. It said that Jack Kapp, the Brunswick record man, wanted to hear me play. This looked great. I knew they wouldn't send for me unless something was in the wind, so by next day I was on my way to St Louis, where I changed trains for Chicago. When I arrived I was cold and tired, but went direct to the studio and sat down and played.

I had been in the habit of making up my own things when asked to play. Out of this training, and the way I was feeling beat, came two originals titled *Drag 'Em* and *Night Life* — the first a blues, the other a faster piece. These were the first solo records I ever made. So far as I can remember it, the session took place in 1930. I know the record was released early in '31 and I never received a recording fee nor any royalties from it, though the record sold quite well. I tried to get some loot, but was fluffed to Mayo Williams, then a kind of artists' manager and connected with some publishing house or other, who in turn fluffed me to the executives. Many years after, I threatened to sue, and stopped the sale of a record that had been reissued ever since 1931 and was even included in the Forties in an album of 'barrelhouse piano'.

That record didn't make my fortune, but it made my name in a double sense. I had been born Mary Elfreda Winn, and had played as Mary Winn until I became Mary Williams. It was Jack Kapp laid the 'Lou' on me. Perhaps he figured plain Mary wasn't enough for a recording artist, whereas Mary Lou was right on the beam. Anyway, Mary Lou went on the label, and Mary Lou it stayed. Until today, few people knew I wasn't born with that name.

Being still broke after the session, I moved in with Mary Kirk, Andy's wife. The Bear (as we call winter time) was in Chicago and it was very cold. Mary provided food and clothes and was the kindest to me. Once again I travelled with Kirk, and it was at the Pearl Theatre in Philadelphia that I joined the band full-time. Kirk had decided to use two pianos, and I was to play the second — a small upright.

Over the two pianos Kirk had a shed-like enclosure built. On top of the shed stood the drums, now presided over by Ben Thigpen, whom we had picked up near Toledo, Ohio. It was tough going; I was used to a large piano, but our regular man, Jack, had the Steinway and I was doing my best with what seemed like a two-octaves 'Tom Thumb'. And I could hear practically nothing but the thunder of drums overhead. This routine had lasted about a week when Jack failed to make the show one night. I graduated to the grand — and solo honours — and it seems my playing surprised everyone in the theatre, including Sam Stiefle, who owned the place. Jack later had hot words with Stiefle, ending in his taking two weeks' pay and a ticket home. I stayed on as the orchestra's pianist and arranger and must have gone around the world (or the equivalent distance) a thousand times a month on one-night dates.

These things happened in 1930, and Blanche Calloway, Cab's sister, was fronting the band at the Pearl. Blanche behaved like Cab on stage, and I heard that she was the originator of his style. Though Blanche was short on voice, she had personality to spare, and I got a kick from her versions of *Let's Do It* and *I Need Lovin'*. Stiefle secured Victor recording dates for Blanche and the band, and we cut those two songs with her, also *Sugar Blues, Casey Jones* and some original things. I always wondered what became of the cheque for these dates; none of it came my way, but I was getting used to that by now.

We played at the Pearl for many months with Blanche, meeting such top Negro performers as Ethel Waters, Bill Bailey and Butterbeans and Susie. Eddie Heywood, Sr, was accompanying the Butterbeans act, and he gave me plenty of constructive advice.

After parting from Blanche Calloway, we returned to Kansas City to open the Winnwood Beach Park Ballroom with a somewhat altered personnel. On trumpets we had Irving 'Mouse' Randolph, great musician from St Louis, and Harry 'Big Jim' Lawson and Earl Thompson. The trombonist was Floyd 'Stumpy' Brady, and the reeds were John Williams, Johnny Harrington and Slim Freeman. Andy Kirk played tuba, Ben Thigpen was on drums, myself on piano, and Bill Dirvin on guitar.

It was one of our great bands. With Randolph leading the brass, no music was difficult to read. I could pass out arrangements on the stand during the evening and they'd be read right off. Our engagement was a riot, causing the rival Fairyland Park to employ Bennie Moten in self-defence. Kansas City in the Thirties was jumping harder than ever. The 'Heart of America' was at that time one of the nerve centres of jazz, and I could write about it for a month and never do justice to the half of it. Lester Young, who had worked with Walter Page and Bennie Moten, was blowing cool sounds at the Subway on 18th Street. This was a small place with only one entrance: really a fire-trap, yet groovy. The first time I heard Lester I was astounded. It took him several choruses to get started — then, brother, what a horn!

A wild 12th Street spot we fell in regularly was the Sunset, owned by Piney Brown, who loved jazz and was very liberal with musicians. Pianist Pete Johnson worked there with bass and drums, sometimes with Baby Lovett, a New Orleans drummer who became one of Kansas City's best. Now the Sunset had a bartender named Joe Turner, and while Joe was serving drinks he would suddenly pick up a cue for a blues and sing it right where he stood, with Pete playing piano for him. I don't think I'll ever forget the thrill of listening to big Joe Turner shouting and sending everybody night after night while mixing drinks.

Pete Johnson was great on boogie, but he was by no means solely a boogie player. It was only when someone like Ben Webster, the Kaycee-born tenor man, yelled 'Roll for me ... come on, roll 'em Pete, make 'em jump,' that he would play boogie for us.

In the summer Kirk's band worked only from nine to twelve at night, and afterwards we would drive by the Sunset — John Williams and me and the five or six that rode with us. Pete might be playing something like *Sweet Georgia Brown* or *Indiana* when we got there. I'd go home to bath and change, and when I got back, ten to one Pete would still be jamming the same tune, and maybe some of the guys wailing along with him.

Hot Lips Page was the life of many a Kaycee jam session. After a soloist had blown nine or ten choruses Lips would start a riff in the background which the other horns picked up. Not many arrangers could improve on Lips when it came to backing up a soloist.

Of course, we didn't have any closing hours in these spots. We could play all morning and half through the day if we wished to, and in fact we often did. The music was so good that I seldom got to bed before midday. It was just such a late morning occasion that once had Coleman Hawkins hung up. Fletcher Henderson came to town with Hawkins on tenor, and after the dance the band cruised round until they fell into the Cherry Blossom where Count Basie worked. The date must have been early 1934, because Prohibition had been lifted and whisky was freely on sale. The Cherry Blossom was a new nightclub, richly decorated in Japanese style even to the beautiful little brown-skinned waitress.

The word went round that Hawkins was in the Cherry Blossom, and within about half an hour there were Lester Young, Ben Webster, Herschel Evans, Herman Walder and one or two unknown tenors piling in the club to blow. Ben didn't know the Kaycee tenormen were so terrific, and he couldn't get himself together though he played all morning. I happened to be nodding that night, and around 4 a.m. I awoke to hear someone pecking on my screen. I opened the window on Ben Webster. He was saying: 'Get up, pussycat, we're jammin' and all the pianists are tired out now. Hawkins has got his shirt off and is still blowing. You got to come down.' Sure enough, when we got there Hawkins was in his singlet taking turns with the Kaycee men. It seems he had run into something he didn't expect.

Lester's style was light and, as I said, it took him maybe five choruses to warm up. But then he would really blow; then you couldn't handle him on a cutting session. That was how Hawkins got hung up. The Henderson band was playing in St Louis that evening, and Bean knew he ought to be on the way. But he kept trying to blow something to beat Ben and Herschel and Lester. When at last he gave up, he got straight in his car and drove to St Louis. I heard he'd just bought a new Cadillac and that he burnt it out trying to make the job on time. Yes, Hawkins was king until he met those crazy Kansas City tenormen.

Off and on, I was with Andy Kirk right through the Thirties and up until 1942. Enough characters passed through the band in that time to fill a book. And if I could set down everything that happened, it would probably turn out a best seller. Tenormen, as I have said before, were in good supply in Kansas City. We certainly had our share of them. After Slim Freeman, we used Buddy Tate, Ben Webster, Lester Young, Dick Wilson and Don Byas.

It was when we returned to Kaycee for a summer season at Harry Duncan's Fairyland Park ballroom that Ben Webster was added. What a wild cat! I remember him first as a spoiled youngster from one of the county's most respected Negro families: a family of lawyers and other professional people. From the moment I met him I was fascinated because he was always up to something. Then, too, I liked his tenor. If he felt over-anxious, Ben would play roughly, distorting a style which was already full of vitality. It seemed to me he played best when he was either sick or tired.

Ben was really bad boy pick, always wrong. Sometimes John Williams yelled at him on the stand to stop experimenting and play. But after being around with the guys a while Ben became less boisterous, which made me like him better. We used to walk for miles together, and he always took me to jam sessions. At one place, called Val's, we ran into Art Tatum. Art had a radio programme, also a job in a dicty private club, but preferred wailing at Val's after hours. It was Val's every night then. Whenever I wasn't listening to Tatum I was playing — Art inspired me so much. Chords he was throwing in then, the boppers are using now. And his mind was the quickest.

Art usually drank a bottle of beer while the other pianists took over, and didn't miss a thing. For instance, there was a run that Buck Washington showed me (Buck, of the Buck and Bubbles team, played a lotta piano, especially when out jamming. Everything he did was unusual). Now Art heard me play this run, which consisted of F, E flat, D flat, C; (octave up) C, B flat, A flat, G; and so on all the way to the top of the keyboard. When he sat down he played it right off. Other pianists had heard and tried, but taken time to pick it up.

I can remember only one man who sounded good following Tatum. His name was Lannie Scott, and he was the most popular pianist in Cleveland, until Tatum came to Cleveland. Then Lannie lost his popularity.

In Kaycee, though, we had a kind of counterpart of Tatum, an ear man called Sleepy who played almost as much as Art, and in the hard keys — A natural, B natural, E natural. Another unsung piano player was Lincoln, known as a three-chord man. His harmonies were the worst, yet he was terrific with the beat. Martha Raye, then eighteen, stopped in Kansas City on her way to Califonia and got hung up listening to Lincoln's nasty beat. She stayed close on two weeks, and was down at the clubs digging the music and singing like mad night after night. Martha hated to leave, nearly missed doing her picture. That was how Kaycee would get you, for there were always places open and music to hear.

Besides the players I've mentioned, and Bennie Moten, Count Basie, Pete Johnson, Sam Price and Clyde Hart, there were three girl pianists apart from myself. One was Julia Lee, who took little part in the sessions; another I recollect only as Oceola; the third was known as Countess Margaret. Countess was a friend of Lester Young, and when I was sick for a time, Kirk sent for her to take my place for a month. The tour got her, I fear, for she died of tuberculosis before she had done very much, though I hear she was quite good.

Two other pianists I met in Kaycee during the mid-Thirties were Tadd Dameron and Thelonius Monk. I was to get to know both of them well in New York in later years. Tadd, who came from Cleveland, was just starting out playing and writing for a band from Kansas. Though very young, he had ideas even then that were 'way ahead of his time. Thelonius, still in his teens, came into town with either an evangelist or a medicine show — I forget which.

While Monk was in Kaycee he jammed every night; really used to blow on piano, employing a lot more technique than he does today. Monk plays the way he does now because he got fed up. Whatever people may tell you, I *know* how Monk can play. He felt that musicians should play something new, and started doing it. Most of us admire him for this. He was one of the original modernists all right, playing pretty much the same harmonies then that he's playing now. Only in those days we called it 'Zombie music' and reserved it mostly for musicians after hours.

Why 'Zombie music'? Because the screwy chords reminded us of music from *Frankenstein* or any horror film. I was one of the first with these frozen sounds, and after a night's jamming would sit and play weird harmonies (just chord progressions) with Dick Wilson, a very advanced tenor player.

But this is getting ahead of my story. Our next added attraction was Pha Terrell, a good-looking singer who helped to make Kirk's band the hot proposition it soon became, though he never got recognition for doing so. Pha was naturally lucky with females, as all of them — from schoolgirls to schoolmarms — drooled over his smooth, pleasing voice.

As for Ben Webster: he stayed with us two or three years — longer than he'd stuck with anyone — then quit to join Cab Calloway. Until he had gone I didn't realise how much I would miss him. Then I lost 25lb, as I could not eat for some time.

Lester Young replaced Ben, and sensational as he was, never fitted the band like that big Webster sound had. In truth, Ben could blow more in two bars, so far as soul and 'story' are concerned, than most men can in a chorus. Of course, being accustomed to the big tenor tone, I thought at first that Lester's sound was anaemic. But soon I learned to appreciate what he could do, for he was a master at improvising solos of five or fifteen choruses, never repeating.

Lester wasn't with the band too long before he left and went over to Basie, with whom he had worked previously. Basie had, some time before, quit the Moten band to form his own small group. Then along around April of 1935, Bennie died. It seems that a young intern operated on him for removal of tonsils, but something went wrong and the operation killed Bennie. So Basie drew several of Moten's men into his outfit and built the band that blew up a storm at Kaycee's Reno Club.

While the Count was getting this group together, he sent out for Jo Jones on drums. I loved to see Jo teaming with Walter Page, the bassist. Page showed Jo what to do and when to do it, and it was really something to dig these two great musicians. I have caught Basie's orchestra at times when there was no one on the stand except Page and the horns and, believe me, 'Big One' swung that band on his bass without much effort.

Meanwhile, we continued our one-nighters, working our way back East to Baltimore, Maryland, where we landed in a beautiful little club called the Astoria. Joe Glaser caught our band and promised to do something about it. He had us come to New York after the engagement, securing a record date on Decca for the band. Never have I written so many things so quickly in my entire career. I must have done twenty in one week, including *Cloudy*, *Corky* and *Froggy Bottom* (both new arrangements), *Steppin' Pretty* and *Walkin' And Swingin'*.

For nights I could not leave my room, having my meals brought in to me. And at 7 a.m. I was up again for another session.

I had begun to think my arrangments were not worth much, as no one ever wanted to pay for them, and Andy, I knew, could not afford a proper arranger's fee. But the work paid off in the long run. Whenever musicians listened to the band they would ask who made a certain arrangement. Nearly always it was one of mine. *Walkin' And Swingin'* was one of those numbers musicians liked to play. I had tried out trumpet combining with saxes to make the sound of five reeds, and this was different and effective. So other bands took up the arrangement. Our band paid 3 dollars for the arrangement, Earl Hines 10, and the Casa Lomas 59; which totals 63 dollars — wow!

We made these records in 1936, with the new and superb tenorman Dick Wilson, who had joined us before the tour. We had Booker Collins on bass (Kirk having finally decided to use string bass), and wonderful Ted Brinson on the guitar. In between band sessions, I cut my first Decca solos, including *Isabelle* and *Overhand*. We were still supposed to be incorporated, but after our first big record we were no longer that way (smile). The more I asked about it, the dumber everybody got.

Glaser put us in a Cleveland ballroom, where we broadcast nightly over a national hook-up with America's top sports commentator. What power and money can do! We stayed until the name of Kirk was ringing from coast to coast, also three of his stars — Pha Terrell, Dick Wilson and (let's face it) Mary Lou Williams.

After our first release, *Froggy Bottom*, which was a fabulous seller on the juke boxes, we were booked into Harlem's Apollo Theatre. At this time I met luscious Billie Holiday, then just catching on like mad with her early records. She and Teddy Wilson's combo, with Ben Webster's crazy horn, really went together. Pha had a crush on Billie, but was too bashful to visit her alone, so I was made to go along with him. I have been fond of Billie ever since, for I have always felt tremendous warmth and kindness in her.

By now, Dick Wilson had become my special buddy; perhaps tenor players were my weaksness. He was a handsome cat, and when we weren't jamming in his room it was generally full of girls. One night, scuffling around Harlem, Wilson and I fell in the Savoy. After dancing a couple of rounds, I heard a voice that sent chills up and down my spine (which I never thought could happen). I almost ran to the stand to find out who belonged to the voice, and saw a pleasant-looking brown-skinned girl standing modestly and singing the greatest. I was told her name was Ella Fitzgerald, and that Chick Webb had unearthed her from one of the Apollo's amateur hours. Later I learned that Ella never once forgot Chick for giving her the break when others turned their backs — others who wanted her when success came.

By the time we returned to Kaycee, to Fairyland Park, all that could be heard on the juke boxes was *Froggy Bottom*. That particular tune was being played all over the country, and as a result our band started hitting like mad on one-nighters.

I often wonder what an agent would do if he had to travel with the band he's booking. After the release of our Decca records, in 1936, the Kirk band travelled five or six thousand miles a week on one-nighters all through the South, repeating most of the dates before coming West again. For nearly three years we toiled across Georgia, Mississippi, Alabama, the Carolinas, Tennessee, Louisiana, Oklahoma and Texas. I shall never forget some of the beautiful stretches of country, nor the many attractions of New Orleans.

We got little chance to hear the local musicians, though, for we arrived in most places in time to play, and left right afterwards. I have gone to sleep with my fur coat on, near to freezing, and woken up in the car hours later wet from perspiration in the sub-tropics of Florida.

Our sidemen were making only eight and a half dollars a night, and paying two or three bucks for a decent room. Since they had gone through hardships to keep the band intact, I thought they deserved at least 15 dollars. I made 75 a week, with arranging, and think Pha Terrell got even less.

This didn't make me feel any too good, and I began to lose interest in the project, particularly as we repeated in so many mosquito-infested States. Sometimes I sat on the stand working crossword puzzles, only playing with my left hand. Every place we played had to turn people away, and my fans must have been disappointed with my conduct. If they were, I wasn't bothering at the time.

By now I was writing for some half-dozen bands each week. As we were making perhaps 500 miles per night, I used to write in the car by flashlight between engagements. Benny Goodman requested a blues and I did *Roll 'Em* and several others for him. One week I was called on for twelve arrangements, including a couple for Louis Armstrong and Earl Hines, and I was beginning to get telegrams from Gus Arnheim, Glen Gray, Tommy Dorsey and many more like them.

As a result of Benny's success with *Roll 'Em* (I received recognition as the composer), our band had to start featuring boogies. One I wrote was *Little Joe From Chicago* — dedicated to Joe Glaser and Joe Louis — and this turned out a big seller when we recorded it in 1938.

I guess our group and Lunceford's did more one-nighters than anyone. Jimmy's trumpet man, Paul Webster, once played with us, and bet me they had travelled more miles than we had. I'd show him either the itinerary or the speedometer and win the bet. That itinerary I have kept for when I want to look back on the impossible!

I remember jumping from St Louis to Canada: over 750 miles in one day. We played St Louis until 3 a.m., slept and left for Canada around 11 a.m., and arrived at ten at night — one hour late for the job.

Eventually we worked our way round to Pittsburgh. As soon as I reached my home town I was told about a great young pianist just coming up. When I asked my brother-in-law who this was, he said it could only be Erroll Garner, then going to Westinghouse High School with my niece. I arranged to visit a friend's house to hear Erroll, and was surprised to find such a little guy, playing so much. And he did not even read music. The next few days were spent just listening to him. He was original then, sounding like no one in the world except Erroll Garner.

At one point I tried teaching him to read by giving him first whole notes, then halves, then quarters. I soon found he didn't want to bother, so I skipped it but tried to guide him any way I could, as others had guided me. I realised he was born with more than most musicians could accomplish in a lifetime.

Our tour took us to Oklahoma City again. Jack Teagarden had given me his family's 'phone number, so I called Norma Teagarden and she came to our dance. Norma talked about a remarkable guitarist named Charlie Christian, who played electric guitar and was raised in Oklahoma City. Norma is supposed to have taught Christian music, and she told us he could play everything from jazz to the classics. His favourites were *In A Mist* and *Rhapsody In Blue*.

Our guitarist, Floyd Smith (who replaced Ted Brinson), considered he could improvise with the best of them, and the guys in the band were anxious to see what he'd do after hearing Charlie. So after the dance everyone tore out to the club where Christian worked. I rode there with Pha Terrell, and when we got in the two guitarists were down with it: Floyd playing his head off for two choruses, then Charlie taking over — very cool.

For a while it was a close call, then Charlie decided to blow. He used his head on cutting sessions, the way Chu Berry used to do, taking it easy while the other musician played everything he knew, then cutting loose to blast him off the map. Never in my life had I heard such inspired and exciting music as Christian beat out of his guitar. Poor Floyd gave it up and walked off the stand. Charlie played for us till daybreak.

I knew many leaders, including Benny Goodman, had tried to get Christian. Up to now he had refused to leave Oklahoma. But feeling that he and jazz should have a break, I asked him would he leave to join B.G. if I wired New York. Finally he said: 'Okay, if you say so, Mary.' I wired John Hammond right quick, and John (who had heard Charlie previously) got together with B.G. In the summer of '39 Christian made the move, and Benny thanked me on one of his broadcasts for getting him for the band.

At this time I was feeling really dragged so far as Kirk's outfit went. I could not play or write my best for thinking about my share of the loot, and my sacrifices before we made a hit. All my piano solos I turned over to Floyd. I had gotten sick of playing the same ones long ago. Our repertoire consisted of recorded hits, and the solos had to be exactly like those on the records.

I had plenty of offers to leave, but turned them down. Though dissatisfied, I still felt loyal to the band. All the same, Pha and I caused so much annoyance through asking for raises that the 'Golden System' decided to add more stars and oust us completely. Henry Wells, who played fine trombone and sang a fair ballad (though he was no Pha Terrell), joined a little later. And the next star to be added was sensational June Richmond who could break up the coldest audience. How I enjoyed her act.

Don Byas came into the band, and now we had two great tenormen — Don and Dick Wilson. I think it was these two who kept me in the band, for I got real kicks out of jamming with them. I began to feel better.

We were booked into the Grand Terrace in Chicago, the place made famous by Earl Hines with the best band he's ever had. Omer Simeon was on clarinet,

George Dixon and Walter Fuller on trumpet, Budd Johnson on tenor, Quinn Wilson (bass), and the late Alvin Burroughs on drums. Earl had gone out on the road, and we went in with twenty-five chorus girls and a big floor show. The engagement was sensational. We must have stayed there six months, and I jammed night after night, Chicago being second only to Kansas City for inspiration. Even those chorus girls swung like mad while dancing!

Going to session upon session with Dick Wilson, I became ill and was carted off to hospital. At least fifteen young interns visited me daily, and I had a radio, record machine, and so many flowers they were lined up along the corridor. I did not get much rest there. The interns offered to pay for my board and room if I stayed another week. I went home to Pittsburgh to convalesce, and after a time rejoined the band.

We must have repeated on our Southern dates about 100 times. Practically everyone was ill from travelling when we got an offer to go into the Cotton Club (on Broadway), by now operating on its last legs. Before this engagement, Harold Baker joined us on trumpet. It seemed our brass section was wilder than ever ... with Harold, Big Jim Lawson, Howard McGhee, Henry Wells and Theo Donnelly. Every section hung out together and tried to outdo the others. On the stand, the rhythm was always pushing and telling each other to get on the ball. After the date, we'd say: 'We were really going, but you guys ... huh!' Of course, when a new arrangement was brought out we found time to help each other.

At the end of the Cotton Club deal, John Williams decided to stay in New York and go into the barbecue business with Mary Kirk. He made a few more dates and left the band. He and I were nearly through, anyway. Don Byas also left and was replaced by Edward Inge.

I began to notice that Dick Wilson was looking ill. Then he started disappearing upstairs during intermission. When I took him a drink, I'd find him stretched out on a divan. One night Wilson stayed home, and Harold Baker and I decided to visit him. He was in bed ill, too sick to eat. I ran across the street and got a doctor, who said he should be in hospital. When Dick heard this he wanted to get out, said it would be the end if he went into hospital. He must have known he was dying.

The band left New York shortly after for a Southern tour, and the next we heard was that Dick had been taken to hospital. In a couple of days, they said, he looked like a skeleton, and soon afterwards died. This happened towards the close of 1941, when Wilson could not have been older than thirty.

The next months were my last with Andy Kirk. For twelve years with the band I'd known swell times and bad ones, but barnstorming and the 'New System' of management were bringing me down. Looking back, I can smile at our life on the road. Towards the end, though, there was no more brotherly love. I had lost so much through thefts that for a solid year I had to sleep with everything I owned. When someone broke in my trunk and took earrings, Indian-head pennies and silver dollars which I cherished, I decided to leave.

Dragging my trunk off the bus, I drove to Pittsburgh. Within two weeks, I heard from Harold Baker, who said he'd be coming through Pittsburgh and would stop by and see me. He stopped by all right. The band did not see him any more. Next thing, we both received letters from the union. I countered this move by stating that I would make it very unpleasant for the 'New System' if I answered. Nothing further happened to me. Baker was fined a few pounds, I think.

So ended my long association with the Kirk orchestra. Harold and I stayed in Pittsburgh, forming a six-piece combo which had Art Blakey on drums and Orlando Wright on tenor. While rehearsing, Art told us of a terrific singer over on Wylie Avenue. I visited the club and was taken off my feet to see a guy who could sing so pretty and look so handsome. Girls were swooning all around the place, which was packed. Billy Eckstine was the handsome cat, and when I had a chance to meet him I found he lived near me out in East Liberty. It was a pleasure to talk to such a nice cool gentleman.

We rehearsed the new outfit every day, Harold Baker and myself, and through John Hammond contacted some people who were able to find us work. Our first job was in Cleveland, at Mason's Farm, and the combo went over well enough for us to be kept on from August to October — way past the summer season.

Tadd Dameron and most of the musicians around came out to hear us. When Duke Ellington hit Cleveland, all the guys dropped by Mason's Farm. And they liked Harold so much they hired him. Later I learned why he decided to go. There had been a little dissension because he was not from Pittsburgh. It seemed my guys wanted all Pittsburghers in the combo, and had almost come to blows about it. So Harold went to Duke, and I said nothing though I thought plenty.

After he had gone. Art Blakey and the rest had me stop by Pittsburgh to pick up the greatest (they said) on trumpet. We arrived in New York with 'The Greatest'. He couldn't even blow his nose! I must have auditioned every good trumpetman in NY. No one had realised the value of Harold Baker. He could play ten choruses solo and fall back into a fast-moving ensemble without splitting or missing a note. The new trumpetman would split anything. We were playing tricky arrangements that called for a bit of reading, and I could not even find a sound reader on trumpet. I felt depressed and made up my mind to join Harold as soon as I could.

Duke's band was in California. When it came to New York, Harold and I went off to Baltimore and got married. I travelled with Ellington, arranging about fifteen things for the orchestra. They included *Trumpet No End*, my version of *Blue Skies*, which I suppose was written early in '42 but not recorded until some years later.

I hope Duke always keeps a band, for he is a genius who gets the best results out of musicians. And what strange guys they were: half of them didn't speak to each other. Too many stars, I guess. When they were speaking, and felt like playing, they'd rearrange some of the band's oldies spontaneously right on the stand. Basie's is the only other band I know capable of doing this.

I moved around with Duke's orchestra until we reached Canada, and I came close to freezing. Then I caught the first train out to New York leaving Harold with the band.

Now I want to write what I know about how and why bop got started. Monk and some of the cleverest of the young musicians used to complain: 'We'll never get credit for what we're doing.' They had reason to say it. In the music business the going is tough for original talent. Everybody is being exploited through paid-for publicity, and most anybody can become a great name if he can afford enough of it. In the end the public believes what it reads. So it is often difficult for the real talent to break through. Anyway, Monk said: 'We are going to get a big band started. We're going to create something that they can't steal, because they can't play it.' There were more than a dozen people interested in the idea, and the band began rehearsing in a basement somewhere. Monk was writing arrangements, and Bud Powell and maybe Milt Jackson. Everyone contributed towards the arrangments, and some of them were real tough. Even those guys couldn't always get them right.

It was the usual story. The guys got hungry, so they had to go to work with different bands. Monk got himself a job at Minton's — the house that built bop — and after work the cats fell in to jam, and pretty soon you couldn't get in Minton's for musicians and instruments. Minton's Playhouse was not a large place, but it was nice and intimate. The bar was at the front, and the cabaret was in the back. The bandstand was situated at the rear of the back room, where the wall was covered with strange paintings depicting weird characters sitting on a brass bed, or jamming or talking to chicks.

During the day-time, people played the juke-box and danced. I used to call in often and got many laughs. It is amazing how happy those characters were — jiving, dancing and drinking. It seemed everybody was talking at the same time: the noise was terrific. Even the kids playing out on the sidewalk danced when they heard the records.

That's how we were then — one big family on West 118th Street. Minton's was a room next door to the Cecil Hotel and it was run by Teddy Hill, the onetime bandleader who did quite well in Europe, and who now managed for Minton. Henry Minton must have been a man about fifty who at one time played saxophone and at another owned the famous Rhythm Club where Louie, Fats, James P., Earl Hines and other big names filled the sessions. He had also been a Union official at Local 802. He believed in keeping the place up, and was constantly redecorating. And the food was good. Lindsay Steele had the kitchen at one time. He cooked wonderful meals and was a good mixer who could sing a while during intermission.

When Monk first played at Minton's there were few musicians who could run changes with him. Charlie Christian, Kenny Clarke, Idrees Sulieman and a couple more were the only ones who could play along with Monk then. Charlie and I used to go to the basement of the hotel where I lived and play and write all night long. I still have the music of a song he started but never completed.

Sometime in 1943 I had an offer to go into Café Society Downtown. I accepted, though fearing I might be shaky on solo piano since I had been so long with Andy Kirk's band and my own combo. I immediately made some arrangements for six-pieces to accompany piano. At my opening people were standing upstairs, which I was glad to see. Georgia Gibbs, who was just starting out, was in the show with Ram Ramirez (composer of *Lover Man*), playing piano for her. Pearl Primus was also in the show, and Frankie Newton had the small band. I was sorry to hear of Newton's death just recently. He was a real great trumpetman, always very easy on the ear.

During this period Monk and the kids would come to my apartment every morning around four or pick me up at the Café after I'd finished my last show, and we'd play and swop ideas until noon or later. Monk, Tadd Dameron, Kenny Dorham, Bud Powell, Aaron Bridges, Billy Strayhorn, plus various disc jockeys and newspapermen, would be in and out of my place at all hours, and we'd really ball. When Monk wrote a new song he customarily played it night and day for weeks unless you stopped him. That, he said, was the only way to find out if it was going to be good. 'Either it grew on or it didn't.'

I considered myself lucky having men like Monk and Bud playing me the things they had composed. And I have always upheld and had faith in the boppers, for they originated something but looked like losing credit for it. Too often have I seen people being chummy with creative musicians, then — when the people have dug what is happening — put down the creators and proclaim themselves king of jazz, swing or whatever. So the boppers worked out a music that was hard to steal. I'll say this for the 'leeches', though: they tried. I've seen them in Minton's busily writing on their shirt cuffs or scribbling on the tablecloth. And even our own guys, I'm afraid, did not give Monk the credit he had coming. Why, they even stole his idea of the beret and bop glasses.

I happened to run into Thelonius standing next door to the 802 Union building on 6th Avenue, where I was going to pay my dues. He was looking at some heavy-framed sun-glasses in a shop window, and said he was going to have a pair made similar to a pair of ladies' glasses he had seen and liked. He suggested a few improvements in the design, and I remember laughing at him. But he had them made in the Bronx, and several days later came to the house with his new glasses and, of course, a beret. He had been wearing a beret, with a small piano clip on it, for some years previous to this. Now he started wearing the glasses and beret, and the others copied him.

Out of that first big band Monk formed grew people like Milt Jackson, J. J. Johnson and Bud Powell. No one could play like Bud, not until he recorded and the guys had a chance to dig him. And even now they cannot play just like him, for I believe he is the only pianist who makes every note ring. The strength in his fingers must be unequalled. Yet I am forced to the conclusion that Monk influenced him as a kid. He idolises Monk and can interpret Monk's compositions better than anyone I know. And the two used to be inseparable. At the piano Bud still does a few things the way Monk would do them, though he has more technique.

Yes, Thelonius Monk, Charlie Christian, Kenny Clarke, Art Blakey and Idrees Sulieman were the first to play bop. Next were Parker, Gillespie, and Clyde Hart, now dead, who was sensational on piano. After them came J. J. Johnson, Bud Powell, Al Haig, Milt Jackson, Tadd Dameron, Leo Parker, Babs Gonzales, Max Roach, Kenny Dorham and Oscar Pettiford. Those men played the authentic bop, and anybody who heard the small combo that Dizzy kept together for so long in New York should easily be able to distinguish the music from the imitation article.

Often you hear guys blowing a lot of notes and people say: 'They're bopping.' But they are not. Bop is the phrasing and accenting of the notes, as well as the harmonies used. Every other note is accented. Never in the history of jazz has the phrasing been like it is in bop. Musicians like Dave Brubeck come up with different styles which may be interesting. But they are not bop. Personally, I have always believed that bebop was here to stay. That's one reason I tried to encourage the original modernists to continue writing and experimenting.

Right from the start, musical reactionaries have said the worst about bop. But after seeing the Savoy Ballroom kids fit dances to this kind of music, I felt it was destined to become the new era of music, though not taking anything away from Dixieland or swing or any of the great stars of jazz. I see no reason why there should be a battle in music. All of us aim to make our listeners happy.

When I had been working in Café Society for a year I decided I needed a vacation, and took off July and August to do some writing. Moe Asch, the best recording man in the business, wanted me to do a session. I have always admired Asch. The poor guy never quite made it financially because he was too nice to musicians. He would pay their price even if he had to sleep in the rain. And he never told a performer how to record or what to do. If you only burped, Moe recorded it.

He thought up bright albums of children's records and all types of folk-song, as well as jazz, and hired good cover artists. The major companies used a lot of his ideas. Moe would treat the musicians he recorded to big steak dinners and drinks. Some deserved this, many did not. In fact, we ruined a couple of sessions from being too high.

I am grateful for the things that Asch did. He submitted my music to all the New York libraries, he paid me for recording musicians I had heard in Pittsburgh, and he encouraged me to record my *Zodiac Suite*, which sold and is still selling. Sessions for Asch brought me more royalties than I've had from any other record company, and gave me the freedom to create.

I met a very talented artist named David Stone Martin, and asked him to do a cover for one of my albums. Through this he received additional work with Asch, and people soon noticed his outstanding work. Today he is well known in the jazz world for his illustrating and record album and sleeve designs, and in the high brackets for picture sales. He has not forgotten me, and always credits me with his first step to success. We are very good friends.

Another friend from this period was Gjon Mili, the photographer who worked on the jazz short, *Jammin' The Blues*. Gjon tried to get a good picture of me for some while without succeeding, but finally made it with five studies — one of which went on display in New York's Modern Art Museum. Naturally I was delighted to see so many people looking at me, amazed, no doubt, by the quality of Mili's photography.

Meanwhile, I was back at the Café; elsewhere in New York bop was really moving. Al Haig, with Ben Webster's band, was bopping nicely on piano and going to school to study more theory. Soon he was blowing with Gillespie, Parker and the rest.

About now I met Babs Gonzales, the only original singer bop produced (to my mind). Babs was wailing in his highly personal way, and wailing with the pen as well as the voice. He was writing a book about bebop, and in between bouts of writing was coining all kinds of hip expressions for a famous New York disc jockey. Unluckily for Babs, the book got away from him; stolen, he says, by a publisher.

One day I heard that Erroll Garner was opening the following week at a place on 52nd Street. I could hardly wait to hear him again, and got away between shows to catch his opening. He was playing more than ever before, yet seemed to me to have got on a Tatum kick, playing fast runs and all. I reminded Erroll of his own original manner of playing which I had admired so much when he was working in Pittsburgh. Before very long I was glad to hear him back on his old style.

In those times, Garner made a habit of going over to Inez Cavanaugh's apartment, an inspiring spot for musicians where Erroll used to play and compose all day. She told me he once sat gazing at a subdued table lamp of hers, then composed something to fit the mood, which he titled *Lamplight*. Often he gets ideas for his pieces from some object or scene that happens to catch his attention.

Some unpleasantness came up on the job about this time, so Erroll went out to California for two years or so. When he returned to New York he was astonished by the reception he got. He had thought of the Three Deuces as just another job, he told me later, and was surprised to see it full of people like Robert Sylvester, Barry Ulanov and Leonard Feather for his opening. Garner had not realised the impact made by his bestseller, *Laura*, in the East. And to back this up, he had dozens of sides with small companies, all of which released his stuff at one time in an attempt to cash in while *Laura* was still hot. So far as jazz pianists go, I guess Erroll has become the fastest seller on records in the world. And he surely deserves this success, for he is a fine and distinctive player.

Unknown to Erroll, I often won small bets on him. You see, many people have the idea that he lacks technique and cannot execute difficult passages. I have been able to prove them wrong. Garner is modern, yet his style is different from bop. He has worked out a sound of his own, doing four beats in the left hand like a guitar. He often uses bass and drums but can play alone and still promote a terrific beat. I like his playing for several reasons, primarily because it is original and has more feeling than almost any pianist I can think of. To me he is the Billie Holiday of the piano. Some musicians put him down because he does not read music nor indulge in a lot of senseless modern progressions. But these are not the important things in jazz.

What would jazz piano have done for inspiration without Earl Hines, Teddy Wilson, Bud Powell, Monk, Tatum, Garner and the older giants like Willie The Lion Smith, James P. Johnson and Fats Waller? Without these individualists, many of today's pianists wouldn't be playing anything, for they lack the power of creative thinking. Garner has been an asset and inspiration to the jazz world.

Teddy Wilson I would call a genius. He has studied a great deal, and it is reflected in his playing, but the study has not been allowed to impair his individual style. Many people forget that jazz, no matter what form it takes, must come from the heart as well as the mind. Regardless of what technique he may have, a jazzman must be able also to tell a story. I can never admire a robot pianist whose runs flow straight from his studies instead of his feelings.

For short periods I would be out of the Café, on concert tours and such, and then go back. I had become like one of the fixtures, and was treated like a member of the boss's family. On Sunday nights we had a little party, just the staff and a few musicians. Hazel Scott, Thelma Carpenter, Billy Strayhorn, Aaron Bridges and Lena Horne and friends would come by and we'd have the most enjoyable time.

The only drag in New York was the many benefit shows we were expected to do — late shows which prevented me from running up on 52nd Street to see my favourite modernists. Sometimes Johnny Gary (the valet) and I would dig a boogie character coming to take me on a benefit. We'd tear across the street to the 18th Hole and hide real quick under a table till the danger was past.

All this time, Minton's Playhouse jumped with cool sounds. People had heard about Monk and were coming from all over town to see what was happening. Teddy Hill had named Monk the 'High Priest of Beebop' (at first that spelling was often used), and this title attracted disc jockeys and newspapermen. I cannot remember who gave bebop its name, though it was explained to me that the word was derived from the sound of the modern drummer dropping bombs. Klook Clarke was one who developed the bop method of drumming, and Art Blakey was bombing away very early. Sometimes Art's moving so fast you cannot see his hands: he's a crazy drummer.

Some players, like Art and J. C. Heard, seem to have been born bopping. J. C. played so much drums when he was with Teddy Wilson's great band that they had to hold him back in order to get a good solid beat going. And Art was about the same when I met him — we had a difficult time with him on ballads and straight dance things. He was a real eager-beaver.

Few creative artists can explain or analyse what they write or play because musical ideas come to them spontaneously while they're playing. I have heard Garner and others, listening to a play-back on a record date, say: 'I didn't know I made that passage.' Jazz is created in the mind, felt in the heart and heard through the fingertips.

My reason for feeling that bop is the 'next era' music is that it came about spontaneously in the same way as our blues and classic jazz, or any other music that a race of people produces. And I contend that bop is the only real modern jazz, despite the contentions of the copyists of Stravinsky, Hindemith and Schoenberg. The swing era produced smooth eighth notes which many of our theoreticians are still playing. The phrasing and timing of bop puts it in a different category altogether. The American Negro musician of today is born to this new phrasing, just as in the past he was born to the rhythm and phrasing of ragtime or boogie and naturally played those styles of music.

Bop has become a powerful and, I believe, permanent influence on our native music. The guys who originated it were as gifted as the creative musicians of the Thirties and the eras that came before. I have known older musicians discourage them, speak badly of the music. Perhaps these older players feared for themselves and their positions. If so, they were being ridiculous. If some of them were to add a few modern changes here and there in their own work, it might revive their inspiration and help them avoid the danger of artistic stagnation. The sooner the older players and fans accept the new music the better it will be for everyone concerned with jazz. It does not mean that Duke, Louis, Count, Teddy Wilson and the rest will lose out completely. Without a war in music we can all survive. For, regardless of whether the music is bop or something else, it will have to have the jazz foundation — a beat!

For four or five years I worked at Café Society, mostly Downtown but finally graduating to the Uptown Café on 59th Street when Hazel Scott left there to marry Adam Clayton Powell. The Uptown Café was a modern-style beautiful room with the bandstand in the back faced by a cute little balcony that seated fifty people or maybe more. Mildred Bailey, Eddie South, Lena Horne, Josh White, Phil Moore, Eddie Heywood, Pete Johnson, Imogene Coca and Susan Reed (with her zither) were among the artists who would work there. And for quite a while Edmond Hall had the band there, with Irving Randolph on trumpet and Jimmy Crawford on drums. They played music as good as any I ever heard in a chic club. Often I spotted Benny Goodman in the room, digging Edmond's clarinet. But for all its looks, the Uptown Café was nothing like Downtown — though it catered for the same kind of Eastside crowd: movie stars, millionaires and the elite. Downtown was groovy, more relaxed than Uptown.

During these New York years I had an idea I would like to hear an orchestra of sixteen or so pieces play my *Zodiac Suite*. Barney Josephson agreed to give the concert for me at Town Hall, and I decided to use oboe, flute, horn, tenor sax, ten or twelve strings, piano, bass and drums. Ben Webster played tenor, Al Hall bass and J. C. Heard drums. The rest were from studio orchestras. The concert attracted a pack of musicians, newspapermen, disc jockeys and theatre people, and eveything went all right until we got to the special arrangement of *Roll 'Em*, our only jazz number. The long, drawn-out strings threw some of the other musicians: I think the conductor lost the place, and for a moment I thought we'd had it. Everyone seemed to be playing a different page, and I'll never forget Ben Webster's big eyes fixed on me. I thought I would blow a blood vessel any second. I remember yelling: 'Count eight and play letter "J".' Somehow we got out of *Roll 'Em*.

After the concert I was sick for about a week, could not work. Then I went down to the Town Hall for the records Barney had paid to have made of the concert. For the first time in the history of the hall, the records had been stolen. I never found them, and so never heard how my music sounded. And I'd spent some 500 dollars for copying and other matters, though Barney backed the concert.

Being determined, I nevertheless tried it once again. Norman Granz had blown into town with fresh ideas on jazz presentation. He broke into Carnegie Hall and took New York by storm. I had built up a nice solid following by now, and Norman invited me to do a concert for him. When I told him what I wanted in payment he blew his top, said I wasn't worth anything to him and that he knew a town where none of my records ever sold. First I was hot, then I laughed, and since that time I have learned to like Norman better.

I couldn't get my price so I took scale and compromised with a deal by which I could perform three of the Zodiac things with the New York Philharmonic Symphony. I was determined to hear my work played by 100 paper men. Mr Rybb, who booked all the concerts in Carnegie, immediately started on the concert details. I had only eight or nine days to work, and a hundred pieces to score for, so I got an old friend, Milton Orent, to help out. Milton was a clever bass player and arranger who wrote some things for Kirk, did *Otto, Make That Riff Staccato* for Duke, and wrote the lyrics of *In The Land Of Oo-Bla-Dee*.

The day before the big night, Milton had to leave town for his summer job. I stayed up the best part of the night working on a blues for the orchestra. I had already arranged *Libra*, *Scorpio* and *Aquarius*, dedicating the last to President Roosevelt. The blues was an idea that came on at the last minute. I called Milt, a hundred miles away, and asked, 'What about having the symphony play a jazz piece?' His reply was: 'Don't do that, Pussycat.' I took no notice.

It was 6.30 p.m. when I began this piece of craziness. Before I knew it, it was seven in the morning and I had just finished copying for the five basses. After grabbing a few hours' sleep, I made the 2 p.m. rehearsal.

Everything went down okay on the *Zodiac*, then Mr Rybb asked, 'Anything else to rehearse?' Shakily I made preparations with the female conductor, who knew little of jazz, and anyway seemed scared of the hundred guys sitting in front of her. I think this was her début, too: at this point we were both shaking like dogs with distemper.

After the intro., I had four choruses of fast boogie, then oboe and trumpet playing written solos: last, but not least, I gave the thirty-six violins two bop choruses, and I must say they tackled them bravely.

At the concert that night the performance was quite sensational. The boys in the symphony applauded louder than the audience and, to prove they meant it, carried on like mad backstage. I went home much elated, and this time I did not forget my slides (recordings). In fact, I asked Inez Cavanaugh and her husband, the Danish Baron Timme Rosenkrantz, to guard them for me.

By this time I had worked almost six years straight. Now, for a while, I'd take it easy and ball. After I left the Café I turned down work that would have paid £400, and was told I should be in a strait-jacket.

I decided to find out what people and conditions were like in the slums of Harlem: things I'd never had the chance to really dig before. This was a mistake. I got mixed up with the wrong characters. When someone gave me a line I swallowed it hook and sinker. The next thing, someone I considered a friend had got me in a swindle. I was having fun like a babe in the woods: lost so much money, which I regularly drew from my postal savings, that the authorities thought some goon was blackmailing me.

From Lennox to 125th Street and 8th Avenue I cruised all over Harlem. Never had I been in such a terrible but fascinating environment, among people who roamed the treets lamping for someone to devour. Truthfully, it was fascinating to watch one race of people live off each other. I wondered why the shrewd brains never ventured Downtown where the real gold was.

New York, anyhow, is no place for slow thinkers. It's a town where if you relax and act nice and normal, something happens: a town where you don't dare take a vacation. You must be on the ball or move out to the country.

After playing around awhile, I realised I must work again. I secured several record dates — luckily getting some new sounds going, which enabled me to tour Chicago, Boston, Philadelphia, Pittsburgh and Atlanta. As a result of disappearing for six months, it was like starting from the bottom all over again. But I began getting jobs on radio and television, and was soon kept quite busy.

When Benny Goodman came to New York I went to rehearsal, taking several arrangments along. I found that Teddy Wilson would be teaching during the summer, and was asked if I'd take his place. I joined Benny. He had Wardell Gray, Stan Hasselgaard, Red Rodney, Billy Bauer, Mel Zelnick (drums), and a wonderful bassist whose name I've forgotten. I played weekends with the sextet, which sounded fair but never quite made it except one night when Benny went home early and left us to finish. The guys blew like mad this particular night.

Unfortunately, when Benny was on the stand he often made musicians feel uneasy by the discouraging look he gave them. Perhaps he wasn't happy then.

Around this time Monty Kay had an idea to open a place on Broadway where the Hurricane used to be. The idea came off, and he named the place Bop City. No wonder: it was an enormous joint which held at least a thousand people. Later, I took my trio there to accompany Billy Eckstine. It was this same Monty Kay who afterwards ran the Downbeat Club, another cool haunt. He was the ideas man in the club business. Whenever I went there, Monty offered me three of four weeks, and I finally took him up on it. I alternated with the great Billy Taylor. He made me feel like playing, for I was raised on competition. Oscar Pettiford and Klook Clarke were the rhythm men, and when I'd played half an hour I would bring Kal Winding, Zoot Sims and Kenny Dorham on the stand. There wasn't a set with the trio when we didn't compose on the spot.

Three months passed and Oscar left to return to one of his old jobs in Snookie's, near 6th Avenue, taking Klook with him. The new section wasn't bad, perhaps, but after what I'd had it annoyed me. One night I gave up, asking Billy Taylor to play for me while I went upstairs to listen. 'If they don't sound any better with him,' I told myself, 'I'm cutting.' They didn't and I split, but had to return later as that was the only way I could get paid for three of four days' work done. When I got back I was given a raise.

Next thing, I received an offer to come to England. Several times I refused, then made up my mind to go, getting permission to leave my job for thirty days. That was November of 1952, and I'm in Europe yet.

Joe Bushkin

Joe Bushkin, famed jazz pianist and sometime cornet player, will be known to many buyers of piano and 'mood' albums, also to followers of Bing Crosby. Senior berets may remember him all the way back to Bunny Berigan, Billie Holiday, Eddie Condon, Lee Wiley, Sharkey Bonano and Muggsy Spanier's historic Ragtimers. In London in 1970, making a fruitless attempt to present his Live Jazz group at the Royalty Theatre, he spent some merry hours with me — and such jazz friends as Ken Brown — and did much talking and taping at the Chelsea flat of American-in-Britain Ernie Anderson.

Joe said he was born on 7 November 1916, 'on the same day that President Wilson was re-elected'. His home was at 64 East 103rd Street, between Park and Madison. 'We lived in the neighbourhood that started the numbers running,' he recalled. 'It was East Harlem. When they talk about jazz coming from Storyville and wine from France, it should be noted that royalty arrangements came from my part of town. Dutch Schultz and his numbers gang were the originators of that dodge and a number of others as well.

'My old man had a marvellous barber shop. There were three chairs, all of which were fully occupied nightly, from the time he closed until he opened, by three policemen from the 104th Street precinct, one of the toughest stations in the city. I especially remember a cop named Schwartz. Everyone loved him. If the fuzz is out, this cat was in. So much so that my old man gave him the key to the shop. Next thing you know we had three slot machines in the back — in exchange for letting the all-night duty cops use the joint as a hotel suite. This was during the Prohibition days, and there was a lot of alcohol used in that shop to make various hair tonics and lotions. Schwartz knew all about that.

'My dad had originally been a cellist in Russia. He came to America in 1909, and the story I always got from him was: "You're lucky, you're a fortunate kid."

'The very first band I ever saw and heard play was Elmer Snowden someplace in Harlem and that gave me a fusion reaction. It was like seeing the Dead Sea scrolls. I must have been about eight years old and the teacher told us to write what we wanted to be when we grew up and I wrote, "I want to be a piano player in a band". I was thinking of the piano player with Elmer Snowden who seemed to be having a marvellous time. There was a family piano in our flat and I was always convinced that it was there to keep me off the streets where some violent things were going on. I actually saw a kid tossed off the roof of a six-storey tenement into the street right before my eyes.

'We lived on the third floor and there was a gal on the fourth floor and her name was Sarah Brodsky, I'll never forget her. She was a good looking chick and must have been about seventeen. I was about nine. I occasionally used to annoy my old man by playing the East Harlem version of Chopsticks. He then decided that I should take piano lessons. Seeing Sarah Brodsky on the stairs every day convinced me that he was right. But my Dad was trying to talk me out of taking lessons from Miss Brodsky and this aroused my youthful suspicions because this Sarah Brodsky was really stacked.

'I managed to talk my old man into letting me take lessons from Miss Brodsky at half a buck a lesson, considerable money for those days, but my old man laid some free haircuts on her brother and father and the price went down to 35 cents. I used to go upstairs to her place twice a week, Wednesday and Saturday. I needed Sunday to rest up from that lesson.

'I really enjoyed those lessons even if they did keep me off the streets. Then one day at school a young music teacher named Miss Stritch said, "All of those who are taking music lessons please raise your right hand." I did with a number of others. When she asked who was studying piano about eight hands shot up, but not mine. I took a rain check on that one. When she asked who was studying brass instruments five hands went up — three trombone players, a tuba player and a guy who couldn't make up his mind. That was me. So, when I heard there were no other trumpet players, I said, "trumpet".

'I ran to the barber shop that afternoon and got my old man to take me over to the local school of music. He left a cat hanging in mid-air with a mud pack — that takes a while to dry. It was a 25-cent a lesson school where they sold you a trumpet on time. The professor would give you a half hour of misinformation.

'The pretty music teacher at school said that they were going to start rehearsals for the new band right after Easter vacation. This gave me five weeks to learn the instrument, which I'm amazed to say didn't seem to phase me in the least. Other kids read the comics but I remember that what really interested me was any ad about music.

'The school was at 116th Street and 7th Avenue, deep in black Harlem today, but then a white section. A corner building with some draughty studios, you signed a contract for the instrument and the 25 cents a lesson for three years until ready for Carnegie Hall. I can't remember playing the Arben method. I saw that later on Chuck Peterson's music stand with the Dorsey band at the Paramount. Bunny also worked with the Arben method and so did Benny Baker. This school charged 75 cents for the advanced trumpet method which meant you were getting ready for the Street Cleaner's Band.

'The landlord of our tenement block, a Mr Kossoff, whose son was studying with Josef Llevine in Vienna, used to come to the house to pick up the rent money. If you couldn't make the rent he would talk things over with you and come to some arrangement. When you paid him, his way of saying thanks! was to show you the latest postcard from his son.

'On one occasion old Mr Kossoff was away on a trip and this son, who was in New York on vacation, came by in his place. This young man turned out to be one of the most amiable people I have ever met. It is due to him that I consciously realised I wanted to play the piano. (Subconsciously I wanted to be a horn player.) I happened to be practising when young Mr Kossoff came by that day and he listened to me from the doorway of the living room. I knew that he was about to embark on his own career as a concert virtuoso. My Dad was thrilled at this interest and signalled to me to go into one of my more rehearsed pieces immediately but Mr Kossoff waved this aside. He walked over to the piano and said, "Do you know all these notes?" and he pointed to C, C sharp, D, D sharp, etcetera. "If you go into the next room," he asked, "and I strike a note, can you tell me what it is?" "Sure," I answered. I went into the kitchen and closed the door and he started to strike notes on the piano which I was able to call correctly. Then he started to strike two notes, then three, four notes, then chords, all of which I named.

'I didn't realise I was doing anything worth mentioning. He then started to get slightly crazy on me and throw a little Scriabin at me, and I didn't miss it. I should have been playing Vegas, I could have cleaned up. He was amazed, and spoke to my father explaining that he wanted me to study with him. He didn't even want to be paid but my father wanted to pay him and struck a bargain with him, which was a purely nominal sum. Anyhow, nominal or not, it was a whole lot of haircuts. I had one lesson a week at his place on Riverside Drive and he insisted on my coming back a second day each week on the house for a brushup, as he called it. And of course my Dad was cutting his hair for zero too.

'It seemed too easy for me, I recall. I used to con him into playing the piece first, then I would just slide through it. By that time I was into my early teens and there was just too much going on to practise the way I should have. There was never any question of being able to read, however, and we got into some pretty hard pieces. We went through the Hanon book, the Schirmer versions of some of the standard classical numbers, some Scarlatti, all of the Chopin ballades and the études.

'That summer, after Easter, I still didn't want to play the piano. I was only interested in the trumpet and I used to go on Friday nights for my half hour lesson. The minute the teacher went out I would be playing some of the things I was hearing on the radio. *What'll I Do, Alexander's Ragtime Band, Tin Roof Blues*, all fell into my library right there.

'Luckily, living in East Harlem we were exposed to some good records. My Dad and Mom went to see Bill Robinson one night at the Lafayette Theatre in Harlem. Fletcher Henderson's band was playing the show and rocking on back. One of the acts was Fats Waller. My Dad came home, opened the window and threw out all the Paul Whiteman records plus everything by Irving Aaronson and his Commanders. I said, "Give them to the Salvation Army". He said, "These aren't good enough for them." He really flipped. He went out and bought every Fats Waller record he could lay his hands on, or anything that was related to it.

'There was a very special hood that I thought was the best dressed cat in town. He was so sharp it was ridiculous. He came in and heard the Fats Waller records playing in my father's barber shop. He said, "If you like that, dig this!" And then he put a Louis Armstrong record on — *West End Blues*. It was too much. When we got *Sugarfoot Stomp*, that was the swingingest barber shop in town.

'That summer Mr Kossoff decided I should live in Mount Vernon, a suburb of the city, so that I could put in more time with him. He had a son about my age, who did not play the piano. It was a whole new atmosphere to me. They had a concert Bechstein piano and I think my preference for that instrument dates back to that time. When school started again I had to go once a week for my lesson in Mount Vernon. This meant taking a train up to 241st Street, then a trolley car for twenty minutes, then a long walk.

'The weekly marathon to Mount Vernon always ended up in one of two ways. Coming back I would get off the train at 135th Street, which was where the Lafayette was, or at 125th Street which was where the Apollo was. In any case nobody seemed to be reading in those places, whether it was Mills Blue Rhythm Band, Andy Kirk and his Clouds of Joy (with Mary Lou Williams) or even Lucky Millinder.

'I was about fifteen when I was asked to leave the Dewitt Clinton High School, 79th Street Annex, after lasting out three months as a freshman. I then went down to Textile High, a vocational school which had a swimming pool in a brand new building, on 18th Street between 9th and 10th Avenue, a very rough section. I immediately joined the band on trumpet because I was playing the lead part of *Strike Up The Band* like crazy. Then one day at rehearsal something happened in the 'bone section. Somebody obviously misunderstood the *del signo* and there was a tumult.

'Since I was usually the principal villain all the heat was turned on me. The instructor who was leading the band took out after me and I just ran around the auditorium two or three times. Obviously I had a longer stride than him because I went right out the door and down into the subway, horn and all.

'By this time, with the barber shop connection, I found out who needed a piano or trumpet player. My main victim was a guitar player who I was crazy about because he was actually smaller than me, and I was really short for my age. His speciality was Italian weddings and he hired me whether there was a piano in the hall or not. I had plenty of Fats Waller choruses to fall back on and once in a while, when I visited my cousin on those Friday nights, I heard an Eddie Duchin record or two.'

By now it was 1932, and Joe joined Frank Lamarr and his orchestra at the Roseland Ballroom as a substitute for the pianist who was ailing. When the pianist got better, Joe wound up on second trumpet, playing the jazz solos.

'When I got the piano chair back I decided I didn't need those stacks of piano parts piled up on the piano — they obstructed my view of the young ladies on the dance floor. I got rid of the piano book by sitting on the parts, which just about brought me up to the right height. As far as reading is concerned, once I was playing in a band there was little reason for me to read. The band played simple tunes. What was there to learn? All I can say is that Lamarr loved it; he told me he thought the band was getting to sound like Isham Jones.

'Later on I got a reputation: "He can't read because you don't see any parts on his piano!" I encouraged this attitude, and when I joined Tommy Dorsey in 1940 I took all the piano parts out of the fibre case and filled it with dirty laundry and other items. Eventually they stopped even giving me the parts.'

During his two years with Dorsey, Joe made over 100 recordings with the band and began composing. He recalled the way he came to join the band:

'Berigan was in the band and knew that the pianist, Bob Kitsis, was going as he'd been fired publicly about three times.

'So Bunny suggested I came in for the last set. He said Tommy had fired

Kitsis and so far as he knew I was the only player for the job. Those days, Bunny used to get drunk every night. But he played hell out of the trumpet and always sat upright and walked straight and kind of stiff. He'd stumble off the stage at the finish looking like Field Marshal Rommel.

'So I showed up there and Bunny called me up behind the band. Dorsey didn't see me. He'd heard me play but didn't really know me, and he was drinking then. I got up there in the trumpet section and started playing.

'Dorsey had his back to the orchestra and when he heard me he turned round and asked "Who's that playing?" Bunny answered: "That's Joey Bushkin!" And T.D. said: "Kid, you're hired — on piano."'

For most of his early years in the business, Joe played more for kicks than cash. He says the first job that brought him any prominence was at the Famous Door in 1935 and '36. Berigan was the leader and the group was regarded as one of the hottest little bands in New York. Joe's co-players included Bud Freeman, Eddie Condon, Dave Tough and, from time to time, Teddy Wilson.

In spite of the good jazz, the Door attracted so few customers Joe says the musicians were afraid of becoming snowblind from the glare of empty table-cloths. But musicians came to sit in. Artie Shaw was one, and that's how Joe came to be on the Billie Holiday session. Billie was still singing at the tables in Pod's and Jerry's Log Cabin and it was her friend, Bernie Hanighen — writer of *When A Woman Loves A Man* and *If The Moon Turns Green* — who talked Columbia into putting out titles by Billie and her Orchestra on its cheap Vocalion label.

'We made that first version of *Billie's Blues, Summertime, No Regrets* and, oh, I forgot the other one. She sounded just beautiful and looked the same way.

'How do I feel about Billie? I feel about her the way I feel about Louis Armstrong as a singer and a trumpet player; the same as I feel about Bunny Berigan or Lester Young. What she did was the same as what they were doing — — she made a song her own.'

Bushkin recorded with Berigan on several occasions in 1936 and worked with his band off and on until well into 1939. They were close friends and for a time Joe lived with Bunny, sharing his problems which were mostly financial. When he joined Tommy Dorsey, his new boss asked what he got with Bunny.

'I said I was supposed to be getting 90 dollars a week, but I thought it was a secret between him and his lawyer,' says Joe.

'So Dorsey said: "Okay kid, you get 90 dollars." That was guaranteed, but we got 25 dollars extra for a three-hour record date and something extra for whatever we did except the regular network broadcasts.

'Then they took 10 dollars a week off for the uniforms — we used up six suits a year. I didn't go for this as I didn't like the cut of 'em, or the colours.'

By this time Joe had begun to write songs. His first, *Oh! Look At Me Now*, was recorded by the band in January, 1941, with Frank Sinatra, Connie Haines and the Pied Pipers. It reached Number One on the American Hit Parade. Sinatra was then the band vocalist and one of Joe's assignments was to rehearse him in all his songs as the singer didn't read music. They've been comrades ever since.

Buddy Rich was the drummer and, according to Bushkin, often turned up late for the first set which Dorsey didn't play. T.D. was meticulous about punctuality and fined anyone he caught who wasn't on time.

'The fine,' said Joe, 'was that you had to buy booze for the whole band, which cost a lot of bread. Now Buddy was late for that first set nearly every night. But Tommy wasn't there and nobody every finked on him.

'As it happened I was always on time, except about twice. Once I was terribly late and that was when I had a fight with Buddy Rich. When I appeared Tommy stopped the band and said: "You used to play with us."

'Well, I was late and I had the wrong uniform on. It was Tuesday, after the Monday off, and we changed to the light suits. But I hadn't been home all night and I woke up somewhere uptown of course, so I was wearing the wrong uniform. I was happy to buy the booze.

'Anyway, he called the waiter over and made it pretty tough. George Arus and Chuck Peterson drank Canadian Club: a bottle of that. Somebody else had a bottle and so on. A case of Coca-Cola and, finally, a bottle of wine for Buddy Rich.

'"Cancel the wine," I said. Tommy wanted to know why and I told him: "Not for that cat. He was late every night when you weren't there. I refuse to buy him wine. Let him pay off first."

'The waiter arrived with all the bottles and the wine was there. So I sent it back. Afterwards, Buddy and I went out in the park and beat the shit out of each other. Well, it was a fighting band.

'Dorsey came out and tried to stop the fight, which I wouldn't have minded because I was getting the worst of it. But he wasn't worried about us. "Take the jackets off," he shouted. "The jackets. We got another programme to play."'

Looking back on his British experiences, Bushkin recollected that Waller introduced him to the subject of England and English musicians. 'Fats played *Bond Street* and other items about London. I knew that when he wasn't playing in Harlem he was probably in England, which gave me a high impression of the place. In 1953 I came over when John Huston first opened "Moulin Rouge". I had never made Europe before. I took a vacation for three weeks and got home five months later.

'The very first musician I met in Britain was Jack Parnell, and I met him with Ernie Anderson. Jack was playing a one-nighter and I went out to catch him with his big band. My timing was perfect — I arrived just as the band hit the first note of *God Save The Queen*. Jack played an arrangement on that I'll never forget. All the chords were elevenths and thirteenths. It was really spread out. The band was so great it was hard to believe.

'When I was here then there were some jazz clubs but the scene was sort of confused to me. But on this trip we went directly to Ronnie Scott's. Everybody in New York and Los Angeles knows what's happening at Ronnie's because what's happening there is usually more important than what's happening back home. It is today like what Birdland used to be before it became an underground garage.

'There was a time when anybody who played jazz came from New Orleans.

And a critic has called me "Chicago Style". I don't know what that means because I came from under the El at 103rd Street. But these days the whole world knows that some of the best jazz musicans playing are British.'

After living in Britain for a while in late '69 and early '70, Joe went back to the West Coast and returned here professionally as Bing Crosby's accompanist in September of 1977. The Bushkin Quartet appeared with the Crosby Show *for a London Palladium season plus a few outside dates. On the eve of the tour Joe spoke to me about Bing.*

'This whole thing started with that Christmas TV show with Bing Crosby and Fred Astaire. It was one afternoon in the studio when things got a little out of control. There was some problem about lighting and we weren't getting too many takes in. It was a big set and there was a lot of running about in an attempt to get this show on the road, and the whole thing began to remind me of Groucho Marx,' Joe remembered.

'It was a tremendous comedy except that a fortune was being wasted for Bing's company while a couple of jerks were trying to change a baby spot into a pin spot, or whatever the hell it was. There was a lot of technical dialogue and not much action going on.

'I was getting tired of standing around. I'd drunk about thirty cups of coffee and was getting a little acidity problem, and I figured the best way for me to waste some more time was to just go up and play some piano.

'Where I had to play was supposedly in Bing's music room at his home. There were steps up to the piano and back of it a library of records and tape machines and so forth. That was the scene. So I sat down and started to play *Wrap Your Troubles in Dreams.*

'I don't know why I went into that, but subconsciously I did it in a key where it lay well for him. He sings it around C, D flat or something.

'Bing was at the back getting a cup of tea, and he came walking up with this paper cup of tea in his hand and stood by the piano. I was into the middle part of the tune and he starts singing, and all the noise stopped in the studio because he was just singing softly, you know, with the piano.

'So I went from *Wrap Your Troubles* to *I Surrender, Dear,* and a bunch of tunes like *Please,* that he dug, and he went on singing. And, next thing you know, his wife, Kathryn, and the kids came over and sat on the steps. The studio men got the lights straight, and now they're ready to shoot the scene, and Bing is going to keep the medley going. Now he's throwing tunes at me.

'And while I'm playing piano during this lighting panic, Bing asks me if I'd like to bring a quartet up to the Pebble Beach Pro-Am, which is the biggest golf tournament in the United States. He said he hadn't sung a tune at his own Pro-Am Celebrity Tournament in eight years. He'd get up and talk, and so on, but apparently hadn't sung a song at his own thing in all that time. And this year (1975) he was going to do a medley of thirty-five tunes.

'And that was the whole show. We opened with a number, and Bing got up and sang about thirty songs, which absolutely clobbered 800 of these great golfers. Fractured 'em. Then Bing said we had to do a concert with this thing, you know. So we got the family together, because they had the material from the various shows that they did; the orchestrations were already written, practically, and he got Nelson Riddle, Rosemary Clooney, and my quartet with Herb Ellis on guitar. And we had a show.

'And I must say this: with the music I love playing, I'll do it for nothing or get paid. With Bing I'm getting paid and I really enjoy being with the guy. It's a kick, and everything has been first class.'

Bushkin, as I have tried to imply, feels an almost unlimited admiration for Crosby, whose skill and professionalism and sheer enthusiasm for music he finds stimulating and endearing. Bing, I noted on the last Palladium visit, occasionally looked surprised or amused at what Bushkin (or maybe Johnny Smith) was playing during the medley.

'Well, yeah, right. We used to change it every show, and we threw him a couple of times. But he loved it. He said: "Throw some curves." He's like Babe Ruth, man; he loves a fast ball or a curve or something unexpected.

'Bing is absolutely one of the guys in the band, like any guy doing a solo. He's no different than Bunny Berigan was playing solo trumpet. Consequently I enjoy every minute of it, and I'm sure he does. He'll go anywhere in the world with this quartet.

'In fact, what's come up is to just go out with the quartet. It's such an easy thing. We can travel in two cars; all we need is a van for the amplifier and the drum set.

'And Bing would love to be in the same automobile as the quartet, so we could be talking about jazz musicians and old times. When I did that Christmas show with him and Fred Astaire, that was the Bing Crosby Projects, his company, that's paying for it. Yet he was hanging up shooting in order to ask me about the guys.

'He asked me about Bobby Hackett, when I saw him last, and so forth, and we talked about all the cats he knew. That's his thing, you know. He reminisced a lot about Jack Teagarden, of course, and Condon. He loved Eddie Condon.'

I said Bing had always been a singer who appreciated superior jazzmen, players such as Louis Armstrong, Eddie Lang, Joe Sullivan, and the Dorseys, and loved working with groups like Bob Crosby's Bob Cats. Joe put it to me that Bing just preferred good musicians, a preference which should not surprise us.

'He always asked for us on the record dates when we were session men, and that's natural, isn't it? I mean, if you have a choice of hanging out with Broadway Rose or Sophia Loren I think you're going to take Sophia.

'Most good singers feel that way. Tom Jones wouldn't make a move without Jack Parnell on his TV show, would he? And as a matter of fact, when I was over here in 1970 I went out with Phil Harris to the studio to see Jack and the guys, and noticed they were all the great players — Stan Roderick, Bobby Orr and many old-time players who'd worked with Ted Heath and the Palladium band, and so on.

'And Tom Jones, in the States at the height of his popularity, was considered a big pop-rock guy, and I figured he'd have a bunch of kids behind him. But when I mentioned it, he said: "Look, when that red light's on and you want those notes you don't get no young kids; you get the guys who can play, you get the pros".'

I wondered when and how the Crosby-Bushkin association began, and Joe said that the Crosby connection went way back to when he recorded with the singer.

'I made a lot of records with him. I did recordings with him when I was with Tommy Dorsey's band in '40 and '41, and then when I was a studio piano player after the war — you know, I was staff pianist in early 1946 — Bing called in and he got Eddie Condon, Bud Freeman, George Wettling and myself, and a bunch of guys he specified for a record date at Decca. He did *Personality* with me and some other tunes.

'And I played piano for Bing as far back as 1940 on the *Road To Morocco* soundtrack. That's when Dorsey's band was on the West Coast, and we played at the Palladium in Hollywood. Bing wanted Tommy's band to be on the main title track of the picture, which had Victor Young's orchestra, so it was really quite a scene.

'This was an immense studio with a big symphony orchestra, Victor Young's, and the Tommy Dorsey band, and man there were some sounds going on.

'Anyway, Bing dug my playing. He picked up on it right away; I guess it reminded him of whatever piano playing he liked to hear. So I got to know him real well around that time.

'At that period I began writing songs: *Oh, Look At Me Now, How Do You Do Without Me*, a lot of songs for the Dorsey orchestra, and through this activity I got to know a lot of the songwriters and publishers.'

A lover of well-constructed songs, he is still into composing. He's not too keen on the protest-song genre, though, as he has never seen songs as a weapon.

'I'm not one of those cats who believes in asking, when told that such and such a singer is a very good act: "Never mind that, can he march?"'

Hoagy Carmichael

Bandleader, jazz pianist and vocalist of radio, record, stage and screen renown, and great composer of jazz songs and standards — to be all these things was a lot for one man to achieve and remain unbumptious and friendly. But Hoagland (known variously as Hoagy, Hugo and Hogwash!) Carmichael not only won fame and deserved it, he took the kicks of a busy life with equanimity, good humour and not a trace of 'big time'. His Stardust Road book suggested he would be sardonic, terse of speech and mildly crazy about jazz. Film roles made him out a saturnine character of philosophical bent. It was a great buzz for me when I met him in August 1948, and realised he was a reasonably normal American: a good talker and a great story teller, and a quieter dresser than most. This is what I wrote then.

First thing you notice is that he's smaller than you thought. In conversation he reveals an admiration for the men like Bix, Louis and Trumbauer (who were important musical influences) but no signs of craziness about jazz. It's just a part of the enjoyment on hand.

'About a month before I left home,' he told me, 'I got in a taxi and told the driver to take me to the Negro section of Los Angeles to see what was happening. When we passed a joint with the name Kid Ory up outside, I said to the driver, "That'll do for me." Inside I found a club like a cleaned-out grocery store, with a small platform at one end on which these elderly coloured musicians were playing the old jazz tunes. The pianist, I remember, looked particularly sleepy, but his hands went up and down those keys ... wham!'

On stage Hoagy is himself — a very relaxed character. His is an unusual presentation for British variety, but effective. Making a personal appearance at the Carlton Cinema last Friday (at the première of RKO's *Night Song*, in which he has a featured role as a bandleader), Hoagy talked to friends until a minute before time, then sauntered on without having thought of anything to say beyond his opening sentence. But his gift for ad libbing got the crowd.

In *Night Song* Hoagy is seen singing and playing (clarinet as well as piano) and netting a fish caught by Merle Oberon.

About the fishing scene he told me: 'Those trout sure were difficult to keep alive. Something wrong with the water in the studio tank, I guess. Anyway, they died, and whenever we tried to shoot the scene, up came a lifeless trout. Eventually they persuaded one to keep going long enough for me to net it. This fish flapped a couple of times.' Hoagy undulated his hand twice, twisting his features into a typical grimace, 'and then quit. You know what that shot cost? Fifteen hundred dollars a wiggle.'

I think this story illustrates Hoagy's mode of speech, his sense of humour and attitude towards fame and films, as well as anything I know. Of course, you need to hear him tell it, but if you are familiar with his records you can imagine the morose accents of the Hoagian drawl.

His wife, Ruth, whom he married in 1936, corroborated my impression that her husband is a glutton for golf rather than work. They live in about three and a half acres on Holmby Hills, California, with their two sons — Hoagy Bix, aged eight, and Bob, who is two years younger. Says Ruth: 'When Hoagy comes home from golf — which is nearly every day — he goes straight to the bar, has his drink, then looks around to greet me and anyone else who may be visiting.'

It's when Hoagy starts talking about songwriting that he really expands.

'It's a lot of fun writing songs,' he told me. 'Anyone who has the urge to should try. Contrary to general belief, the doors are wide open in the States. And one thing is certain: write a song about Texas and you're apt to make a lot of money.'

Hoagy himself hasn't specialised in songs about the Lone Star State or, indeed, in any kind of romantic song. He made his name after serving a pretty long apprenticeship, with pure melody numbers like *Stardust* (written before 1928) or melodic swingers like *Washboard Blues* and *Riverboat Shuffle*. None of them had words at first. Mostly the lyrics were added by someone else later on, but if Hoagy couldn't get the words he wanted he'd write them himself or alter the other fellow's.

'To get words to fit the melody and idea of a song just right is *the* most difficult thing,' Hoagy claims. 'So I'm writing my own words quite often. Not because mine are that good, you know, but because I can at least get the feel of my own music.'

Hoagy's latest, written for the London Casino show, is a bouncy leg-pull about a monkey and a cannibalistic king. Tentatively double-titled, Hoagy is leaving it to British audiences to choose between *The Monkey Song* and *King Bebop's Dream*. Probably the lay public miss the satire of Carmichael's bop singing in this number, but they like the crack about the king's stomach-ache: 'It must have been somebody you ate!'

A jazz song? Well, that depends largely on how it's performed, of course. Maybe I, as a frustrated jazz lover, would say not. But Hoagy says 'Yes,' and he after all, has heard more jazz songs than I've had hot dinners.

'I don't have any patience with the narrow jazz boys — no patience *at all*,' says Hoagy emphatically. 'You can't separate jazz and popular jazz and swing music. I don't think you can separate music at all ... not properly. It's all one, really, all leads out of the one thing. Do I make myself clear?'

He lifts a quizzical brow. 'The thing's clear to me all right. None of my songs could have been written without I'd had a jazz background. But that doesn't mean I try to write jazz. I write *melodies*, and those tunes are conditioned by my musical environment, which means some were directly inspired by jazz, others weren't.

'Many have been big hits, so they are commercial if you like. But I never in my life sat down and tried to write a *commercial* song. As a matter of fact, several of my songs were turned down for years as "uncommercial": *Judy* was one I wrote years before I dared turn it loose on the public — because I knew thay wouldn't take it at that time.

'It isn't a question of my having "progressed" from jazz to something else. In the early days I wrote *Stardust* (which I played in a very different fashion on an early Gennett recording from the way it's usually played to-day) and also some more obvious jazz tunes. Then I wrote songs like *Rockin' Chair, Lazy River* and *Georgia,* and a lot of slow melodic numbers. Later I did *Hong Kong Blues* and *New Orleans,* which I think are jazz. Anyway, I can tell you it took a jazz education to enable me to write 'em.

'So when I once read a piece in which the writer said "Hoagy no longer writes jazz — he's left the fold," and so on, I said to myself: "That's a young feller wrote that." All I reckon to do is write a melody (and maybe words to go with it). I do my best to write a good tune. And that's all I ever did. There's licks associated with old-style jazz and bob licks to-day: there's fashions in them. But all the hot licks in the world don't mean a thing compared with a good melody. In music you've got to have good melody — that's what I believe.'

Before leaving the topic, it is worth recalling a dozen of the less publicised Carmichael compositions — *March Of The Hoodlums, Boneyard Shuffle, Sing It Way Down Low, Old Man Harlem, Charlie Two-Step, Moon Country, Thanksgivin', Ballad In Blue, One Night In Havana, Daybreak, Poor Old Joe* and *Memphis in June.* The great majority of these have been recorded by swing bands. Hoagy recalls that Duke helped him out by using *Hoodlums* at a time when his writing was not bringing in much money. Goodman, of course, recorded the *Ballad In Blue* (a charming 'mood' piece), but that was a few years later when things were beginning to go well for Carmichael.

It was in 1937 that he had his first film part — as a piano player in *Topper*. Paramount had him under contract to write music, and he was collecting on one or two hits. *Lazybones, Georgia, Rockin' Chair* and *Little Old Lady* have been steady breadwinners for Hoagy, and *Stardust* still brings him in a regular ten thousand dollars yearly . *Ole Buttermilk Sky* is his latest money-spinner in the States. He has penned a total of eighty songs, about half of which have clicked.

On records Carmichael has attained the status of an old music-master (witness the reissue of his pre-war version of *Hong Kong Blues* and *Riverboat Shuffle* on the current batch of American 'Special Edition' discs). These sides were released here on Columbia and, with *New Orleans/Two Sleepy People* on Parlophone, helped make his name with casual collectors.

The serious ones already knew his scatting on *Walking The Dog* and *I Must Have That Man*, his cross-talk with Louis on Armstrong's *Rockin' Chair*, his vocals on that same tune and *Georgia* by his own band, and his warm effort on the Hotsy Totsy Gang's *High And Dry*. Later, there were *Sing It Way Down Low, Lazy River* and *Little Old Lady* and *Washboard Blues* — the last two vocals with the Casa Loma Band.

I talked about all these to Hoagy, and he was surprised that I preferred the earlier *Hong Kong* and *Shuffle* to the recent Brunswick versions. 'Just trying things out then,' he said. 'Trying for an idea, not getting it.' I agreed that his new release of *Riverboat Shuffle* was good, wished that the US Decca folks would use more of those trio or solo piano backgrounds instead of the big bands and 'Whoo-Whoo' vocal groups. 'I don't need a band behind me,' Hoagy grinned. 'Only a beat.'

On both *Hong Kong Blues* discs he uses his famous mandolin-attachment piano 'to give a battered effect to the music.' On the new *Shuffle* he's accompanied by Buddy Cole, white pianist who plays on his radio programmes, and the record is Hoagy's jazziest for some time. 'Good people, we've got *Milenberg Joys* in a special orchestration,' yells Hoagy. And one of the breaks goes: 'Mr Hawkins on the tenor'.

'Yeah, I just put the line in for fun this time,' he said. 'You know, people in the States are not as informed about jazz as they are here. I couldn't talk to anyone over there who knew as much about my records as you do.'

Today, jazz boys don't go for Hoagy's records like they did. Maybe the material isn't so good; certainly the background music has slipped. But there isn't much difference in the voice, and the swing's still there.

The wonder is, though, that he draws the cash customers to the record counter. Hoagy is a singer getting by without a singing voice; his sorrowful voice, confidential style and relazed phrasing hypnotise listeners into acceptance of singing which is almost soliloquising in rhythm. Maybe his screen personality helps sell his records and radio act. Whatever it is, they certainly sell and will go on selling. To me that is good, because I like Hoagy better than the floppy-bow brigade.

Guitar

Eddie Condon

Though not himself a heroic figure, Eddie Condon was one of my personal jazz heroes from a young age — me, not him. His records sounded good, and in photographs the dandyish character with patent-leather hair looked okay, too. Also he sounded (when you could hear him on records) a strong, firm rhythm man on banjo or guitar. I learned later on he felt that guitar was not really a solo instrument, and I was able to confirm that he was an intelligent, articulate man, also a survivor in spite of the damage he inflicted on his physique. Some people did not care for his fly attitudes, his publicising of alcoholic drink, or his casual behaviour in charge of a band — what he sometimes referred to as 'stern leadership'. Myself, I liked it all well enough.

Here are my thoughts on a jazz-lover who made himself an important catalyst in a swinging situation, also a useful spokesman for jazz and satirical commentator with voice or pen. They were first written down and used in part in an obituary in Melody Maker *of 11 August 1973. But this is a longer, different piece.*

Eddie Condon might justly have been dubbed Father of Chicago Jazz. He may not have been the first to make records in what came to be known as Chicago Style, but he was certainly among the first. And the 1927 McKenzie and Condon Chicagoans sides — *China Boy, Nobody's Sweetheart, Liza,* and *Sugar* — effectively defined the new approach for a generation of white musicians and jazz fans.

A batch of records cut in Chicago at this period showed what this particular way of playing was, and suggested where it had come from.

Charles Pierce's band and the Jungle Kings, with Muggsy Spanier and Frank Teschemacher, preceded the Chicagoans on record by a month or two. Condon was playing banjo with the Kings, and he took part in several more historically important sessions by exponents of Chicago Jazz. It wasn't that he was making records in Chicago for very long; he moved to New York in '28 and had little to do with the Windy City after that. But he remained faithful to the broad principles of the music-making which engaged his attention there back in the early Twenties.

In some respects characteristically white jazz, inspired by recordings of the Original Dixieland Jazz Band, Bix and the Wolverines and New Orleans Rhythm Kings among others, it was at the same time based partly on the musicians' open admiration for artists like Oliver, Armstrong, the Dodds brothers and Bessie Smith.

Condon once stated that his bunch of Chicagoans were raised on Bessie's records, and this is confirmed by Bud Freeman, at any rate, who invariably includes the singer among his influences and cherished memories.

I suppose one of the remarkable things about Eddie Condon was his dedication to this special kind of middle-road Chicago-Dixieland, later to be nicknamed Nicksieland because of its association with Nick's in Greenwich Village.

Another was his enthusiasm for, and judgement of, musicians who excelled at creative melodic improvisation within the idiom he saw as real jazz.

Condon was no revivalist, and had hard words for some of the elderly bands of New Orleanians which came to prominence with Bunk Johnson ('I've got to give them credit for being able to stand up', was one of his comments).

And according to Humphrey Lyttelton, described by Eddie as 'a reconstructed Etonian', when Condon first listened to the New Orleans revival music of Turk Murphy's Band he snapped: 'After two hours of this I'm almost ready for some bop. Well . . . not quite *that* ready.' He cared little for bop, or anything beyond it in a way-out direction. In the early days of his first club on West 3rd Street, opened with the help of his publicist and friend Ernie Anderson, there was the oft-quoted occasion when a waiter dropped a tray of plates and cutlery. Eddie looked up from his drink and ordered: 'None of that progressive jazz in here.' When he launched Condon's in December of 1945 and a reporter asked him the capacity of the club, Eddie replied: 'Oh, about 200 cases.' I don't suppose he repeated that crack, or his recommended hangover cure — 'Take the juice of two quarts of whisky' — but other people did. He was a pithy, instinctively funny conversationalist who seldom told any story the same way twice. He didn't need to. If the alcohol loomed large in the Condon mythology, it was because he enjoyed booze and jazz and liked to talk about his favourite subjects (he also spoke approvingly of women sometimes, particularly of his wife, Phyllis).

Annoyed at his refusal to take the doctor's advice on cutting down on the sauce, Phyllis drew up a list of famed jazzmen who had died from the demon drink. She thrust it at her ailing husband who studied it briefly and observed: 'They haven't got a drummer.' Eddie had a love-hate relationship with percussionists. Overpowering drummers were on the hate list, also those with a time-keeping problem. He felt unlimited affection for guys with one ear for light and shade, and another for who was playing what around them, and the ability to keep the music alive and kicking at all times. Dave Tough and George Wettling were two that filled the bill. Commenting on one old 'Commodore' gang, he explained to me: 'What really made the band, though, was Jess Stacy on piano and George Wettling on drums.' Here, we got the hint of a Condon theory, although he disliked all theorising about the music, for he also said: 'A good band is based on good drums and good piano. Give me a good piano and George Wettling and I'll give you a good band, anytime.'

Fortunate for us, therefore, that when Condon hit London early one Tuesday morning in January 1957, he had a bemused George Wettling in tow, as well as Messrs Davison, Cutshall, Wilber, Gehman, Schroeder and Gaskin. I do recall someone later that day demanding to know: 'How's your drummer?' And getting from Condon the unexpected answer: 'He comes on like *We The People*'.

This being Eddie's first visit to Britain (and the only one, as it happened), he attracted a fairly large and varied reception committee to London Airport. Despite the cold, and even snow I believe, there was a band to greet him — it included Lyttelton, Mick Mulligan, some of their bandsmen, Beryl Bryden with washboard, Diz Disley, plus the *Melody Maker* and sundry fans. Condon, doubtless bewildered by an impromptu jazz rendering and our strange appearance, asked if this was Belgium. Reassured, he consented to enter a limo and be carried off to his West End accommodation. Along with Mulligan, Lyttelton, Richard Gehman (Eddie's co-author and drinking mate) and Ernie Anderson, I accompanied the guitarist-bandleader to the hotel in Piccadilly.

It was still quite early and the man at Reception asked Eddie if he would like to breakfast. Being ignorant of the rules, he enquired if it was possible to get whisky for breakfast.

'In an English hotel, Sir, a guest can get alcoholic refreshment at any hour of the day or night,' he was informed. The bandleader turned a bleary eye in Gehman's direction. 'Dick,' he announced, 'I'm taking out papers.'

This was the prelude to an alleged press reception in Condon's rooms which seared itself on my memory, as indeed did the tour itself.

While the leader reclined gratefully on his bed, fully dressed and with hat tilted forward on his head, right-hand man Anderson offered refreshment to anyone willing. After a check, he lifted the 'phone and ordered: 'Half a dozen large whiskies please.' The recumbent figure muttered: 'Add half a dozen large doctors.' Members of the press began to be admitted, and more drinks were dispensed. One or two brave souls attempted questions, such as why Eddie took no solos. 'I don't play solos for a purpose; I don't know enough about guitar,' was one muffled response. Pressed further, he opened his eyes and declared: 'I'm a saloon keeper, not a guitar player.'

At one stage he said mildly: 'If you fellows think I'm a total abstainer you're probably right — with the exception of a few open jugs of spirit now and again.' This struck a chord in my mind. Didn't Eddie have a sign over the door of his first club stating 'Total abstinence is not obligatory in this establishment', or advice to that effect?

As the party thinned, one of the remaining reporters raised his voice impatiently, seeking usable quotes. Lifting his head slightly, the honoured guest made a sideways gesture and told him: 'Right ear deaf. Shout into the right side but whisper in the left.' Finally a worried Daily with deadline to meet asked if

Mr Condon would object to answering questions from a sitting-up position. Peering from under his brim, Eddie promised to do his best. 'But I'm not really an athlete,' he complained. One or two celebrities had rung through by this time and it dawned on Condon that he was in demand. Another knock on the door. 'That'll be Bix Beiderbecke's mother,' said this slice of Chicago jazz history.

That evening saw a reception for Condon and colleagues at the Jack of Clubs in Soho, complete with 'the daddy of all jam sessions'. Eddie, in high spirits now, mentioned that he called his band of wandering minstrels the Barefoot Gang. 'We only wear shoes on the stand.' Earlier I heard: 'One thing I want to ask you English fellows — where do you hide your booze?' And on downing Scotch: 'There's only one better drinker in America, Toots Shaw.'

On the Wednesday, armed with tickets, expenses and a survival kit, I wound up at Kings Cross Station shortly before midnight with family and friends for an unofficial see-off party. The Barefeet, minus leader, were bound for Glasgow by the night express. I was sharing a sleeping carriage with Geo Wettling (as he usually signed his name), who had spent part of the day buying Burberry suiting, an overcoat and tweedy sportsman's hat. George was proud of his new possessions and, after a few convivial snorters with his fellow passenger, tucked himself into the sleeping berth wearing the full Burberry kit — all but the hat.

Glasgow in the morning was nothing to write home about but after signing in and procuring scoff and a wash and brush-up, a volunteer contingent made its way somewhat unsteadily to the local airport to meet 'Slick' Condon, as he was once nicknamed. Having elected to carouse in comfort in London and fly to his first gig of the tour, he was in good shape as he emerged on to the blustery airfield, gangstery hat back on his head and coat blowing in the wind. As Lyttelton and I advanced, salutations were cordial. Humph was clad in a long, heavy greatcoat (inherited from his father as I recall), for which he was noted, and both of us had bottles protruding from our pockets. I'm not sure what Eddie said to me, except that it had to do with his not requiring the address of my barber, but he greeted Humph warmly with 'I'm not going to ask you who your tailor is; who's your distiller?'

And so it was all 'go' again — back to the hotel, reunions with the barefoot mob, meetings with the good and great to whom Condon was a type of jazz prophet and saviour. I remember only fragments of the repartee, but it does me credit that I jotted some of it down in the trusty reporters' notebook. In the hotel: 'Can we have brunch? Some matured whisky'; on seeing Geo Wettling: 'Hello, the king of the xylophone players'; to Ernie Anderson: 'Is that the manager unpacking? I think I'll call you Ralph' (no, I don't get that, either).

A Scottish fan came up to ask where Wild Bill Davison could be located. 'Bull?' queried Condon. 'He's been invited back to London for a drink.' And introducing writer Gehman: 'He's my night-damager.'

During a rest period in the suite, pianist and former bandleader Billy Mason was ushered in. A longtime admirer of Eddie's type of jazz, Mason made him a present of a bottle of rare and ancient straight malt. 'That, my dear fellow, is medicine,' said Mason in reverent tones. After an interval, Anderson asked what we'd all like for a 'taste'. Without hesitation Eddie replied: 'I love medicine on the rocks.' Not for the first time it was brought home to me that the saloon keeper was smart with the verbals. On producing a jug of water from the bathroom, he asserted: 'Ah, the water's soft in Scotland. I hope the booze is hard.'

However, much besides the whisky and wisecracks in Condon's career was memorable. I have space only to refer to a few facets.

He organised and/or participated in several of the earliest racially mixed record dates: the Hot Shots of '29, Fats Waller's Buddies and some Louis Armstrong's. He made a flock of very worthwhile records under his own name, on many of which he felt proud to sit-in and 'pluck the old pork chop', and helped to familiarise collectors with the work of a succession of original and talented instrumentalists. Included among this list of musicians are Frank Teschemacher, Bud Freeman, Max Kaminsky, Bill Davison, Joe Sullivan, Gene Krupa, George Wettling, Bobby Hackett and Jimmy McPartland; and a great many more — from Pee Wee Russell and Edmond Hall to Muggsy Spanier and Jack Teagarden — and also that sweetly warm singer, Lee Wiley, became identified with Condon at various periods and in different ways. His love of really good swinging players never waned.

During the depression years Eddie, like hot jazz, knew some very tough times. He appears to have fought hard to keep himself and Condon-style music alive, and whenever an opportunity came by he followed it up tenaciously, involving himself in ground-breaking jazz broadcasts, concerts at New York's Town Hall (some of them televised) and eventually in running, or fronting perhaps, his club in Manhattan's Greenwich Village. And, of course, he continued taking his special kind of Dixieland into the record studios, on tour and into any joints that would pay. It is wholly typical that for his long series of radio 'Jazz Concert' presentations he inserted into his contract this statement: 'In order to preserve the unrestrained ad lib qualities of this music, the artists may depart from the formal programme at any time.' The artists he respected played in their own way.

On one recording of such a concert we hear the dapper bandleader welcoming to the microphone Lee Wiley, an old regular returned to the fold. 'It's nice to see you're back,' he remarked cheerfully. 'Not to mention your front.'

So, as a musician and entrepreneur, raconteur and self-publicist, Eddie put the stamp of Condonia on a type of jazz expression which many of us recognise as Chicago-Dixieland or Chicago Jazz — even if no such specific style ever existed. No matter the name, the stuff was generally tasty and highly rhythmical, and what we heard on the British concerts was as good as I'd expected, and sometimes better.

That evening the Gang kicked-off the tour in St Andrew's Hall. Attendance was excellent and the show struck me as being the sort of informal, action-packed clambake which lived up to the night-club host's reputation. Not surprisingly he played very little guitar, which provoked several shouts such as 'Why don't you play more?' or 'Can't you take a solo?' Eddie remained good-humoured and made some off-the-cuff rejoinders which were amusing but largely unheard. He tended to wander about the stage asking members of the troupe what they had in mind to play, before announcing the tunes in rather terse Condonese. This caused a bunch of the natives to get restless, and one of the lads called out: 'You're drunk; why don't you go home?' At once Eddie rasped back: 'If you'll let me have your key . . .'

As I might have made apparent, Albert Edwin Condon could be hard going, especially for teetotallers. His manner had some of the surface grit and sharpness of a city slicker, and his witticisms were mostly deflating in an amiable way, often self-deflating. He had no use for pretentiousness, and a person who put on airs around him was living dangerously. But he was able to describe the sound of Beiderbecke's horn as 'being like a girl saying yes!'. What I experienced of the man, backed up by what I've heard of him from intimates, leads me to support Red McKenzie's nomination of Condon as 'one of the nicest guys in jazz.'

Anyway, that night, after the Glasgow debut, Humphrey Lyttelton and I drank drink for drink with the band at Norrie McSwann's, though Eddie was using a pint jug for a glass, and lived to see him carried out.

'I think that's one up for England,' said Humph, raising his glass to me. And it was; two actually, but only just. Of the two bands, British and American, he and I were the only ones able to stand.

About ten years before, the doctors gave Condon ten years to live. He knew what it was about and continued to take his Scotch as health allowed. Last time Ernie Anderson visited him, Eddie dug into his quart as they talked of old times. Presently he complained that his stomach hurt and wife Phyllis said that of course it did after all that whisky.

'It's nothing to do with whisky,' said the indomitable Condon. 'Laughing's given me a pain.'

Bass

Joe Benjamin

The sight of Joe Benjamin on the bandstand was, to me for a couple of decades or more, comforting. He represented professionalism, solidity and extra qualifications, such as accurate, firm stopping and the ability to put down clean, buoyant bass lines, which guaranteed that this particular rhythm section was going to be, at any rate, well based. Joe, like his mentor George Duvivier, bowed and plucked skilfully and could be relied upon to swing.

I first ran into Benjamin in the very young Fifties, when he was part of Lena Horne's musical unit in Britain, then again during '54 as bassist with Sarah Vaughan. He was one third of a formidably fluent trio completed by pianist Jimmy Jones and drummer Roy Haynes. I got along excellently with all of them, and remember Joe as being very welcoming in his quiet, undemonstrative

*way. He cared deeply about music, of course, also about standards and be-
haviour — personal and communal.*

'The way society conducts itself?' I once asked.

'Or misconducts itself, wouldn't you say?'

*I can still hear the voice in my mind's ear, calm and quizzical. J.B. was handy
with words as well as musical notes, and possessed a gentle turn of humour
which, I assumed, helped him maintain equilibrium in face of the worst that
road-life could throw at him. His speech style bordered on the formal, as when I
sought an explanation of the 'Crazy Joe' tag during this interview (dating from
November 1971).*

*'I shall have to disappoint you,' he said gravely. 'I never have been able to
find that out, either.' Certainly there was nothing visible on Joe's respectable
and serious surface to indicate anything idiotic down below.*

*By the time he reappeared here in April of 1957 with the Gerry Mulligan
Quartet, it was in the nature of a reunion with the Jones family. He continued
over the years to treat us as mates, even if long-distance ones, and we liked him
very much. So the news of his death (in Livingstone, New Jersey, of a heart
attack) in January 1974 caused unusual upset in our household. Only two
months or so previously I had been breakfasting with him at the Caledonian
Hotel in Edinburgh, following an Ellington concert the evening before. Over
porridge, boiled eggs and tea he related stories about faraway places worked by
the band, talked of the making and breaking of string basses and the playing of
them, and discussed the merits of various artists — intelligently, sometimes
dismissively, always without rancour. He seemed an orderly, tolerant man, one
of the gents of jazz.*

Musicians once associated with Duke Ellington are inclined to remain associated with him — often on an off-and-on basis. Joe Benjamin (once referred to
by Sarah Vaughan, for hidden reasons, as 'Crazy Joe Benjamin') is a newish
member of the orchestra with old associations. Asked on the recent British tour
how long he had been with the band, Joe replied: 'Since January 1970 officially,
but unofficially I go back a long way. I've been in and out of his payroll for
years.'

Benjamin, who worked as a music copyist for many well-known people, has
done copying for Ellington on numerous occasions. He did some of the work
on the *My People* production and played bass on the recording as well as in the
show. Also, he was Mercer Ellington's bassist in 1946, and once played second
bass with Duke's band at a '51 concert. And, in his phrase, he has been on
standby many times since then.

Now he's the regular bassist, close to clocking up two year's experience in an
exacting position. And he takes his place in a long and distinguished line which
includes Wellman Braud, Hayes Alvis, Billy Taylor, Jimmy Blanton (an early
inspiration to Joe), Junior Raglin, Oscar Pettiford, Wendell Marshall, Jimmy
Woode, Aaron Bell and Ernie Shepard.

Joe's immediate predecessors were, in reverse order, Vic Gaskin (who came to
Britain with the band in late '69), Paul Kondziela, Jeff Castleman and John Lamb.

Knowing Benjamin to be a highly regarded session man, with plenty of dates in the book, I had been a little surprised to see him following Victor Gaskin into 'captivity'. Joe agreed he had been fortunate enough to have a sufficiency of bookings for radio, television and recording sessions, even symphony work, to keep him feeling contented and artistically fulfilled. This last is important to him. As he put it: 'I like to be able to do many things in the profession, just so I can feel at ease with myself.

'When you can feel at ease doing that, you begin to believe you're doing well in this profession. Like Clark Terry, Milton Hinton, George Duvivier ... any time, any day, anywhere, anything, they can handle it.'

These are names of people Joe greatly admires — 'the kind of guys I came up with' — and his ideal is to be up to what they can do musically. This, then, was his point of view. What happened to change it? Joe said it was the circumstances that happened.

'It's very easy to explain. A great deal of the musical activity I was concerned with began shifting from New York to places like Los Angeles and Tennessee and Alabama. It began to diffuse. I was still busy, you understand, but not so busy. And then, for about the umpteenth time, the phone rang with somebody from the Ellington organisation asking if I'd join the band. This time I agreed, but after considerable thought.

'In my years in the profession, I felt, I'd had everything but this particular depth; I'd had enough experience to tackle this, but was I ready? Of course I had doubts about pulling up roots; and then I thought about my long-term association with the Ellington family and organisation, going back years.

'After all these deliberations, I asked myself if I was really sure at this point in my life that I knew enough about music and whatever was necessary to fit into this exceptional organisation, to play with these particular musicians. I'm of an age to choose what I do with my life. So I considered the matter fully. If, I thought, I can make a contribution to the orchestra, I'll join. If not, I won't.

'It wasn't easy to decide. Can I contribute anything to a man who has been a genius for all those years? I thought about the times I'd done copying for the band. For how long? We can go back to 1947 without second thoughts. And I did the original copying on *Harlem* around 1949 or '50.

'These are some of the reasons it took so long to decide. How much do I love Duke? Will I devote my life to his orchestra? He plays his music, not mine or yours, his music. You cannot come into the band looking to be great. You're joining an institution and you need a great deal of dedication for this job. It winds up being that.

'After you have decided, and joined the band, then of course you find it rewarding. Ellington alters things while you're doing them, and that's what keeps you interested — if you care, and I do. We'll play the same arrangement at two concerts and it will sound different.

'Duke's done so much for the world in general, and I feel honoured to be an integral part of his orchestra. I feel now that I'm supposed to be here, and I think I am.'

So that is the story of Joe's joining. The facts of his first engagement are these:

'I was standby, as I told you, and got this call from the office. Gaskin had left and the band was on its way to Japan without a bass player. "Come in, we need you," they said.

'Well, I made my mind up and had to rush to get my passport and visa. I joined within two or three days for that tour which went to Manila, Taiwan, Burma, Hong Kong, Australia and New Zealand.

'The first notes I played with the band were in Tokyo. That was an initiation, as it were.'

Was it a difficult initiation, I wanted to know.

'Yes,' said Benjamin with unaccustomed brevity.

Slam Stewart

*Often you will hear Slam Stewart praised for his ability as a novelty man —
because of his special ability as a simultaneous hummer and bower of rather
snappy little jazz improvisations delivered in well-pitched octave unison. In
truth these are pleasant, rather humorous diversions which have become so
much second-nature to this distinguished bassist that at rehearsals or between
takes he can sometimes be heard firing out little unison messages of the
'Alrighty o-reeny' type to his leader or session brothers. But Stewart's curious
trademark sound must not blind us to his conventional musical attributes. He
has always been much more than a novel soloist, and more than just a bowing
bassist though his arco work is exemplary.*

*A conservatory-trained player with wide experience of music of various kinds,
he is an excellent technician, plucking or bowing, who also commands the
natural beat and sense of time and tempo essential to successful jazz-making.
This feature dates from 1981.*

In his *Dictionary Of Jazz* (1954) Hugues Panassié wrote of Slam that in a rhythm section 'he plays pizzicato with great mobility and varied accentuation which gives his playing a biting swing which few bass players have equalled.' This reliable swing-power as well as many instances of his singing-bass technique can be appreciated on scores of records ranging from 78s made with Slim Gaillard in 1938 to relatively recent albums with Bucky Pizzarelli or Major Holley or Illinois Jacquet's band.

The Stewart discography includes items by Slim and Slam and Slim's Flat Foot Floogie Boys (1938 to '41), the Royal Rhythm Boys trio ('39), pianist-singer Una Mae Carlisle ('40), Fats Waller ('43), Lester Young ('43) and then strings of recordings with Coleman Hawkins, the Art Tatum Trio, Don Byas, the Johnny Guarnieri Trio, Gillespie Sextet, Goodman Sextet and Orchestra, Erroll Garner, Red Norvo and groups of his own from '44 onwards.

Slam is a listening musician and a gently humorous one, and these qualities – – together with his solid training and quiet brand of showmanship — have kept him in demand throughout the ups and downs of a career stretching over nearly half a century. And the novelty aspect has proved to be a very minor goldmine for the bassist from Englewood, New Jersey, ever since he teamed up with guitarist and funny man Slim Gaillard in the late Thirties, and the duo fathered a big-seller with the unlovely title of *Flat Foot Floogie*. The vocal-and-instrumental solo method of Stewart's plus the 'schoolerooni, fruiterooni' school of vocal jive (the 'vout' language) devised by the duo fascinated radio audiences, record buyers and other listeners during '38 and '39. The vouty slang became part of the hip idiom, and you can still hear offshoots of it today in the conversation of many veterans of the Swing Era.

Slam bows his head and smiles almost wistfully when you quiz him about the Slim and Slam days and his reputation as 'one of the wits of jazz' — as he has justly been termed. He acknowledges the importance of the three-days-a-week radio programme the guitar-bass duo did for WNEW's Martin Block back in '37. Block took over their management and toured them in theatres across the nation, and though Stewart worked with other groups — including the Spirits of Rhythm early in 1939 — and formed his own trio in 1940, he continued to play dates with Slim until the latter was drafted in '42. The old team was reunited years afterwards at the South Bay Festival and, later again, at Monterey.

The first time I met Slam Stewart — he narrowly escaped a meeting in Paris during 1948 when I was forced by impending paternity to abandon a visit to the Paris Jazz Festival that May — was around 1960. He was then in Britain with Rose Murphy, with whom he had a long musical association dating from 1956 or '57, and they were touring the US army camps in various parts of Europe. Slam, born Leroy Elliott Stewart on 21 September 1914, told me then that the violin was his first instrument and that he studied it for several years from the age of six or seven.

'I played pretty well for a child but wasn't too interested in the sound of the squeak-box. I decided to make the bass violin my instrument while at Senior High School in Englewood, and then I studied for a year at Boston Conservatory. I had already played in local combos, and after graduation I worked with bands around Boston such as Jabbo Jenkins, Dean Earl and Sabby Lewis.

'In one of these combos was an alto player doubling violin and when he took a fiddle solo he used to sing or hum along with it in unison. It was an effect he'd dreamed up, and I thought if he can do that with a little violin, why shouldn't I do something like it on string bass?

'Pretty soon I was trying it out, humming and bowing but singing an octave above the bass part. I kept practising the trick and had started humming with one of the local groups even before I left Boston. The boys didn't think too much of the idea, as I recall.'

Talking in Belfast recently about Slam's contribution to the potential of the string bass as an articulate solo instrument Illinois Jacquet and Slam began rapping about Ray Perry. Not a well-known name (though known to me because of a recommendation by Panassié years ago), Perry, from Boston, Massachusetts, worked on alto sax and violin with Dean Earl's Band among others in the mid-Thirties and subsequently made a limited name for himself with Lionel Hampton's Band, playing amplified fiddle with an attack said to be reminiscent of Stuff Smith's. Perry was the man whose vocal-violin unison inspired Slam, and it was agreed in the Belfast night that he was a gasser on electric violin. Perry died in the autumn of 1950 and spent the last few months of his professional life in a group led by Illinois.

Stewart began knocking harder on life's door in 1936 when he left Boston and joined a band led by trumpeter Peanuts Holland.

'I heard that Peanuts needed a bass player in Buffalo, so I ventured out there and got the job — my first fully professional gig. While I stayed with that band I kept on developing my bowing, whenever they gave me a solo. Then I went back to New Jersey and started jamming around and seeking work in the New York clubs.'

It was then, in 1937, that Slam ran into Gaillard 'in one of the uptown places' — probably Jock's Place — and the idea of the bass and guitar routine took shape. As Slam remembered it: 'He had a radio programme, playing guitar and singing, and he invited me to do a show with him. It was the first time we had played together, but we fell into it with each other.

'He played lead and I played rhythm bass, then one or two solos with my new singing-and-bowing style. It was just the two of us going at it by ear, but disc jockey Martin Block was so impressed he signed us up.

'We decided then and there to team up and began looking for a name. Seein' that I was slammin' around on the bass fiddle, and that the word went nicely with Slim, "Slam" was produced. Before that I was generally known as "Bass-y". No, I never did hear of another Slam.'

Right after they got together, the pair created *Flat Foot Floogie With The Floy Floy*, which became something of an international hit as a 'crazy' song. Backed with *Ti-Pi-Tin*, this first Slim and Slam platter was issued over here on Parlophone. It made the team a well-known name among record collectors everywhere, and I read somewhere that the *Flat Foot* song was buried in the time capsule at the 1940 World's Fair as an example of American music of that era.

'But we didn't do too well out of that record,' Slam said in his mild, rather sleepy fashion, although he allowed that the publicity helped the duo to get work until its break-up in '42. And, of course, he is never quite permitted to forget it. I have heard him deliver several different refinements on the theme over the years since he began visiting Europe regularly. At lunch on the day of my departure from the Belfast Festival, the bass veteran was preparing for a new version to amuse the audience at that evening's 'Remembering Jazz At The Philharmonic' presentation. He goes into a vamp at the end while intoning things like 'flat foot', 'sugar foot', 'left foot', 'slew foot', 'fat foot', 'tender foot', 'big foot', 'stocking foot', 'bare foot' and 'swing foot'. It's an old bit of Slam show business, this.

'I go through all the different feet,' he said thoughtfully over the lemon and orange cheesecake. 'Not sure I remember them now.'

'There's satchel foot,' I suggested, 'and kipper foot.' He brightened up a bit, nodded approvingly, and added: 'Pussy foot ... and then of course there is black foot, and a few more I'm not certain I should mention tonight.'

It was after Slam joined the army that his sidekick 'got close to Art Tatum and joined his trio in 1943'. Slam and Tiny Grimes were the original co-members of the trio, and I guessed that playing bass with Tatum must have numbered among the less cushy forms of musical employment.

'Art Tatum ...' Stewart mused over the name and said in his far-away voice that he had quite a few memories of the encounter.

'Of course when I first joined Tatum I was the most frightened bass player that ever existed. Because, as you are aware, Tatum was all over that piano; he was a genius. So when I went with the trio I was scared, naturally. He'd make so many changes and I'd try to keep up with him, you know.

'I learned a lot from Art — I was with him until the following year, and then again later in the Forties — and got to the point where I just kept my ears open real wide and listened very carefully to everything he was doing. Which is very important you know. And I learned to understand what Art was playing and finally got to a point where I was able to follow him very well. I made quite a few mistakes in that time but finally I did things right.

'Yes, I had quite a few solos and he offered them to me. I didn't ask. He told me to go ahead and take solos, yes. And I must say — regardless of the fact that Art, in my estimation, was the greatest of pianists, well, one of the greatest anyway — I will say that many times when I was taking my solos I couldn't concentrate too well.

'That was because Art, he didn't complement me while I was soloing. Like, most pianists will comp you, you know, but he wasn't one for that, all over the instrument like he was taking a solo also while I was taking a solo. So that was kind of tough. It didn't quite fit with me because I couldn't think ahead too well, and a lot of times I didn't manage to get out all that I wanted to do solowise.

'But I didn't mind it a bit because that was the way Art was, and he was a giant. I just went on and tried to close my ears to what he was doing at the same time as I was soloing. It was quite a challenge.'

While agreeing that there may never be another quite like Tatum, Slam insisted there could be some other giants coming along. There had already been other piano greats like Duke Ellington and Erroll Garner, 'and don't forget Oscar Peterson who loved Tatum'.

Slam went on to name another pianist I would know, Dick Hyman. 'He came up to my home one time to do a concert with me at the college, at the State University at Binghampton, my home for the last twelve years or more. The concert was some kind of a dedication to Garner and, of course, during that programme Dick played a number that sort of copied Erroll's style, beautifully done. And then he copied Art Tatum for a couple of numbers, doing almost exactly what Art used to do. Which is difficult, and I thought Dick did a wonderful job. I was playing with him. I know.'

Slam, still a jazz enthusiast at sixty-six, is a nice wise-looking man, with a quietly expressive voice and plenty of patience. He's been around, seen most of it if not all, and learned to suffer the slings and arrows with a quiet kind of fortitude. In Belfast with the Jacquet band, he was worried at the start about the instrument he was going to use — since he hadn't risked one of his own on a flight to Ireland. By the time opening-day run-through was due he still didn't know if a bass fiddle was there to meet him. It was, but the bridge was too low and he couldn't pick properly, also the steel strings were not to his taste, but no panic, only a mild complaint. Expert help arrived to solve the bridge problem; however, it was stated authoritatively that no gut strings were available in Belfast. Slam shrugged, said 'Okay, let's try it,' and got on with the job for the rest of the week in his modest, thoroughly professional fashion.

Later that night, during a vodka-break in the band room, Slam explained some of his feelings about bassmanship, amplified and otherwise. He had no thoughts of quitting, not even foreign festivals and similar distant jobs. 'No, sir, so long as people ask for me, I'll turn up and play. That's for sure. I very much enjoy playing. As for amplification, even now — working for Illinois — I'm using the house system. Which, if I have a good bass, picks up very beautifully, you know.

'Of course in certain cases, if I'm using someone else's bass — and especially when they have steel strings on it, and I use gut strings — it's kind of rough for me and I love to have an amplifier so I won't have to work too hard plucking, because I do a little damage to my fingers.

'But outside of that I haven't had much use for amplifiers. Many times in the Forties I did things with Benny Goodman, and while I was with Benny he didn't care particularly for those amplified basses, so the only amplification I used was the house system.'

Stewart has worked with symphony orchestras, chamber groups, in movies, on Broadway and in television, as well as with college workshops and countless jazz combos, and has received awards and citations from sources as far apart as *Down Beat* and President Ford. Serge Koussevitsky once described Slam's playing as unique and fantastic.

For 'straight' work he uses what he refers to as his 'pet', a fairly old German bass which he purchased back in '58. It is three-quarter size, he says, but is very special, 'beautiful indeed'. Ray Brown and George Duvivier are names Slam mentioned among bass players whose work he has admired. As for Illinois Jacquet, in whose band Slam has operated off and on for a year or two, he expresses a sincere and long-standing admiration for the bass wizard.

'In the first place he can play, and in the second place Leroy — that's his real name — is a gentleman. Number three, he listens to me and respects my ideas, as I respect his. To me he's sort of like a professor. He decrees on just about everything that's happening when he works with me. I really respect his *discipline*.'

FIVE

Singers

Billy Eckstine

I knew 'Mr B.' by reputation ever since he sang Jelly Jelly on a 1940 Earl Hines recording. I made his acquaintance when he started appearing in Britain, and discovered that he loved talking about Hines, Armstrong, Ellington, Basie, Parker, Dizzy, Billie, Ella, Fats Navarro and anything to do with the modern-sounding band of his own which the bookers kept saying wasn't commercial (he gave it up after some three years). When Eckstine was in London during 1954, playing the Finsbury Park Empire, I went backstage two or three times to interview him on my old reel-to-reel tape recorder. A dressing-room is not the ideal place for conducting a long interview. Billy, however, is no ordinary subject. His fluency and high spirits, intelligence and fly-paper memory, combined to overcome all normal obstacles. All I had to do was set the reels and his mind rolling, sit back and enjoy, and now and then prompt. On the tapes his tremendous good humour and love of the sounds that gas him are plain to hear. I hope some of this gusto comes through the printed pages.

Fabulous people? I've met plenty. Some, like Dizzy, Bird, Sarah Vaughan and Budd Johnson, worked with me; others were friends and artists whose music I admired. Yes, I have lovely memories of the days when I sang with Earl Hines and later when I led a band of my own.

As good a place as any to start, I suppose, is the period just before I joined Hines; that is around 1938. I had been working in different little spots. Like when I left my hometown, Pittsburgh, and went to Buffalo, New York, to work in a club. Stuff Smith, Peanuts Holland and those guys were playing in this club, the Moonglow, and I was MC of the show and singing ballads and jump tunes.

I stayed around Buffalo about a year and a half, at the Moonglow and the Little Harlem, then went to Detroit — to a place called the Club Plantation. Cecil Lee had the band there, with Gerald Wilson and Howard McGhee on trumpets.

Cecil used to be third alto with McKinney's Cotton Pickers, and I think he took over the band when McKinney died. I know he still had Kelly Martin on drums and the wonderful trombonist Jake Wilder, who later died. A great player.

From Detroit I can bring you up quickly to the Hines band. Budd Johnson had always been a real good friend of mine, back from the days when he arranged for Gus Arnheim, and when he came to Pittsburgh we used to hang out together. One day Budd came through Detroit with Earl's band, and he asked: '"B." why don't you come to Chicago?' I hadn't been to Chicago so far, and Budd told me 'There's no one around there singing. Why don't you come on over there? You can make yourself some loot.'

Up till then I hadn't made above about 20 bucks a week, so I was glad to get over there. I stayed in Chicago about a couple of years, working at the Club De Lisa and other places. The vogue then was to have a Breakfast Dance on one day of the week. Every club in Chicago, at some time or another, would have a Breakfast Dance, with the show going on at 6.30 in the morning.

One spot there, the 65 Club, had a Breakfast Dance one morning, and they had a little combo with King Kolax on trumpet, a kid named Goon Gardner, who could swing like mad, on alto, John Simmons on bass and Kansas Fields, drums. It was more or less a jam show, for after the show all the musicians would blow in there. We were standing around one morning when a guy comes up that looks like he just got off a freight car; the raggedest guy you'd want to see at this moment. And he asks Goon: 'Say, man, can I come up and blow your horn?'

Now Goon was always a kind of a lazy cat. Anybody that wanted to get on the stand and blow, just as long as Goon could go to the bar and talk with the chicks, it was all right with him. So he said: 'Yes, man, go ahead.'

And this cat gets up there, and I'm telling you he blew the bell off that thing! It was Charlie Parker, just come in from Kansas City on a freight train. I guess Bird was no more than about eighteen then, but playing like you never heard — wailing alto then. And that was before he joined Jay McShann. He blew so much until he upset everybody in the joint, and Goon took him home, gave him some clothes to put on and got him a few gigs. Bird didn't have a horn, naturally, so Goon lent him a clarinet to go and make gigs on.

According to what Goon told me, one day he looked for Bird, and Bird, the clarinet and all was gone — back somewheres. After that I didn't see Charlie for, I suppose, three years: not until he came up to New York with the McShann orchestra. There used to be a joint in New York, a late spot up on 38th, called Clarke Monroe's Uptown House, where the guys all jammed. I had learned trumpet — fool-around with it, you know — and used to go out and jam at Monroe's. Bird used to go down there and blow every night, and he just played gorgeous.

Now by this time I was with Earl Hines, who was starting out with his new band. Budd Johnson and myself got this band together for him, and it was all young guys — Scoops Carry, Franz Jackson, Shorty McConnell, little Benny Harris and guys like that.

The war was on, and a lot of the guys had to leave to go in the army. So we sold Earl the idea to go up and hear Charlie Parker. Now Budd Johnson had left the band and we needed a tenor player. Charlie was playing alto, of course, but Earl bought him a tenor and turned Charlie over on tenor, and we got Bird in the band then.

We had about three weeks off to shape this band up, and we were rehearsing every day at Nola's Studios and going up to Minton's at night to jam. Bird couldn't get used to this tenor, used to say: 'Man, this thing's too big.' He couldn't *feel* it. One night Ben Webster walks in Minton's and Charlie's up on the stand and he's wailing on tenor. Ben had never heard Bird, you know, and says: 'What the hell is that up there? Man, is that cat crazy?' And he goes up and snatches the horn out of Bird's hands, saying: 'That horn ain't s'posed to sound that fast.'

But that night Ben walked all over town telling everyone: 'Man, I heard a guy — I swear he's going to make everybody crazy on tenor.' The fact is, Bird never felt tenor, never liked it. But he was playing like mad on the damn' thing.

As a matter of fact, we had another kid on tenor and he could blow. Thomas Crump, from Gary, Indiana, right outside of Chicago. Crump could wail, too, but he went into the army and made a career out of it.

Now I'll tell you a funny thing about Bird when we were with Hines. He used to miss as many shows as he would make. Half the time we couldn't find Bird: he'd be sitting up somewhere sleeping. So he often missed the first shows, and Earl used to fine him blind. You know, fine him every time he looked at him. Bird would miss the show, Earl would fine him. We got on him, too, because we were more or less a clique. We told him: 'When you don't show up, man, it's a drag because the band don't sound right. You know, four reeds up there and everything written for five.' We kind of shamed him.

So one time we were working the Paradise Theatre in Detroit, and Bird says: 'I ain't gonna miss no more. I'm going to stay in the theatre all night to make sure I'm here.'

We answered: 'Okay, that's your business. Just make the show, huh?'

Sure enough, we come to work the next morning, we get on the stand . . . no Bird. As usual. We think: 'So, he said he was going to make the show and he didn't make it.'

This is the gospel truth: we played the whole show, the curtains closed, and we're coming off the band cart when all of a sudden we hear a noise. We look under the stand, and here comes Bird out from underneath. He had been under there asleep through the entire show!

Another thing happened at the Paradise. You see, Bird often used to take his shoes off while he was up on the stand, and put his feet on top of his shoes. He wore those dark glasses all the time he was playing, and sometimes while the acts were on he would nod and go off to sleep. This particular time, the act was over and it was a band speciality now. So Bird was sitting there with his horn still in his mouth, doing the best bit of faking in the world for Earl's benefit. Earl used to swear he was awake. He was the only man I knew who could sleep with his jaws poked out to look like he was playing, see? So this day he sat up there sound asleep, and it came time for his solo.

Scoops Carry, who sat next to him in the reed section, nudged him and said: 'Hey Bird, wake up, you're on.' And Bird ran right out to the mike in his stockinged feet; just jumped up and forgot his shoes and ran out front and started wailing.

Oh, we used to have some wonderful times in those bands.

I didn't make a record until the year 1939. That was with the Earl Hines band, and the first vocal that meant anything was *Jelly Jelly*. I'll tell you how that one came about.

We used to do a lot of travelling in the South, and down there you had to play plenty of blues. Earl never had a blues singer in the band, so he just used to get up and play the thing on piano and I sang a whole lot of blues choruses — made them up as I went along. We were doing a session one day, the time we recorded *I'm Fallin' For You*, and we had an instrumental that the recording company didn't like so well. They asked Earl: 'Earl, have you got anything commercial you can do instead? How about a blues?'

We said: 'Gee, we don't have anything off-hand; maybe we'll do that thing we've been jamming.' I reminded Earl that we hadn't any original lyrics for it, and he says: 'Go outside and write a lyric while we're trying to cut this thing down to three minutes.'

So I went out into the anteroom and wrote off the lyric to this thing we recorded and called *Jelly Jelly*. It was really a fill-in, as I say, and we figured nothing's going to happen to it. But the thing sold — I don't know — hell, it's gone almost to a couple of million now. By this time it is some kind of collectors' item in the States, and regardless of where I go I still have to do it when I'm home. Still got to do *Jelly Jelly* on all concerts, because they still ask for it. And it's fourteen years old.

That was made before we had the young band. I remember that Budd Johnson and Franz Jackson were in with us then, and Scoops Carry. Benny Green, he came in a little later. We got Benny out of high school. We needed a trombone player, so Earl held some auditions for the different players. Benny was still going to Du Sable High School, where they had a wonderful music teacher called Walter Dyer, who made some real great musicians from out of Chicago. Youngsters that have come up like Gail Brockman and those boys, they all studied under him in the school band.

So Benny had studied with Dyer, and was in the marching band. It was a funny thing: Benny had a good lip and could read well, but he couldn't make it in Earl's band because he was too scared; absolutely scared to death. He stayed about two months and they had to let him go. When we came back to Chicago the following year, and wanted a trombone player again, Benny came in the band once more and blew everybody out. Nobody in this band could hold a light with him. That year's confidence did it, you see.

Now I must tell you a funny bit about Sarah Vaughan. I got Sarah in the band, you know: found her in an amateur show. It happened this way. I had a money order I wanted cashed. It was after five o'clock and there was no place to cash it. Then it dawned on me to go into the Apollo Theatre and see Mr Schiffman, the manager in there. It was Amateur Night, and there's something I hadn't done before and haven't done since — go into the Apollo on Amateur Night. Believe me, Bedlam is in this joint on Amateur Night, every Wednesday. You can get water thrown on you ... anything. So nobody even thinks of going in there.

I don't know why I went in to the audiorium; it must have been a stroke of Fate. Anyhow, they said Mr Schiffman had gone around to Frank's to get something to eat, would be back in a few minutes. So I thought I might as well watch the show while I was waiting.

Well, I'm sitting there watching, when from Left Field they introduce this little girl, and she's going to sing *Body And Soul*. She walks out on the stage, just a little skinny thing with a brown skirt on. It is Sarah, and she's about seventeen then.

So help me! When she opened up her mouth I started sliding down in my chair. I couldn't believe this, what I was listening to. Right afterwards I went backstage and grabbed her, said: 'Look here, I want to talk to you.' She was just as naïve and scared as she could be: right away she figured somebody was giving her a big deal. So I explained that I wanted to have Earl hear her, and I took her number and everything. To Earl I said: 'I have just left the darnedest thing you ever heard in your life — a girl singer.' At that time we had a girl — a very pretty girl — but she couldn't carry a tune in a bucket.

The result was that Earl agreed to go and hear Sarah. She had wrecked the house that night, and the Apollo had given her a week's work. Incidentally, it was with Ella Fitzgerald, who was booked there the next week. So she and Ella appeared on the same bill — Ella the big star and Sarah the kid, the amateur.

Anyway, Earl says: 'Yes, she can sing' — and has her come down to Nola's where we were rehearsing. Now I had told the band about this little chick, how I had never heard anything like it, and the guys were teasing me. You see, I have never liked chicks singing, because chicks always try to be cute and they forget about what's happening. I mean, they rarely stop to think: this is music, after all; it isn't television.

So when Sassy comes down to the studio, the band looks at her curiously. It was after we'd finished rehearsing for the day, and the guys were packing up their horns when she came in, looking young and and kind of ordinary with her hair up on top. Most of the guys were doubtful, and some of them said: 'Man, are you kidding?'

At that time the number one song was *There Are Such Things*, that Tommy Dorsey had recorded, with Sinatra singing. Earl sits down at the piano and says: 'Do you know this, honey?' And starts playing *There Are Such Things*.

Sass took the mike they had in this little recording studio, and started singing. You could see the guys stop their packing to stare at each other. By the time she had finished, all of them were around the piano — looking at the homely little girl who was singing like this, just wailing.

When Earl saw the reaction of all the band, she was *in*. That's how Sarah came into the band. She hadn't worked professionally before: she'd been singing in churches.

As you know, she plays piano, so Earl had two pianos on the stage, and he'd lock the backs of them together. While he conducted, Sarah would sit up there and play just the chords. Then Earl would bring her down to sing, and, boy, she wrecked everywhere we went. She was singing about like she does on records, but more straight tone then. Some things were a little cold, because of this straight tone, but she and the boys in the band got together, we got real tight, and she was soon singing beautifully.

Myself, and guys in the band like Shadow Wilson, Bird and Diz, Bennie Harris and Shorty McConnell, we raised Sarah and showed her practically everything that the music business was about. Later, when she was in my band, if she came late for a job we didn't bother to fine her. I never would fine Sarah if she was late. I'd turn her over my knee and whip her ass. She wouldn't often be late after that. And when she did come in late she looked around cautiously. Because one of us was behind the door to grab her and beat the hell out of her. So Sarah just came up right as a bunch of the guys: just as a musician.

But I'm getting a little ahead of my story here. I told you how I got into the Hines band: now I'll tell you how I left it.

As I said, we used to travel in the South much of the time, because that was the most lucrative field for Negro bands. We'd do three months of one-nighters through the South and into New York, where we'd probably work the Savoy, then turn around and go right back through the South and into the Grand Terrace, Chicago, again.

Everybody got tired of the South, of course, and we used to complain when Hines said we had to work this place and that place down there. But after having a band of my own I can understand how it was: I can see how tough it was for him to find location spots.

To get back to the point: up to that time I had been with Earl going on five years. He said he was going back down South again, and I told him: 'Hell, no! I don't want to go down South any more, Earl.' I'd just gotten married, so I said: 'I think I'm going to stay around in New York and work down 52nd Street.' So I put my notice in, and when I did nine of the guys put theirs in, too. Shad, Dizzy, Bird, Bennie Harris — just nine of them. Sarah didn't leave at that point, but she came along later.

That first band I had: that was a pretty fabulous bunch of guys. As I said, about nine of them came over from the Hines band, and when all of us left, that was when Earl got the brainstorm. He added a whole lot of strange things to his orchestra — a gang of girls playing fiddles out of tune; oh, he had a real conglomeration: about thirty pieces as I remember, and these chicks playing fiddle.

But first I went to work on 52nd Street, at the Onyx Club. Now let me see: Dizzy Gillespie had a little group there, with Budd Johnson, Max Roach, Oscar Pettiford and, on piano, Clyde Hart — modern all the way and writing like hell. They used to alternate between the two of us. When I was singing I had John Malachi on piano, and Dizzy's rhythm would back me. Now John Hammond was right there on the jazz scene then, and Hammond sent me to New York booker Billy Shaw to see what Billy could do for me.

At that time, frankly, Shaw had never heard of me. He'd been booking Earl, but I guess he didn't know everybody in the band. Anyhow, he came into the Onyx to catch me, and asked me where I had been working. I said with Earl for five years, and told him about the records that we'd been moving along on: *Jelly Jelly, Skylark, Water Boy, Stormy Monday Blues*, things like that. He wanted to see what the promoters thought, and sent out wires saying: 'Are you interested in having Billy Eckstine?' He sent out forty wires and got back answers from about twenty-five of them, wanting to know what the dates were.

Now there was a band around St Louis by the name of George Hudson, and they got the idea for me to take this on, as it was an organised band, and front it on gigs. When I talked it over with Diz and Budd Johnson, they said: 'Man, if you're that much in demand, why not start a group of your own? 'Cos when you've finished the dates with this guy and come back home, then you won't have no band.' Which made sense.

I gave the idea to Shaw, and he sent out, saying: 'The price of the band will be 600 dollars a night. Send the deposits in and we'll give you the dates.'

The money they sent for deposits I used to buy music, and to get the band going. First I got Diz for MD, then tried to get most of the other guys that left Earl. But by that time the Army had jumped in and taken Shadow Wilson. So I didn't get Shad. Bird, meanwhile, had been working with Andy Kirk and Noble Sissle, but by this time was back in Chicago. I called Bird from New York and asked if he wanted to come in with me. And Bird had all the eyes in the world to come in the band.

I went into Chicago to get Jerry Valentine, Gail Brockman, Tom Crump and Shorty McConnell, and brought Bird back. We came back into New York to rehearse, and we were all buddies — like I told you before — we were the clique. We knew the style of music we wished to play.

We wanted another alto player, and it was Bird's idea to send for a kid called Robert Williams: Junior Williams out of Kansas City, who had played along-side Parker with Jay McShann. So when we got him we needed a baritone player. Leo Parker (no relation to Bird) had been playing alto up to this moment, but I went down town and signed for a baritone for Leo and put him on it.

So the reeds then were Bird, Junior, Leo, Tommy Crump and Gene Ammons (who had been playing in Chicago, too, with Kolax). While we were in rehearsal the Army took Crump, and I got Lucky Thompson to make the first band.

Then, in the trumpet section, we had Brockman on first, Dizzy, Buddy (who also used to play with McShann) and McConnell; and on trombones: Benny Green, Scotty (Howard Scott, out of Earl's band) and Jerry Valentine.

The rhythm was John Malachi (piano) and Tommy Potter (bass), who I'd taken from Trummy Young's little combo, and Connie Wainwright on guitar. Only three when I started. I had no drummer: I was waiting on Shad, and as I say, the Army had grabbed him.

After we had rehearsed some three weeks, came our first job — in Wilmington, Delaware. And I don't have a drummer. I've got a whole new band but no drummer, and only two arrangements. But, oh! we had a million 'heads'. The two scores were *Night In Tunisia* by Dizzy, and a thing Jerry Valentine had written. Valentine, who was then one of the most underrated musicians in the business, had done a lot of scores but we had not had time to copy them up yet.

So to Wilmington for our first night. This place is just a little stop about half an hour out of Philadelphia. Diz gets on the train to New York, goes to sleep — and wakes up in Washington, D.C. Now I'm really frantic: I don't have Diz there, and I don't have any drums.

What was happening was this — I used to get up and play drums, but on the slow numbers. Something fast — somebody else would play drums. Anyway, we made the gigs, and worked for a week without a drummer. When we got down to Tampa, Florida, I picked up a kid called Joe, who played drums (well, he could keep time, and we taught him what we wanted him to do). Now this poor kid was ill, had to take injections all the time. He hadn't been with us above two weeks — we were in a hotel in New Orleans — when the guys wake me up one morning and tell me that Joe's sick. I say: 'What's the matter with him?' And they say: 'He's layin' in the bed. He looks real bad.' I go in the room and the guy's dead. So now we're down there with no drummer and I got a dead one on my hands.

At that time Art Blakey was with Fletcher Henderson. Art's out of my home town and I've known him a long time. So I wired him to come in the band, and Art left Fletcher and joined me at the Club Plantation in St Louis. That is where we really whipped the band together — in St Louis. We used to rehearse all day, every day, then work at night. Tadd Dameron had moved into Kaycee at that time, and when we got there he used to work along with us, writing some things for the band like *Cool Breeze* and *Lady Bird*.

Of course, then, the whole style of progressive jazz was just a theory of chords, a new version of old things. Bird was responsible for the actual playing of it, more than anyone else. But for putting it down, Dizzy was responsible. And that's a point a whole lot of people miss up on. They say: 'Bird was it!' or 'Diz was it!' — but there were two distinct things. The whole school used to listen to what Bird would play; he was so spontaneous that things which ran out of his mind — which he didn't think were anything — were classics. But Dizzy would sit there, and whatever he played, he knew just what he was doing. It was a pattern, a thing that had been studied. He's got that mind of his that people often don't stop to figure on.

Now Diz is dizzy like a fox, you know. He's one of the smartest guys around. Musically, he knows what he is doing backwards and forwards. So what he hears — that you think maybe is going through — goes in and stays. Later, he'll go home and figure it all out just what it is. So the arranging, the chord progressions and things in progressive music, Dizzy is responsible for. You have to say that.

Monk, too, was a great creator with his songs and tunes. I knew Monk when he played ten times as much as he does now. I think he has got a little weird in his music today. But I tell you, Monk used to play.

Dizzy left my band in Washington D.C. because he was going to organise his own bunch. He came and told me to go over to the Louisiana Club, where

Andy Kirk was working, because there was a fellow with Kirk called Fats Navarro. 'Take a listen to him,' said Dizzy. 'He's wonderful.'

So I went out to the club, and the only thing Fats had to blow (because Howard McGhee was the featured trumpet player) was behind a chorus number. But he was *wailing* behind this number, and I said to myself: 'This is good enough: this'll fit.'

So I got Fats to come by and talk it over, and about two weeks after that he took Dizzy's chair, and take it from me, he came *right* in. Fats came in the band, and great as Diz is — and I'll never say other than that he is one of the finest things that ever happened to a brass instrument — Fats played his book and you would hardly know Diz had left the band. 'Fat Girl' played Dizzy's solos, not note-for-note but his ideas on Dizzy's parts, and the feeling was the same and there was just as much swing.

Fats stayed with me, I imagine about a year and a half. Then, when we went out as far as California, he decided he wanted to stay in New York and work his card out. So I got in touch with Miles Davis; he was out there working in a group with Bird, who also had left me by now.

I'd like to tell you about Miles. When I first heard him he was working in St Louis, which is Miles' home. He used to ask to sit in with the band. I'd let him so as not to hurt his feelings, because then Miles was awful. He sounded terrible, he couldn't play at all.

But by the time we got to California he had blossomed out. He'd been going to Juilliard, in New York, and playing with Bird, so he came in and took over that same book, the solo book which was originally Dizzy's. Miles stayed with me until I broke up, which was in 1947.

I was losing a lot of loot with the band because — well, it is history now — the people were not quite ready for that type of music. It was still a dance-crazy public, and we were playing music that was a little bit too wild for them to dance to. The concert field was not like it is now. Today, the band could have made it, because we would be able to play strictly concerts.

Singing has been the big thing in my life since around 1932, when that particular bee bit me in Washington. The singer that inspired me — probably most of you have never heard him. He was with Don Redman's band 'way back, and his name is Harlan Lattimore.

Latty was just fabulous. To me, he had one of the greatest voices that I've heard since or before. He had a nice, warm sound, and he was a smooth baritone. As I was a kid at school when he came to Washington, I used to follow him around like a good dog. Yes, Latty was more or less the guy that inspired me.

Another, slightly later, source of inspiration was Pha Terrell. Now, there's a guy! Pha was really my buddy, and when he came to town with Andy Kirk's band I used to hang with him all the time. Up until Pha came along Negro male vocalists almost always sang blues on records. There wan't one specialising in ballads. Pha came up with *Worried Over You, Clouds, Until The Real Thing Comes Along*, and all those pretty things, and they were so soulful and melodic that he was a definite inspiration also. But Pha's voice was a little higher than mine.

Pha was really wonderful and, aside from singing, man, that cat sure could fight. Boy, he could wail! That's another funny thing: for same weird reason, people used to think that all male singers were ... well, kind of on the lavender side. I used to get in fights all the while to disprove this. Every time Pha and I met, after I'd gone with Earl Hines, we would say: 'Who you got to your credit lately?' and have a laugh about it.

We were together in Chicago once, where they have those 'Jitney' drivers, that pick up passengers on each corner in cabs for a dime. Pha was driving down Michigan Avenue, and one of these Jitney drivers saw someone waiting. So he stopped right in front of Pha, who ran into the back of him. Next thing, this guy jumps out of his cab with a crank handle. Now Pha was a real quiet-spoken fellow, and he said: 'What's the matter, daddy? We're going to talk, we ain't gonna fight.'

The driver gives him a lot of choice words, and Pha says: 'Man, you're crazy,' and turns to walk away. The guy thinks: This is all over — and he puts back the crank.

Then Pha turns round and hits this guy and knocks him right over the hood of his cab ...

The thing the average person didn't realise was that Pha used to be a pug. Sure! he was in 'Golden Gloves', and all of those things, and could fight like mad! He wailed this guy all over 55th Street. We had a ball out there with this Jitney driver, I'm telling you!

Now, let's see — singers. Which brings me right along to Nat Cole. First off, I don't think there's anybody around who can read a lyric like Nat does. I love the style Nat has, the really warm feeling. It may seem funny, but I feel about Nat the same way I do about Louis Armstrong — in singing. I mean, Louis hasn't got 'a voice'. And fundamentally Nat hasn't, either. It is the warm sound and soul you hear from both that makes you say: 'This guy is singing hell out of that song.' Nat has that intimate, bedroom style of singing that fractures me. I can truthfully say I have everything he's made, and I like to put his records on when I'm sitting quiet at night.

I mentioned Louis. Now I like modern music: to me, it's so fresh, and it's an inspiration. It's something that is always new, always fresh in your ear. I don't particularly like the stereotyped Dixieland music, but then I don't think of Louis as being an old-time musician. I think of Louis as being a pillar in music. A person of whom you can say: 'Here's the guy that did it.' Right now, whatever he plays to me sounds good. Maybe the modernists won't go along with me on this, but I wouldn't care, because I love Louis. And his singing gasses me. He sings some of the hardest songs and makes them sound good. Sometimes Dizzy plays something of Louis's and another thing I know for a fact: Dizzy idolises Pops. And Pops digs progressive music. I know he doesn't dig it as far as trying to play it, but I know he likes Diz and Diz admires him.

But for the other singers — I like Perry Como. I like his relaxed style. He doesn't go out to prove anything, but just to sing a song. And then I like Sinatra — the breathing and the technical things Frank does.

Then for the girls, I've already said that I'm no admirer of chick singers, as a rule, and also that Sarah Vaughan is my girl. And Ella Fitzgerald, she can do no wrong for me whatsoever.

I faintly can remember Bessie Smith in Pittsburgh, but that was when I was a real young kid. When I remember her best is after I went to Washington to school, after I had become sort of fascinated with music. And I can remember one thing of hers that always did impress me; any time I hear her name I think of that. Where I used to hear her sing, she would come out after she'd maybe sung a fast blues — she'd go off the stage and then come back for her big song, a real slow blues, you know, the real drag blues. She'd step out of the wing and start singing the song very slowly, and as she finished each chorus she'd just take a slight step towards stage left. And each chorus she would take another step, so by the time she had finished like that she would be on the other side of the stage and off into the wing. But boy, you couldn't hear your ears from then on. And between one side of the stage and the other she sang about twenty choruses of the greatest blues you ever listened to.

Finally, there's Billie Holiday. She can do no wrong to me, neither. I can't think of anyone with more soul than Lady Day. Lately they haven't given her many good things to do, but if you want a real styling on a song, there's nobody to out-style Lady.

Before I finish I'd like to give credit to a guy that taught me what I know about music. When I joined Hines I could hardly read a note, and it was strictly through Budd Johnson, tenor player and Musical Director of the band, that I learned. Budd is perhaps the most underrated musician around. You can walk in Birdland any time and find him right there with all these small, progressive jazz groups. Budd will be up there wailing as much as anybody. And Budd is two years older than I am, which makes him forty-two.

Another thing you can credit to Budd: he put a saxophone in Ben Webster's hand. Ben was a piano player in Corsekana, Texas, and Budd came through there with the George E. Lee band. Budd was playing C-Melody then, and Ben said he wanted to learn saxophone. So Ben went out to a pawnshop and bought one of those C-Melody instruments, and Budd showed him the scales and so on. When Budd next came through there, four or five months later, Ben was wailing the hell out of it: you know, this raggedy old C-Melody! Next time Budd saw him he was in Kansas City, playing tenor with Benny Moten or one of those bands.

About jazz and music generally, my view is that you cannot close your mind and say I don't want to listen to this or that. Because if you can't appreciate the bad for being bad, you can't appreciate the good. If you turn a deaf ear to everything but one style, pretty soon it's not going to work out.

Music is something to be felt and appreciated and enjoyed. When people go to a night club or concert I think they go there to be entertained. They don't expect to go to school, and they don't expect to hear a whole lot of dissonances and things that they cannot figure out. I know myself, with an open mind, that there are one or two new groups in the States that I cannot follow. I cannot tap my foot to their music because I can't find the tempo. I like swing, and I don't want the music to swing for two bars and then I'm wondering where the hell it went.

Count Basie — now there's a band. This band he's got now. I swear it's the greatest he ever had. I just worked 120 cities with him. And, man, this cat's got a band. Everything about it is good: swing, intonation, the right kind of guys.

I'm all in favour of progressive music, but I guess it's hit a stumbling block just now. At the start of it there was so much fire, and every new record was a brand new thing. But now it has reached the point where there's nothing creative about most of the records that come out.

You take the average guy, say, in a jam session in London, and he's playing what he's heard. But you want somebody to play, not what he's heard, but his *development* on what he's heard. It's no use playing just the same things you've heard on records, because pretty soon those riffs become stereotyped — the same as the old cliché Dixieland riffs.

Now about modern drumming. I dig 'bombs' when they are dropped at the right time. The big trouble with drummers playing progressive jazz is that too many think: 'boom ... this is it.' 'Wham' ... They'll drop a bomb in the middle of a guy's solo. The guy's got his mind all cleared on what he's playing when here comes a thunder jumping from nowhere. So all of a sudden he forgets what he wanted to play. It's confusing.

Now you take Kenny Clarke, Art Blakey and the best ... they don't throw bombs unless they mean something. While the horns are taking a breath, the drummer fills up a gap. That's what bombs were for originally. In other words, they fill out the music, and maybe set a pattern for you to think up something on. For instance, if you ever listen to Diz humming something, he hums the drum and bass part and everything because it all fits in with what he's doing. Like *Oop-Bop-Sh'Bam*. That's a drum thing. And *Salt Peanuts* was another. It was a drum lick; that's the reason Kenny Clarke's name is on it.

Which only leaves me to say — Farewell, you crazy people!

Billie Holiday

To write about Billie Holiday, even to think of her, is to fill my mind with recollections of a love affair with a voice. When I think back on the time it started, the middle 1930s, this was no exceptional thing. I had dug Bessie Smith (only one or two records) very deeply, was strongly attached to Mildred Bailey, and occasionally entranced by Ivie Anderson, Ella Fitzgerald and Connie Boswell. And Lee Wiley was inspiring lovely emotions. But with Billie it was different, and almost instantaneous. One of her earliest vocals, heard on the air, made a powerful impact and sent me looking for a Holiday purchase. Trumpeter Johnny Claes, my former bandleader and a close friend, used to order all the month's jazz realeases from a wholesaler across the road from his flat off the Tottenham Court Road, pick them up on a Saturday morning and take them home to play one by one, with hardly a break except to change discs. Often I would be there for this audition, and the next play-through included One, Two, Button Your Shoe *and* Let's Call A Heart A Heart, *by Billie and her orchestra on the Vocalion label. Claes was particularly intrigued by the singer's bit of banter with Cozy Cole at the start of* One, Two, *and that side of the disc got played repeatedly. As swiftly as possible I obtained this marvellous record, also* Billie's Blues *and* A Fine Romance. *From then on it was a Billie a month for me except when the available funds had to be diverted to Roy Eldridge, Mildred Bailey or an outstanding release by Louis or Duke, Basie, Goodman, Henderson or Lunceford.*

I was hooked on all Billie's qualities of sound and style, on her almost indolent improvising, on the freshness and rightness and special rhythmic thrust of each interpretation, on the fact that she never came across as slick, artificial or winning in a little-girl way. I remain hooked on her until this very day. Before long I latched on to the 1935 Wilson-Holidays and thought them at least as good, and even more optimistic-sounding. On all of them — it hardly needs saying now — the band playing was of the same high calibre as the singing. In those days it was *something* to hear a vocal chorus which stood shoulder to shoulder with instrumental contributions by Eldridge, Wilson, Webster, Goodman and such jazz aces. The records were easy to love, and I quickly came across other receptive listeners, in various parts of the country, who were addicted to that curiously expressive voice and lagging delivery. In the years that followed, around the turn of the decade, I concerned myself with 'rhythm clubs' (giving record recitals at many of them) and corresponded widely with other jazz fanciers. Often I would be put in touch with collectors such as Charles Fox in Bournemouth or Albert McCarthy in Southampton with the advice: 'He's a Billie enthusiast and likely to interest you.'

Later on, but before the day of long-play reissues, I met by chance a collector who used to specialise in lecture-recitals on Billie Holiday. I had not seen him in years but within minutes he was telling how he had acquired four very rare Billies. 'I could get copies for you and bring them over on the bike next weekend.' He was as good as his word. He knew I wanted them. None of us then would have believed that when they were made, our heroine was broke. That is how it was with us — 'real Billie men', or 'Bix men' or 'Louis fanatics' or a blend of all three or something similar — in Britain during the 1930s and early war years. In the USA the Wilson-Holidays found a ready market in the jukeboxes, so she was popular there to a certain degree in the middle to late 1930s; but I doubt if she enjoyed the same serious appreciation and faithful following as she had on the English side of the Atlantic. She wrote of her pleased surprise at being famous in England in letters to local admirers. Albert McCarthy received such a note from her, and I can tell you we studied it with awe and envy.

It is not possible for today's younger listener to experience all the revelation Billie's recordings provided in those far-off, memorable times. But those records confirm that she was as good and original as we thought, and worth the praise heaped upon her by other singers as well as writers and those many thousands grateful simply to have seen or heard her. The 'group' recordings made under Wilson's or Holiday's own name between 1935 and 1939 include some of the absolute best of small-band-with-vocal jazz put on wax before the advent of the LP. Quite a few rank, in my opinion, with the most delightful jazz-song performances ever cut. The records show, too, how influential Billie was in re-shaping jazz and popular singing. Though she was inimitable, her style affected performers as disparate as Frank Sinatra and Dinah Washington. Her influence worked in varied and subtle ways, not only in her approach to lyrics, her use of tone, pitch and vibrato, her reconstruction of a melody and laid-back swing, but in her visual delivery of a number. Among scores who inherited fragments of her artistry are Peggy Lee, Carmen McRae, Abbey Lincoln, Annie Ross, Marilyn Moore, Cleo Laine, Carole Sloane, Norma Winstone, Anita O'Day, Maria Muldaur, Phoebe Snow, Sylvia Sims, Marie Bryant and Maxine Sullivan. Even Mildred Bailey's phrasing was never quite the same after she heard Lady Day. The same could be said for dozens more, especially if we delve into the vocalising of many lesser-known women singers in Britain, Germany, Scandinavia, Canada and even (I'm told) Japan. Jazz singing, however, being founded on American speech, is the hardest jazzcraft for Europeans to master; thus the paucity, and some would say total absence, of non-American authentic jazz voices.

To prove Billie was the most complete *jazz* singer of all time is no easy thing. Unquestionably her singing was a natural extension of her speech — as indeed was Armstrong's — and was unique because *she* was unique. Though this statement can be broadly applied, it is nonetheless significant. Stanley Dance pointed out to me that many women of that time — Billie, Cue Hodges, Helen Procope were examples — spoke in a way that now seems peculiar to their period; and it went into music. The same could be said of such people as Jelly Roll Morton, Sammy Price and Earl Hines, from different parts of the country, who had a way of speaking that belonged to a time rather than a place.

When we discovered Billie, and the delectable taste of her talking voice, she was three parts mystery. Career details were not then known to us, and her age was uncertain. She just arrived from nowhere, sounding almost fully mature. Her personality, her nature were uniquely laid bare on records from the start. And, growing up with her disembodied voice we became exceedingly interested in the charmer so generously exposed on shellac. When the first photograph appeared in a Vocalion catalogue I remember being surprised though not displeased by the smiling, chubby face surmounted by a large-brimmed tilted hat. Later, her looks became more familiar from images of a slimmer, beautiful woman usually sporting a white gardenia in her hair.

Years passed and I naturally wished to meet the object of my infatuation and I knew she wanted to visit Britain, but I had a long wait. By the early 1950s I had learned a great deal about her from books and periodicals, also from sightings in musical shorts and in the misleading mock-jazz film, *New Orleans*. I knew the seductive voice had changed with her appearance, the revolutionary vocal approach had become mannered, and that the dramatic power had managed to increase as a compensation. In some repects, at least, her craftsmanship was improved; and when finally I met the Lady she spoke with assurance of being able to do things with a song she could never have achieved in girlish days.

One day, late in 1953, I received news from Leonard Feather that Billie would hit Britain in February 1954 at the close of a European tour of his 'Jazz Club USA' package, in which she was the star.

The rest of the company couldn't play here, because of the policy of the musicians' unions involved, but concerts were fixed for Billie and she was able to use pianist Carl Drinkard.

Billie was due to arrive at London Airport from Paris on Monday, February 8, following three weeks in Scandinavia, Germany, Switzerland, Holland and France. I made arrangements with *Melody Maker* to drive out to Heathrow to greet her and to 'cover' her in general, as chance permitted. Reports of the tour had been favourable. Need I say that I looked foward impatiently to meeting, at last, the Princess of Harlem, as they were calling her in France?

The red-letter day came and I drove to the airport well before mid-day, armed with a photographer and half a bottle of whisky. Both could be useful, I knew, as a means of breaking the ice, and both were to come in handy. Stories of Lady Day's uncertain temper and 'unreasonable behaviour' crossed my mind as I drove. Parking near the Arrivals lounge, I felt the *frisson* of an imminent adventure — eager anticipation tinged with apprehension.

I had not long to wait. A commanding figure, recognisable on first glimpse, emerged from the Customs Hall. She was clad almost from neck to foot in a luxurious, blonde fur coat topped by a tight-fitting woolly hat, and was following through the barrier by three men. It transpired that they were — in priority order — husband-manager Louis McKay, her pianist Carl Drinkard and dancer Taps Miller who chanced to share the same plane from Paris.

The singer looked tired, cold and resentful, as though she had suffered many fools in the recent past. Not wanting to be added to the total, I greeted her with measured warmth, politeness and a degree of reserve I was far from feeling. I was honoured, I said, to make her acquaintance. It was no lie. First impressions? They were all I had expected and more — quite apart from the amount of mink. I saw an imposing woman of average height (she was 5 ft 5 in, I believe) — an inch or two taller than I had guessed — with handsome, well-boned features and an intolerant, faintly mocking expression. She seemed to me less lean in the face than I had gathered from the *New Orleans* screen image. Her speaking voice was slurry, a little cracked in tone, and 'meanly attractive'. What she said inclined to the brief, hip and pithy. She had dignity and natural magnetism and I thought I perceived in her an odd amalgamation of naïvety and experience.

She was moderately friendly, though understandably detached, and her manner thawed when I referred to mutual acquaintances such as Marie Bryant, Helen and Stanley Dance and Mary Lou Williams. Everyone who warranted it was introduced to everyone else and we secured a few photographs.

I got off to a poor start by suggesting a shot with Drinkard and Taps (the latter had caused a hold-up at French customs by being checked for drugs, which had infuriated Billie). In addition, this delayed her progress to the waiting limousine. She signalled her impatience to be moving but something guarded me that morning and she agreed to the picture with a resigned lift of the eyebrows. Her glance clearly warned me: 'You're taking chances, buster; let's get it over and blow.'

Now, it isn't the simplest act in the world to present a half of Scotch to a proud-looking woman who is at once your jazz heroine and a virtual stranger – – and, by now, also shut away in the rear of a hired car. Worse, she was refusing to look in my direction. But faint heart never won fur-coated lady.

Opening the door gingerly I proffered the bottle, asking whether it was too early for a taste and apologising for the lack of glasses. The look of menace was replaced by a smile. I don't think she spoke but she slid forward and the bottle vanished into the mink, just as her retinue entered the limo. Then the car was driven away in the direction of London.

A press reception had been fixed for early afternoon at the Piccadilly Hotel, where Billie was staying, and the questioning was under way when I arrived. Already the star was looking harassed. The lay-press gents — minimally concerned with her musical accomplishments — wished to know about her drug habit and prison sentence. As I entered she smiled across the room and told Louis McKay: 'There's the man who saved my life out at the airfield.'

The reporters knew she had been imprisoned on narcotics charges, and that she was not allowed to sing in any New York 'cabarets' because the Police Department had withdrawn her cabaret card. They questioned her closely, and exclusively so far as I recall the occasion, about her troubles. 'Are you still on dope, Miss Holiday?' asked one pressman pointedly.

Billie ignored the question, but explained that she had served her time for the offence and expected to be able to start off again with a clean slate. 'I can't work in any places in New York that sell whisky', she said. 'Why whisky? It's a city ordinance or something. I guess they're stuck with it. I'm trying to get my police card back. You know, I'm not the only one: *some* kids have been in trouble two, three times ...' [here she named a well-known girl singer who was not, as it happened, black] '... and are still working. So why pick on me? Somebody's got a hand in it somewhere; some kind of politics. That's what I'm squawking about'.

Interrupting another question, she answered: 'No, I don't think it's because I'm a Negro. I just don't dig it. I guess somebody has to be the goof.'

I should cut in on the story here to say that Billie, to judge by what I knew of her, was not obsessed by race relations and colour bias. She was, I think, a 'race woman' in the sense that she refused to imitate 'white' manners, modes of speech and standards of conduct, and ridiculed those that did. But she was in no way a 'professional Negro' or, for that matter, a professional personality of any kind. What she believed, she said: and what she believed was most likely to be the result of her personal experience. In Billie's experience, the police were part of a system which was subject to bribery, political pressure, gangster pressure, moral prejudice and all the weaknesses of mankind. She thought the withholding of a police card was unfair, but she wasn't prepared to attribute it to Jim Crowism on the part of the cops. Perhaps it was due to Billie's intransigent nature, more than anything. As Josh White once said of her: 'She'd had to fight all her life, and most people hate fighters, I can tell you.'

Whatever the Police Department's motives may have been, Billie didn't want to talk about them this first afternoon in London. Her face often bore an expression of deep sadness and, as often, one of dissatisfaction tinged with a smouldering kind of explosiveness; at this early stage in our acquaintance I thought I could detect danger signals. Billie's answers were becoming briefer now.

'I suppose your friends are still fighting for you', said one Daily.

'You know, we don't talk about it, we *forget* it', she told him meaningfully.

Rescue was urgently called for and I told the company at large that I didn't suppose Miss Holiday had travelled all this way to give a lecture on narcotics. I asked how she had come by her nickname, Lady Day (though I knew the answer), and she shone upon me a real smile and expression of gratitude. Would she be singing *Strange Fruit* at her concerts? I followed up. Then, whenever a drugs question began to rear its head, I interposed a query about her programme or records or accompanists.

Billie saw what I was up to and seemed appreciative. Though able to look after herself, physically and verbally, she felt uncertain in strange surroundings, among alien accents. She told us how Lester Young named her Lady (Day) and her mother Duchess. 'I named him the President, and actually I was also Vice President ... of the Vipers Society, you know. We were the Royal Family of Harlem.'

As the conversation warmed up, with assorted references to ofays and spooks, Pres and Pops, Bessie and the Queen (Dinah Washington), a few pressmen left. 'Who the hell was *that* guy?' she asked about the principal inquisitor. 'He couldn't say nothing but "dope"'.

When I told her he was the *Daily Blank*, she did a bit of swearing. 'Well', she said with an air of finality, 'I was just about ready to run his *Daily Blank* ass out of here'.

She laughed at this, drank a little Scotch and looked offended. 'I hate it without ice,' she said.

While somebody rang down for ice-water, Lady Day mused over Lester:

'Now that's been going on since around 1938,' she told us. 'I was given that title by Lester Young, the President. I was with Basie's band for a time, and Lester used to live at home with my mother and me. I used to be crazy about his tenor playing, wouldn't make a record unless he was on it. He played music I like, didn't try to drown the singer. Teddy Wilson was the same, and trumpet player Buck Clayton. But Lester's always been the President to me; he's my boy — and with him I have to mention Louis Armstrong and Bessie Smith. Many's the whipping I got for listening to their records when I was a child.

'I used to run errands for a madam on the corner. I wouldn't run errands for anybody, still won't carry a case across the street today, but I ran around for this woman because she'd let me listen to all Bessie's records ... and Pops's record of *West End Blues*.

'I loved that *West End Blues*, and always wondered why Pops didn't sing any words to it. I reckoned he must have been feeling awful bad. When I got to

New York, I went to hear him at the Lafayette Theatre. He didn't play my blues, and I went backstage and told him about it. I guess I was nine years old then. Been listening to Pops and Bessie ever since that time. Of course, my mother considered that kind of music sinful; she'd whip me in a minute if she caught me listening to it. Those days we were supposed to listen to hymns or something like that.'

By this time, most of the daily Press had stolen out. Billie didn't seem worried by their departure. 'Some of those guys were getting me a little salty,' she explained to us. 'I didn't come three thousand miles to talk about that shit. It's ended.'

Before leaving, we asked Billie when her British visit would be over.

'I'll be here until Tuesday, I reckon, after that I'm not sure,' she said. 'We've been offered so many jobs — Paris, Africa, even some Variety in England. Daddy' — here she looked across at husband Louis — 'hasn't made our plans yet, but we have a good offer back home.'

Louis McKay added that getting back into New York cabaret could mean upward of $75,000 a year. Billie said: 'It's not just the dough, it's the principle of the thing. To me, it's unfair.'

On the way out of the hotel, we said goodbye to Billie's accompanist, Carl Drinkard. He joined Billie in Washington in 1949, his first recording with her being *Crazy He Calls Me*. Said Carl: 'I've been with Lady nearly five years. You know something? Her singing still amazes me.'

That evening, at her invitation, I returned to the hotel with Betsy, a Decca record player and a bunch of new and old Holiday recordings. She and Louis were in bed but not sleepy. For a few hours we played music, smoked and drank a little, and chewed the fat. Billie loved hearing the old sides, and reflected in outspoken terms a spontaneous stream of thoughts about songs and musicians she had worked with. All fascinating to us, of course, and rewarding to someone who had hoped fervently to strike up a sympathetic relationship with the prime enchantress of his first jazz decade.

Of Lester Young, Teddy Wilson, Freddie Green, Louis, Bobby Tucker, Annie Ross, and Ben Webster she spoke fondly, ladling out praise to instrumentalists who accompanied a singer unselfishly and helpfully. Now and then a bitter note intruded (she was contemptuous of phonies in any walk of life), and sometimes she allowed personal considerations to colour her assessments. At the sound of Buck Clayton she announced: 'Prettiest cat I ever saw.' When Roy Eldridge cropped up in the conversation, she surprised us by confiding: 'He stole my cherry, you know.' But she smiled appreciatively when Little Jazz's mean trumpet snaked from the grooves. Almost more abrupt was her confession on Sid Catlett: 'Honey,' she told me in solemn tones, as a Leavisite might deliver an important critical judgement. 'Big Sid . . . biggest dick I saw in my whole life.' I was certainly impressed.

Chatting with Billie, as you can guess, was a kick. I never heard her put down a really good singer, though she could be very cutting about the duds and those she supposed had slighted her. Some entertainers, Lena Horne and Ella Fitzgerald among them, she evidently loved as friends.

On the subject of people who are generally acknowledged to have copied aspects of her performing style, she was strikingly tolerant. She viewed the imitations as a form of fondness and admiration, and she spoke affectionately of Peggy Lee, though retailing some scurrilous remarks about Peggy's presentation made by a world-famous actress (Tal Bankhead in fact) who had sat next to her at a Peggy Lee performance.

In the course of the next few days, I travelled around with Billie and her husband, and got to know her quite well. I saw a good deal of Billie's 'temperament', but during that week she was more often happy than low, though the smallest upsets would soon get her storming. At her first rehearsal, with Carl Drinkard and several British musicians in a Leicester Square club, she was angry about some mislaid music parts. She settled down grimly to the job of running through her programme, saying nothing except what was relevant to it, and singing only the minimum amount necessary to a productive rehearsal. Even so, it was my first 'live' audition and I was absorbed and moved by it.

As soon as it ended, I had to return to work. And I left without speaking to Billie, mainly because she was arguing with someone and looking thunderous. Maybe her pianist was having a hard time that day. He took me aside and explained: 'If Lady likes you, she'll do anything in the world for you; but if she don't — look out! I mean, when she's feeling evil, don't cross her. Because if you do, she's going to hit you ...' He weighed me up in his mind before continuing: 'And if she hits you .., let's face it, she's going to knock you down'.

It was a friendly warning, though I never needed it. Like most artists, Billie Holiday liked to be appreciated. Next time we met, she said: 'I saw you digging me'. And after her opening concert in Manchester, she remarked on the 'awareness' of the English audience. I realised she was gratified but nevertheless puzzled by the extent of our admiration and knowledge of her work.

For me it was the start of a friendship I found as touching as it was surprising. I chauffeured her when needed, ran errands, took her out for food and drinks, and visited her and McKay at the hotel. I saw as much of her as I could — and hold on to my job — and as she had taken instantly to Betsy we were able to go on the town as a foursome — invariably augmented soon after the first few glasses had been emptied. Mostly we talked about music, booze, sex, drugs, politics, gangsters, film actors, club owners, writers and Café Society; also about dogs, or clothes and shopping. Billie nursed a belief that many of the mishaps and misfortunes befalling her were due to 'politics', by which she seemed to mean the machinations of nebulous forces connected with an underground fellowship of bookers, managers, cops, lawyers, taxmen, pushers and assorted authorities.

Her own life-style, probably responsible for much of the disorder swirling about her person, she defended stoutly as 'my own damn business'. Sadly, she accepted responsibility for her habits, while fully conscious of the fact that dope suppliers (at times husbands or lovers) had leeched most of her earnings, and continued to amuse herself in her chosen fashion. I say 'sadly' only because the immoderate use of stimulants shortened her life. This she foresaw, naturally, and accepted. She wasn't unhappy about it while we were with her in '54, and it is necessary to correct impressions of a tragic lady with morbid interests, very rough language, and a taste for bad husbands and depressing songs.

Some of these things, yes; however she enjoyed drinking and narcotics, and the men while they lasted, and smiled (inwardly at any rate) while singing *What A Little Moonlight Can Do, I Only Have Eyes For You, Them There Eyes* and one or two others. More wistful items like *Willow Weep* were uplifting, too. Her bearing on stage was something to see, and in the street she also looked stunning. Her language could be savage, it's true, but usually to the point. She was bright, tough, realistic, stylish, transparently sincere most of the time and lovable for much of it.

She fitted comfortably into a quiet corner of the Studio Club in Swallow Street late one afternoon, looking swish in a ski suit newly purchased from Simpson's, plus the familiar knitted cap, and making cute faces for 'Daddy' as he popped off a few shots for the family album. Beryl Bryden, just in from France, tracked us down via a call to my home and joined the appreciation society. Billie took a sort of child-like pleasure in this open admiration she found in England, and accepted the compliments without demur. When my brother-in-law, alerted by telephone of this impromptu 'sundowner', came in and paid his heartfelt respects, he ended by asking if he could have the honour of getting her a drink. 'Yes, I'll have a treble brandy with a cointreau float,' she said.

Later that night we moved on to the Stork Club, almost next door, for food and drink 'on the McKays'. After some champagne-celebrating Beryl suggested that Billie sing, which I thought unwise as Lady had told me she hated 'sitting-in' at sessions. Billie reversed the request and Beryl — reluctantly for her — obliged with *Billie's Blues* in front of its now-legendary creator, who gave every sign of feeling overjoyed and flattered by the rendering. Eventually Billie was persuaded to sing two or three with pianist Danny Turner's trio — which she judged to be with-it. When we collected our coats in the small hours I heard her remonstrating with the captain to the effect that if those goddam people knew what she was paid to sing professionally, they'd have brought champagne on the house. Instead they had given Louis the whole bill. I never discovered the outcome of that dispute but Billie was accustomed to winning her fights, and I thought her to be in the right. In any event, the night was not over.

Most times, whatever we put foward in the way of outings was okay with the McKays; if he had something better to do, he opted out. We would very much like to have entertained them at Primrose Hill. When I invited her, however, for the second time, she explained that she never went to people's houses. Asked why, her reply was typically honest: 'Because the drinks don't come up fast enough, honey, and you can't leave when you want to.' Oddly enough, at the Stork we had met Dick Kravitz from *Esquire* mag; he knew Billie from somewhere and spoke about getting her on the Esky cover — a big deal to her. He twisted her arm, or McKay's, and it was agreed we'd all motor over to Regents Park and sink a bottle or two at the elegant home of Vasco

Lazslo, the noted painter, who not unnaturally had to be prised from his bed in order to receive the unexpected revellers. I remember little of consequence about that conversazione except that soon after we were seated a plaintive voice demanded: 'Who's pouring the damn' drinks here? They ain't comin' up very fast.' When Billie began carousing she wanted to *carouse*.

Another day, when Billie was pursuing an idea for an evening binge, I told her we were booked for a sort of dinner-convention laid on by a trade organisation known as the Jazz Record Retailers Association. It sounded a stiff affair, I warned, guessing she wouldn't want to know, but of course she would be welcome to accompany us. They were jazz people, after all, including several Holiday freaks: I knew that for a fact. To my astonishment she accepted on the spot. The JRRA committee, after initial consternation, readily agreed to lay on an extra place at the set dinner. Made a last-minute guest of honour, and treated with reverent courtesy by the record dealers, Billie exuded charm and patience during the business hocus pocus and established an easy rapport with the company on her own serene terms.

Seeing the photographs now I'm struck by the surreal nature of the occasion — worthy British collectors like me, Doug Dobell, Pete Payne, Stan Wilcox, Morris Hunting, Mike Butcher and Dave Carey politely fêting the greatest woman jazz singer alive at a formal feed in an upstairs room of a middle-class restaurant in Bloomsbury, London. Taking her there was, I guess, one of the most quietly spectacular achievements of my jazz-hacking years.

Lady Day's brief concert tour kicked off on 12 February. This is part of what I wrote in Melody Maker *of 20 February 1954 under 'Max Jones Spends A Holiday With Billie'.*

When Billie Holiday stepped onto the stage of the Free Trade Hall last Friday, the applause must have frightened the porter in the Midland Hotel up the street. The almost unbelievable had happened. Lady Day was behind a Manchester microphone, wearing a black dress with a gold thread in it, diamond necklace and earrings, and a patch of silver-sprayed hair a little to one side — where the gardenias used to be pinned. She smiled slightly in acknowledgement and rocked into *Billie's Blues*, then a fastish *All Of Me*, a beautiful *Porgy*, *I Cried For You* (which began slowly, then whipped up), and a rather weird *Them There Eyes* on which she and pianist Carl Drinkard seemed to travel separate ways. This was really it —for me and, I'm sure, most of the 2,000 people there. I had gone into the hall with the conviction that Billie was the best lady singer still on the jazz scene. So the performance was a confirmation rather than a discovery. She looked calm and happy until the microphone gave up on *Blue Moon*, her eighth number. She then gave us *My Man* unaided by electricity, and retired before doing the encores, *I Only Have Eyes For You* and *Strange Fruit*. The band, with Drinkard, Tony Kinsey, Dick Hawdon, Don Rendell, Tommy Whittle and Ronnie Ross variously featured, provided what I thought was the best support she got on her short tour.

And Billie's own performance moved me more than any of her others —

perhaps because it was my first Holiday concert; perhaps because the hall was good, the crowd dead silent, and I was positioned to catch every vocal inflection and every gesture of face, hand and shoulder.

Now and again she announced a song, looking surprised the first time when applause broke out before she had reached the title. Afterwards, she told me:

'I never speak on the stage, once did 36 songs at Carnegie Hall and didn't say a damn' word. I just felt happy with this English audience ... diggin' everything I was doing. I guess they wanted to hear my talking voice as well as my singing.' The idea of this seemed completely new to Billie.

We went back to the hotel and celebrated Lady Day's first British concert. Carl Drinkard, Doug Tobutt (of the Harold Davison office) and the Flamingo's Jeff Kruger were there, and later Harold Pendleton came over from the hall, full of regrets for the faulty mike.

'Forget about it,' said Billie. 'That was such a sweet little guy who came out and apologised and brought me another mike ...' (this one didn't work either) ... 'he apologised so much I felt sort of as if I'd ruined his show. When you go back be sure to tell him I love him.'

Billie was in top form for the celebration, posing for innumerable pictures taken by husband Louis McKay (an almost non-stop photographer who even takes pictures out of the airplane windows), taking photos herself, and talking with relish about Basie band days.

Naturally, she spoke of Lester Young and of his battles with section-mate Herschel Evans. 'Normally I don't go for those saxophone battles,' she said, 'but those cats really hated each other, and it kept them both blowing all the time.

'They were for ever thinking up ways of cutting the other one. You'd find them in the band room hacking away at reeds, trying out all kinds of new ones, and anything to get ahead of the other.

'Of course, Herschel had the great big beautiful tone: Lester had less tone, but a whole lot of ideas. Once Herschel asked Lester: "Why don't you play alto, man? You got an alto *tone*." Lester tapped his head: "There's things going on up there, man," he told Herschel. "Some of you guys are all belly."'

On Saturday, soon after midday, we left for Nottingham, where Billie was appearing at the Astoria Ballroom.

Rehearsal was called for five, and Carl Drinkard — who, like the Aga Khan, is worth his weight in platinum on these occasions — went through the routines with the rhythm men from the resident Derek Sinclair orchestra.

They were Ken Pye (drums), Jimmy Luke (bass) and Don Sanford (guitar), and as things were going smoothly Billie slipped out to boost her spirits, with a tomato juice and several milk chocolates.

Like most performers, she never eats a meal for some hours before a concert.

Then she went off on a shopping expedition, via the local pubs, with wife Betty, and took considerable pleasure in buying pyjamas and other things for 'my Louis', as she called him. Presented with the bill at Marks and Spencer, Billie hauled up her skirt and produced a roll of notes from the top of her stocking (shades of Bessie Smith), observing that 'It's safer there.'

The two women had escaped while I watched rehearsal, so I started doing the round of local taverns. I had checked out only three before I found them in the far corner of a bar, laughing at life over two large drinks. 'I knew he'd track us down, honey,' she observed in her special voice which conveyed a kind of fond derision.

I called up liquid reinforcements and joined the table in the 'Horse and Groom', which Billie thought looked just like the pubs she had seen in films made in England. Soon we got onto her nickname, Billie.

'I was a real boy when I was young,' she explained, 'and my old man called me Bill. You see — he wanted a boy and Mama a girl, so they were both satisfied. My real name's Eleanor, but almost everyone calls me Billie, excepting Basie and Billy Eckstine. To this day they still call me William.

'Of course, if I go to my home town, Baltimore, someone will shout out "Eleanor". And nobody answers. I'm looking round and thinking "where the hell's Eleanor?"'

That evening Billie did two sets at the Astoria, one around nine and the other about 10.45. Each was of five songs, and for the second spot she brought out two we hadn't heard at Manchester: *What A Little Moonlight Can Do* and *You're Too Marvellous*.

Being a ballroom, the place was noisy: too noisy for proper appreciation of Billie's subtleties. But the place was packed to capacity, the atmosphere was festive, and nobody got too upset when the mike played up through a couple of numbers. I think Billie was expecting it by now.

In Nottingham then there appeared to be a surfeit of girls and women, (because of the lace industry, I was informed). Walking round the balcony between sets, Billie eyed the dancing throng with a sardonic expression. 'Hey! Look at those bitches dancing together,' she told Betsy with obvious enthusiasm. The scene added something to her knowledge of the Old Country, and you got the feeling these were the types of ordinary people she understood and felt to be square and not too corrupted.

I had offered the McKays and Dougie Tobutt a lift in my car back to their London hotel, wishing to save them time and trouble. I should not have done it.

With a Sunday rehearsal before them, she and Louis packed quickly and got into the car, expressing the hope that Jones would find the swiftest night route to London. 'You probably won't hear a word out of me until we get to that hotel,' Billie promised, and fell immediately to sleep.

She was awakened only too soon, in deep, dark country, to find the car stationary, bonnet up and wreathed in steam. In an effort to promote American standards of heating, I had shut the radiator blind for too long; the hose had blown off, and the last of the water was now gone with the wind.

As it happened, there was no garage open for 46 miles, the way we were going, and only the unstinted help of a Bingham policeman, who (clad in pyjamas, coat and slippers) brought up reserves of water and tools, got us mobile by one in the morning.

Lady Day, I could sense, was sorry she hadn't gone by train, even though she doesn't much care for trains. 'I like flying,' she'd told me earlier. 'I'd fly across the street if they ran a service for it.'

As we lumbered off, hissing like a Stanley Steamer from the leaks in the joint, I asked incautiously if Lady was all right.

'No, I ain't,' she said promptly. 'I'm cold and disgusted. Take me to an airstation, a railroad station, anywhere there's something *goin'*. Only get me out of this car.' After a resigned silence, she inquired: 'How much damn' farther we got to go?'

Before I could whisper the dreadful truth, Doug Tobutt — with fine managementship — said soothingly: 'We're nearly there, Lady, it's just a few miles. You go to sleep.' I dipped the headlights in time to miss a signpost. It read: 'London 110 miles.'

We stopped repeatedly to replenish the cooling system, and when the cans were empty I resorted to extreme measures in order to get us to a café on the Great North Road. Waking up again, Lady demanded suspiciously: 'What's he up to now?' Betsy admitted I was peeing into the radiator. Billie subsided with some profanity, but I believe she liked me for that. At the café, Doug, Louis and the Joneses slunk inside for refreshments, leaving the legendary body sleeping and dishevelled on the rear seat of the Ford. We looked up apprehensively every time the doors swung open, McKay seeming to be as scared as the rest of us. But Billie slept on, and we resumed the stop-start progress.

We bade the McKays a brief goodbye at the Piccadilly Hotel at 5.30 a.m. on Sunday. That afternoon, Billie rehearsed hard with Jack Parnell's band, and in the evening gave a splendid performance of 15 songs at the Albert Hall, ending — as she likes to do — with *Strange Fruit*.

Despite bad lighting and the odd tricks of the hall that make drummers' off-beats hit your ears like bad on-beats, Billie gripped an audience of some 6,000.

Billie had discarded some of her underclothes during the long night ride (while feeling unwell), and these Betsy washed and pressed in time to return to their owner at the Albert Hall. Lady reacted with genuine gratitude and surprise, as though such little kindnesses were still unexpected. Feeling uneasy, I said nothing until offering her a whisky in the interval.

Once more, and again that night at the Flamingo Club, she proved that her relaxed, expressive singing brings freshness and added meaning to any worthwhile pop-song. Her style has outlived several 'new' vocal styles and will probably outlive many more. Dill Jones told me: 'Billie is one of the most poised women I've ever seen, and unquestionably the greatest jazz singer I have heard since Louis.'

Don Rendell, another admirer, rushed from work to the Flamingo to accompany Billie (at her invitation), got there just in time, but was unable to press through the crowd to the bandstand.

After the show, I found Billie and Don toasting each other in the band room. 'You know Don?' she said to me. 'He's my boy.' To Don she said: 'I still love Max in spite of that car ride.' I hope she means it.

She enjoyed the acclaim she received in Europe — later she said the crowd of 6,000 at London's Albert Hall gave her one of the greatest receptions of her life

— and she worked as hard as her health would allow to earn it.

Saying goodbye to Billie was like saying goodbye to an old friend who values you despite your faults. She had said to Betsy one day: 'I know Max loves me, but can you stop him talking me to death?' I hoped she would forgive me for that and the car journey; and I believe she did because on November 11, 1958 I received a telegram from Paris at my Primrose Hill address. It read: 'AT HOTEL DE PARIS TILL THUR EVENING LOVE BILLIE HOLIDAY'. Next day I telephoned her there. She sounded dragged, said there was nobody who spoke the damn' language, and asked: 'Why aren't you here?' I should have gone at once, but the paper didn't want to release me or pay expenses and I was as usual strapped for cash. Betsy's advice was to draw out what savings I had, sod the MM, and do what I could for the dispirited singer. I have always regretted not taking her advice.

Soon Henry Kahn in Paris was telling me she wanted to come to London and stay here. Since separating from McKay she no longer wished to live in the States. 'I want to settle in Britain because I love the people,' she declared. 'They do not just call me a singer; they call me an artist and I like that.' After a tour round France, Kahn reported, Billie would go to Italy, then probably prepare to come to London.

Without warning, late in February 1959, I heard from Harold Davison's office that Lady Day was scheduled to appear in a London TV show. I checked arrival time, hotel booking and so on, then drove out to meet her plane. It was the prelude to a few more hectic days in her extraordinary presence. And the lasting friendship I felt had been struck up in '54 resumed as if there had been no interruption. But this time Billie was separated from Louis and the mink coat, was showing signs of increased strain, and was clearly dissatisfied with her domestic and professional life. Nevertheless, she was an often diverting, always interesting, companion. I guessed she was ill but her defiant nature would not allow her to give in, just as it would not allow her to feel apologetic about her need for drugs. She spoke repeatedly of her desire to live over here and, at the time, she was serious. Back home again it might have been a different matter. I never really knew. I tried to arrange record dates but had no luck. It was a sort of tragedy she couldn't have got over here while there was a chance of regular work.

Again, I spent most of my waking hours with her, collecting her on the morning of the programme to take her to rehearsals (no one had laid on a car), shopping for vodka when we reached the studios (she was meticulous about paying for bottles, handing me the cash in dollar bills), and lending support through the day. Singers Beryl Bryden and Yolande Bavan, and the faithful Betsy, all turned up at Granada to lavish help and attention on their favourite. In fact, we formed an ad hoc Holiday Supporters Club, bent on giving her the best care we could. One event I cannot forget was taking Billie to the Downbeat, a musicians' hangout in Soho. She wanted to sing, and a spontaneously formed group accompanied her in several songs. The club telephone rang in mid-song, and when a Hooray Henry customer prolonged his 'phone conversation, an enraged Kenny Graham (bandleader, tenorman and Holiday worshipper) moved swiftly towards him and carried the protesting Hooray bodily away to enforced silence. The act somehow typified the hold Billie exercised on all *her* people. This is what I wrote about other aspects of that final visit (*Melody Maker*, 28 February 1959).

Billie Holiday looked almost as surprised to find herself in London on Sunday night as I felt at seeing her here.

'The whole thing was a rush. We only heard about this TV date two or three days ago,' she said when she was safely off the Jet Clipper. 'That's why I couldn't let you know in time. I knew damn well you'd be here anyway.'

The TV date was for 'Chelsea At Nine'. On Tuesday, Lady Day sang *Porgy*, *Please Don't Talk About Me* and *Strange Fruit* at the Granada Theatre in the King's Road.

The last was accompanied largely by her pianist, Mal Waldron. The others had the full support of Mal and Peter Knight's orchestra. The entire show was filmed, and viewers will see it in March.

On a song that measures up to her, she can communicate the mood with an almost painful intensity. Part of it is 'soul', part is expert timing. Then there is the troubled tone — Ethel Waters said she sings as though her shoes are too tight — and what Steve Race described last week as 'the curiously instrumental quality of her vibrato'.

The subject of vibrato came up spontaneously, while the Lady relaxed one evening at the Club Caribe in Leicester Square.

Proprietor Alex Graham maintained a flow of recorded music, and when one of the LPs got under way, Billie demanded to know: 'Who is that? Sounds as though she's crying. She reminds me of Judy Garland with that vibrato.'

It turned out that the owner of the vibrato was Roberta Sherwood, and Billie went on to tell us:

'When I got into show business you had to have that shake. If you didn't, you was dead. I didn't have that kind of vibrato, and when I sang people used to say: "What's she putting down?"

'I always did try to sing like a tenor, or some horn. That big vibrato fits a few voices, but those that have it usually have too much. I just don't like it. You have to use it sparingly. You know, the hard thing is *not* to sing with that shake.'

I read Billie some of the things Miles Davis said about her to Nat Hentoff in 'An Afternoon with Miles Davis' in *The Jazz Review*, December 1958. Among them: 'I love the way she sings ... like Lester Young and Louis Armstrong play ... she doesn't need any horns. She sounds like one anyway.'

Bille smiled faintly and said: 'That's how I *try* to sound; I didn't know I succeeded.'

The record that brought Billie close to the gramophone was one called *Out There With Betty Carter*, on the Peacock label. Betty Carter used to be billed as 'Miss Bebop' when she sang with Lionel Hampton, is now known as 'Lady Cool'.

Billie listened a long while in silence before saying: 'I love her. She's really got something. On the slow tunes her diction's bad — that's the onliest fault

I've got to find. I think she's crazy — she can scat like Leo Watson. You remember Leo?'

I did, of course, but Betty Carter was new to me. This didn't surprise Billie, who suffers from no delusions about the British public, though she likes working to it.

'Betty's five years ahead of her time,' Lady said, to clear up the situation. 'They don't dig her even in America, so you know they won't dig her here.'

The possibility of making Europe her headquarters is still much in Billie Holiday's mind. I reported last November that she contemplated settling here, and she insists now that she will buy a house in London and work in Britain, France, Sweden ... 'wherever the opportunity arises'.

The reason is simple. 'I can't get my police card to work New York, so how can I make it there?' she asks. 'America won't *let* me work, so I'm going to make it in Europe or somewhere.'

Billie argues that she's paid for any offences she's committed, and expiated the deeds. She wants a fair chance to go on earning her living. The withholding of a police card means she is unable to work in New York clubs.

On the face of it, her case sounds reasonable. 'I'm Billie Holiday,' she explains. 'Singing's the only thing I know how to do, and they won't let me do it. Do they expect me to go back to scrubbing steps — the way I started out?

Anyway, she had no further opportunity of making the move. Soon reports were coming in regularly of her deteriorating condition. At the end of May she collapsed and was taken to hospital, suffering from liver and heart complaints.

Still harried by the authorities, she died in degrading circumstances at 3 a.m. on 17 July 1959, with 70 cents in the bank and 750 dollars in large notes strapped to her leg. She was, by her reckoning, only 44 years old. And I was halfway through a letter to her when friends telephoned to say she was dead. Though half expecting it, I was devastated by the news.

But still, we have those many lovely or disturbing recorded performances. They will pleasure my ears for the rest of my life and those of future generations for all time, I guess. On a personal note, again, I will always gladly and sadly remember that at her birthday party on April 7 that year, Lady asked the BBC's Barrie Thorne to pass on to me her 'undying love'.

And Maely Dufty, who said she contributed a large chunk to *Lady Sings the Blues* with her then husband Bill Dufty, wrote to Dave Carey in a letter of December 1962: 'Please tell Max Jones that Billie, during the two months at the hospital (and I was with her till the end), often spoke about him with much affection. Tell him to drop me a line.'

Later, while living in London, Maely called me to say how greatly Billie had felt wanted, and how there were 'Holiday freaks' who loved her, when she was in England. Max was high on the list of the constant lovers. I suppose I feel as gassed about that as any tribute received in a lengthy and misspent life on the jazz case.

Sarah Vaughan

To my mind, Sarah Vaughan possesses the most sumptuous voice of anybody in jazz and, has the control, expressive flexibility and range to enable her to project this splendid instrument into space with commanding confidence. I nursed a kind of furtive appreciation of her clarity and cleverness right from the start — which for me was the 78 of Mean To Me *and* Signing Off *on Continental — despite suspicions that some of the startling intervals and melodic shifts displayed there were vocal shock tactics, studied rather than logical phrases. By the time she arrived in London, during 1950, for her first British tour, I felt she had added to her considerable attainments. This doubtless meant I was catching up with 'the greatest new voice in jazz'. Meeting her, with husband George Treadwell and right-hand man Johnny Garry, and attending rehearsals, a BBC interview with Denis Preston, and sundry concerts, I soon joined the unofficial Vaughan Appreciation Society. Hearing her in person, working with the band and then before an audience, made a difference to my perception of her expressive technique. Getting to know her a little meant penetrating barriers of reserve, dignity and, no doubt, justifiable distrust, and coping with a keen, often oblique sense of humour. She didn't laugh a lot, as I recall the visit.*

Since those days I have heard Sarah, and spent time with her, in many different locations: theatres, restaurants, festivals, green rooms, Sunday dinners, late-night parties, and various hotels in Britain and elsewhere. She has changed and is much more relaxed and sophisticated than the woman I encountered thirty-seven years ago. Her voice and style have undergone modifications, too, though they belong indubitably to the same, apparently gauche *youngster of the mid Forties, and Sarah has developed into, quite simply, one of the most gifted singers in the world. Steadily she has enlarged her repertoire, and one of her recent achievements (as I write) is an album titled* The Planet Is Alive . . . Let It Live! Sarah Vaughan Sings Pope John Paul II.

I have tried, half-heartedly because of her resistance to questioning, to interview this phenomenon in places as disparate as Chatham's Central Hall (in January 1972) and the China Theatre in Stockholm (in May 1956). This piece dates from July 1981, with an insertion from seven-and-a-half years earlier. In it the mature Miss Vaughan reluctantly re-trod some common ground.

'Let's see. Who was I with then? Charlie Parker, Dizzy Gillespie, Benny Green, Dexter Gordon, Gene Ammons, Fats Navarro, Art Blakey ... and I could go on. All those guys. It was just like going to school. So that's how fortunate I was.'

Sarah Vaughan was looking back to her professional beginnings — not a thing she particularly cares for — and recalling some names from the Billy Eckstine Band of '44 and '45. On the road with that company must have been school-of-life with a vengeance.

'Yeah, one girl and sixteen guys; what the hell.' A girlish gurgle followed. 'What else can I say? But as a musical education: Oh, my goodness! How lucky I was. That's the best experience I'll ever have. If I hadn't had that I might now just be, well, I don't know. And I could do it over again, just that part. But after that I could skip a whole lot of it.

'But then — I was about eighteen when I first went to Earl Hines, and the next year I joined Billy's new band — everything was new to me. I'd never had so much fun. Yes, I had lots of fun in there, and yet I was shocked — scared to death really,'cos I didn't really know all this sort of thing went on. You know, I was just a young singer from Newark.'

On an earlier occasion, in the Mayfair Hotel in 1973, we had been speaking about her youthful musical preferences in an off-hand manner — she usually tended to retreat if asked directly about 'influences' exerted by other vocalists – – when she suddenly advanced a name which was totally unexpected by me at that time.

'Judy Garland,' she said,'was the singer I most wanted to sound like then; not copy but get something of her soul and purity. A wonderful young voice; and another I admired was Marian Anderson.'

I guessed she was out listening to groovier sounds as well, during her school-days in New Jersey. She answered: 'You bet. I used to play hookey from school to hear music, and at night too. I wasn't supposed to be at dances but I was — listening to all that good music like Ella Fitzgerald and Chick Webb. I would sneak over to New York and hear the bands at the Savoy Ballroom.' Then she added sweetly: 'I was just a baby then.'

The information about Garland did, I admit, set me listening to the wonder miss with fresh interest. I came to repect the qualities that had excited Sarah's curiosity and approval.

'But I'm telling you,' she insisted, 'I wasn't so much on listening to singers; I was more of an instrumentalist. If I'm to talk about influences, I always wanted to sing like a horn plays. 'Course I have a lot of favourite singers that I like — Ella and Billie, and I used to admire Jo Stafford and some others — but the instrumentalists were what I listened to most. I listen to them still ... Charlie Parker, you know, Lester and Dizzy, guys like that. I prefer horn players to singers.

'So far as being influenced in what I'm doing — not copying, I hate that word — well, Dizzy and Bird of course, I was raised with them. In fact they were all on that album the gentleman gave me the other night. I heard my voice and didn't believe it. I sound like I was two, but I was twenty. They were things we made on army bases, I seem to remember. 'Jubilee something', I think they were called. That would have been 1944 I guess: Oh, my Lord!'

And today's avant-garde sounds; how much do they inspire the singer?

'Well, I'm not against them but really I don't know what's happening. I don't understand the high stuff, when they go up in the heavens. I don't know how they know where they are. But they must do; they start and finish together. I'm not putting it down, but I can't tap my foot to it and I like to tap my foot up and down. I like to dance, and I can't dance to that.'

In my experience of her, and it stretches back some thirty years, Sarah Vaughan has seemed to feel about interviews like most people feel about eating tripe. But at the Grosvenor House last week she was at her most accommodating and friendly. She gets bored with questions about the early days, of course. And this you can tell when she says, with a kind of studied politeness, that yes, she sang at the Mount Zion Baptist Church as a young girl; or even: 'I knew you were going to ask me that. Yes, I did; church choir in Newark, New Jersey. And piano lessons at age seven.' The rest of her career lines she is inclined to recite like a child in a history lesson. 'Church choir to the Apollo Theatre, there to Earl Hines, Earl Hines to Billy Eckstine, Eckstine to John Kirby, and then all on my own. And here I am.' Here, at this particular moment, was a press and photo call at Grosvenor House to publicise the week's cabaret season there in which Sarah, Andy Williams and Nelson Riddle were together for the first time. Sarah has been a solo artist ever since 1945/6 and so we can take it she prefers working that way. 'Just say I prefer working' is her verdict. 'Now that I've been in so long, you know, I can work with whom I want to. I have more say-so now over what jobs I do and how I want to do them.'

Meeting Sarah after her relatively long absence from Britain, I was greeted with a hug and a kiss and the assurance that she had remained away these couple of years or so simply because she'd been busy, busy, busy. 'And thank God for that,' she said, sitting down at a table with her glass of iced water. 'I'm very happy about it.' When I asked if I could rest my drink on her table, she replied: 'Yes, but not if you're going to ask me too many questions.' Okay then, but what about the gentlemen accompanying her on this trip? No gents, she assured me. She was foot-loose and so on, her companion on this visit being Blanche Shavers, widow of that excellent all-round trumpet player, Charlie Shavers.

I think Sarah misunderstood me on purpose. I knew she was no longer with Waymon Reed, the former Basie trumpet and flugelhorn player, and had refrained from mentioning him. My question referred to the gentlemen of her trio. 'That's good,' she responded firmly. 'Don't ask me about my troubles.'

Records. That's a nice safe topic. She has been busy again — after a stint of studio de-employment — with the blessed Norman Granz, and to very good effect. The Pablo LP, *How Long Has This Been Going On*, was a cracker; and followed up by two most admirable Duke Ellington *Song Books*. Twenty-one of Duke's tunes were released on the two albums, but a great many remain undone by Sarah. I wondered if further episodes were planned? The unwigged head shook. 'No, I think for a while that'll do it. It was enjoyable for me because the melodies are so good and many of the lyrics are thoughtful. And though I've sung a lot of Ellington songs, there were some on that second album I'd never heard before.'

Another album of luxurious vocals is her *I Love Brazil*, cut in Rio de Janeiro late in 1977 and issued here only to be quickly and mysteriously withdrawn with a request that no reviews appeared. I assume this was because the agreement between Pablo Records and Polydor had run its course. What could she tell about this? Nothing, it transpired, because she had not known of its appearance in this country and speedy disappearance.

'I'm glad you told me. I wondered why it was withdrawn. The thing is, I own the record. It's my album, produced in Rio by Aloysio de Oliveira. I leased it to Norman, you see, for three years. So I can't understand why it was only out here for a hot minute.'

Sarah returned to Brazil, a land she is most partial to, late in '79 and made another set with the same producer.

'What about that second Brazilian one, *Copacabana*? she enquired. I told her that I hadn't got it yet, but was on its track.

'You don't have it? Well I'll be durned. But I've done some other things. Well, I made an album three of four months ago with Count Basie and his band, and that should be coming out very shortly.'

How was Basie?

'Oh, looking good. You know he's not as free as he used to be but he's still got the old charm and magnetism.

'I'm also recording in February for Columbia. We're recording the Gershwin programme that I do at the Hollywood Bowl with the Los Angeles Philharmonic.'

That, I surmised, was done by arrangement with Norman Granz. Sarah laughed loudly. 'You better believe it,' she said.

'And then I think I'm going to record *Porgy And Bess* here; I'm recording with Nelson Riddle. Well, I guess it'll be here in London. I don't know how he's going to do it, but I know it'll be one of the most interesting things I've ever done. I can hardly wait.'

The next time I saw Sarah, after her opening night at Grosvenor House, I learned that the album of *Porgy* songs would have to be recorded later on. The wait would be longer than she had thought, but her enthusiasm was undimmed. This is not, apparently, to be a two-name set such as *Porgy And Bess* by Cléo Laine and Ray Charles.

'I just don't know yet how it's going to be; it's all left up to them. Fortunately I read music, so it won't be too difficult. And I've already been to Nelson's house in LA and we ran through a few things. Thank God I can read music.

'But we're not going to do the play, the opera. No, no, no. I guess I'm going to have to be the other person or people.' She laughed and said: 'The other peoples ... well, I think there's one little thing in there I might be doing with Joe Pass; and I'll probably record that when I get back home.

'I told them I really don't want it to be a jazz-type setting. It's still got to have the Gershwin feel. And I can tell you it's going to be very, very different.'

Allowing that she is hoping for a production which possesses other than jazz qualities, would she consciously vary her approach when tackling this material?

'The way I'll approach it,' she answered, giving me a one-of-those-questions look, 'is the only way I know, whatever way that is. Don't ask me to describe it because I can't. I just get up and do it. It's not planned. I don't think in terms of jazz this, or jazz that. Music has too many labels. There's this artist does this and that one does the other; there's rock-jazz and there's plain rock, and folk-rock and there's jazz. There are so many titles: soul and soul rock, un-soul rock, London rock. I just don't know no more. I don't understand.

I call it all just music. In the old days it was different. And I hate being labelled.'

During the week I was given the latest Vaughan on Pablo. *Copacabana*, with its Brazilian rhythm section, reflects her growing fondness for the music of Antonio Jobim and similar composers. When we spoke about this she admitted to being beguiled by the music of Brazil but was quick to point out her long-standing constant affection for the songs of the Gershwins, Porter, Ellington, Arlen, Berlin and other great songwriters. Whatever she sings, so long as it is good of its kind, she gets pleasure out of it. LBC's Keith Howell, who was sitting-in with Sarah, asked at this point if she had one special favourite out of all these writers.

'Oh, there are so many. You know, when you ask me a question like that my mind goes blank. Because there are so many good composers, and so many that people don't know about.

'Come to that, there are so many good musicians around that people don't know about; so many good singers they don't know about; so many good anything.'

Her idea of a song that's good of its kind might take in anything from the spiritual, *Motherless Child,* to the Mann-Mitchell pop, *Passing Strangers,* which proved a big success when she made it on a duo album with Billy Eckstine. Funnily enough, Sarah said, it was a hit in Britain but not anywhere else.

'At home, if I bring that song out, nobody knows it's not a new number. It sold a bit back in the Fifties, but was revived over here about ten years later, and I didn't even know it. One day Billy called me from London and said: "Guess what, Sass? We got a hit record. I thought I'd let you know." That was *Passing Strangers*. And I was shocked to smithereens. Now, every time I come over here, I have to learn that song again because I forget that they love it so much.' *Strangers* could be considered — if we were employing labels — to rank with Sarah's more commercial offerings; that is, those aimed at the wider public. Even so, the way that she interprets it, together with the character of her voice, gives the performance a style which can interest jazz tastes. No one expects a jazz masterwork. I said as much, and the singer showed surprise. *Send In The Clowns* is her current choice of top-pops: 'It has so many meanings, that song. It says you're not feeling too good, or something.'

She asked: 'If I sing *Send In The Clowns* does it sound like jazz to you?' I said it was good popular music, also a performance which had a feeling of jazz about it on account of her phrasing and the nature of her tone and vibrato.

'Oooh,' she intoned, disbelief writ large on her face. 'And what if I sing *The Lord's Prayer*? What would you say about that? Does that sound jazzy to you? Well, I've known that record for years and it veers towards the legit. *Touché!*'

'That's a difficult one, Sarah,' I admitted. 'It's one record I don't think of as jazz-slanted.'

She appeared mollified, and said: 'Thank you. Neither is *Clowns*. How could you say that was jazzy? Perhaps you're thinking of my record. I sing *Clowns* differently now. I've just done it with Count Basie, ha, ha, ha. It's the way that I'm feeling is the way that I sing it.'

Because of her musicianship and superb vocal equipment, Sarah Vaughan should not in my view be trapped, or tempted, into performing petty song material which trivialises her amazing talent. Not that it is my place to tell her how to do her job, and I've been careful to avoid such a gaffe. Nevertheless, ever since I first asked her to leave *Broken Hearted Melody* out of an up-coming set she has chilled perceptibly at any reference to best-sellers, pop junk and so forth. Though she keeps a weather eye open for suitable new songs she denies striving for what she termed 'hitty records'.

She assured me once that she had cut so many tunes she didn't know precisely which ones had been recorded. 'I know most were songs I liked, because anything I dislike I don't bother about, even if I feel sure it's going to be a hit. Some of the stuff they suggest, I refuse to do.'

Because it is not worth doing?

'Because I don't dig it, you know. I would just rather sing what I want than look for a new hit record. I guess it's like you; you wouldn't want to write about someone you really don't like. Right?'

'Not enthusiastically,' I said, agreeing up to a point. 'But it's not as simple as all that, is it?'

'I'm not heart-broken if I don't have a hit.' Sarah sounded wistful. 'But I guess a hit would help. It makes the money go up a bit.'

Dinah Washington

Despite her twenty years of exposure on records Dinah Washington never achieved real popularity in Britain, and critical reaction to her broad talents internationally was less than intense. Twenty–three years after her death, her interpretative ability is winning creeping acclaim. This portrait of 'The Queen' is an amalgam of pieces I did for record sleeves, stories for the Melody Maker, *and new material drawn from the singer's one short stay in London. So in complete form it appears for the first time.*

Few possessions benefit a jazz singer more than the gift of individual sound and delivery. Dinah Washington's style was as markedly personal as anyone could wish. I dare say she could be recognised by those with an ear for jazz as easily as any woman who ever slammed out blues or ballad — except perhaps Bessie Smith and Billie Holiday. For both those artists she expressed admiration to me on several festive occasions.

Dinah was her own woman, as the cliché has it (and this time it is apposite), and no doubt breathed something of her personality into a song right from the start. But style is not plucked from nowhere. The most important formative influence on her was exerted at St Luke's Baptist Church in Chicago, where she sang and played piano from the age of eleven or twelve. Dinah spoke fondly of her early involvement with religious music. I have to say that in later life — she was thirty-four when we met — it needed a leap of the imagination to visualise this hard-bitten, defiant, highly-sexed and worldly woman as youthful choir-mistress Ruth Jones, which she once was at St Luke's some time before 1942. Even without her testimony, or knowledge of her history, it would still be crystal clear from the voice and declamatory manner heard on records that here was a singer out of the black church. Dinah, however, liked the look of the secular side of the vocal territory, its greener life-style and rewards. She became, she said, an avowed disciple of Billie Holiday, and admitted 'imitating Lady on a few early records'. Bessie Smith was not in the picture then. Ruth Lee Jones never saw Bessie in person; nor did she hear any Bessie recordings in her youth.

Dinah had been active in church music for six or more years, though straying outside its boundaries from time to time, and showed she could 'do sanctified' any time she felt like it. She talked knowledgeably about Mahalia Jackson, Sallie Martin, Della Reese, Clara Ward and Rosetta Tharpe, and despite a sharp-edged humour which embraced just about any topic, never derided gospel music in my hearing. Indeed she resented those who attempted the idiom without having either a gospel background or, in her estimation, aptitude for the style. An idea of her outlook on this can be gained by a *Down Beat* 'Blindfold Test' conducted on her by Leonard Feather during the Fifties. After listening to four girl singers (they included Jane Russell and Connie Haines) rendering *Do Lord*, Dinah indicated that she didn't care for them 'playing with a sacred song', which she considered to be in poor taste. 'That really didn't kill me,' Queen Dinah stated. 'I think that's terrible. I don't give that *no* rating. And I don't know who it is. But they should all be punched in the face!'

She herself sang *The Lord's Prayer* for Mercury in 1952 but reckoned she 'didn't fool with it'. I cannot say I was able to pin down her precise criterion for sincerity; however, like the enthusiast who loves but can't define jazz in words, she recognised it when she heard it.

'If I have to, I can go to church,' Dinah used to emphasise. And, as I've said, she could prove it. She did so one evening in our house in London's Primrose Hill, warmed by cognac and chat about Georgia Tom Dorsey, Sister Rosetta, Marie Knight and the Ward Singers. Taking over the piano she interpreted a couple of spirituals in properly fervent manner, the voice nicely complemented by gospel piano. At the end, she turned from the keyboard and announced with challenging firmness: 'That was better than Rosetta Tharpe.' I don't believe we contradicted her. Dinah was not a favourite choice as someone to take on if you wished to get along with her, as I devoutly did. Not that she was hostile. She could be very friendly and outgoing, also generous, but her nature included a quarrelsome, aggressive streak and a fairly acid strain of humour; and we were newly acquainted. A friend and colleague of mine, living in our home at that time, found Dinah objectionable. I suppose much depended on how you reacted to her boisterous idea of fun; and on how she responded to you.

Dinah could be wickedly funny, and she and Beryl Booker (her pianist on this visit) had the makings of a stellar jazz-comedy team, with Fats Waller undertones, when in the mood. In the course of the unplanned gospel recital, after a late-luncheon *chez* Jones, Dinah threw out many musical and behavioural references to Sister Rosetta, then a popular figure with British audiences. I thought the mimicry good-natured. In any event she did not clown-up the musical substance of the act. Ms Booker bounced over to the piano when the Queen vacated it, and gave us Beryl's version of *Girl Of My Dreams*, replete with Wallerisms and assorted grimaces. She reinterpreted the song as *Gorilla Of My Dreams*.

To my mind Dinah was as natural an entertainer as, say, Armstrong and Waller, both of whose jazz-making she appreciated; not of the same calibre, no doubt, but the same kind of showperson. She performed whether on-stage or off, for money or nixes, in her own spot or messing in someone else's. She could count on the ability, confidence and that spontaneous combustion needed to vanquish all but the fittest. I think she had the killer instinct, too, which helps a performer survive in the showbiz jungle.

This, and her sarcastic tongue and fiery temperament, were not character-istics likely to top the list of anyone looking for a mate, or maybe an employer. She impressed me now and then as being like a human bomb with a short fuse, primed to go off at the drop of an insult or fancied slight. And yet she could be the most stimulating and attractive company: kind, sociable, amusing and delightfully barrelhouse. At other times she was, I suppose, difficult. She never cussed me out, though, or lost her temper with me. I saw her flare up, but was lucky enough to be a bystander at the battles. Of course I didn't work for her, was only around her for two weeks. The experience carved a notch in my memory. In that fortnight we came to know her unexpectedly well. So far as the Joneses were concerned the Queen was not only approachable but warmly matey to a degree wich proved wearing on the mind and physique. That I dug her singing she very soon learned; however she acted chummy before realising that, and by Day Two was affability personified.

My intro to the Washington flair had arrived early — with Leonard Feather who brought me a bunch of 78s on one of his Forties return trips to the homeland. The records included, memorably, Sarah Vaughan's *Mean To Me* and *Signing Off* on the Continental label and the four sides he made with Dinah (for Keynote in December '43) which launched her disc career. Though hardly enchanting, these initial studio shots at blues singing hinted at an artist of promise. Besides that, the small band with Joe Morris, Arnett Cobb and Hampton sounded groovy enough to make at least two of the titles worthy of many replays. From then on, and there was a bit of a wait, I kept an ear open for Dinah Washington.

Then, one day in 1959 she was due in London for the first time. I set out with a *Melody Maker* photographer for the West End hotel in which, we had been informed, she would be staying for at least twelve days. My frame of mind was hopeful; I looked forward to the encounter. And the chunky trouper lived fully up to expectations. Her manner struck me as quite engaging, combining gaiety and verve with a touch of impetuosity; we were soon on first-name terms, and beyond. During the informal interview–photo session she poured brandy liber-ally and regaled us with a string of pithy comments on music and the world at large. Several were unprintable in a paper aimed at youth.

Also installed in this Oxford Street hotel suite were Beryl Booker and another female member of the Queenly entourage. Ms Booker soon proclaimed herself beat after their long journey and retired to bed. Dinah scorned all suggestions of rest and, to prove her powers of endurance, executed perky dance steps and swung around the smallish room pulling faces for the photographer's benefit and suggesting (as I put it in the *Melody Maker* then) 'various robust poses' for the camera. Seated once more, with bottles at hand, she chatted animatedly about husbands and children; how she felt about being categorised; what she thought of singers as dissimilar as Bessie Smith and Annie Ross. Annie she knew and liked. ('That's my buddy; she's crazy.') Bessie she came to know and esteem, through records, perhaps in the early Fifties. 'I listen to her now and don't hear nothin' wrong. She had some good songs, and a crazy piano player.' The player was James P. Johnson, and I guessed that *Back Water Blues* was one of the few recordings by the Empress that Dinah was familiar with.

About now she broke off to telephone New York, motioning towards the bottles and telling us not to leave. She spoke of her two sons — Bobby, then ten years old, and George, twelve, who played drums — saying they had just made their theatrical debut at New York's Apollo. 'I closed there on Thursday night. My kids were on too. They stole the show and made themselves 125 dollars apiece. If they don't join me here soon I'm likely to get dangerous.' They didn't and she did. However, the boys might have joined her when she left England and went to Sweden for two weeks or so. I am not sure. I do know she 'phoned them often, though not so often as she rang me.

At first meeting it was evident that the singer was prepared to be friendly, until bitten as you might say. On the subject of emotion in music, she said the earthiness and heated feeling drew her to Bessie Smith's records. This down-to-earth honesty was what she went for, that and the indomitable spirit behind the big, rich voice. There would be no point in trying to copy the voice and style, even had she wanted to, for Dinah's voice was higher-pitched and more nasal and she lacked the amplitude and magnificent expressiveness of the great blues artist. In any case, an ambitious Fifties R&B star would have no use for an idiom which had fallen out of public favour. People tended to equate the earthy quality with bluesiness, she thought, and this led to her being categorised as a blues singer, and billed 'Queen of the Blues'. Whereas she had actually started out in devotional song and popular music and still regarded herself as a popular singer. Those who attached a blues label to her were in error.

'I like to sing, and I'll sing ballads, church songs, blues, anything,' she explained forcefully. 'I'll sing *Eli Eli* if you hang around. To me the important things are soul and conviction. You've got to have a feeling. That *Back Water Blues* of Bessie's that I did, I had tears in my eyes. Someone came up to me right after I'd finished and I had to say: "Sorry, I'll see you later." Whenever I sing *Back Water* my friends practically have to carry me off the stage. Rock-and-Roll you can have, but I like real blues. You can break loose on those.'

Before I left the suite, promising to return next day with Betsy, Dinah indicated that she was also proficient in the kitchen — with pots and pans. 'Let me fix you a meal, and I'll give you something to write about. I love to cook and I really can burn.' She spoke the truth. Next day we took her 'marketing' in Soho for good chickens, pork chops, various vegetables and a large, oval frying pan. Dinah insisted she could not do her best without a proper skillet. Armed with this and fresh supplies of liquor, we all (including the faithful B. Booker) drove back to NW3 for a lengthy session of cooking, eating, drinking and music.

The preparation was not a solemn ritual. Records spun, ranging from Louis Jordan and Lionel Hampton to the Queen's Own, and elecited cries of approval or dismissal plus a few shrewd comments from the visitors. Dinah spent much time in the adjoining kitchen, from which came increasingly inviting smells. Periodically a well-rounded figure in apron emerged, brandishing the hot skillet and demanding: 'How about another brandy for the cook?' Each request, as I recall, was accompanied by a ribald remark or coarse gesture. If the conduct sounds somewhat gutbucket, I'd say that's the persona the Queen's records would lead you to expect. The abbreviated title, often altered to Queen D or simply D, had been conferred by her peers for talent, not refinement. She prized it, and it suited her temperament and pride, if not her deportment. In my limited experience, she queened it for all she was worth — which was a great deal.

I should add that Dinah was not given to getting sloppy-drunk. Stroppy-drunk would be nearer the mark. She liked indulging in food and drink, pill-taking, music-making and other social activities, including sex, according to bawdy tales she related. Intolerant she might have been, but seldom dull. She was not a placid person.

By this time we had been adopted as unofficial family, Dinah was on the telephone daily with suggestions for some kind of get-together — at our place, her hotel, or elsewhere; usually all of them in succession. Her instincts were companionable and hospitable. She loved to be on the go, and be the centre of attention, and thus seemed ever on the boil, trying to live up to overflow level. Her motto might have been 'anything for a rowdy life', but in a quiet hotel in a strange city even this veteran battler found it tough to stir up very much in her immediate vicinity. Because we were a lifeline, perhaps, we were able to relish several sensational down-home feasts at home, in the company of the Misses Washington and Booker plus sundry guests, including Abbey Lincoln, drummer Dave Bailey and bassist Bill Crow. Dinah's culinary reputation must have preceded her, because none of the fellow diners took long to accept the telephoned invitation. At all these musical round-tables Dinah presided with spectacular good-humour, enjoyed her display of prowess as cook, hostess and dispenser of a distinctive, not to say obscene, line in jokes and patter.

It felt, over the long run, as though the Queen was seldom off the phone and sometimes her invitations amounted to regal decrees. One evening we received an urgent summons to straighten out a medical problem. Being now under a certain strain I retired to bed, leaving the women to untangle what looked like a stressful situation. Dinah stated she was ill but could not get the hotel medico to attend her. We had no idea how many times he'd been called up before, but there it was. Betsy, who had struck up an instant rapport with the singer, asked what the difficulty might be. 'That doctor's a prejudiced motherfucker,' explained the Queen succintly. My own surmise was too many pills mixed with whisky. I did not envy the doctor.

Something had to be done, however, and Bet set off for the hotel, no more than twenty minutes drive away. Such a mercy mission could have been accomplished within an hour and a half, including both journeys. But that was not Dinah's style. Well after midnight a weary wife returned to report the patient more-or-less recovered, sitting up in bed taking nourishment and, minus the platinum-blonde wig, looking like a handsome picture of Bessie Smith. She had found the Queen feeling sorry for herself and complaining of stomach pains. The doc turned up, failed to diagnose the trouble, and refused to prescribe. Outside the door he said (quietly) that in his opinion 'there's nothing wrong with her'. It transpired that Booker and the Girl Friday were out that night. Dinah disliked solitude.

The up and down life continued, and we escorted the sparky singer to her two gigs: a TV appearance for Granada and an informal BBC *Jazz Club* airing connected with Leonard Feather, who was here on holiday. London was almost snarled-up with jazz visitors that month; others I'd spent time with included singers Helen Merrill and Abbey Lincoln, and we also conducted Dinah to Granada's TV theatre, where Abbey was performing for *Chelsea at Nine*. Another eventful outing was to the Blue Lagoon niterie in Soho, to catch Helen in cabaret there. The broadcasts and the meeting with the beautiful Lincoln passed off well enough, while our descent into the Lagoon can best be described as a revelation.

At the Lagoon, we were to see Dinah, in the ample flesh, motoring along in top gear. Helen Merrill had started her set before we plunged in. She was singing in her quiet, sensitive fashion, seated on a stool. Spotting us at the back of the room she announced that 'America's Queen' was in the house, and invited her to oblige with a number. Knowing Dinah's propensity for walking into a place and taking it over, I thought this risky on Helen's part. And so it proved. Up shot Dinah, followed closely by the trusty Booker, determined to give her all and knock the customers' socks off with the vivacity of her performance. Not only did she belt it out to dynamic piano support; she clowned around, swopped licks with Beryl at the keyboard, and ended up taking turns on string bass and vibes. In short, they blew up a storm. It was the whole act condensed, an extremely hard blitz to follow. I realised this was one of the ways Dinah got her highs, and noted mentally that to the old adage about not appearing on bills with children or animals could be added 'or with triple-threat prima donnas like Dinah Washington'.

Out in the street I remonstrated gently with her for trying to disrupt the show of the headliner, expecially when said star was a non-aggressive artist like Helen. Totally unrepentant, Dinah retorted: 'Shit, the broad invited me up there and got what she asked for.' It was one of the faces of Dinah; she didn't go out of her way to curry favour and generally believed she was in the right. Not surprisingly, she earned renown as a hard nut who showed deference to nobody, certainly not husbands. Nevertheless she had a ready supply of affection, though not located on the surface.

Among other sides to this singer were her professionalism and insistence on being free, so far as that is possible in the business, to choose artistic directions. Time and again she asserted independence: 'People who call me a blues singer don't understand what I do. I used to specialise in blues with Hamp's band, and I still sing 'em. But I'm not restricted to one thing. I think of myself as just a singer.'

The question of when and why she began featuring blues is still hazy. I'm not even sure who dubbed her Dinah Washington or Queen of the Blues. Facts of her early life that we know are these: she moved from Tuscaloosa, Alabama, to Chicago while still an infant, later attended Wendell Phillips High School and, during her term as a gospel exponent, won an amateur talent contest at Chicago's Regal Theatre, aged fifteen. She carried on with church music and bided her time. When seventeen she got married, the first of at least seven weddings, or so she assured me (name of husband number one was not diclosed). Apparently it left little impression on her. The contest success eventually led to local club engagements, but nothing significant. 'What inspired me to try once more was hearing Billie Holiday, always my favourite, at a Chicago night spot.' If D was consistent about anything it was Lady Day. 'I love her,' she told me. 'Perhaps you've heard me mimic her on *Lover Come Back to Me*?'

Dinah found employment at the Garrick Lounge in '42, doubling the cloakroom with a vocal spot. She stayed nearly a year and it provided the springboard she needed. Also the job resulted in her change of name, though how it came about is unclear. Red Allen heard her at the Garrick and passed the word to Associated Booking Corporation boss, Joe Glaser. He went to see, and introduced her to Lionel Hampton who offered her a place in his band. Good going for a singing hat-check girl. It was 1943. One version has it that club owner Joe Sherman altered her name when he put her on the Garrick stage. Others claim Glaser recommended a more saleable handle. Hamp told me himself it was his idea to turn plain Ruth Jones into the more up-market DW. Leonard Feather, who played a decisive part in advancing her career later that year when he cut the four tracks for Keynote, says: 'Glaser always claimed it was he, not Lionel, who changed Dinah's name, and I believed him.'

In order to sell a nonentity, Leonard laid on a sextet from Hamp's orchestra to back her on the records. He remembers: 'She joined Lionel's band early in '43 and was definitely singing only ballads and pop songs with him. It was my idea that she would sound great as a blues singer and, as you probably know, I wrote or re-wrote all those songs for her. (I had written a couple — *Evil Gal* and *Salty Papa* — in male versions for previous records). She behaved fine on the session, and seemed to enjoy having a little freedom with a small improvising group.'

The neglect by Hamp of Dinah's glowing capabilities is rather mysterious. She started out with the band at a reputed salary of some £20 a week in English money, remained with it for three years and recorded almost nothing, though she sang with the band at many concert and theatre dates, besides taking part in a series of filmed programmes known originally as telescriptions and entitled *Showtime at the Apollo*. Of the Keynote session, Feather also recalled that Lionel arrived before it was an hour old and sat in on piano and drums, although he and his wife had been opposed to the whole idea. When the discs were issued, as by the Lionel Hampton Sextet with Dinah Washington, 'all hell broke loose' and labels had to be reprinted without Hamp's name on them. 'But by now,' as Leonard put it, 'they could have sold if they had been printed in Swahili. The unknown singer within a few weeks had become a juke box queen, and *Evil Gal* my (and her) first hit song.'

The new juke box star can be heard wailing *Evil Gal Blues* — written by Feather and Hampton, according to label credits — on Hamp's Decca-Brunswick album of the *All-American Award Concert* of April, 1945. 'It was quite a while before Lionel really took advantage of the success of the Keynotes,' Leonard told me. 'But she finally got to record another blues of mine, *Blow Top*, with a contingent from his band. By the time I put on his Carnegie Hall Award Concert in the spring of '45, where she did *Evil Gal*, she had become a big star and she left the next year with Joe Glaser's blessing and management.'

If the lady had been dragged by Hamp's reluctance to stick her in the limelight, she'd got over it by 1959. With him she gained profitable training in vocal technique and stagecraft. This she acknowledged. 'Lionel,' she said, emphasising that last syllable, 'taught me the value of showmanship. With his band I learned what this business is about.' With Hamp, too, she was groomed for the Queen of the Blues role, a step up the celebrity ladder despite misgivings about type-casting. At a mention of the title, on the Soho streets one sunny day, she adopted a slightly indecent pose and cried: 'Call me Queen of the Juke Boxes, honey. I finally got a hit but I practically had to whip those disc jockeys to get it.' Privately I had judged Dinah capable of whipping many a man, having taken on board colourful stories about her answering the door to an unwelcome visitor and greeting him with a loaded pistol. And she gave grudging confirmation of the account of her striking a husband (probably her fourth) over the head with his saxophone. To his anguished complaint, she is alleged to have replied: 'Well, I bought it for you, didn't I?' It's not hard to understand why strong men shrank from her wrath, and logic.

Her muscularity did not prevent Dinah telephoning me from the hotel bed one morning about 5.30 to accuse the night porter of insulting her by offering her sex. Far-out information to receive at any hour, and in my befuddled state I narrowly avoided asking who this hero could be. I did proffer congratulations, upon which the hurt tone changed to indignation. Would I come over right away and sort matters out as she was upset? No procrastination; the chips were down and it was now or never. So, gathering wife and clothes about me for protection, I zoomed to a dawn-empty Oxford Street to do what I could.

To imagine Dinah as a picture of injured innocence, glass in hand and defenceless in a distant land, is to conjure up a Marx Brothers scene. To me it was the wild leading the mild. She was neither a shy nor modest woman, but pride had been hurt and she valued her dignity. She'd been grossly insulted; what was I going to do about it? The facts, as I interpreted them from her story, were that she had 'sent out for a bottle of whisky' in the small hours and the night man — delivering same and discovering our singer bare except for a shortie nightie — had drawn a perilously false conclusion. It led to the alleged sexual advance. Hard words were used.

While Betsy calmed the storm, I approached the janitor downstairs. He struck me as being apprehensive, as well as Irish and not entirely sober, and we skirted around the subject for a while before reaching the reason for my presence. Agreeing that he might have been out of order while tired and rushed off his feet, we parted. I tried to intercede in his favour upstairs and Dinah heard me out in a spluttering kind of silence, looking as though she suspected betrayal. When next I called on her at the hotel, and made tactful enquiries, the man had gone. I learned that Dinah had modified the old advice: Don't get mad, get even. She did both. No wonder she wanted to title her projected autobiography 'Evil Gal'. It made sense. And I wonder what became of the plan. This extraordinary singer, who was somehow programmed for a short, hectic career, deserves a larger-than-life biog.

A few more memories seek release from the DW brain-file. At the BBC *Jazz Club* broadcast, during the run-through, she was soon being asked to sing one of her old blues numbers. She had little chance of escaping from the blues net. This programme came her way only by chance, as Feather reminded me. 'The BBC thing was really a lucky accident. Vic Lewis had put a band together to do a programme of my tunes, and Helen Merrill was supposed to be guest singer. However, Helen goofed and hours before showtime I still hadn't heard from her. I ran into Dinah and Beryl on the street and asked Dinah if she would mind stepping in, which she did quite graciously.' I remember the singer being given a note by Leonard, probably with the lyrics jotted on it, which she took up on the stand with her. And she announced, before naming her closing number, that Leonard had asked her to do such-and-such a song but she wasn't going to. Possibly this was typical Dinah conduct, too.

Viewed with hindsight it is astonishing that this visit by so exciting a singer received scant publicity and created very little fuss in jazz circles here. Nobody from the Entertainment Establishment — or any other establishment for that matter — fêted Dinah. I imagine her recording of *What A Diff'rence A Day Made* generated sufficient noise to secure this European trip. But she was neither a big-enough popular name nor respected jazz figure to warrant red-carpet treatment from either camp. So it was a minute body of enthusiasts that found out she was among us, and took the trouble to meet her.

One devotee who did was British vocalist Beryl Bryden, an indefatigable jazz lover who was always *au fait* with what was moving on our scene. We met Beryl Bryden with the Queen at the television studio and on one or two excursions, and Dinah was entertained at her flat. Unforgettable, except in its multifarious details, was a voyage around Soho and the West End one 'rest' day. We did a tour of shops and pubs, the taverns being whistle-stops in D's prolonged search for collard greens to supplement an up-coming meal, and after closing time embarked on a club-crawl. Our intention was to continue carousing through the afternoon, at such joints as would serve us, until opening time came round. At one point our party came to rest in a Greek café in what is now London's Chinatown. To enliven the action Beryl Booker commandeered the corner piano and Dinah was soon attacking *Send Me To The 'Lectric Chair'*, an unexpected choice considering the hour and the surroundings.

No one could accuse Queen Dinah of belonging to the I-don't-sing-unless-I'm-paid brigade. This was a facet of her outlook on life much appreciated by us and, I am sure, many people unknown to me. At another juncture, as we made our way along Oxford Street, we came upon the Happy Wanderers (a familiar sight in London) busking in the roadway. A delighted Dinah said: 'I've got to sing with them,' and proceeded to lead the band up past Selfridges' belting out *I Can't Give You Anything But Love* — one of the few songs common to both repertoires. Beryl Bryden had needed to push the buskers a bit to get them to accept a parade leader. 'I explained she was a very famous singer from the States. They'd never heard of her.' Bryden can provide a visual *aide-memoire*: some photographs taken on our junket, including Dinah and Wanderers and Betsy with D, snapped under the Eros statue in Piccadilly Circus. And I have one of Dinah signing her autograph for a chap who sprang up and recognised her in Brewer Street, Soho.

Still, it remains puzzling why she was un-newsworthy. Even in '59 she was a star who had been recording for some sixteen years. Perhaps the not-specialising operated against her.

There are rumours of her being capricious, to put it mildly, but on the other hand the jobs she did in London were undertaken in a firmly professional if spirited way. And we have Feather's word for it that her behaviour was fine on her very first studio session. Then, too, around 1959 and '60, Dinah and Brook Benton collaborated on a number of recordings, some of which notched up enviable sales. The two had worked together occasionally, and A&R man Clyde Otis decided to team them on records. The word is that the sessions ran fairly smoothly, no serious hang-ups.

'She could be difficult, they say, but we got along very well in the studio,' said Benton who, at our first meeting, named Dinah as one of his two favourite women singers. And of the mistakes in the routine of *Baby, You Got What It Takes* — they lead to Dinah observing 'You're in my spot again' — he assured me; 'Not that much rehearsal went into the actual recording dates but quite a bit went into that particular song. As it turned out, the take with the goofs sounded better than some of the others. No, the goof wasn't intentional; we were playing around really, you know, testing as we went along. Frankly, some of the time we didn't even know they were taping. We were like having a dry run. And when they put it out, *Baby* sold a million for us.'

These stories tend to rebut the charges of tempestuous conduct, in the studio at any rate. Dinah was not a solemn grafter; but when the show started she knew what she was doing. Nothing interfered with her clear enunciation.

But let me draw the reminiscences to a close: we had many good times with her just talking and laughing; she loved laughing about people and also liked laughing at herself. She spoke fondly of Ella Fitzgerald very often, also of Billie and Annie Ross, and expressed great respect for Charlie Parker, I remember. As to her childhood, part of it in the South, so far as we were concerned she kept that a closed book, which was more than could be said for her love life.

Before the end of her stay in England I had again taken to my bed, dented in health, when the Queen rang through to state that we were all going to the Palladium to call on the Peters Sisters, and following it up with a night at the Astor Club in Mayfair. Not one to be baulked she went off happily with my wife who, nearly exhausted too, regretted she would be unable to complete the itinerary. She was promptly dosed with one of D's wake-up pills, which did its work. She was not able to sleep properly for two days and nights, and swore that the Queen downed these uppers by the handful. The outing was of course riotous.

This all-night binge was just about Dinah's last stroke. A day or so afterwards I had the pleasure of driving her, on her own, to Heathrow Airport on a fine morning — in my Zephyr convertible with the top down. In her fur coat and blonde wig, with a white crocheted cap on the back of her head, she was something to look at, and listen to as she ran through the vicissitudes of five or six marriages and several irregular liaisons. Aside from the first forgotten man there had been husbands called Grayson, Jenkins and Chamblee (the last celebrated on *T'ain't Nobody's Business* when she ad-libs the line, 'If Eddie and I fuss and fight'), and a new one named Rusty Mallard had just been received. I heard all about the briefly happy couples, and why this one and that had to go. And one, at least, who got out from under before being chopped. Then, with a big embrace and sardonic bow, the Queen was gone to be 'processed'. I never laid eyes on her again, but a couple of days later I was awakened at 5 am by the telephone bell. The caller was D, in Stockholm, saying her husband had joined her and I was to say hello to Rusty, who was something to do with taxis. 'Hey, what's the matter with you? You asleep?' she asked.

I've indicated my esteem and regard for this artist. If it was the unique, exuberant talent which had captivated me in the first instance, it's true to say I liked her still at the end of two weeks which felt as though they had added two years to my age. In drawing attention to what might seem like eccentric traits, I am not trying to portray her as a 'character', simply recounting the biographical fragments of her life known to me personally. Beryl Bryden, asked later what she had thought of Dinah, said enthusiastically: 'Lovely, a right nut. Of course I admired her voice, but I wish she'd been given better material to sing, and more often with good jazz backing. She had so much jazz feeling.' In this remark lies a clue to the mystery of the disregard shown by most jazz pundits for Dinah Washington's output. She was saddled with quantities of dull, even dog songs — selected I am sure (like the accompanists in most cases) by supervisors and producers in the eternal quest for the hit — and she did her damndest by them. Usually it resulted in something worth hearing, but is was not always enough. She had sharp ears, natural musicianship, expressive phrasing and the utterly relaxed approach needed for true swing.

A jazz singer? Who knows? She was a jazz person, that's for sure. Dan

Morgenstern once wrote that she had, he thought, annoying mannerisms at times but was a shouter 'who fought bad material with jazz weapons'. The trouble was, for many critics, that she'd dirtied her hands with musical trash. She was young when she died, and at that time I was still hoping she would find a producer (Norman Granz perhaps) who could help her make records which 'blow away' all but the stoutest rivals. Sadly, it was not to become reality. When we read of the champion's sudden, unexpected death — on 14 December 1963 at her home in Detroit — we were shocked but not astonished to read of an unmarked bottle of pills found at her bedside. She lived for fewer years than Billie or Bessie, or Mildred Bailey who died at forty-four. Jazz singing can be a high-risk profession.

Index